DEMOCRACY AND AUTHORITARIANISM IN PAKISTAN

The Role of The Military and Political Parties

Shiraz Sheikh

KNOWLEDGE WORLD

KW Publishers Pvt Ltd
New Delhi

ISBN 978-93-89137-24-8 Hardback
eISBN 978-93-89137-25-5 ebook

Published in India by Kalpana Shukla

KNOWLEDGE WORLD

KW Publishers Pvt Ltd
4676/21, First Floor, Ansari Road
Daryaganj, New Delhi 110002
Phone: +91 11 23263498/43528107
Marketing: kw@kwpub.com
Editorial: production@kwpub.com
Website: www.kwpub.com

Printed and Bound in India

Contents

Tables and Figures

For Mother

Acknowledgement

I would like to express my sincere gratitude to Prof. Ajay Darshan Behera for mentoring me and stimulating academic discussions which have proven to be instrumental in the final result of this study. Despite ideational differences he has always been helpful and offered his invaluable advice and guidance and enriched the manuscript with his objective scrutiny and conceptual criticism.

My heartfelt thanks are reserved for the soulful Dr. Mathew Joseph C., the Coordinator of the UGC-Centre for Pakistan Studies at the MMAJ Academy of International Studies, Jamia Millia Islamia. He has always been forthcoming in critiquing parts of my manuscript and sharing his expertise on the subject. He motivated me and created the ambience in the workplace which helped me to develop this book.

This work has come to its shape not only by extensive sources referred in this book but also as a result of various academic and informal discussions. Recalling all the people who generously devoted their time is not possible. Nevertheless, I would like to place on record my gratitude to Prof. Mohammad Waseem, Prof. Ishtiaq Ahmad, Prof. Andrew Wilder, Dr. Maya Tudor, Amb. Husain Haqqani, and Dr. Ayesha Siddiqa who took out time to give me insights about the democracy, political parties, economy, military and civil-military relations in Pakistan. I would like to express an especial thanks to Dr. Moeed Yusuf and Prof. Philip K. Oldenburg who had multiple discussions about my research, connected me with other scholars and shared research materials.

I am also thankful to the competent authority at the Jamia Millia Islamia as it kindly accorded the permission to publish part of my work submitted as doctoral thesis to the university. I am immensely thankful to my publisher Kalpana Shukla at the KW Publishers for talking time to converse and to transform the manuscript into this book. I would also like to thank Sushant Gayen for looking after the manuscript and seeing it through the press.

I would also like to acknowledge the support rendered by the argumentative tribe of my friends. With them I had the most illuminating scholarly conversations at various stages of my study. I am indeed thankful to them for their intellectual company and their unconditional support and unflinching faith in me.

I am indebted to my mother (the late) Sufia Khatun, who imbibed, patience and respect for knowledge in me through the folklores of her cultural roots. Most especial thanks to my brothers, my *Bhabhi* Najma, and my nieces for their care, affection and faith in me which enabled me to bring this book to its conclusion.

Any omission, misinterpretations and error in methods are mine.

New Delhi **SHIRAZ SHEIKH**
2019

Abbreviations

AIML	All India Muslim League
ANP	Awami National Party
APDM	All Parties Democratic Movement
APMSO	All Pakistan Muhajir Student Organisation
ARD	Alliance for Restoration of Democracy
BC	Before Christie
BNR&R	Bureau of National Research and Reconstruction
CDNS	Council of Defence and National Security
CEC	Central Executive Committee
CENTO	Central Treaty Organisation
CII	Council of Islamic Ideology
C-in-C	Commander in Chief
CJP	Chief Justice of Pakistan
CML	Council of Muslim League
COAS	Chief of the Army Staff
COP	Combined Opposition Parties
CSP	Civil Service of Pakistan
DC	Defence Council
DCC	Defence Committee of the Cabinet
DG	Director General
EBDO	Elective Bodies Disqualification Order
FSF	Federal Security Force
GHQ	General Headquarters
HDO	Higher Defence Organisation
ICC	International Cricket Council
ICIJ	International Consortium of Investigative Journalists
ICT	Information and Communications Technology
IDP	Internally Displaced Person
IJI	Islami Jamhoori Ittehad
INC	Indian National Congress

ISI	Inter-Services Intelligence
JCSC	Joint Chief of Staff of Committee
JUH	Jamiat Ulema-e-Hind
JUI	Jamiat Ulema-e-Islam
JUI-F	Jamiat Ulema-e-Islam (Fazlur Rahman)
KPK	Khyber Pakhtunkhwa
KTC	Karachi Tanzeemi Committee
LFO	Legal Framework Order
MMA	Muttahida Majlis-e-Amal
MNA	Member of National Assembly
MQM	Muttahida Quami Movement
MRD	Movement for Restoration of Democracy
NAP	National Action Plan
NC	National Council
NDP	National Democratic Party
NDU	National Defence University
NJC	National Judicial Commission
NRO	National Reconciliation Order
NSC	National Security Council
NSF	National Student Federation
NWFP	North West Frontier Province
PAT	Pakistan Awami Tehrik
PCO	Provisional Constitutional Order
PEC	Provincial Executive Committee
PEMRA	Pakistan Electronic Media Regulatory Authority
PML	Pakistan Muslim League
PML (J)	Pakistan Muslim League (Jatoi)
PML (N)	Pakistan Muslim League (Nawaz)
PML (Q)	Pakistan Muslim League (Quaed)
PNA	Pakistan National Alliance
PNS	Pakistan Navy
PONM	Pakistan Oppressed Nations Movement
PPB	Provincial Parliamentary Board
PPO	Political Parties Order
PPO	Press Publication Ordinance

PPP	Pakistan Peoples Party
PTI	Pakistan Tehreek-e-Insaf
PWC	Provincial Working Committee
QML	Muslim League (Qayyum)
RAW	Research and Analysis Wing
RPPO	Revised Print and Publication Ordinance
SG	Secretary General
TNSM	Tehreek-e-Nifaz-e-Shariat-e-Muhammadi
TTP	Tehreek-e-Taliban Pakistan
UDF	United Democratic Front
UNHCR	United Nations High Commissioner for Refugees
US	United States

Introduction

Pakistan was created as a homeland for the Muslims of the subcontinent with a promise of setting an example of ideal political order. In the course of time, its political order appeared most chaotic and unstable in the region. In seven decades of its political history, its rulers could not develop consensus over a political order acceptable to all. More than half of its independent history has been ruled by non-elected regimes. In the first decade Pakistan was ruled by the civilians, but they were not elected. The military came to power for the first time in 1958. Thereafter, the country oscillated between democratic and military regimes. The military has ruled the country for a longer period than democratic regimes.[1] A substantive part of democratic rule was also been under indirect shadow of the military.

The dominance of the military started soon after the creation of the state of Pakistan. The initial deterioration of the political process and the dearth of political leadership facilitated the military to become the central power at the national level. When Pakistan came into existence, Muhammad Ali Jinnah, the founder of the country continued with the viceregal system and became the Governor-General of Pakistan. Jinnah pronounced that the country would be governed under a democratic setup, but before the transition from authoritative viceregal system to procedural democracy could be completed, he died. Following Jinnah's death the Muslim League which lacked a social base in Pakistan failed to transform itself from a movement to a strong political party. It ceded power to a more competent bureaucracy – comprising mainly of Muhajirs – and the country was ruled by a civil-bureaucracy instead of elected politicians.

Having a sense of their numeric vulnerability in a majoritarian democracy, where each citizen's vote counts for one and a greater number of votes determine the winner, the civil-bureaucracy remained wary of democratic politics. This systematic, shirking from electoral politics, undermined the already weak democratic institutions. The constant tussle between the political parties, which demanded democratisation and authoritative bureaucracy determined to hold onto power, created political instability in Pakistan. Amid this political confusion the military found its opportunity to intervene in politics. General Ayub Khan staged the first coup in 1958 and ruled under martial law until June 1962. A constitution was framed in 1962 to civilianise General Ayub's regime. The new constitution enabled him to rule even after the withdrawal of martial law. His rule came to an end by another military coup in March 1969 by General Yahya Khan who handed over power to Zulfikar Ali Bhutto in December 1971 after the military defeat in East Pakistan.

After more than a decade-long military rule an elected government was formed in 1971. Bhutto, the leader of the PPP, was sworn in as the Prime Minister of Pakistan. To come to power, Bhutto used populist politics by using popular slogans like *roti, kapda aur makaan* (bread, clothing and shelter), and harnessed the discontent of the growing number of working class disenchanted with elitist politics to rise to power. Despite riding to power on the shoulders of popular slogans, Bhutto's arrival did not herald any significant change in a predominantly feudal country. The democratically elected government of Bhutto was overthrown by General Zia-ul Haq in 1977. His military regime ruled the country for the longest period under martial law in Pakistan's history. In 1985, Zia allowed political parties to contest on a non-party basis but political power remained with him.

After the death of General Zia in a mysterious air crash, Pakistan went back to the democratic system in 1988 which showed some hope for the regeneration of democratic institutions. This period was mired with political distrust and democratic regimes were uncertain of their fate. The democratic regimes were largely concerned about salvaging their position rather than improving the conditions of democratic institutions. Nawaz Sharif and Benazir Bhutto, leaders of the PML (N) and PPP respectively, also showed authoritarian tendencies while dealing with political opposition. The period saw power struggles within and between different institutions representing civilians and military spheres. Before Pakistan could relish the fruits of the second democratic experiment, it ended with a *coup d'état* by General Pervez Musharraf in 1999. The coup was a consequence of a political crisis which paved the path for military intervention. General Musharraf officially appointed himself as the President of Pakistan in 2001 and ruled till 2008 when once again the political order transited to civilian rule from a military regime. Since then democratically elected governments, have maintained power with successful transition of power in 2013 and 2018.

There are many reasons attributed to the decline of democratic institutions and the rise of the military as the dominant political institution in Pakistan. A weak political institution was one such reason which led to the downslide of democracy in Pakistan. Pakistan inherited weak political institutions as a colonial legacy which allowed successive military dictators to manipulate the codified rules to their advantage. Institutions like the legislature and judiciary remained weak in Pakistan. For the first two decades after Pakistan's creation, no direct election at the national level was held and thus the legislature was not directly elected.

The nature of civic and political culture pervading in feudal and tribal societies is also seen as one major reason for authoritarianism to develop in Pakistan. Historically, these societies were also not acclimated to modern democratic systems. It is argued that regions which comprised Pakistan underwent different colonial experiences. From the very beginning the British administration in India had its operation in united Bengal, while parts of Punjab and North West Frontier Province (NWFP) were under indirect rule. The British colonial authorities penetrated this region through the bureaucracy and political agents and never tried to disrupt the customary practices, therefore people of this part were not accustomed to a democratic model of governance, and therefore the foundation of political culture upon which democracy could rest, remained weak. Pakistan adopted the parliamentary form of government and federal system without building the institutional foundations necessary for its operation.

Scholars have also argued that the military was the most developed and organised institution inherited by Pakistan which created immense difficulties for civilian politicians. It was also the ambition of the military to play an active role in politics beyond its conventional functions. Military officers saw themselves as the saviour of the country and advocated a proactive role for the military to reform society. The military saw itself as the guardian and defender of the idea of Pakistan and unless Pakistan was saved from the political rot, it was not possible to protect the very basic purpose for which it was created. Another reason for the military's cyclic intervention in politics is its economic interest. Over the years the military has created a vast corporate empire to benefit the military fraternity.

Others see Islamic political theory and the conditioning of society anchored in Muslim history as the main cause of authoritarian rule. In Pakistan, which was created in the name of religion, Islam played an important role in the polity. From the very beginning, Islam had become a powerful social force if not a political one. Though Islam is not accepted as a political force and people do not endorse the calls of Islamic parties in the elections, it shapes the way politics is played out. After tasting political rejection in elections, the Islamist parties sought to enter the power structure through the backdoor and supported the military. The military used Islamist forces to curb centrifugal forces such as ethno-nationalism. To attain its goal the military supported, encouraged and nurtured the Islamist forces. This relationship was twofold; the military gave patronage to the Islamist forces and in return received ideological legitimacy from the self-appointed guardians of Islam.

Another argument is that political parties as an institution remained underdeveloped in Pakistan. Political parties and electoral dynamics suffered accordingly, as power was publicly identified with the political executive and bureaucracy while the legislatures were given a subordinate role. Military rule, which became cyclic in Pakistan, created difficulties for political parties to mature and thus democracy always remained susceptible to military coups. Contrary to this argument, this study argues that at the formative phase of Pakistan, political parties had opportunity enough to develop democratic institutions. From the beginning, political parties developed authoritarian tendencies. Political parties either failed in engaging in mass politics or deliberately exhibited authoritarian propensities. This facilitated the military to intervene in politics and establish itself in the power structure. Democratically elected governments got two short spans to develop democratic institutions previously and they failed miserably.[2] The third democratic phase is in progress and exhibits mixed signs of improvement for democratic institutions.

Whatever was the form of regime, the political parties in Pakistan provided the much needed legitimacy to them. This was one precise reason for which even military regimes had their own political parties or system. The political parties played the role of regime legitimisation and stabilisation. Despite their central role, both democracy and parties remained weak in the country. Against this background, the book studies how the political parties in Pakistan despite repeated opportunities to govern the country failed to develop democratic institutions. The study analyses political parties, their origin, growth, leadership, functioning, organisation and social background and its implications for democracy in Pakistan since the first elected government in 1971. The study analyses how and to what extent political parties whether under civilian or military regime are responsible for the decline and progress of democracy in Pakistan; and how their background, leadership, politics and policies are correlated to democratisation and authoritarianism in the country.

To understand this correlation it would be useful to discuss the nature of political parties, outline its typology and theorise its functions and linkages with democratic systems.

Outline of the Book

This study is both analytical and descriptive. It establishes the correlation between political parties and their role in diluting and deepening of democratic institutions in Pakistan. For the purpose of this study, both primary and secondary sources are used.

A substantive number of interviews with Pakistani scholars, politicians, professionals and students has been used as primary sources. In addition non-native scholars on Pakistan were also interviewed to get a broader perspective on the issue.

Other primary sources other than interviews comprised of major ordinances, orders and legal frameworks related to political parties, official compilation of elections and detail results. Party manifestos, constitutions and founding documents also provided vital information on the original inspiration and orientation of parties. Also proving helpful in getting sense of socio-political condition of the country were the Constitutions of Pakistan as well as major amendments to them, Census of Pakistan, Pakistan Penal Code, White Paper issued by government on the functioning of former governments, various official reports on the economic and social status of citizen. The autobiographies, biographies and memoires of civilian and military leaders as well as their speeches and statements also added to the list of primary sources.

The book comprises six core chapters besides the introduction and conclusion.

Chapter I *Democracy and Political Parties: Conceptual Linkages* provides a brief overview of the conceptual origin and evolution of democracy and its inter-linkages with political parties. The chapter discusses the conceptual variants of democracy and political parties. Under the rubric of democracy it theorises the idea of liberal, social and Islamic democracy, while the section on political party analyses the epistemological and ontological origin of political parties and how they are defined in various frameworks. It further analyses the typology of political parties and theoretical linkages between a political party and democracy – liberal or Islamic.

Chapter II on *Authoritarianism, Military and Civil-Military Relations* focuses on authoritarianism, variants of military regimes, why they come into being and what type of civil-military relations they envisage. It tries to explain the origin of a military institution in the modern state system and how they play a professional and political role in different contexts. In addition to this, it tries to trace the evolution of military institution in Pakistan and theorises the variants of civil-military relations in Pakistan. The first two chapters should be seen in combination as they overlaps in each other's boundaries and collectively explain correlation in theoretical framework. Along with providing conceptual correlation between the political parties, democracy and authoritarianism it explores the theoretical possibilities of determining logical conclusion when these variables are collectively analysed.

Chapter III *Political Parties in Pakistan: Origin, Evolution and Electoral Participation* provides a specific mapping of political parties in Pakistan. It contextualises the historicity of the conditions in which these parties emerged and what their political interests are. It analyses the importance of the 'founding moment' of the institution and what specialised role they play. This chapter studies the origin and growth of political parties in Pakistan and analyses the pattern, on which the political parties have developed, and, affects the growth of democratic institutions. It also examines the composition and organisational structure of the parties and their way of functioning.

Chapter IV *Society, Leadership and Social Base of Political Parties* has two parts. The first part explores the process of social formations in Pakistan. In this it examines the origin and growth of tribal, feudal and *salariat* societies and strives to establish the linkages between society, state and electoral equations. The second part focuses on the social background of the leadership to understand the ideological and political orientation of the party. Furthermore, the chapter looks into the social and political constituencies (class, caste, sect, regional and ethnic identities, tribe and *biradari*) of the parties to understand their political base. It helps identify the segment of society from which they originate and the segment's interest they mobolise and protect.

Chapter V *Political Parties and the Two Civilian Interludes* studies how political parties have determined the trajectories of democracy and authoritarianism in Pakistan since the arrival of the first elected regime till the beginning of the last military regime. The chapter explores the traditional role of representative functioning, their adaptive capabilities, and their stabilising roles as initiator, manager and consolidator of political changes related to democracy in the given period of the political parties. The chapter specifically looks into the politics of parties in the period of Zulfikar Ali Bhutto, General Zia-ul Haq's regime and the second democratic interlude under Benazir Bhutto and Nawaz Sharif — and also analyses how their politics had implications for democratic development. The chapter also examines the impact of personality-centric politics on democratic institutions and how the issue of survival and antagonism between political parties shaped the political system.

Chapter VI *From Military Rule to Democracy: Political Parties' Third Chance to Consolidate* specifically covers the period of the last military regime of General Pervez Musharraf and thereafter the two elected regimes of Pakistan Peoples Party under Asif Ali Zardari and the Pakistan Muslim League (Nawaz) under Nawaz Sharif. It tries to decipher the style of military rule in the post-Cold War period and how the military devised new methods to legitimise its exercise of power in the civilian domain. The recent period of elected regimes, which is in progress, is analysed in a framework of continuity and shift of politics of parties. It analyses coalition politics which was different from alliance politics of the past and helped deepening the democratic roots in the country. In the final assessment, the chapter tries to see if there is hope for democracy on the basis of the pattern of politics of parties and military's tactical manoeuvring.

Notes

1. The first decade after its creation Pakistan was ruled by a non-elected civilian leadership. In 1958 the military staged its first coup under General Ayub Khan and ended civilian rule. He established a military regime which continued for more than a decade. He was dislodged by General Yahya Khan in 1969. His term came to an end in 1971 when Zulfikar Ali Bhutto became the first elected Prime Minister. Bhutto's civilian regime was short-lived, being brought to an end in 1977 by General Zia-ul-Haq. His military regime lasted for a decade and came to ruin in 1988 with his death. Thereafter four civilian regimes managed to survive for a decade until the military struck back in 1999 under General Pervez Musharraf. His military regime was ousted in 2008 and civilian regime returned to the helm of power again.
2. Political parties' first chance to govern the country and consolidate democratic institutions came in 1971 when the PPP formed the first elected government. However this government could not complete a full tenure as elections were called before time. The election outcome was never accepted by the political opposition which led to the military's intervention. The second democratic interlude from 1988 to 1999 was relatively longer but highly unstable. During this period elected governments were dismissed prematurely and in 1999 the military seized power again.

1. Democracy and Political Parties: Conceptual Linkages

...there is no democratic theory – there are only democratic theories.

— Robert A. Dahl [1]

There are competing interpretations over the meaning of democracy. Contemporary scholars of democracy treat it differentially than their ancient counterparts. The ideas of democracy emerged in ancient societies and gradually found practical expression in modern societies of Europe. Democracy is defined as both a procedure of electing government and also as a form of governance. It is argued here that democracy is variable rather than a static arrangement. In conceptual terms the Schumpeterian dictum of "Creative Destruction"[2] which he applied to explain "evolutionary process" of capitalistic institution can be applied to exhibit similar progression within democratic systems. As Joseph Schumpeter argued that industrial advancement destroys the old economic structure and replaces it with a new one, this chapter argues that with new innovations in technology and political theory, democracy also moves beyond the recognised *modus procedendi*.

The second part of the chapter discusses the nature of political parties, outlines its typology and theorises its functions and linkages with democratic systems. The third part of the chapter focuses on the debates on Islamic democracy. It examines how various elements essential for a democratic state are interpreted in the Islamic model of democracy. It further discusses the concepts of caliphate (*khilafat*), nation (*ummah*), sovereignty and authority in reference to an Islamic state. It also tries to see the degree of theoretical compatibility between what is called Islamic democracy and the popular understanding of democracy.

Conceptual Evolution of Democracy

This section attempts to establish that democracy is a variable which gets impacted by new innovations with regard to its principles and methods. This section examines the conceptual evolution to see how democracy took birth and was reformed in the course of time with new ideas shaping its outlook. Since democracy is a variable and not a constant, it can be argued that it gets reshaped and reformed by organic growth of institutions. Historically it has been seen that states which adapted to new changes and continued with a reformed setup strengthened, wherein the closed systems like monarchy and autocracy crumbled after a span of time. This section is an attempt to demonstrate how these changes were accommodated theoretically.

There is a sort of general agreement among the scholars of democratic history about its origin from Athens. It is difficult to answer why democracy first took roots in Athens. However Simon Harniblower has argued that it is the existence of "preconditions" which facilitated the budding of democracy.[3] One such precondition was the existence of slavery which allowed free time for the "elite citizen" to have active political careers. The second condition was the emancipation of 'serfs,' that created small-holders who could then become citizens as the eligibility for citizenship was widened from aristocratic lineage to the possession of property. Harniblower, however, argues that although this system was far from democracy it did open up the path of democracy. In 500 B.C. King Solon constituted a council of 400 elites which was later replaced by the council of 500 whose task was to ponder on the matters of governance.[4] King Solon latter established a popular lawcourt, the *heliaia*, in which one had the right to appeal against any unjust decision of the magistrate. After Solon, a short period of anarchy followed until King Kleisthenes, who brought participation of villages and tribes into the Council of 500, thus making the council much more representative.

During its imperial peak, Athens exported democracy around the Aegean Sea. But during the Peloponnesian War the democracy was under severe strain, but once the war ended democracy was restored. It then became more efficient – although less democratic.[5] The Athenian Democracy established the institutions of juries and more participatory councils. Although the Athenian system was a form of direct democracy, it disenfranchised more of its population – women, slaves and workers – than it enfranchised.

Apart from the physical institutions which existed in Athens, many Greek philosophers also reflected on political theories with regard to democracy. The *Republic* reflected that the "*polis* existed to express and secure the good of its citizen."[6] Due to the existence of *polis* a tension between the personal and the civic emerged. The civic identity of citizen and non-citizen of the *polis* helped the citizen attain their due through the instrument of the *polis*. Conceptually "the *polis* was valued for its ability to secure the good of its members through the preservation of freedom and order..."[7]As the traditional hierarchy weakened during the time of Kleisthenes, the citizenry attained power through voting rights to express their view collectively to come to a consensus on their leadership. In this sense the political rights of *demos* provided legitimacy to decision-making.

Political philosopher like Plato and Aristotle argued that the *polis* had a role to play in the well-being of humankind. Contrary to this view the early Greek philosophers like Antiphon, Socrates and Callicles, who were of the view that political order was not necessary to attain the well being of humankind believed that the *polis* had actually corrupted an individual's understanding of self-interest by turning them into a civic man.[8]

The Athenian system of democracy which was practiced in a limited scale for a short period did not have a radical influence on other European states until the beginning of the middle ages. The political changes which came about in middle age Europe replaced the monarchy completely with a parliament, or accorded the monarch a ceremonial role— as in England. The church was separated from the matters of the state. Gradually legislature, executive and judiciary were also separated and accorded specific powers. Citizens were accorded voting rights to elect their representatives through periodic elections for a limited tenure. Another specific feature of European democracy was that it evolved largely in industrial settings; consequently more feudal Eastern Europe remained untouched by the liberal democratic revolutions.

By the dawn of modern history, states which were on the course of being democracies, like England, became a large republic and thus direct democracy was not possible. The transformation of absolute monarchy into parliamentary democracy compelled them to adopt, indirectly, a popular representative form of government. During this period, only those who owned a certain amount of land could vote. In the towns, only the wealthiest had the right to vote. As a consequence, only wealthy men and landowners could become members of parliament. The parliament became the stronghold of the wealthy; as a result, the interest of the masses were overlooked. The political reforms of the 19th century extended the right to vote from propertied men to all men, and later, to women.

Jeremy Bentham and Stuart Mill were two modern political scientists who advocated for representative democracy. To prevent the government being above the interest of the people, Bentham and Mill advocated universal franchise and representative government. C. B. Macpherson regarded Bentham and Mill's view of democracy as a model of "protective democracy", in which the purpose of government is to protect the interest of individuals and the principle of the civil code implies that the purpose of law is to ensure the security of the labourer and the fruit of their labour.[9]

To secure the interest of the people, Mill propounded the idea of developmental democracy. In modern European conditions when the society was divided into working and employing classes by capitalistic competition, Mill observed the deteriorating plight of the working class which could make them antagonistic to the establishment and thus he thought of doing something to change the situation.[10] He propounded a democratic model that would contribute to human development. His ideal of democracy was a moral system which "promotes human development better than any other political system."[11] Mill recognised that capitalism produced class inequality which was incompatible to his model of democracy.

Democracy offers incentives to participate in the political process to retain the citizens' interests which are at stake in the operations of government. The class inequality of industrial Europe was of an antagonistic nature, and the numbers in the working class was higher than in the owning class. The democratic maxim of 'one person, one vote' maximises the interest of one class and negatively harms the other. To balance this, Mill introduced the idea of 'plural voting' and exclusion of many groups from voting. Mill's idea of 'plural voting' contradicted his earlier proposition of representative democracy. This model reduced the idea of incentives of participation in the political process as it minimises his idea of greater participation and more self-development.

Those who claimed to be democracies largely denied voting rights to women, slaves and the property-less populace. This situation is contradictory to one of the three criteria of democratic process set out by Robert Dahl. In his opinion, a democratic process is deficient unless people have adequate and equal opportunity for effective participation for expressing their preferences as to the final outcome.[12] The irony of universal suffrage is that women were given voting rights very late in England whereas the Afro-Americans were accorded this right only few decades ago.

The critics of procedural democracy prioritise substantive democracy, i.e, the rightness of outcome of decisions, over the process by which decisions are reached. Arend Lijphart sees the consensus model as more inclusive than majoritarian rule, which is exclusive, competitive and compromising.[13] In his view the majoritarian model is best suited to homogeneous societies, wherein the consensus model is appropriate for plural societies.[14] Like Lijphart, Dahl also exhibits his dislike for majoritarian rule as he sees this model as an effort to arrive at a mere compromised outcome between "the power of majorities and the power of minorities."[15] The remedy to this situation he finds in the Madisonian axiom of attainment of "non-tyrannical republic."[16] The axiom is based on the philosophical point that if external checks are not in place, individuals who are in power may tyrannise others. The tyranny is defined here as "severe deprivation of natural rights" and external checks as "application of reward and penalties."[17] It is already been discussed earlier that power has to be separated and diffused among the organs of the state, which constitutes the core of these external checks.

Dahl identified majoritarian democracy with political equality and popular sovereignty. He regarded democratic organisation if the process of arriving at government policy met the condition of political equality and popular sovereignty. His objection to populistic democratic theory is that it all focuses on how to maximise two goals – political equality and popular sovereignty – considering other goals to them. Besides prioritising two goals above others, populistic democratic theory also does inform how to maximise these goals in the real world.

A very trenchant criticism of liberal democratic theories comes from Joseph Schumpeter. In *Capitalism, Socialism and Democracy*, he criticises the notion of democracy as "...institutional arrangement for arriving at political decisions which realises the common good…" as old doctrine of democracy.[18] Instead viewing people as a repository of political power, as old theories of democracy suggest, he sees democracy as an "institutional arrangement for arriving at political decisions in which individuals acquire the power to decide by means of a competitive struggle for the people's vote"[19], that is to say, that the struggle is for leadership to exercise power. One of the newest theories of democracy, which resembles the oldest model of direct democracy, is "deliberative democracy," which is defined as an "association whose affairs are governed by the public deliberation of its methods."[20] In Joshua Cohen's conception, deliberative democracy is "…an ongoing and independent association – in which – …free deliberation among equal is basis of legitimacy, and …members regard each other having deliberative capacity."[21]

The essence of modern democracy is the belief that the base of democracy is the people themselves. That is, the only legitimate basis for instituting any system of political decision-making and any system of law is the will of the people. The concept of modern democracy cannot be defined within fixed parameters. There are multiple understandings of what should be the nature of democracy. With this caveat that any definitional effort would make the concept of democracy more reductionist we try to understand democracy – for the operational purposes of this study – through two broad categories – political freedom and civil liberties. These two categories briefly constitute elements of democracy when put together.

Political freedom, in a democracy, is a cluster of political rights which allows individuals or groups of individuals to choose their ruler or ruling party. The cluster includes one's right to elect and to be elected for the constitutional position without interference from any individual or group. In a federal form of government it also means devolution of power, i.e. all power should not be concentrated with one individual or party. All the elected bodies are only representative of powers and not the repository of power and people are the source of power. In the name of enforcing civic conduct, no group should hold onto power depriving people's right to choose their legislature by a meaningful process.

Civil liberties are a set of measures which ensure freedom and justice. Civil liberties and political freedom are two sides of the same coin and inextricably connected. They advocate both collective and individual rights. These include freedom of expression, association, assembly and freedom of religion. It also does promote an impartial judiciary. To ensure civil liberties it is essential that no one should possess multiple authorities, i.e. the power to make laws, implement laws and dispense justice. Interference in an independent institution's space by another authority endangers civil liberties.

So far we have discussed the historical, political and philosophical aspects of democracy. In addition it needs to be emphasised that the core of modern democracy rests on the principle that people have control over decision-making and all franchised citizen are equal to exercise this control. A state is only to be considered as democratic if the government is chosen by the franchised citizen through publicly approved methods for a limited tenure and remains accountable to the people. It is also important in a democratic setup that decisions which determine the fate of the people are not taken without reflecting on the interest of the public. There should be proper channels of the accommodation of voices of civil groups which are not necessarily elected but represent public concerns. A democratic government adopts persuasion and discussion as conflict resolving-methods between the competing forces rather than the use of force and violence.

Constitutionalism is essential for any democracy, which ensures that all people are aware of the fact that which organ of the state possesses what right and responsibility. This makes the authorities much more transparent. A democratic state also guarantees civil liberties and specially the protection of minorities living in that state. A state does not qualify to be democratic if, the views of minorities are constrained and their political and socio-economic potentialities are impaired through majoritarian tyranny. There has to be some power-sharing mechanism through which minorities could access public office and have a say in policy-making. In addition to these features, which collectively define and explain the nature of democratic state, it should be emphasised that people need to realise that they are the spirit of democracy and their participation in governance is a quintessential necessity.

The Origin and Definition of "Political Party"

In earlier times, the term 'faction' was the term used to refer to what we understand as 'party' today. In his analyses, Giovanni Sartori noted that etymologically and semantically these two terms do not express the identical meaning.[22] Both the terms originate from Latin and their usage in political lexicon had negative and pejorative connotations. The word 'faction' is derived from *facere* (a verb which means to do or to act) but used negatively and associated with groups whose behaviour was considered harmful. The term 'party' was also derived from a verb *partire*, meaning 'to divide.' It conveyed the idea of a "party" and in analytical construct became pejorative. Nevertheless, the term 'party' gradually entered into common usage and is defined differently by scholars. Before defining what a political party denotes in contemporary scholarship, it will be useful to see how and when it originated.

Historically, political parties took root in Europe. The germination of the concept was the corollary of political transformation followed by the Glorious Revolution of 1688 and French Revolution of 1789.[i]

It was the period when monarchies began to transform into representative republics. In the US, where monarchies and aristocracies were absent, the process of democratisation and party politics differed from European experiences. The process of democratisation also coincided with industrialisation in both the continents. According to Hans Daalder "the modern political party...can be described with little exaggeration as the child of the industrial revolution."[23] Industrialisation provided certain social pre-conditions where parties could emerge and grow. Joseph LaPlombara and Myron Weiner called political parties a "symbol of political modernity" which developed with the notion of incorporating the public into the system of political power.[24] In their understanding:

> The political party materialised when the task of recruiting political leadership and making public policy could no longer be handled by a small coterie of men unconcerned by public sentiments. The emergence of the

i. The Glorious Revolution was an elitist realignment of power in 17th century England. In 1688 the political class came together and overthrew the monarchy in England and established a system of parliamentarianism with limited voting rights. On the other hand the French revolution of 1789 was a popular uprising against absolute monarchy and French aristocracy. It brought radical change to the French polity by establishing republicanism, citizenship and civil rights committed in the name of liberty, equality and fraternity. Both these revolutions oriented the future political course of European nations towards nomocracy and later democracy.

> political party clearly implies that the masses must be taken into account by the political elite. Either out of commitment to the ideological notion that the masses have a right to participate in the determination of the public policy or the selection of the leadership...[25]

In reference to the growth of European political parties, Maurice Duverger observed two processes. The first was the Electoral and Parliamentary Origin of Parties. Within this paradigm parliamentary groups were the first to be created, then appeared the electoral committees and the third stage was a permanent linkage between these two components. Thus he stated that "Indeed there were political assemblies before there were elections" and "... the second evolved from the first more or less gradually."[26] The second process was the Extra-Parliamentary Origins of Parties. These associations were not parties in the traditional sense and their activities lay outside elections and parliament.[27]Contrary to the first process, parties in this paradigm were the secondary product. Associations such as trade unions, student organisations, religious sects and philosophical societies evolved first, and then followed formal parties from them. Max Weber had also developed a sequence of evolutionary stages of the parties. In his scheme, it follows as aristocratic cliques, small groups of notables and a plebiscitarian democracy.[28]

Near similar observation was made by Giovanni Sartori in his masterful work *Parties and Party System*. In his sequence of party development, the party government during the 18th century remained external and uninvolved in the sphere of governance. The party operated in the ambit of government but did not govern thus it was not party government but a "responsive government."[29] In the scheme of a representative system, the parties were extraneous and inimical and only at a later stage when large-scale enfranchisement of voters occurred, did the parties compete to mobilise voters, thus leading to the crystallisation of the party system.[30] Other scholarly points of views on the origin of political parties differ on the stages of development. In some cases, Duverger and Sartori's ideas also do not corroborate.

In certain cases both the process of democratisation of suffrage and the institution of parliament occurred simultaneously while in many cases "democratisation of suffrage outpaced the transfer of responsibility to the legislature."[31] The variation occurs due to the institutional obstacle and institutional incentives in a particular country. The development of parties was determined by the stringent laws which inhibited freedom of expression and press and formation of free association to put forward their views. This varied from country to country and therefore the evolution of parties also significantly differed. In this epistemological context parties evolved. What the term 'party' signifies depends upon the strand from which it is examined.

Scholars of political parties have developed three approaches based on their interest, ideology and popular choice. In the interest paradigm that what a political party strives to seek a very pragmatic definition was provided by Robert Huckshorn that: "A political party is an autonomous group of citizens having the purpose of making nominations and contesting elections in the hope of gaining control over governmental power through the capture of public offices and the organisation of government."[32] Among other prominent scholars who view parties from this lens is Joseph Schlesinger. He defines party as "a group organised to gain control of government in the name of the group by winning election to public office."[33] John Aldrich sees party "as coalitions of elites to capture and use political office." For Leon D. Epstein a party meant "any group, however loosely organised, seeking to elect government officeholders under a given label."[34] This idea sees party as an instrument to gain political power to perform certain objectives.

Duverger had defined parties on similar lines; however, he described them as faction. In his view the role of these factions "is to win political power and exercise it."[35] LaPlombara and Weiner did not see party as a loose organisation with the sole purpose of exercising power. Both suggested certain characteristics for an organisation to qualify as a party. A party in their opinion requires: continuity in organisation, coordination and regular communications between local and national units, determination to capture power, and mobilisation of popular support.[36] The definitions in this strand are more focused on the operational part of a party. The second strands of definitions are pertaining to the ideological dimensions of a political party.

Edmund Burke and Ronald Regan emphasised on the ideological roots of party politics. For Burke a "party is a body of men united, for promoting by their joint endeavours the national interest, upon some particular principle in which they are all agreed," while for Regan people group "together in a political party because of certain beliefs of what government should be."[37]The principle and belief are important component of such association. Religious parties sometime fall in this category. Members join and vote for them, while even being aware that they will not win, but because they believe in their principles. The third strand of definitions focusing on popular choice, fall between these two. They see political parties as a bridge between society and government and their purpose is to influence the policies of the government.

Sartori's definition serves as a catalyst for this model. He defines parties as "the central intermediate and intermediary structure between society and government."[38] One of the scholars advocating this paradigm, Anthony Downs sees political parties as mediating instruments with the purpose of mobilising voter choices to influence the governmental policies. Downs defines a political party as "a coalition of men seeking to control the governing apparatus by legal means"[39] with a purpose of attaining common agreed goals.

Theorising Party Types

Given that the societies are dynamic and their socio-political structures are not static, developing a uniform typology of political parties will not reflect the real world conditions.[ii]

Most of the prevalent conceptual categories of political parties were developed on the empirical field of the West. However a generic classification of political parties is shaped-up on the basis of some fundamental characteristics. The political parties are classified on certain fundamental distinctions such as their structure, social origin, ideology, leadership, objectives and policy orientation etc. The literature on party types was the central theme of scholars of political parties around the second half of the twentieth century. Maurice Duverger (1954), Sigmund Nuemann (1956) and

ii. The majority of the none-European states were colonised for some period of their history. The process and timing of decolonisation of British colonies in Asia, Spanish Americas, Dutch East-Indies and French Indo-China and West Africa differed. Their socio-economic conditions varied. The creation of political parties inthese colonies before and during the process of decolonistaion was a colonial construct with varied objectives. The main purpose was either to use these parties as their agent to control the natives or transfer power to them during their retreat. Therefore, the functions of these superimposed parties which had no organic origin could not be equalised with their European counterparts. However, they were the most important tool of political modernisation in their respective territories.

Otto Kirchheimer (1966) in their separate works developed party typologies which became the classical paradigm of analysing party categories. In the later decades of the 20th centuryAngelo Panebeanco (1988) and Piero Ingazi (1996) added more categories to the list of party types.

Based on the party characteristics and existing typology, Richard Gunther and Larry Diamond have developed a genus of "Species of Political Parties."[40] This genus has fifteen ideal-type species of parties. It encompasses all the broad available party-types and adds a new typology to the list. It reapplies the old components of available concepts to create a new typology. They emphasise that parties are a product of their social and technological context which are subject to change. Their party genus is based on three criteria. The first of these is the party's formal organisational design. In their view, some parties are organisationally thin and some are thick. Their membership styles are inclusive (open to all) and exclusive. Some depend on traditional modes of interaction and some prefer to adopt new means of communications to reach their supporters. The second criterion is the programmatic commandments or orientations of the party. These orientations may have ideological roots in religion, nationalism, political philosophies or they may not have any well-defined programmatic commitments. They work generally to serve a particular group. The final criterion involves party strategy and its attitudinal norms, whether the party is tolerant and pluralistic in its behaviour and respects the rules-of-the-game or whether the party has an anti-system attitude and proto-hegemonic objectives.

In their new party typology they have five broad types of parties such as elite parties, mass-based parties, ethnicity-based parties, electoralist parties and movement parties. Within these broad types there are sub-types of party species with minor similarity and differences with reference to three criteria stated earlier. In this section we will briefly discuss these party types.

The first major type is the Elite Parties, which is further divided into two subtypes. The Elite-based Parties, according to the authors are those "whose principal organisational structures are minimal and based upon established elites and related interpersonal networks within a specific geographic area."[41] They lack programmatic commitment and are not ideological. These parties are generally tolerant and collaborative within parliament and do not have hegemonic ambitions but they are not necessarily democratic. The first subtype party is the Traditional Local Notable party. Origin of such parties is traced to the 19th century with limited suffrage in semi-democratic regimes. They did not adopt extensive organisational campaign and were more concentrated on their own homogenous constituencies to gain power. The second subtype is the Clientestic Party. Such parties appeared when "the traditional local notable party was subjected to challenges from newly enfranchised segments of the electorate within societies undergoing industrialisation and urbanisation."[42] These parties served as instruments of new notables and were based on personalistically based support. They had weak organisational structure, ideology and programme and largely coordinated among the niche group of notables.

The second major type is the mass-based parties, further divided into six sub-types. Mass-based parties were the corollary of industrialisation and were "externally created party" which "emerged as a manifestation of the political mobilisation of the working class in many European polities."[43] Such parties have a base of "dues-paying" members who are always active. The party influences the social sphere of citizenry and is active through various affiliate bodies such as trade unions, youth clubs and religious organisations. The party penetrates through organisational networks from local to national levels. These networks serve as engines of political mobilisation and fraternisation. Further, the six subtypes of party species are largely classified on two distinctions. First, to what extent the parties are committed to party ideology, programmatic commitments. Second, what is the political attitude of the party, whether it is politically tolerant and pluralistic and agrees to operate within a democratic system or it has a hegemonic agenda and wishes to impose its programmatic commitments on the society.

The first subtype of mass-based party species is the Pluralist mass-based parties and Proto-hegemonic mass-based parties.[44] Pluralist parties strive to secure office through elections in order to attain their programmatic objectives. Their mobilisation of voters depends largely on building a mass membership base. In contrast to the pluralist parties, the proto-hegemonic parties are more disciplined and have active commitments to the party objectives and are ready to participate in electoral and extra-parliamentary conflicts. Therefore "recruitment of members is highly selective, indoctrination is intensive, and acceptance of the ideology and short-term party line is demanded of all members."[45] The second is the Class-mass Party.[46] Its mobilisation and membership basis remains within its class constituency. While they attempt to bring potential members into their fold, unlike the previous subtype, indoctrination and ideological conformity is less intensive. Within the organisational structure, power is located in an executive committee.

The third sub-types are the Leninist Parties, whose purpose is the systemic overhaul of the prevailing political structure by imposing a revolutionary change in society. This type of party sees itself as a vanguard of the masses and "organised expression of the will of society."[47] It has a secretive and closed structure base. Membership is highly exclusive and warrants unquestioning obedience. Indoctrination is intense. Followed by this, the next sub-type species, is the Pluralist Nationalist Parties. Such parties are based on mass-membership. The support base is generally found among individuals who see themselves as distinct national groups. They may take moderate preferences with regard to economic and religious policies, but may adapt an anti-system stance on the issues of territorial governance.

The fifth sub-type parties are the Ultranationalist Parties who have proto-hegemonic aspirations. For such parties, the core is the promotion of ideologies which admire race and nation above individuals. They despise minorities and believe in coercion and often rely upon uniformed party militia. Such parties are closer to Leninist parties in terms of member-base, indoctrination and objective of seizing power through electoral process or outside the system. The last subtype species of mass-based parties is the Fundamentalist Party. Such parties strive to recalibrate the state and society according to their own interpretation of religion. The party- programmes are standardised as per the party's reading of religious doctrines and are imposed on society. Such parties work on the belief that there is no separation between the state and religion. Party structure is usually hierarchical, absolutist, and members are supposed to be loyal and disciplined.

The third major party species are the Ethnicity-based Parties. Such parties are not very strong structurally. These parties have distinct electoral logic, and, contrary to mass-based parties, do not promise programmes for all the segments of society. Their objectives are parochial and centrally focused on their ethnic groups. They seek to mobilise votes only from within their own group. They see the state apparatus as an instrument to advance benefits to their specific electoral clientele. The fourth major party type encompasses parties under the class of Electoralist Parties. There are three sub-type species under this class. They share similar structural design and strategy but differ in their ideology, programmatic commitments and their political attitude to the other players and the system as a whole. Parties in this category do not nourish very strong ideology. They are more active during elections and use modern technologies and professionals in their campaign. They do not have rigid membership procedure and party candidates are selected on their personal traits.

The first sub-type species under this party type is the Catch-All Party. It is pluralistic and tolerant ideal-type party. It is not ideologically grounded but electorally oriented. Its organisational structure is not strong and depends largely on the central leadership. Its sole purpose is to mobilise votes during the election and secure office. The catch-all parties usually position themselves as moderate and liberal centrist. Their policy commitments are not rigid and changes with public opinion. These parties heavily rely on charismatic personal traits of their candidates. The second sub-type in the sequence is the Programmatic Party. It is similar to the catch-all parties in respect of the structure and preference of candidates on personality attributes. But it differs in terms of having strong programmatic and ideological commitments. Unlike the former, it sometime, resorts to a narrower mobilisation within its core constituency. The third and most purely electoralist party is the Personalistic Party. Its central motive is to provide electoral platform to its leader to win election and govern. It has a very shallow and opportunistic organisation and may change its name in each election. It is largely leader-driven and instead of ideology and programme, it mobilises votes through the charismatic attributes of the party leader.

The last major party type in the genus of party species is the Movement Parties. It has two sub-type parties. Conceptually, they overlap between the party and movement. They have fluid organisational traits and membership is open to all. The first sub-type is Left-libertarian Parties. Such parties are 'post-materialist' in their political attitude. They reject the primacy of economic issues and are characterised by "a negative consensus that the predominance of markets and bureaucracies must be rolled back in favour of social solidarity relations and participatory institutions."[48] Organisationally, it is based on loose networks of local support, membership is open to all and policy preferences are not rigid. The last sub-type of this species is called Post-Industrial Extreme Right Party.[49] It is the distinct response to the conditions of post-industrial society. It is based on hierarchical leadership structure and leader's directives are unquestionable. It concentrates its line of attack on state's policies for the relative plight of the society. Such parties are xenophobic and intolerant of migrants.

The Parties' Democracy Connection

The brief discussion above has outlined the ontological meaning of political parties, their epistemological origin, their characteristics to qualify as a party as well as their typology in a broader sense. Now for the purpose of this study it is imperative to understand the essentiality of parties in a democratic system. Historically nomocracy and democracy or, in other words, constitutionalism and parliamentarianism emerged much before parties came to existence. Despite the fact that the origin of democracy is older than political parties, in present times parties have become indispensable to the functioning of democracy. Therefore, an obvious question which flows from this historical fact is why political parties were created and how they became essential to the functioning of modern democracies. The answer to this question also outlines the very premise of what linkages democracy and political parties share. Interestingly political parties did not originate on their own, but were created by politicians who were running the business of governance without political parties. Then why did they create political parties in the first place?

The answers lie in the observation that democracy being a political process is driven by institutionalisation of political parties. If democracy is a political process that organises societal interaction and also the government "of the people, by the people, for the people"[iii] then people are entitled to participate in the process of democracy. By this logic the citizens who are to be governed and whose social life is to be organised by the very process

iii. In the simplest but most powerful definition, almost one and half centuries ago in his address at Guttenberg, Pennsylvania, 17 November 1863 the then US President Abraham Lincoln defined democracy as the government "of the people, by the people, for the people," Abraham Lincoln, *Lincoln: Speeches and Writings 1859-1865* (New York: The Library of America, 1989), p. 536.

have to be involved. The collective choice of the citizen was to be taken in consideration by allowing them to participate in the political process. At the time of direct democracy and a small social setup it, to some extent, had the possibility of involving majority of its citizens. Thereafter, societies became too big to be governed by direct forms of democracy, so democracy itself transformed to indirect and representative form to allow maximum participation. Now the question was through which mechanism collective participation could be ensured. This mechanism was political parties whose very origin was to represent the collective interest of the mass which elected their members to the parliament. In the thesis of John Aldrich's who studied the origin of American political parties, they were created as new institutionalism resolving the problems of social choice and collective choice.[50]

Aldrich however carefully underlined that the *raison d'être* behind the creation of political parties was the set of incentives politicians have seen; then the parties could be used as an instrument of achieving a politician's goal of winning.[51] Therefore it could be deduced that parties were created for purely functionalist purposes. The instrumentality of political parties to represent the public choice and their interest institutionally makes them a connecting link between the governed and the government. This very nature of political parties being functionalist, whether in the government or outside the government, makes them central to the workings of modern democratic systems. The principal function of a party is democratic consolidation. The term "democratic consolidation" in its originality meant stabilisation of democratic political process and making democracy "immune against the authoritarian regression."[52] The consolidation process included range of items such as:

> ...popular legitimation, the diffusion of democratic values, the neutralisation of anti system actors, civilian supremacy over the military, the elimination of authoritarian enclaves, party building, the organisation of functional interests, the stabilisation of electoral rules, the routinisation of politics, the decentralisation of state power, the introduction of mechanisms of direct democracy, judicial reform, the alleviation of poverty, and economic stabilisation.[53]

Who was supposed to carry these tasks? The political parties emerged as the answer by carrying out multifold functions and leading to the ultimate regime legitimisation and stabilisation. Their functions ranged between multiple dimensions. More than half a century ago, V. O. Key, in his seminal work on political parties in America, outlined major functions of political parties in a democratic system. He broadly classified the functions of political parties into four major cyclic stages namely: the parties as organisation, parties in the electorate, parties in government and parties in the legislature.[54]

In the first stage of "parties-as-organisation" they have functions of recruitment of leaders to participate in the electoral process as well as to hold political offices. They are also responsible as organisations for the training of a class of political elites and nurturing them as current and future leaders who will be the vanguard of the democratic system. The parties-as -organisation are also instrumental in 'aggregating and articulating' the public interest by giving them organised voice. In the next stage the "parties-in-the-electorate" parties carry the functions of 'educating citizens' about political issues and process. Another significant task is to simplify choices for voters by making politics accessible to them. They are supposed to generate the symbol of loyalty and provide anchorage for political identification. The last function of parties in this stage is to campaign and mobilise citizens to participate in the electoral process. In the third stage of "parties-in the-government" – the ultimate objective of parties – they are supposed to carry out the function of 'creating majorities' through consensus or coalition to form a stable government. Thereafter parties have a responsibility to 'organise and stablise' the government by creating a consensus or seeking the cooperation of individual legislature. Parties in the government are responsible to formulate public policies and devise mechanisms to implement them. In the stage of "parties-in-the-legislature" the parties are also expected to organise dissent and opposition and offer an alternative choice if possible. Parties here are collectively responsible for providing stability to the government and act as responsible actors.

In the array of functions of parties Richard Kartz through his recent work added "coordination" as one of the most important functions. A party in Kartz's view serves as a coordination tool "within government, within society and between government and society at large."[55] Coordination within government means to maintain discipline and communication within the party's parliamentary members; bridging between legislative and executive branches. Coordination within society involves organising political activity with citizens. Lastly coordination between society and government is linking the representatives of public office and citizenry.[56]

On the basis of the above discussion the functions of political parties can be summarised as follows: aggregating and articulating social interests in the political system; recruiting and training the next generation of the political class; developing programmatic content and building public opinion; campaigning and participating in the election; educating and socialising the citizens about the political process and making them participate in the electorate process; occupying political offices through legitimate means and exercising political power; criticising anti-people polices as an organised group of dissenters; and consolidating and legitimising the political system. Because of these range of functions, a political party becomes indispensible to the working of present democracies. Both are critical to each other like a conjoined twin, if separated their chances of survival is minimal. On this premise political parties, in the scheme of this study, are taken as the primary and the central variable whose role and acts are correlated to measure the trajectories of democracy in Pakistan.

The Islamic Debate on Democracy

The following debate focuses on the discourse germinating in the context of democratic governance within Muslim scholarship. It largely analyses within the framework of political theory and does not intend to examine the textual merits of Islam, rather it concentrates on how Muslim scholarship has contributed to it theoretically. It also focuses on how the scholarship, with regard to democracy, transformed in temporal and spatial settings. It is recognised in the beginning of the debate that the scholars belonging to different sects and nationality offered contradictory perspectives. In this theoretical discussion the happenings in the 'real world' are deliberately not given much space, however they are used in fragments for empirical substantiation.

This is largely an ontological study with selective writings which received prominence in literature and shapes the perspective of the academic world.

The concept of Islamic democracy is debated here, as Pakistan is the case study. In Pakistan the debate is still ongoing on how to govern the polity, despite having adopted a Constitutional form of democracy. Some political parties, largely the Islamist parties and one military regime, argued in favour of a *Shariah* state. They also shaped the narrative that Pakistan should be governed on the basis of democratic principles of Islam. This has certainly impacted the social and political order in Pakistan. For this very reason, in this section we look into the theoretical debates from which these forces derive their legitimacy. What this section tries to analyse is how the Muslim scholarship perceived the concepts of nation and nation-state, sovereignty and authority, state and its organs, and how they collectively influence their understanding of democracy.

The application of the term 'state' in the framework of political theory while making simultaneous reference to the Islamic state means how a certain set of principles would guide the ideal of governance. Since Sunnite and Shi'at political theories do not agree on the principle of separate notion of Caliphate and Imamate, the debate largely revolves on the point of confluence. Most of the debates originate in certain contexts of a historic past which were subject of change. The modern political language does not offer a complete explanation of these principles. Having said that, it is also important, to examine the application and continuation of these understanding in the present discourse.

If we agree on the view that the Quran is didactic and an ethical book no such disagreement arises among various scholarships. The ambiguity emerges when the Quran is also considered as a book of political guidance. Since there is no absolute trace of the origin of the concept and nature of the state scholars have rationalised their interpretations with ambiguous meanings. What is found in this brief debate is that thinkers have no consensus on the nature of the Quran whether it is only a didactic and ethical book or it is also a book of political and economic guidance.

When it comes to the political debate on the nature of the Islamic state all debates concentrate on the period of the Caliphate. Apart from this, it is difficult to find other spatial and temporal references which add to the clarification on the nature of the Islamic state. Anything which did not have Islamic origins was not incorporated and thus deprived the independent and organic growth of the theory of the state. Barring a few exceptions, the impact of changing Muslim political debate is non-reflective on present Muslim republics, kingdoms and dictatorships. Scholars have endeavored to convince the masses that their political affairs are not wholly decided by the faith alone. The popular notion holds that even in the sphere of political affairs everything is already drafted and thus it does not warrant further enquiry. But this brief debate would demonstrate that the quest to trace the origin and nature of Islamic state were made by the scholars and it is still evolving.

The Caliphate

Ibn-Khaldun, in his seminal work *Al-Muqaddima,* attempted to provide a nuanced socio-political analysis of history of the 14th century Arab world. His arguments possess both an Islamic and a philosophical tone. His analysis of the Bedouin (Arabs) nomad society and its progression to urbanised sedentary civilisation is set within a sociological and ethnographic framework. In his observation the natural corollary of nomad life is a group feeling (*al-asabiyah*). This group feeling matures and metamorphosis into a royal authority (*al-mulk*). This group feeling is a necessary condition to establish a political authority which will defend the nation. In the latter part of *Al-Muqaddima* when he makes a case for the Caliphate he contradicts the sociological phenomenon which he thought was natural.

On the Caliphate, Khaldun argued that the purpose of the political laws was to consider worldly interests while the intention of the Lawgiver (Muhammad) was to consider the welfare of mankind hereafter. To attain such a state, it was required by the masses to follow the religious law. "The authority to do so was possessed by the representatives of the religious law, the prophets. Later on it was passed to the Caliphs who took their place."[57] In Khaldun's view to exercise the Caliphate meant to cause the masses to act as required by religious insights into their interests in the other world as well as in this world.[58] Khaldun further explains that according to the Prophet, the worldly conditions are to be considered in relation to their value for hereafter, therefore the Caliph who substitutes him must protect the religion and exercise political leadership of the world in accordance.[59] He considered the Caliphate and Imamate as an institution and person who heads this institution as the "caliph" or "Imam".

Ibn Taymiyah, who is considered an early authority on this subject presented a similar but a different point of view on this matter. For Taymiyah it was the faith, and not state, which was the foremost consideration of religion and the Prophet did not establish any State. Taymiyah though had similar views on the Caliphate that it was a form of a state and possessed sovereignty and quoted the Prophet that Caliphs are "those who revive my *sunnah* and teach it to the people."[60] But he had a different opinion with regard to the institution of the Imamate. While on the Imamate he argued the establishment of Imamate is a doctrinal as well as a practical necessity.[61]

However, both Ibn Taymiyah and Ibn Khaldun have stated that *Mu'tazilite* and *Kharijites* were opposed to the position of the Imam and they argued that they only observed the religious law. *Kharijites* argued that "they are interested only in the application of '*Shar*'. If this law can be applied by the community without the help of a superior there is no need of an Imam."[62] Khaldun further argued that the Imamate is established by a general consensus and is a community duty and is left to the discretion of all the competent Muslims.[63] The debate on the Caliphate largely concerns Sunni scholarship as Shias do not accept the Caliphate. The Shia opposition to the Caliphate is on the basis of *Risalat as-Saqifah* and the sermon of *Ghadir Khumm*. The Shia argued that the Prophet preferred Ali, and that the Imamate was transmitted to him through the implied preference of acts he was chosen for. They consider the Imamate as "*lutf*" (grace) of Allah towards his people. In their view:

> since God is the absolute ruler of the universe and has placed certain responsibilities on mankind for the good of His creation, it is, therefore, incumbent on Him to appoint someone (an imam) to enforce His law and execute His decrees, because He does not look into all these affairs personally.[64]

The *Mu'tazilite* possessed an entirely different view from both Shi'ate and Sunnite. In their opinion the necessity of the institution of Imamate is proved by reason and not revealed by God. In the present time, the views of the *Mu'tazilite* have faded and been replaced by more conservative schools of thought.

Like Ibn-Khaldun and Ibn-Taymiyah, Al-Mawardi, who is considered as the founder of *Shafi'at* school of though deliberated on the subject of Caliphate. He believed that the Quran has obligated the necessity of establishment of the Imamate. He did not distinguish between the institution of the Caliphate and Imamate. Al-Mawardi's political ideas were derived from his treatise on state administration and political thought, the *Al-Ahkam al Sultaniyah.* According to his understanding of the Muslim society and Islam "the institution of the Imamate is necessary as a requirement of the *Shari'ah* and not as a requirement of reason"[65] and for the Muslims it is an obligation to appoint an Imam.

On his understanding of the period of the Orthodox Caliphate, Al-Mawardi arrives at the conclusion that an Imam must be either elected or nominated. He also enlisted certain conditions for being qualified to be elected as an Imam. He also makes clear the qualifications required for those who can elect.[66] The principle of appointment of a successor by a ruling Imam is principally embodied in the Shi'at tradition, wherein the *Kharijites* were opposed to it and advocated for democracy and universal franchise.[67]

Sovereignty and Authority

Within the theoretical timeline of Western political thought with regard to the formation of the state as an institution, it is agreed upon that it germinated as a social contract. It resulted from the agreement between the Leviathan and the masses. The Leviathan was omnipotent and omnipresent had control over all, but was accountable to none. He derived his legitimacy from that social contract. His power was absolute. But as societies advanced and became more complex, his authority was diluted and became the subject of the "will of the people" and was accountable to the masses.

In varying contextual settings, various forces evolved which shaped and determined the nature of legitimacy. Such forces were of an economic, social and coercive nature. Divine force was another such force, which is the subject of this deliberation. The discourse on divine force and the authority determines the nature of legitimacy in many official Islamic states. However, empirical observation does vary. Scholars may make many theoretical distinctions among authority, power, legitimacy and so on, this has created ambiguity and rulers have manipulated this in their favour.

In the framework of the Leviathan, who becomes the arbitrator of social affairs of those who chose him, due to human nature, Khaldun argued that they would need someone who would act as a "restraining influence and mediator in every social organisation" to maintain peace and this person will have superiority over group feeling and his superiority is recognised as "royal authority" (*al-mulk*).[68] Royal authority means superiority and power to rule by force. It is more than just leadership and something natural to human beings because of its social implications.[69]

This idea of royal authority is similar in the works of Ibn-Taymiyah. On the basis of a *hadith* (which is of apocryphal origin) of the Prophet that says: " the *Khilafah* after me will last only thirty years, after that it will become dominion (*mulk*)"[70] Ibn-Taymiyah built his theory that after the prophetic succession it will be an ordinary *Khilafah* "*mulk*" (dominion, sovereignty or kingdom).[71] Ibn-Taymiyah's distinction between the *mulk* and the Caliphate, according to Qamaruddin Khan, is not of much significance as the functions of both the institutions are similar.

In his study of the Bedouins, Khaldun states that "Arabs are natural groups which by necessity exist in civilisation" and these nomads aspire for urbanised sedentary life.[72] As discussed earlier, as this group had a group feeling it was also necessary to have a leadership. In his view, the leadership over people who share a given group feeling cannot be vested in those who are not of the same descent. According to him leadership exists only through superiority and group feeling. After presenting his sociological study of leadership among the nomads and sedentary people of the Arabia, Khaldun talked of divine authority. In his view those who possess royal authority it is granted to them by God. "Political and royal authority are (God's) guarantee to mankind and serve as a representation of God among men with respect to his laws."[73]

Ibn-Khaldun, Ibn-Taymiyah and Al-Mawardi have also described certain qualities needed to acquire authority among the *Ummah*. According to the classical writings of all, a Caliph who will govern the affairs of the Muslim community (the *Ummah*) has to be of *Qurashite* descent.[74] With this common assumption for Ibn-Taymiyah they were concerned also with other qualities such as infallibility, for Al-Mawardi it was justice, learning, integrity of physical senses and organs, wisdom and bravery and for Ibn-khaldun it was generosity, the forgiveness of error, tolerance towards weak, hospitality towards guests, the support of dependents, maintenance of the indigent, patience in adverse circumstances, faithful fulfillment of obligations and liberty with money.[75]

Since Ibn-Khaldun, Ibn-Taymiyah and Al-Mawardi completed their treatise before the ferocious expansion of Muslim rule in the non-Arab territories, and before the establishment of great Sultanates and Emirates, their focus remains on the period of the Orthodox Caliphate and extended period of the subsequent Caliphate of the Abbasid, Ummayids and the Fatimids. Since the Caliphate and Imamate remained their referral period, they deliberated on the nature of leadership and authority of a Caliph, which also shaped the ideas of modern scholars on this subject.

Among the contemporary scholars, Ali Abd Al-Raziq has recognised the distinction between the Prophetic state and the rule following his celestial repose. This distinction is also visible in Ibn-Taymiyah's work, and according to the implied argument of his thesis, the Caliphate and the Prophetic state were distinct on the basis of their objectives. In his view, the purpose of the Prophetic state was to build a just social order wherein the objective of Caliphate was to establish a just political order where Islam could thrive. In terms of authority, Al-Raziq argues that the prophecy is something other than royalty where prophecy is one sort of dignity and royalty another.[76] In his opinion, the Prophet was only an apostle of God, and his purpose was religious and he did not made any appeal for political government. And therefore one should not equate prophetic sovereignty with temporal political sovereignty. The prophet may have performed a role similar to that of a king but his governance was of this world and also concerned with the world hereafter. On this basis, Al-Raziq argued that the authority of the Prophet over the Muslims was the authority of apostleship; it had nothing to do with temporal power.[77] He further argued that the purpose of the prophetic mission was to spread a universal religious message and to build a human unity on the basis of faith and not a state unity on the basis of a temporal authority. Unlike, Al-Raziq who made this distinction, Abul Ala Maududi considered Islam as a political unity and also as political order established by the Prophet. Since Maududi communicated in the idioms of modern political science he clearly shared his view on the concept of sovereignty and authority.

In Maududi's theory of Islamic state, sovereignty belongs to God, "none is entitled to make laws on his own authority and is obliged to abide by them, the right vests in Allah alone" [78] which is extended to the entire universe and over all people. He interpreted that the sovereign is one who has the ultimate power to make laws and impose his will; therefore it is natural to see human-made legislation in conflict with the laws of God. And it is not possible for the two systems of government to go together. In Maududi's understanding "laws come into existence by the will of the sovereign and binds people to obey him but here is no law to bind the sovereign and he himself is absolute authority."[79]

In Maududi's concept of the Islamic state, he recognised the Prophet and latter *Khalifa* as the deputy of the sovereign who was given limited sovereignty under the suzerainty of God.[80] They were the chosen ones and were supposed to enforce the laws of god. Maududi interpreted that the chosen ones "who has have the authority in whatever capacity among Muslims deserve obedience. It is not correct to dispute with them and disrupt the life of the community."[81] He does not seem to question the source of authority and urges the people to submit to anyone who has the capacity to exercise power. Maududi grants religious sanction for the use of force stating, "Allah prevents all those things using the power of the state, which the Quran does not prevent."[82] He further says,the "reforms that Islam wants to introduce cannot be introduced just by preaching. To implement them, political power is needed."[83] He diverted the concept of sovereignty towards a divine ambiguity for certain reasons.

Nation and Nationalism

Within the conceptual framework of democracy, which strengthened its roots in modern nation-states, the concept of nation and nationalism becomes a quintessential element. Scholars of nationalism have interpreted it in several ways. There are various defining markers of nationalism which shapes its nature. These markers are temporal and spatial and depending on a context any marker may become deterministic of particular nationalistic feeling. An empirical observation of South Asian states exhibits varying defining markers or forces which took precedence over others in their formation. One of the causes of the partition of India stemmed from the "two nation theory" based on religion. In the formation of Bangladesh, the cultural nationalism of "Bangla" took precedence over their Muslim brotherhood. Within India many states were reorganised on the basis of linguistic nationalism. The objective of this discussion is to debate how Muslim scholarship sees the concepts of nation and nationalism.

Before discussing the understanding of nationalism in Muslim scholarship, it is imperative to briefly examine its understanding in Western thought. A very authoritative definition of nationalism was given by Benedict Anderson. In his book *Imagined Communities*, Anderson defined nation as "an imagined political community." It is imagined because the members of even the smallest nation will never know their fellow members, meet them or even hear of them, yet in the minds of each lives the image of their communion.[84] This imagined community despite all its inequalities and contradiction is conceived on the basis of comradeship.[85] The concept of Muslim community or *Umma*, as one united community, is also very similar to this idea and it will be discussed in detail later.

Ernest Gellner also considered the 'nation' as an elusive concept but he explained that the nation exists when members of it share the same culture and recognise each other belonging to the same nation.[86] The concept that nations are natural and God-given is a myth in Gellner's view and it is the nationalism "which sometimes takes preexisting cultures and turns them into nations, sometimes invert them and often obliterates preexisting cultures: that is reality."[87] An identical position was also professed by Eric J. Hobsbawm who believed that "nationalism comes before nations. Nations do not make states and nationalism but the other way round."[88] According to Hobsbawm's theory of "nation as invented tradition" there are 'constructed' or 'invented' components which turns individuals into a nation.[89] Within the paradigm of "invented tradition" Hobsbawm identifies three major innovations. The first innovation is the development of a secular equivalent of the church – primary education. Second is the invention of public ceremonies and third is the mass production of public monuments.[90] The combine of all these innovations helps in producing individuals who believe that they are a part of that tradition.

Unlike Anderson, Gellner and Hobsbawm, who considered it imagined, elusive and invented, Ernest Renan and Joseph Stalin considered nationalism as more dynamic, regenerative and a tangible project. For Renan if nations have begun they will end or be replaced.[91] He identified 'nation' as morality, a grand solidarity constituted by historical consciousness. And it is an 'everyday plebiscite' and it remains till individuals affirm it.[92] Similarly, Stalin argued that a nation is not a racial or tribal but a historically constituted community of people.[93] For Stalin a nation is a "*historically constituted, stable community of people, formed on the basis of a common language, territory, economic life, and psychological make-up manifested in a common culture*"[94] (italic in original). In the absence of any of the elements a nation will be incomplete and presence of all these characteristics itself qualify for being a nation.[95] Similarly in Hugh Seton-Watson's view it was a practical necessity and the formation of national consciousness in new nations was a deliberated project of educated life.[96]

On nationalism, Anderson argued that it is a political creed that underscores the cohesion of modern societies and legitimises their claim to authority. Nationalism in Anthony Smith's opinion is a more practical ideology which places the nation at the centre of its concerns to attain three generic goals – national authority, national unity and national identity – and a nation cannot survive without the sufficient degree of all three.[97] This brief discussion tries to give us some understanding of the conceptual origin and practical necessity of nation and nationalism. Through this framework, we shall examine how Muslim scholarship, particularly in South Asia, conceived the essence of these two concepts.

The concept of nation and nationalism among the Muslim thinkers remained ambiguous. It has been always unclear that how in an Islamic state all the groups becomes part of a nation. This ambiguity arises due to the various interpretations given to the term '*Ummah*', used in various verses of the Quran.[98] The term is popularly used to denote the Muslim community. Now if the *Ummah* is only a religious community of those who follow Islam are in an Islamic state, how do other religious communities form part of this *Ummah*? Although they share the same historical past, language, culture and ethnicity, their rights and duties conceptually varies.[iv] Secondly, different ethnic communities, for example Arabs, Persians, Tatars or Turks, followed

iv. In an Islamic state, Muslim and Non-Muslim identities were formed on a religious basis and were addressed differently, extraction of taxes from them had different mode, and their duties toward the defense of state were not uniform.

Islam, but formed their own nations in a political sense. In the Quran the term was not used to denote the community of believers in territorial or ethnic sense. Therefore, there is not much contestation on the understanding that it is used to describe the Muslims.

When Muslim scholars encountered the Western political idea of nation and nationalism, especially during the time of European colonialism, they propounded different theoretical formulations. On the practical question of the possibility of Arab unity and Muslim unity Sati Al-Husri agreed that Arab unity is much easier than Muslim unity and capable of realisation.[99] The concept of Arab unity means political unity and the concept of Islamic unity defers from Muslim brotherhood.[100] He recognised a pragmatic contradiction to attain Muslim unity. To have unity among Muslim states the first prerequisite is that they should have political organisation. Political unity in the Muslim world which existed in the beginning did not withstand the changes of circumstances for any length of time. The Caliphate of Abbasid and Ummayids could not unite them politically. Al-Hursi observed that even during the Caliphate and after independent political units were formed, Islam still spread in many countries without the Caliph's authority. The idea of Arab unity or nationalism emanates from the natural social forces – language, history, geographical contiguity and from any external artificial views.[101] This is an identical view to Ibn-Khaldun's sociological idea of group feeling (*al-asabiyah*).

Similarly, when South Asian Muslim scholars faced the crisis of political positioning they advocated different ideals of nationalism. The concept of nationalism and Islam in the sub-continent was debated between Hussain Ahmad Madani and Muhammad Iqbal in a charged environment of the freedom movement. In 1937, Madani made a statement that "in the current age, nations (*qaumean*) are based on home lands (*autaan*), not religion."[102] In the following days, Urdu dallies such as *Ehsan* and *Al-Aman* published it using the term *millat* instead of nations. According to Barbara Metcalf this gave Iqbal an opportunity to insist that the Muslims needed a political unit of their own.[103] Iqbal criticised Madani for his statement that nations are formed by lands and the Indians are advised to accept that view.[104] Iqbal argued that the country is a geographical term which changes with time, wherein Islam is a social order and both the concepts do not clash. Iqbal accused Madani with the charge of persuading Indian Muslims to adopt:

> That religion and politics are entirely separate, and if the Muslims want to live in this country, they must understand religion to be a merely private affair which should be confined to individuals alone. Politically they should not regard themselves as a separate nation. They should rather lose themselves in the majority.[105]

This accusation was a reflection of Iqbal's understanding that polity and ideal are not separate entities, rather that Islam is a blend of both, and he argued that Islam does not bifurcate between private and worldly affairs and church and state are organic to each other.[106] Iqbal further argued that the term *qaum* used by Madani is unfounded in the Quran which used the term *millat* and *Ummat*. And unbelievers can also have their own faith and *millat* but cannot be the part of *Ummat*.[107] Responding to Iqbal's charges Madani argued that during the time of Prophet when he migrated to Medina from Mecca a covenant was signed between Muslims and non-Muslims. The agreement provided the same rights and privileges to all the signatories beyond their faith. They formed a composite *Ummah* against the enemies. They were called *Ummah* and that is the basis of Madani's composite nationalism.[108] During the same period Maududi also contributed to the debate through his writings.

Unlike Iqbal and Madani, Maududi's arguments and perspective on nationalism and Islam was very straightforward and without ambiguity. In his view "in their aim Islam and nationalism are diametrically opposed to each other."[109] He argued that nationalism divides man on the basis of nationality and the principle of Islam renders equality in the sphere of economics, politics and legality; however, it remains empirically apocryphal in his text.[110] He condemned nationalism for it being a satanic principle against the principle of morality embodied in the holy book. In his view the law of God (the *shariah*) aims to develop man into a moral framework and nationalism demolishes this framework.[111] Throughout his text the approach remained one-dimensional and laid emphasis on the moral character of the individual and not on the political necessity of the collective. He did not perceive it as a coherent force necessary for the formation of the nation-state. Having said that it must be acknowledged that the works of Iqbal, Madani and Maududi had made an intensive contribution in the way it shaped mass perception in Pakistan.

Islam and Democracy

In the foregoing discussion we have analysed the debates on key political concepts from the perspective of Islamic political theory within the paradigm of democratic governance. With the help of concepts like sovereignty, nation, nationalism and caliphate (state), discussed in the previous section, the debate can be now carried over to the relationship between Islam and democracy. It is important to understand this link, because Pakistan, which oscillated between democratic and authoritarian rule, also struggled to create balance between the political role of Islam and democracy. Political parties, both of a secular and Islamist nature, used the force of Islam in shaping their agenda and programmes. In the subsequent chapters we will examine how political parties used Islam to gain and maintain power. Before that it will be useful to explore the general conceptual literature regarding Islam and democracy.

This debate germinates around a question posed in simple lexicon and that is, are Islam and democracy compatible? Amos Perlmutter raised a question in his debate "is Islam fundamentalist or otherwise, compatible with liberal, human right oriented, western style, representative democracy?"[112] And he answered in the negative. A very strong criticism has also come from an Iranian scholar, Hamid Paydar, whose accusation was that the religion and religious government has inherent animosity toward democracy and both cannot be combined unless Islam is thoroughly secularised.[113] Fatema Mernissi, also says that "humanistic ideas – freedom of thought, the sovereignty of the individual, the right to freedom of action, tolerance – were propagated in the West through a secular school" and with rare exceptions, Muslim-majority countries never called themselves secular.[114] But there are two perspectives on this – of those who reject the compatibility, and those who see no contradiction in Islam and democracy.

In the spectrum of two extreme points of views prominent scholars like Sayyid Qutb, Abul A'la Maududi and Hamid Paydar are on the side of incompatibility and the counter-point of view is held by Abdolkarim

Soroush, Fathi Osman, Rashid Ghannoushi, Murad Hofmann and Mohammad Khatimi. Egyptian scholar Sayyid Qutb had utter contempt for the confluence of Islam and democracy. In his work *Milestones*, Qutb shares that accepting democracy is like "infidelity (*nizam al-kufr*) or polytheism (*shirk*), because democracy meant worshipping, as supposedly, the sovereign, both the individual citizen and his state."[115] In Murad Hofmann's view, Qutb's position is shaped by the factor that the term democracy emerged in the western world and is imposed by them on their colonies for civilisational mission and also due to the semantic of the term. Democracy is understood etymologically as "the rule of people" i.e, the sovereignty of the people, which is contradictory to the sovereignty of God,[116] therefore both cannot coexist.

Rejecting the incompatibility perspective Iranian scholar Abdolkarim Soroush came up with the idea of "Democratic Religious Government" in a philosophical and epistemological framework. Soroush differentiates between the religious and democratic government on the point that in democratic governments the "common sense" of the people is the arbitrator of conflict, while in religious governments this task of arbitration rests with religion.[117] He further explains that "the combination of religion and democracy is an example of the concordance of religion and reason…" and in democratic governments the arbitration "is left with common wisdom; in religious society, it is left to the religion" and if the array of natural rights, the prerequisite of democracy, are included in religious knowledge the result will be religious democracy.[118]

On the question of secularisation of Islam, Soroush states that this view stems from the perspective when liberalism and democracy are equated and democracy doesn't require believers to abandon their faith. Religious governments stem from a religious society and such a government is the guarantee of both religion and democracy.[119] Like Soroush, Murad Hofmann also see no necessity of secularism to be a democracy and if it is the prerequisite then democracy would be unacceptable to Islam.[120] Maududi also held a similar perspective and developed the theory of "Theo-democracy" where both could coexist.

Maududi developed the concept of "Democratic *Khilafat*", because, in his theory of the Islamic state the caliph will be elected and will have limited sovereignty or vicegerency as against the concept of Western secular democracy, in which, people possess absolute sovereignty.[121] In *Isalmi Riyasat*, he interpreted the democratic *Khilafat* as "Theo-democracy" in which the vicegerent enjoys only limited popular sovereignty.[122] In his seminal work, *Islamic Way of Life*, Maududi elaborates more on the concept of democracy in Islam. In his opinion, in an Islamic state all individuals are equal and represent the Caliphate of the God. Therefore, the authority of the caliphate is bestowed on the entire group of people, which fulfils the conditions of *Tawheed* (unity of God) and *Risalat* (Prophethood) and not necessarily to individuals, class or dynasty alone.[123] Such a society in his view "carries the responsibility of the caliphate as a whole and each one of its individuals shares the Divine Caliphate. This is the point where democracy begins in Islam."[124] He distinguishes between Western democracy and Islamic democracy on the basis of popular sovereignty. In the Western democracy people are sovereign and possess absolute authority while Islamic democracy is subservient to the Divine Law and authority is exercised with the conformity of the limit prescribed by God. Apart from his theoretical formulation, Maududi also elaborated on practical ways in which this concept could be realised.

Among the contemporary scholars, Fathi Osman tries to illustrate how the democratic mechanism provides a practical way of implementing the *Shura* – a serious and effective participation in making a decision in the Islamic state.[125] Osman argues in contemporary phraseology of electoral democracy. Referring to the period of the Orthodox Caliphate he argues that "the head of contemporary Muslim state can be elected directly by the people or by the parliamentary representatives of the people, or can be nominated by those representatives as a candidate for or against whom the public then votes..." and "Islam can accept any of that in the interest of the people."[126] On the election of the head of the state, Osman refers to Quranic verses and argues that the Quran says that most people lack knowledge and moral commitment, and may fail to make the right decisions, but it never suggests that a few people will necessarily arrive at a perfect decision. And when there are multiple candidacies, the leader should be elected with a majority as proven by the Prophet's tradition.[127] Maududi also stated a similar opinion long ago.

In his theo-democratic state, if the laws of God need interpretation, Muslims who have the capability of interpretation (*Ijtihad*) are entitled to do so.[128] In Maududi's own calculation the percentage of people with knowledge of Islam is not more than .001 per cent. Practically his suggestion limited suffrage.[129] He further writes that the common people cannot understand their interest and it is a natural weakness of human beings and this weakness is eternal. Islam advocates *Khilafat* (this he translated as vicegerency) instead of sovereignty.

On citizenship, Osman views the process of electing a parliamentary representative is by majority votes and if this does not provide space to minorities they should be given proportional representation and all citizens – men, women and non-Muslims – must enjoy equal rights of voting and have the right to hold positions in the government and administration.[130] Maududi also argued for the equality of all citizens before the legal and criminal law and recognised their equal right to elect a leader or *Ameer* and *Shura* as their representatives through votes.[131] However, he does not elaborate on the procedure of such an election. Vali Nasr critiqued that Maududi's preoccupation with democracy did not stem from his conviction but was an outcome of his debate with Western political thought and his party's participation in Pakistan's electoral politics.[132]

Commenting on multiparty systems in Islamic states, Osman referred to the period of the Orthodox Caliphate and showed that opposing political ideas raised by different tribes were honoured and accommodated thus showing that Muslims in Islamic states can form several Islamic parties but all of them should be committed to Islam. Contrary to his view, Maududi asserted that in an Islamic state, there is no place for differences of opinion or for political parties. And he writes, "If you wish to organise your political and economic life in accordance with the teachings of Islam, then you need not divide yourself into different parties. Only one party, the *Hizb-i-Allah* (the party of God) is sufficient for all these tasks."[133]

Another important issue of democracy is the making of law by the elected legislators which is a contested sphere in Muslim political scholarship. The orthodox reading is that the *Shariah* provides the complete set of laws to manage human affairs and any new law by human discretion (*ijtihad*) would be in conflict with divine law. Osman has argued that the *Shariah* provides the general rules, and if a legislative body in an Islamic state specifies and establishes details of the required law they should not contradict the divine law.[134] Osman—by referring to an argument of a prominent jurist Ibn-al-Qayyim that if a law is just it is inseparable from *Shariah* and makes it a part of it— draws a conclusion that a legislature is a legitimate institution which allows political pluralism to participate in making state law.[135]

In the chapter two perspectives - Western and Islamic Scholarship - on democracy and political parties have been discussed. The first section elaborated on the origin, nature and variants of democracy while the second section deliberated on origin, definition and typology of political parties and attempted to theorise their interlinkages with democracy. The third section specifically discussed the nature of an Islamic state, in which essential elements such as sovereignty, authority, nation (*ummah*), and the process of selection and election of an *Ameer* (the leader) has been debated. The conceptual discussion on these ideational and doctrinal evolution models of governance was essential for two reasons. First, Pakistan was created in the name of an ideal Islamic state based on democratic principles. Since Pakistan has oscillated between democratic and military rule both the civilian and military rulers have used the promises of an Islamic egalitarianism and democratic ideal to legitimise their exercise of power and mobilise their support. Having a clear understanding of these concepts helps in getting what they meant when they evoked these terminologies. Second, since the promise of an ideal Islamic democratic state was ambiguous it was abused by civilian and military rule alike. Here the political parties like *Jamaat-e-Islami* tried to gain power by promising to establish a Islamic state but failed to do so. On the other hand, liberal progressive parties also used the rhetoric of establishing an Islamic welfare state to neutralise the campaign of religious political opponents.

The next chapter discusses the general nature of authoritarianism, specifically the forms of military regimes and models of civil-military relations and their correlation with political system. The chapter will discuss these concepts both in a theoretical framework and as well as in the empirical context of Pakistan.

Notes

1. Robert A. Dahl, *A Preface to Democratic Theory* (Chicago: The University of Chicago Press, 2006), p. 1.
2. Joseph A. Schumpeter, *Capitalism, Socialism and Democracy* (New Delhi: Adarsh Books, 2011), pp. 82-3.
3. Simon Horniblower, "Creation and Development of Democratic Institutions in Ancient Greece," in John Dunn (ed.), *Democracy: The Unfinished Journey : 508 BC-AD 1993* (Oxford: Oxford University Press, 1992), p. 3.
4. Ibid, p. 6.
5. Ibid, p. 11.
6. Cynthia Farrar, "Ancient Greek Political Theory as a Response to Democracy," in John Dunn (ed.), *Democracy: The Unfinished Journey*, p. 17.
7. Ibid, p. 20.
8. Ibid, pp. 28-9.
9. C. B. Macpherson, *The Life and Times of Liberal Democracy* (Oxford: Oxford University Press, 1977), pp. 27-30.
10. Ibid, pp. 46-7.
11. Ibid.
12. Robert A. Dahl, *Democracy and its Critics* (New Delhi: Orient Longman, 1989), pp. 107-9.
13. Arend Lijphart *Patterns of Democracy: Government Forms and Performance in Thirty-Six Countries* (New Haven: Yale University Press, 1999), p. 2.
14. Ibid, pp. 32-3.
15. Dahl, *A Preface to Democratic Theory*, p. 4.
16. Ibid, p. 10.
17. Ibid, p. 6.
18. Schumpeter, *Capitalism, Socialism and Democracy*, p. 250.
19. Ibid, p. 269.
20. Joshua Cohen, "Deliberation and Democratic Legitimacy," in Alan Hamlin and Philip Pettit (eds.), *The Good Polity* (Oxford: Blackwell, 1989), p. 17.
21. Ibid, p. 21.
22. Giovanni Sartori, *Parties and Party System: A Framework for Analysis* (London: ECPR Press, 2005), p. 4.
23. Hans Daalder, "Parties, Elites, and Political Developments in Western Europe," in Joseph LaPlombara and Myron Weiner (eds.), *Political Parties and Political Development* (Princeton: Princeton University Press, 1966), p. 52.
24. Joseph LaPlombara and Myron Weiner, "The Origin and Development of Political Parties," in Ibid, pp. 3-4.
25. Ibid.
26. Maurice Duverger, *Political Parties: Their Organisation and Activity in the Modern State*, trans. Barbara and Robert North (New York: John Wiley and Sons, 1963), p.xxiv.
27. Ibid, p. xxx.
28. Cited in LaPlombara and Weiner, *Political Parties and Political Development*, p.8.

29. Sartori, *Parties and Party System: A Framework for Analysis*, p. 17.
30. Ibid, pp. 17-8.
31. Susan E. Scarrow, "The Nineteenth-century Origins of Modern Political Parties: The Unwanted Emergence of Party-based Politics," in Richard S. Katz and William Crotty (eds.), *Handbook of Party Politics* (London: Sage Publication, 2006), p. 19.
32. Quoted in John Kenneth White's, "What is a Political Party?," in Ibid, p. 5.
33. Quoted in Ibid, p. 6.
34. Ibid.
35. Duverger, *Political Parties: Their Organisation and Activity in the Modern State*, p.xxiii.
36. LaPlombara and Weiner, *Political Parties and Political Development*, p. 6.
37. White, "What is a Political Party?," p. 6.
38. Sartori, *Parties and Party System: A Framework for Analysis*, p. ix.
39. Quoted in John Kenneth White's, "What is a Political Party?," in Katz and Crotty (eds.), *Handbook of Party Politics*, p. 6.
40. Richard Gunther and Larry Diamond, "Species of Political Parties: A New Typology," *Party Politics*, Vol. 9, No. 2, pp. 167-99.
41. Ibid, p. 175.
42. Ibid, p. 176.
43. Ibid, p. 178.
44. This type is directly influenced by Maurice Duverger's branch and cell-based parties.
45. Gunther and Diamond, "Species of Political Parties: A New Typology," p. 179.
46. This terminology was popularised by Otto Kirchheimer in his work, "The Transformation of the Western Party System," in LaPlombara and Weiner (eds.), *Political Parties and Political Development*.
47. Gunther and Diamond, "Species of Political Parties: A New Typology," p. 179.
48. Ibid, p. 188.
49. For detailed analysis of this party type see Piero Ignazi, "The Crisis of Parties and the Rise of New Political Parties," *Party Politics*, Vol. 2, October 1996, pp. 549-66.
50. John H. Aldrich, *Why Parties? The Origin and Transformation of Political Parties in America* (Chicago: University of Chicago Press, 1995), pp. 57-9.
51. Ibid, p. 28.
52. Andreas Schedler, "What is Democratic Consolidation?," *Journal of Democracy*, Vol. 9, No. 2, April 1998, p. 91
53. Ibid, pp. 91-2.
54. V.O. Key, *Politics, Parties, and Pressure Groups* (New York: Thomas Y. Crowell, 1958), pp. 180-82.
55. Richard S. Kartz, "Political Parties," in Daniele Caramani (ed.), *Comparative Politics* (New York: Oxford University Press, 2011), pp. 223-24.
56. Ibid.
57. Ibn-Khaldun, *The Muqaddimah: An Introduction to History, Vol. 1-3*, trans. Franz Rosenthal (New York: Pantheon Books, 1958), pp. 414-5.
58. Ibid, p. 387.
59. Ibid, p. 388.

60. Qamaruddin Khan, *The Political Thought of Ibn Taymiyah* (Islamabad: Islamic Research Institute, 1985), p. 83.
61. Ibid, p. 32.
62. Ibid, p. 28.
63. Competent Muslims are those having authority and "coercive authority," Ibn-Khaldun, *The Muqaddimah*, p. 392.
64. Qamaruddin Khan, *The Political Thought of Ibn Taymiyah*, p. 28.
65. Qamaruddin Khan, *Al-Mawardi's Theory of the State* (Lahore: Islamic Book foundation, 1983), pp. 52-3.
66. Ibid, pp. 26-7.
67. Ibid.
68. Ibn-Khaldun, *The Muqaddimah*, p. 284.
69. Ibid, p. 291.
70. Qamaruddin Khan, *The Political Thought of Ibn Taymiyah*, p. 84.
71. Ibid, p. 83.
72. Ibn-Khaldun, *The Muqaddimah*, p. 252.
73. Ibid, pp. 291-2.
74. Qamaruddin Khan, *The Political Thought of Ibn Taymiyah*, p. 84, Ibn-Khaldun, *The Muqaddimah*, p. 402, Qamaruddin Khan, *Al-Mawardi's Theory of the State*, p. 26.
75. Qamaruddin Khan, *Al-Mawardi's Theory of the State*, p. 26, Qamaruddin Khan, *The Political Thought of Ibn Taymiyah*, p. 139. Ibn-Khaldun, *The Muqaddimah*, pp. 292-3.
76. Ali Abd Al-Raziq, "The Caliphate and the Bases of Power," in John J. Donohue and John L. Esposito, *Islam in Transition: Muslim Perspectives* (New York: Oxford University Press, 2006), p. 24.
77. Ibid, pp. 26-7.
78. Syed Abul A'la Maududi, *Political Theory of Islam* (New Delhi: Markazi Maktaba Islami Publishers, 2003), p. 2. An address delivered at Shah Chirag Mosque, Lahore in October 1939.
79. Zafaryab Ahmad, "Maudoodi's Islamic State," in Mohammad Asghar Khan (ed.), *Islam, Politics and the State: The Pakistan Experience* (New Delhi: Selectbook Service Syndicate, 1985), pp. 95-6.
80. Syed Abul A'la Maududi, *First Principles of Islamic State*, trans. Khurshid Ahmad (Lahore: Islamic Publication Limited, 1967), pp. 26-7.
81. Zafaryab Ahmad, "Maudoodi's Islamic State," in Khan (ed.), *Islam, Politics and the State: The Pakistan Experience*, pp. 95-6.
82. Ibid, p. 106.
83. Ibid.
84. Benedict Anderson, *Imagined Communities: On the Origin and Spread of Nationalism*, (London: Vesro, 1995), p. 6.
85. Ibid, p. 7.
86. Ernest Gellner, *Nations and Nationalism* (New Delhi: Select Book Service Syndicate, 1986), p. 7.
87. Ibid, pp. 48-9.
88. Eric J. Hobsbawm, *Nations and Nationalism Since 1780: Programme, Myth, Realty*

(Cambridge: Cambridge University Press 1992), p. 10.

89. Eric J. Hobsbawm, “The Nation as Invented Tradition,” in John Hutchinson and Anthony D. Smith (eds.), *Nationalism* (Oxford: Oxford University Press, 1994), p. 76.
90. Ibid, pp. 77-8.
91. Ernest Renan, “Qu’est-ce qu’une Nation?” in Hutchinson and Smith (eds.), *Nationalism*, p. 18.
92. Ibid, p. 17.
93. Joseph Stalin, “The Nation,” in Hutchinson and Smith (eds.), *Nationalism*, 18.
94. Ibid, p. 20.
95. Ibid, p. 21.
96. Hugh Seton-Watson, “Old and New Nations,” in Hutchinson and Smith (eds.), *Nationalism*, p. 134
97. Anthony D. Smith, *Nationalism: Theory, Ideology, History* (Cambridge: Polity Press, 2001), p. 9.
98. The verses where the term *Ummah* is used in Quran are: 2:128, 2:143, 3:103, 3:109, 5:48, 7:34, 7:159, 7:164, 11:18, 16:36, 21:134, 43:22, 43:23.
99. Sati Al Husri, “Muslim Unity and Arab Unity,” in Donohue and Esposito (eds.), *Islam in Transition: Muslim Perspectives*, p. 50
100. Ibid, p. 51.
101. Ibid, p. 53.
102. Hussain Ahmad Madani, *Composite Nationalism and Islam*, trans. Mohammad Anwar Hussain (New Delhi: Manohar, 2006), p. 37.
103. Ibid, pp. 37-38.
104. Muhammad Iqbal, *Speeches and Statements*, comp. Shamloo (Lahore: Al-Manar Academy, 1944), p. 204
105. Ibid, pp. 209-10.
106. Mohammad Iqbal, “Presidential Address: All India Muslim League, Allahabad Session, December 1930,” in Mohammad Iqbal, *Speeches, Writings and Statements of Iqbal*, comp. Latif Ahmad Sherwani (Lahore: Iqbal Academy Pakistan, 1944), pp. 3-5.
107. Iqbal, *Speeches and* Statements, p. 213.
108. Madani, *Composite Nationalism and Islam*, pp. 107-15.
109. Sayyid Abulala Maudoodi, *Nationalism and India*, trans. Qammaruddin Khan (Lahore: Tarjuman-Ul-Quran, 1941), p. 9.
110. Ibid, pp. 9-10.
111. Ibid, p. 21.
112. Amos Perlmutter, “Islam and Democracy Simply Aren’t Compatible,” *International Herald Tribune*, 21 January, 1992.
113. Cited in Abdolkarim Sourosh, *Reason, Freedom, and Democracy in Islam: Essential Writings of ’Abdolkarim Sourosh*, trans. Mahmoud Sadri and Ahmad Sadri (New York: Oxford University Press, 2000), pp. 134-5.
114. Fatema Mernissi, *Islam and Democracy: Fear of the Modern World*, trans. Marry Jo Lakeland (Cambridge: Perseus Publishing, 2002) p. 42.

115. Murad Hofmann, "Democracy or Shuracracy," in Donohue and Esposito (eds.), *Islam in Transition: Muslim Perspectives*, p. 296.
116. Ibid, p. 297.
117. Abdolkarim Sourosh, *Reason, Freedom, and Democracy in Islam*, p. 127.
118. Ibid, pp. 131-33.
119. Ibid, pp. 133-5
120. Murad Hofmann, "Democracy or *Shuracracy*," p. 297.
121. Syed Abul A'la Maududi, *First Principles of Islamic State*, p. 27.
122. Zafaryab Ahmad, "Maudoodi's Islamic State," p. 100.
123. Sayyid Abul A'la Maududi, *Islamic Way of Life*, trans. Khurshid Ahmad (New Delhi: Markazi Maktaba Jamat-e-Islami Hind, 1967), pp.43-4.
124. Ibid, p. 44.
125. Fathi Osman, "Shura and Democracy," in Donohue and Esposito (eds.), *Islam in Transition: Muslim Perspectives* p. 288.
126. Ibid, p. 289.
127. Ibid.
128. Ahmad, "Maudoodi's Islamic State," p. 100.
129. Ibid.
130. Osman, "Shura and Democracy," p. 289-92.
131. Sayyid Abul A'la Maududi, *Islamic Way of Life*, pp. 49-50.
132. Sayyed Vali Reza Nasr, *Mawdudi and the Making of Islamic Revivalism* (New York: Oxford University Press, 1996), p. 84.
133. Ahmad, "Maudoodi's Islamic State," p. 108.
134. Osman, "Shura and Democracy," p. 294.
135. Ibid, p. 295.

2. Authoritarianism, Military and Civil-Military Relations

In modern times, different forms of political systems or regimes are practiced. Democracy is one such form of a political system which is discussed in detail in the previous chapter. On the basis of a set of principles and procedures, the rest of the system could be classified into non-democratic systems. Authoritarian regimes are one such form of a political system that is commonly found to be followed by a democratic one. A variantt of regimes is classified on the basis of a citizenery's relationship *vis-à-vis* its governments. Different regimes exhibit peculiar characteristics but certain elements are shared amongst such regimes. It is unlikely that all shared elements be present in any existing authoritarian system. In an authoritarian regime it is either the individual leader or group of leaders (a *junta*: composed of several officers) which represents the ultimate political authority. Like realism, the state's authority and interest is above all else. On the basis of conception of power, the condition in which it emerges and its peculiar features, Juan Linz in his celebrated article *An Authoritarian Regime: Spain*, defined an authoritarian regime as:

> Authoritarian regimes are political systems with limited, not responsible, political pluralism: without elaborate and guiding ideology (but with distinctive mentalities); without intensive nor extensive political mobilisation (except some points in their development); and in which a leader (or occasionally a small group) exercises power within formally ill-defined limits but actually quite predictable ones.[1]

What one can derive from the above definition is that an authoritarian regime limits political participation and competition. Civil liberties are also coercively constrained. Linz points out that political participation is only open to certain groups and "participation of these groups in political power is controlled by certain forces and channeled through different organisational structures."[2] Unlike a totalitarian regime, where an overarching ideology shapes the society, Linz argued that in an authoritarian regime it's the "mentalities" which determine responses of people. Mentalities in his view are more emotional and non-codified ways of reaction to situations.[3] Masses are not mobilised, rather they remain politically apathetic to the prevalent system. Another aspect of an authoritarian regime relates to political parties. In such regimes political parties are created after accession to power; such parties are not well organised and ideologically-oriented—and sections of the elite do not identify with it.[4] The position of the military is paramount in an authoritarian regime and all affairs related to the military are decided by them only. The military men also occupy bureaucratic and political positions.

There are three subtypes of authoritarian regimes identified by the *International Encyclopedia of the Social Sciences*.[5] The first type is *military authoritarianism*, in which military controls the mechanism of government decision-making.[i] The second type is *party authoritarianis,m* in which single party dominates the mechanism of decision-making.[6] The third type is *bureaucratic authoritarianism*, in which the military controls the system but relies heavily on expert technocrats and the bureaucracy.[ii] The major emphasis of the study rests in the combine of both military and bureaucratic

---

i. During the Cold War period such regime types were widespread across the continents. Even in Europe, countries like Spain, Greece and Bulgaria were ruled by such regimes till the late 1970s. The post-colonial South Asian countries like Pakistan and Myanmar had periodic experience of such regimes even in the post-Cold War era.

ii. The term was first coined by Argentinian political scientist Guillermo O'Donnel in the mid-1970s to explain such regimes in South America. In Brazil, the first bureaucratic-authoritarian regime was established by Castillo Brenco in 1964. In the Chilean case, the period under General Augusto Pinochet (1973 to 1990) is recognised as Bureaucratic-Authoritarianism. In Argentina such regimes were formed twice. The first bureaucratic-authoritarian regime was established in 1966 and lasted till 1973. The second bureaucratic-authoritarian regime was formed in 1973 under General Juan Peron and ended in 1976 with the return of absolute military dictatorship. For detailed analysis of these regimes see Guillermo O'Donnel, *Modernisation and Bureaucratic-Authoritarianism: Studies in South American Politics* (Berkeley: Institute of International Studies/ University of California, 1973) and Guillermo O'Donnel, *Bureaucratic-Authoritarianism: Argentina 1966-1973 in Comparative Perspective* (Berkeley: University of California, 1988).

authoritarianism to which Linz phrased "bureaucratic-military authoritarian regime." In such a regime type the government apparatus is controlled by the military and bureaucracy.

A bureaucratic-military authoritarian regime "neither creates nor allows a mass single party to play dominant role..."[7] Even if the formation of a party is allowed it is officially controlled and used to diffuse the political mobilisation. In such regimes the military plays the dominant role and civilian leaders and bureaucracy play supporting roles.[8] Traditional institutions like the aristocracy, church (clergy), and landowners also play important roles. This section explores the debates on the models of military interventions in politics and its consequences. Both the military regime and authoritarian regime are interchangeably used to distinguish from non-democratic regimes.

The rationale of this chapter is to anchor a theoretical setting that will play as a catalyst for further analysis of governance models of Pakistan, which is both a post-colonial and a developing state. The emphasis of the arguments and concepts are largely contextualised for the situations in post-colonial states. In this section there is a theoretical discussion on the typologies of civil-military relations in general with particular reference to Pakistan as well. It seeks to illustrate circumstances in which the military is motivated to intervene in politics.

The causes of intervention may vary from case to case, but few generalities were developed on the basis of some broad comparative surveys. One such cause attributed is the perception of decaying political situation of the target state which brought in the military to intervene in order to protect it from further deterioration. The second general causation attributed to this is the military's organisational strength and its willingness to play an active political role propels it to overthrow the civilian regime – which is either too weak to resist the military's illegal advances or, has lost legitimacy to exercise power. But before examining the causality of the military's political intervention and its consequences it is important to understand how the modern military developed.

On the Origin of Standing Armies

The modern armed forces were raised and equipped to defend the sovereignty of the state against any external aggression. This is the core of the philosophy of raising standing armies. While tracing the roots of the rise of standing armies, Gaetano Mosca in *The Ruling Class*, found that it was the gradual transformation of primitive military forces into the feudal mercenaries which later turned into modern standing armies. It happened due to the transformation of kingdoms into nation-states as basic political unit accompanied by the fundamental changes in the mode of economic production during the Middle Ages in Europe. The men who constituted these armies were from the 'special class,' the aristocracy and landed proprietors.[9] The men who composed the cavalry were either from the aristocratic background or were from the bureaucratic nobility, while those who constituted the infantry were from ordinary social classes.

Samuel Huntington also traced the origin of professional armies from the first decade of the 19th century. In 1808, the Prussian government issued guidelines which opened military recruitment for non-aristocratic public. These new soldiers were chosen on the basis of their education, knowledge and valour.[10] The government formed standing armies for its own protection from the feudal unruliness but became vulnerable to the advances of their own creation.[11] The modern armies were raised to be obedient to the orders of civilian authority but they began to exercise political influence upon the civil authorities. For Mosca, this behaviour was not a prevailing pattern but an exception occurring during social instability and political crisis.[12] This behaviour was more common in democratic armies whose soldiers were attitudinally distinguished from the aristocratic armies.

The soldiers in aristocratic armies were recruited from a certain class and fought for their pride, honour, and passion. They had a closed system of upward mobility based on class identity. Unlike the aristocratic armies, the soldiers in the democratic armies had more equality and possibilities of becoming officers and thus a desire for promotions.[13] This desire follows from their concern about social status which is determined by their position in the army. In Tocqueville's view this desire of advancement is universal and greater but has limited possibilities. This desire is the root cause of war in democratic armies since it creates more opportunities and advancement.[14] In peace times, the honour of the military is lowered, its utility is questioned and its maintenance seems expensive and burdensome on public taxes. But if there are less or no possibilities of war how does the military keep itself relevant and influential? One tested way observed is to involve itself directly in politics through a *coup d'ëtat.*

Before examining the causality of *coup d'ëtat* it is necessary to understand what this French term exactly signifies. The Encyclopedic definition states it as "a stroke of the state" that is to paralyse the nerve ends of government.[15] A more comprehensive definition comes from the works of Edward Luttwak who defines it as a procedure that involves "infiltration of a small but critical segment of the state apparatus, which is then used to displace the government from its control of the reminder."[16] Luttwak observed that a *coup* is a much more democratic affair. Since it is staged against the government and the forces which stage a *coup* are "from the outside but within the state which is formed by the permanent and professional civil service, the armed forces, and police."[17] The aim of a *coup* is the detachment of permanent employees of the state from the political leadership. The *coup* is more possible in modern states with developed state apparatuses – bureaucracy, police, and military – which are disciplined institutional forces and have relative autonomy. In a *coup*, part of this state apparatus is used to seize power. The act of a *coup* in Luttwak's words is "by definition illegal" and is generally the accepted notion. But a very recent study by Ozan Varol demonstrated that a *coup* does not necessarily have to be perceived as ant-democratic. In Varol's observation "not all coups are equally anti-democratic. Some coups are distinctly more democratic than others because they respond to a popular uprising against an authoritarian or totalitarian regime and topple that for the limited purpose of holding the free and fair elections of civilian leaders."[18] Samuel Finer also argued similarly that it is erroneous to consider that all *coups* are anti-democratic and anti-parliamentary.[19] They are sometimes against oligarchies and authoritarian rule.

There is this puzzling and fundamental issue of why military intervenes in politics that needs to be addressed. Finer has proposed two general conclusions to explain this significant question. In his view, it is either due to the presence of preconditions within the target states which brings in the military into politics or, due to the military's willingness to do so as an independent political force. While assessing the military's political strength, Finer noted that the military as a professional body has three advantages *vis-à-vis* civilian institutions. The military possesses superior organisation, it has a monopoly of weapons and, its members are emotionally cohesive.[20] In his assessment of professional military institutions Finer enlisted certain characteristics which explain the military's organisational strength.

Military Professionalism and Political Intervention

The modern military is visibly different from civil institutions in terms of its excellent professionalism. The professional military has a centralised command structure. It is a stratified and hierarchically organised body. There is formal distinction between the superior and inferior ranks which is depersonalised. The military men exhibit and follow a high degree of discipline. Every command is properly channeled and disobedience attracts penalties. The military also possesses communication systems, that are peculiar to it and which are free of civil authorities. In addition to these enlisted features, the military shares some emotional and psychological bonding, the *esprit de corps*, which is strengthened through training and indoctrination.[21] Due to these attributes the military's professional capabilities is superior to that of civil authorities.

Before addressing the question as to why the military intervenes in politics, Finer raises a pertinent question on why it does not intervene and obey civilian authorities when it possesses a far more developed organisation and monopoly over violence. The military's ability to use arms is the unique competence that separates the military from civilians and is phrased as "the management of violence" by Harold Lasswell.[22] According to Finer, the military obeys civilians due to the political weakness of the military. To rule, the military is either dependent on the civil bureaucracy, as it lacks technical ability of administration, or lacks legitimacy to do so.[23] The military finds it difficult to manage complex economic structures compared to primitive economies. To administer complicated societies the military needs to co-opt civilian administrators or its rule is short-lived.[24] Hence, they are dependent on civil authorities for the smooth operation of social and economic institutions. In terms of legitimacy the military simply has no right to govern.[25] Consequently, it employs coercion which leads to the erosion of legitimacy of its political role which is not always recognised. Another problem militaries face after a *coup* is a lack of procedure for the transfer of power, therefore they constantly fear a counter *coup*.

Apart from these political weaknesses, another reason that inhibits the military's desire to intervene in politics is its own professionalism. Today's military officer corps is a body of professionals and the military officer is a professional man. The professionalism of modern military officers separates them from the warriors of the past and that is the determinative force shaping civil-military relations in the modern age. Defining military professionalism in his classic *The Soldier and The State*, Samuel Huntington distinguished military profession as a "special type" of vocation which has three extraordinary characteristics – expertise, responsibility and corporateness.[26] The Military has a social responsibility towards its client, the society, beyond financial motivation. The military professionals are regulated by professional customs and law stemming from certain values.

In modern militaries the officer corps meets the criteria of professionalism. The officer posseses certain expertise acquired through training and experience. The 'officer corps' skills are intellectually complex, and are more than mechanical craft and art.[27] These skills are universal and transcend temporal and spatial settings. Unlike other professions which are regulated by the state, the military profession is monopolised by the state. The military profession is a recent creation of the modern state. The profession of officership is essentially a product of the 19th century's political change. The professional officer is a new social type of modern society. The emergence of this 'new social type' created the problem of civil-military relations in western societies. "The problem of the modern state is not armed revolt but the relation of the expert to the politician."[28] Huntington differentiated the modern military officer from the mercenary and aristocratic warrior of the previous ages on the basis of their approaches to their profession. As already stated above that the criteria of new recruitment were replaced with merit, and class privileges were not considered; the new armies were furnished on a professional model.

The essential component which shapes the military's character is the 'military mind' which is the functional aspect of professional military. It involves three basic elements; its ability, its attribute, and its attitude. Huntington elaborated on the military's ability as its intelligence, scope, and imagination. It was presumed that the military discouraged brainy initiative, and thus was considered a job of low caliber. The second assumption was that to be a soldier one has to have certain mental attributes. The military mind is considered to be disciplined, logical and scientific and not flexible and emotional. Huntington does not advocate these two approaches to analyse civil-military relations, rather he emphasises on the third approach, the attitude of the 'military mind'. The military mind of professionalism has developed through practice of expertise and responsibility.

The role of the military is debated in terms of civilian control and this is measured in the relative power of military *vis-à-vis* the civil authorities. Here civilian control means minimisation of military power *vis-à-vis* civilian power. There are two ways of reducing military power suggested by Huntington. The first way is 'subjective civilian control' meaning minimisation of military power and maximisation of civilian power. The intra-conflict of interests within the civilian group reduces the possibilities of civilian control. Consequently, the maximisation of civilian power means maximisation of a particular group power that is the 'subjective civilian control'.[29] In post-colonial states this pattern of subjective control is commonly found. As opposed to this type of control is an 'objective civilian control' stemming from military professionalism. This type of control means the maximisation of military professionalism which gives relative autonomy to both the military and civilians in their respective sphere. Huntington argued that this professionalism makes the military more "politically sterile and neutral" and a "highly professional officer corps" does carry out the wishes of civilian authorities.[30]

De-emphasising Huntington's thesis that military professionalism may deter military's disposition to intervene, Finer argued that one motive to intervene follows from military's professionalism. The military sees itself more competent and distinct from the state, and thus is motivated to play a political role.[31] Challenging Huntington's thesis that professionalism and political intervention are antithetical, Amos Perlmutter argued that military professionalism leads to corporatism which shapes the military's motive for political intervention. Perlmutter observed that the "corporate professionalism has widened the military's social and political horizons."[32] In his assessment military's corporate and bureaucratic role and orientation is linked to its propensity for intervention in politics. "As a corporate body the military organisation strives for internal control of its profession and protection from external political control."[33] This is close to Huntington's maximisation of the military's organisational autonomy[34] which in Permutter's argument entails exercise of influence in politics.[35] For Perlmutter, the central cause of military's intervention in politics is its corporate orientation. Other factors such as military's social origin, organisational training, capacity and ideology are peripheral to its corporate orientation.[36] Observing patterns of military politics in South American and African states, Alfred Stepan argued that "social origin" and "internal organisation" of military play a significant role in shaping the military's political orientation and motivation to intervene in politics.[37] The intervention takes place when the military's corporate interest is being threatened by fragmented social movements, interest groups, or political parties.[38] Finer further demonstrated that in countries where the officer corps exhibited their willingness to accept the supremacy of civil authorities they generally avoid intervention in politics.[39] Another inhibition in military's intervention is the fear that any such a move may lead to civil war and the military may face its own people.

Grounds for a Coup D'état

The armed forces have a monopoly of arms and have institutional superiority *vis-à-vis* civilian authorities. Although the armed forces have superior organisational capabilities compared to the civilians there are some factors that inhibit it to intervene in politics at will. Having argued that, it is also evident, that from the beginning of the tradition of keeping standing armies as a professional institution, hundreds of military coups have occurred in different parts of the world. Some regions have remained more prone to military interventions in politics than others. Observing these patterns of reoccurrences, scholars of military studies have attempted to explain the causes for *coup d'état*.

Luttwak has listed three preconditions for a coup to be possible. A coup is possible in a country where the majority of its people are deprived of political participation. They have no interest and stake in the politics of the country. They live in a state of acute deprivation, and economic backwardness has made them politically indifferent. For them replacement of one political elite with another ruling elite doesn't signify any change in their lives. They do not relate to the change occurring in ruling circles.[40] Finer has provided almost similar arguments. Such a country in his analysis is considered a country of 'minimal political culture' where power is diffused in various institutions – politicians, bureaucracy, and military – and lack political consolidation. The society is highly fragmented on the basis of tribalism, casteism, regionalism and various other identities. In such a country trade unions are non-existent, civil service is apolitical and political parties do not represent the people but their cliques. The military does not face any organised resistance and intervenes independently without the cooperation of civilian authorities and replaces them completely with military officers.[41]

Huntington who made the proposition that more military professionalism leads to balanced civil-military relations argued in another seminal work *Political Order in Changing Societies*, that "the most important causes of military intervention in politics are not military but political…"[42] The coup takes place in a praetorian system that is the "political decay and institutional disorder," stemming from "general politicisation of social forces and institutions." In such a system, social forces confront each other, political leaders and institutions are not recognised, there is absence of political consensus and power is fragmented.[43] The absence of institutionalised political bodies to exercise legitimate power in praetorian societies creates a power void which is then filled by the armed forces through military intervention.[44] In Linz's observation it is the breakdown of traditional legitimacy which leads to the formation of authoritarian regimes.[45] This response comes due to the erosion of traditional institutions and absence of legitimate political bodies which could exercise power.

The second precondition for a coup to be possible is that the target state has to be politically sovereign and the sole representative of all power. In the cases of dependent states, where the centre of power is located with their ex-colonial masters or allies, it is impossible to have a successful coup.[46] This rule is not universally applicable as Luttwak himself attached caveats before considering it as a general case. A third precondition is that there has to be 'organic unity' among political and ruling elites. If power is diffused it is difficult to seize in a coup contrary to the situation where power is concentrated in the hands of a small elite.[47] There can be dispersed power centres which influence the state. Such power centres could be giant business enterprises or traditional and regional leadership.

Both Finer and Luttwak had a similar but marginally distinct approach in assessing the possibilities of coups. In Finer's argument there are certain political circumstances in which the military finds opportunity to intervene. According to him, military intervention in politics is more likely in situations where exists (1) increased civilians dependence on the military; (2) overt crisis within civil institution; (3) lack of political consensus and power vacuum, and (4) where the military's popularity is higher than the civilians.[48] The intervention follows a certain pattern and is impacted by the level of political culture found in the target state. The higher the level of political culture – rights to govern is accepted, political system is recognised, public involvement within civil institution is strong, and the process of power transfer is publicly approved – the lower is the opportunity to intervene.[49] We have already discussed the features of countries with 'minimal political culture'.

Countries which have 'low political culture' show a different pattern of military intervention in politics than countries with 'minimal political culture'. In such countries the military strive to influence the civilian government through 'blackmail' or 'pressure' using threats. The military generally operates from the behind. With regard to political culture Linz had similar observations as he argued that authoritarian regimes appear in societies "in which liberal institutions, particularly parliamentary institutions, had been introduced but no true party system attracting the loyalty of the population..."[50] Pakistan, the spatial unit on which this study is based, fits in this classification of a country with a level of 'low political culture'. In such a situation, the military intervenes directly and replaces the civilian regime with the military. In such societies, the military is welcomed as existing civilian institutions are discredited and there is no possibility of constitutional change.[51] For Perlmutter the "regimes with a colonial background tend to be more prone to military coups."[52] Generally countries which exhibit 'low political culture' share commonality of being postcolonial states.

In addition to these causes, countries with multi-party systems are also more prone to military coups than those with a one party system. Huntington had observed that "modernising states with multiparty system are, for instance, much more prone to military intervention than a modernising state with one party..."[53] A very similar observation was made by Luttwak that a one party state is not good for coup-making.[54]

Military Regime and Civil-Military Relations

The discussion so far suggests that specific interests, scenarios and situations motivate military intervention in politics. Huntington attributes the degree of military's professionalism and objective civilian control as the key motive. Finer emphasises on the level of political culture existing in the target state. Stepan focuses on the representation of class interests of the military. Perlmutter underscores the military's corporatist orientation and paraetorianism as the motive for military intervention. With a successful coup the military manages to establish itself in the power structure leading to a military regime.

A military regime, in general understanding, would be a government in which the military becomes the repository of all political power. It is not necessary that every military regime will dominate the composition of the government like civil-bureaucrats and politicians and form part of it, however, the final authority resides with the military. What would be the nature of military regimes depends on the nature of the military which will shape it. The contemporary political systems are largely seen in binary of democratic and non-democratic regimes or in dichotomy of authoritarian (military) and civilian regimes. Just as there is no uniform type of democratic regime in practice, military regimes also have their own variations. Any military regime is defined on the basis of the degree of military's involvement in political decision-making and its role in determining the political executive.

On the basis of leadership, the presence of the military in the government, professionalism of the military, and the role of political parties and civilians, scholars have developed an overlapping typology of military regimes. Finer has classified military regimes on the basis of leadership. A regime, in his classification, is a *military regime proper* if the chief executive is a military man and the entire executive branch is dominated by military men installed by a military coup.[55] Finer's second regime type is the *indirect-military regime* which is headed by the civilians but the military controls the government from behind the scene; The third type is the *intermittently indirect-military regime* which results from the capacity of a military's ability to intervene time to time if they desire to do so. The fourth type of regime is the *military-supportive regime* where the chief executive is constitutionally appointed but relies heavily on the military for its survival.[56]

Irrespective of regime types – democratic or military – civil-military relations, that is the relationship between the civilian and the military, plays an important role in all states. For more than a half century the patterns of civil-military relations were primarily enquired within two traditional theories propounded by Samuel Huntington and Morris Janowitz. Huntington's theory was popularised as an 'Institutional' theory, which sees the military and the civilian worlds as separate spheres. Its thrust was to explain how the two spheres operate autonomously and how to ensure civilian control over the military without conflict. The control is ensured through "objective civilian control" as explained in the previous section. Unlike Huntington's Institutional theory of difference of two spheres Morris Janowitz's theory of "Convergence" recognises the blurring of boundaries between them.[57]

To reduce the conflict between the civilian and the military sphere Janowitz introduces the idea of convergence by minimising the difference through the "citizen-soldier ideal" by "…embedding military service within a system of voluntary national service and by programmes of political education that linked the professional training of soldiers to national and transnational purposes."[58] Since both the 'institutional' and 'convergence' theories of civil-military relations were developed in the epistemological context of World War II and within the confines of the sovereign nation-state they are insufficient to explain new complexities and have outlived their utility.[59] In James Burk's view the traditional theories are not equipped to explain the expanded domain of civil-military relations. Both the theories do not explain how new factors such as transnational military alliances and privatisation of security shapes civil-military relations.[60] Two new theories which were developed in the post-Cold War period attempt to bridge the temporal discontinuity of traditional theories of civil-military relations.

Among the new theorists of civil-military relations, Peter Feaver has laid out a civil-military problematique, a simple paradox that "the very institution created to protect the polity is given sufficient power to become a threat to the polity."[61] He attempts to resolve this paradox by applying a new theory of civil-military relations which he called "Agency Theory" based on the principle-agent framework.[62] Feaver defines democratic theory as an epigramme that "the governed should govern", meaning people choosing their political agents, who then rule on their behalf. It was on this principle, that he argued that civil-military relations involve a designated political agent controlling designated military agent.[63] Thus his model prefers authority of a civilian against that of the the military. In his view, civilians remain the political masters regardless of the military's strength. He elaborates on this relation thus:

> In the civil-military context, this means that the military may be best able to identify the threat and the appropriate responses to that threat for a given level of risk, but only the civilian can set the level of acceptable risk for society... Civilians should get what they ask for, even if it is not what they really want. In other words, civilians have a right to be wrong.[64]

But in certain situations the military might shirk from its designated task. This diffidence is a serious setback to the civilian control as it is more nuanced than simply preventing a *coup*. Shirking from designated task does not mean that the military will stage a *coup* but it is serious because "a military could never *coup* and yet still systematically undermine civilian control" by threatening to *coup* and extract concessions, it will be hardly a victory for the civilians.[65] Apart from Feaver's Agency theory, the other theory which has received academic attention in the post-Cold-War period was "Concordance theory" proposed by Rebbeca Schiff.

Against the dominating theory of institutional separation, Schiff's Concordance theory highlights dialogue and accommodation among the military, political elites and society. The Concordance theory argues that three partners – the military, the political elites and citizenry – should aim for cooperative relations.[66] Contrary to the views of the prevailing theory of separation to prevent military intervention in politics, the Concordance theory "encouraged cooperation and engagement among the military, the political institutions and society at large."[67] The Concordance theory explains "which institutional and cultural conditions – involving separation, integration, or some alternative – prevent or promote domestic military intervention." She then argues that there are four indicators of Concordance: (i) the social composition of the Officer Corps; (ii) the political decision-making process; (iii) the recruitment method, and (iv) the military style... and its historical and cultural conditions which shape the relationship among the partners and the indicators. Based on these arguments she draws the conclusion that "if the military, the political elites, and the society achieve concordance on four indicators, then domestic intervention is less probable."[68]

In the preceding sections a theoretical discussion on military, its origin, functioning, professionalism and its causality to political interventions have been outlined. It has given an understanding of general theoretical explanations on the models of civil-military relations and regimes types that can be applied to explain cases in broader sense. Since this study is related to Pakistan's variant of military regime and implications for democracy the following section focuses on the evolution of theoretical models that explains the nature of civil-military relations and regime type in Pakistan. To explain the causality of military interventions and shaping of civil-military relations the following discussion observes how the military in Pakistan evolved as an institution and the factors that caused it to intervene in politics. The discussion attempts to theorise the process and nature of civil-military relations in Pakistan.

Military and Politics in Pakistan

Military regimes are most commonly found in societies undergoing change and lacking legitimate political order and support. They tend to thrive in unstable, politically underdeveloped, structurally non-cohesive, and, in most cases, non-functioning or poorly functioning governments. Military regimes are established to replace weak regimes, weak executives and governments, impose an ideology, and to appropriate economic resources. The instability in the post-colonial societies was primarily the consequence of rapid social change and the rapid mobilisation of new groups into politics coupled with the slow development of political institutions. In many developing countries, the military has been an active political force.

There are numerous causes for military's intervention in politics; they include anti-colonialism, nationalism, opposition to a nationalist civilian regime, anti-oligarchism, the urge to protect the military institution from encroachment and the fear of losing the military's autonomy and power, the desire to promote modernisation and economic development. The variety of reasons for military intervention, however, is insufficient to explain the creation of military regimes that attempt to develop and stabilise the unstable political system inherited from the civilians. There are many varieties of military regimes and the mix of civilian-military authority varies within military regimes and within civilian ones, as well as between them.

In many newly independent states, constitutional rulers had been imposed by external forces and therefore lacked traditional foundations. With the withdrawal of the external forces and the advent of myriad political problems, politicians corrupted the rules of the new political game. The absence of traditional loyalties either to the rulers or to the politicians led to the atrophy of the strength of political organisations. As governmental structures became weaker, intra-elite struggles for control of the state structure intensified and any initial agreement on the rules evaporated. The middle class to consolidate its power, in Hamza Alavi's view, suppresses the threat of lower-class political participation and demands.[69]

According to Ayesha Siddiqa, the likelihood of a military takeover is increased if economic adversity leads to a reduction of military expenditures. Normally, civilian governments are likely to avoid cutting back military budgets and privileges to keep the armed forces satisfied.[70] Although social unrest has served as a catalyst or a pretext for intervention, military centrality may, paradoxically, intensify mass political conflict. When this is observed within the larger framework of post-colonial theory and history of military regimes, there is overwhelming evidence which suggests that each military intervention in politics in post-colonial societies had their own unique empirical and theoretical case. They are distinct to the extent that they cannot be explained or described by any universal theory or model. Each case has its own peculiarity and requires investigation within the context of its evolution.

To understand the case of Pakistan it is necessary to understand its military as it is one of most important institutions in the country. Therefore it is instructive to dwell on the contextual trajectory in which the military in Pakistan originated, to examine its sources of motivation, its collective ambitions and structure. It is important to examine the post-colonial adaptation and changes, in its structure and foundational principle, if any. This would help to understand its structural evolution and its social and political role.

Military as an Institution

The Partition of British India was also accompanied by the division of its armed forces. The idea of the reconstitution of the existing structure and organisation of the armed forces were not in the imperial interest as they feared that it would disrupt the global strategic balance. Thus, Britain tried its best to avoid any such move. But for the Muslim League it was both in theory and practice important that the new state of Pakistan should have an independent army to project her sovereign status. When all efforts to keep the armed forces united failed, all the three parties involved agreed to a joint control of the armed forces which was later divided.

The division of the armed forces followed a communal line, all Muslim majority units were expected to join Pakistan and non-Muslim units were supposed to remain in India. And Muslim officers and lower ranks were given the option to join either country, this option was not given to Hindus thus they were to join India only.[71] Most of the British Indian army officers were trained at the Royal Military Academy (RMA), Sandhurst. It was only in 1932, the government decided to established a military academy at Dehradun to train the Indian officers. Soon after its creation, Pakistan intensified the indigenisation of the army. For this purpose it appointed a Nationalisation Committee to examine the problems of nationalisation and reorganisation. Because the Muslim officers lacked staff experience many British officers were retained by Pakistan.[72] Many of the lower rank officers were given accelerated promotion and a limited number of them were sent to England and the US for specialised and technical training.

Stephen Cohen, in his study of the Pakistan Army after the creation of Pakistan, carefully observed the process of indigenisation which included consolidation, reorganisation, expansion, and training. He classified the 'Officer Corps' of the Pakistan Army in three different generations based on their training and indoctrination. In his generational classification the first generation of 'Officer Corps' was British which was subsequently replaced by the American generation and finally taken over by the Pakistani generation.[73] The British generation of officer corps received their training in Sandhurst before 1932 and in the Indian Military Academy (IMA) in Dehradun till Partition. And when Pakistan was created there remained around five hundred officers in the Military.

For the initial years the British army model and professional structure was continued. "The training pattern of the Pakistan Army continued to be similar to that of the British."[74] These officers reflected their reluctance in non-military activities. The 1950-1965 generation of military men received their training in America or by Americans. "Along with American equipment and training came American military doctrines, American approaches to problem solving…"[75] What the American model did was that it introduced the Pakistanis to a "military philosophy that stressed mechanisation, the lavish use of ammunition and stores, and an informal personal style."[76] In the 1970s, there was a feeling that the American approach might not work always, thus began the search for an alternative strategic doctrine local to the region.

The third generation of officer corps was the 'Pakistani Generation,' most of whom joined after the military was defeated in East Pakistan. The Pakistani generation officers had very little contact and influence of foreign military training. The Pakistani generation officer corps was given training in the Pakistan Military Academy, set up at Kakul in 1948. "The new officers trained in both military and academic subjects."[77] The development of leadership qualities was also given close attention. The new officers are also trained at Pakistan Army's Command and Staff College in Quetta, and the Artillery School in Nowshera.

Composition, Philosophy and Ideology of the Military

The military as an institution established under the British Indian Government had a modern outlook and professional structure. It was professional in a hierarchical sense and the way it accomplished its goal. The British introduced the Commander-in-Chief System where it assumed the absolute control over the defence matter of the country. The C-in-C was responsible to the Governor-General who was under the British crown. The entire institution was hierarchically stratified and each division followed the order from their higher authority.

The British Indian army was designed and developed as an instrument to protect imperial interests in the subcontinent. It performed the functions of protecting its North-West frontier from Soviet expansionism and Afghan intrusion. In the other parts of British India, the army was a necessary apparatus to maintain law and order and also the instrument to ensure timely appropriation of revenues. The army played a critical role to stop the spread of nationalist movements and political agitation against the British Government. After the experiences of "White Mutiny" of 1806, which opened the rift between the British officer corps and civilian authorities[78] and the dispute between Lord Curzon and Commander-in-Chief Kitchener in 1904-1905 the British army underwent a series of reforms.[79] From thereon the British did not allow the military to influence civilian regimes and maintained absolute control over the military and kept it away from politics. The British established proper relations between the two separate spheres of military and civilian influence, while accepting the superiority of civilian leadership which continued till their departure.

The armed forces were supposed to assume a subordinate role to the civilian government and play no political role. And the military didn't attempt to attain such a role until October 1958, when the political leadership decided to use the armed forces to their advantage; it was then the military got the historical opportunity to assume a political role. The first military *coup d'état* in 1958 was the departure point from where the military deviated from its conventional role of defending the country from external aggression for which it was raised and equipped and moved into the political and economic sphere. The first military intervention in politics brought significant changes in its philosophy, ideology and composition which assisted it to transcend the military's conventional role *vis-à-vis* politics.

After setting the house in order the armed forces decided to stay-on to bring change in the society. Cohen notes that the "military regarded itself as the special expression of the idea of Pakistan, and a few officers have advocated activist role in reforming or correcting the society where it has fallen below the standard of excellence set by the military."[80] It is true that the military was initially reluctant, but the political vacuum and civilian invitation brought them in. But it was not the only explanation of their long stay as they had their own ambitions to be active in the political sphere. "... some parts of the military leadership have been excessively eager to seize power and that this seizure at times reflects broader regional, class, and other interest as well as civilian encouragement."[81] The regional interest of the military intervention in politics corresponds to the composition of the armed forces where one regional or ethnic group – the Punjabi – dominated. Pakistan army is predominantly Punjabi in the overall population. Sindhis, Baluchis and *Muhajirs* have less representation wherein Pathans have relatively satisfactory representation among the ranks and jawans.

A Baluch leader, Sardar Ataullah Khan Mengal, expressed his grievances that, "the Punjabis are determined to retain the rest as a colony."[82] Ian Talbot also notes that according to one reading one cause of Pakistan's first military coup was the need to postpone elections which would have endangered the institutional interest of Punjabis.[83] The Punjabi domination is also reflected in the syllabus of the Staff College. Cohen observes that in a strategic lesson taught in the college emphasises the importance of Punjab as it is regarded as Pakistan's "heartland" and other regions as "gateways."[84]

The numerical strength of Punjabis has its roots in the colonial period. The British created the martial race theory, that the people from the region that is Pakistan today, especially the Punjabis and Pathans, were fit for fighting while the people of what is India are good for trade, art and scholarly work.[85] Consequently from August 1914 to November 1918 Punjabis constituted about 60 per cent of the total combatant recruits.[86] With regard to Muslims the representation of Punjabi soldiers was as high as 75 per cent in the old Indian Army before the [Second World War] and even during it they constituted more than half of all Muslims. "Thus, the new Pakistan Army had something like 60 per cent PMs [Punjabi Muslims] as sepoys and in the officer corps..."[87] This legacy has been internalised by Punjabis after the partition. The continuation of this legacy created serious imbalance in the recruitment. As per Saeed Shafqat's estimate of ethnic group strength of officer corps of Pakistan military, Punjabis counted no less than 68 per cent.[88] Shuja Nawaz however observed a significant decline of Punjabi troops in the army. Based on separate GHQ data for soldiers and officers he observed an overall decline of recruitments of Punjabi solders from 68.86 per cent in 1991 to 43.33 per cent in 2005.[89] His study also noted a marginal rise of Punjabi officer corps by half per cent for the same period.

Another change was in the military's perception of its own image. The Pakistani military thinks that it's a one big family, in Ayesha Siddiqa's term a 'military fraternity,'[90] united by a strong sense of *esprit de corps*. The members of the family are dedicated honest soldiers; the military is disciplined and has efficiency to perform. Anatol Lieven commented that the military in Pakistan not only views itself as a different breed than society in general but also inculcate the same feeling to new recruits that they are part of a military fraternity superior to the civil society.[91] The army sees itself both as morally superior to this "class, and far more modern, progressive and better educated."[92] Apart from appropriation of a large portion of the GDP in the form of the defence budget, in the last six decades, the military which considers itself more efficient and competent as compared to civilians have created their own commercial empire.

Through its profit-making ventures – the Fauji Foundation and Army Welfare Trust – the military exploits national resources. The military through its business ventures got engaged in non-traditional roles which are not related to security. The Fauji group runs industries like fertilizer, cement and textiles, and Army Welfare Trust has its own farmland, rice and sugar mills. The military is also running businesses like banks, airlines, hotels and financial agencies. The Fauji Foundation also runs hospitals, medical centres, schools, colleges and technical training centres. The military which was dependent on the civilians for its economic survival in the pre-Pakistan time has developed its own internal economy to support its fraternity.[93] The financial autonomy made Pakistan military self-reliant and gave them a sense of power and confidence over the civilians. The military's commercial interest brought changes in the attitude of the military towards politics. According to Siddiqa it is the Milbus[iii] that causes the top brass of the military to be interested in enhancing their influence in the state's decision-making and politics and increases the military's institutional interest in controlling the distribution of resources.

iii. Milbus refers to all activities that transfer resources and opportunities from the public and private sectors to an individual or group within the military, without following the norms of public accountability and for the purpose of personal gratification.

The fourth change was observed in the military's ideology. Stephen Cohen in his study found that from the beginning the Pakistan army emphasised Islam as a unifying force and developed study materials aiming at transformation of traditional Indian Army patterns according to Islamic principles.[94] Scholars who carefully analysed the Pakistan army noted that the Pakistan Military Academy (PMA), apart from strategic doctrine and professional training runs a programme in "General Islamic teaching including the concept of Jihad."[95] Although the process of indoctrination of the army was much emphasised under the junta regime of General Zia, it began much earlier under the first elected Prime Minister, Bhutto, who described the 'Pakistan Army as the Army of Islam' in 1974 at the Lahore Islamic Summit.[96] The process of Islamisation of the army continued even during the second democratic interlude under two elected Prime Ministers, Benazir Bhutto and Nawaz Sharif.[97] The relationship between Islam, democracy and the military is discussed in the subsequent section.

With the passage of time the military which was characterised as a professional institution with a limited role in civilian affairs as 'aid to the civilian power' moved to the civilian sphere, exhibiting a shift in its philosophy of non-interventionism to reformism. Secondly, the secular character of the old British army which it inherited became relatively religious. Lastly, the composition is now dominated by one ethnic group, Punjabis, which shaped the way politics is played out in Pakistan.

Civil-Military Relations: Pakistan's Experience

To establish a political order of their own, the leadership of All India Muslim League, championed the Pakistan movement in British India. When Pakistan was created, the leader of the movement, Muhammad Ali Jinnah became the Governor-General of Pakistan and ruled the country under an authoritative viceregal system. Before a procedural democratic system could take its roots he died. Following his death a none-elected group of civilian leadership, with the help of bureaucracy, continued to rule till 1958 when they were removed by General Ayub Khan in a *coup*. General Ayub ruled for decade by developing his own political and administrative models. He was ousted in a counter coup in 1969 by General Yahya Khan who handed over power to the first elected Prime Minister Zulfikar Ali Bhutto in 1971. After a short span of democratic rule the military recaptured power in 1977 under General Zia-ul Haq, who later judicially executed Bhutto. General Zia's military rule ended in 1988 when he died in an air crash. Thereafter the country experienced a decade of unstable civilian rule until 1999 when once again the military returned to the helm under General Pervez Musharraf who continued till 2008. All the regimes, civilian and military, devised their own political systems and models of civil-military relations. These models showed a great deal of fluidity and capacity to absorb the shock of their duration in power.

Various models of civil-military relations can be applied to Pakistan theoretically. Ayesha Siddiqa has classified civil-military relations into six models. The models are distinguished on the basis of the "level of military's penetration into the polity, society and economy."[98] She has identified six models of civil-military relations existing in the world which are as follows:

- *Civil-Military Partnership*: Here the military is subservient to the civilian authorities. This is due to the strength of strong political institutions and active civil society. This model is found mostly in stable democracies such as the UK, USA, India, and France and where free market economy is in practice which allows the military to gain economic advantage through partnership rather than operating freely. The primary role of the military in this model is to provide security. The political and economic role of the military is not accepted as legitimate activity. In this model, strong democratic principles inhibit the military to penetrate into segments of economy, politics and social life.
- *Authoritarian-Political-Bureaucratic Partnership*: This model was found mostly in communist states (such as China, North Korea and Cuba) or countries with authoritarian party control (such as Iran and Russia). The political party or the leadership is the repository of all power and legitimacy and armed forces play a subordinate role. The armed forces are supposed to enforce the policies of the top leadership and aid the political leadership in state formation. The military and the political party function under a cooperative framework and support each other for maximum gain of economic share.
- *Ruler Military Domination*: In this model the armed forces replaces the civilian institutions by force and installs itself in direct power permanently. This model is totalitarian in nature and averse to transfer

of power to the civilian leadership. It imposes totalitarian control over the state and society and believes that it can modernise the society through coercion. Many Latin American states of the 1970s fall in this category. These were predominantly pre-capitalist economic models where the armed forces played a dominant role to amass a greater share of resources

- *Arbitrator-Military Domination*: In this model the armed forces assume direct command over politics time to time but shirk from prolonging its rule. The armed forces usually go back to the barracks once the problem is fixed by them. The military in this model has a tendency to rule from behind and is reluctant to intervene until pulled-in by circumstances. The armed forces view themselves as "balancer of power between the various competing political forces. They draw the moral legitimacy to intervene from the self-acquired role of providing stability and bringing progress to the nation."[99] The military performs the role of a political arbitrator and assume a dominant influence in politics. The civil society is highly fragmented and the military controls the state and society. The economy is pre-capitalist in nature and the military plays a dominant role in this.
- *Parent-Guardian Military Domination*: In this model, the military institutionalises its exercise of political power through constitutional engineering or by other legal provisions. This is done through co-opting civilian partners that are dependent on the military for their survival. The institutionalisation of the military's rule becomes important to protect the military's corporate interests which otherwise cannot be safeguarded by the civilian authority. In this model the civil society and society in general is highly fragmented and the military has hegemony over them and the economy is pre-capitalist where the military plays a dominant role. The military constitutionally controls the political system and acquires political legitimacy of a permanent arbitrator. The parent-guardian military model evolves from an arbitrator model thus contains some of the characteristics of the former model, such as building partnership with the civil-bureaucracy. The military justifies its continuation for the exercise of power as a prerequisite for strengthening democratic institutions.

- *Warlord Domination*: It is a political system where the nation-state is on the verge of disintegration giving rise to the power of individual leaders or groups that use coercion to exploit state's resources. Military's character is non-professional and its key role is self-protection rather than protecting the country. In this model the economic system is anarchic and the military is partner of warlords in plundering the society. In this model the "political system is highly clientist where the political, ethnic or group leaders offer patronage to a particular group of people."[100]

Veena Kukreja has also identified three basic models of civil-military relations in theory. Her first model – the Western Model[101] – is identical to Siddiqa's first model – the Civil-Military Partnership. The Western Model is found in highly industrialised countries of Western Europe. Here the military is expected not to play a role in electoral representative politics. The elected representatives attain power through elections and the bureaucracy and military is expected to implement policies made by the political elites. National defence policy remains in the hands of politicians and the military is subservient to them like civil-servants. The established culture of welfare state and institutionalised electoral process are the basis of political power in this model. Accepted legitimacy of civilian power is a common feature which constrains the military from overt participation to compete for political power. In this model, any conflict between civil and military authorities is over policies and not over power. The primary function of the military in this model is to defend authorities not society. These two models, identified by both Siddiqa and Kukreja are found mostly in stable democracies. The military is subservient to civil authorities. The military sees its benefit in partnering with the civilian authorities.

Kukreja's second model – the Communist Model[102] – is similar to Siddiqa's Authoritarian-Political-Bureaucratic Partnership, where the military is dependent on political parties or the leader and usually work in a cooperative model with the party. In Kukreja's view, in this model civilians assert their supremacy over the military. Here the military may be considered as equal partner with the civilian regime, and also the protector of party hegemony. The military is an administrative arm of the party without which ruling-party authoritarianism cannot be sustained. Though the military is subordinate to the party, it does have its distinct institutional and professional value, interest and objectives which seeks to advance within the given rules and constraints of the system.

Siddiqa's Warlord model is to be found mostly in African states. Here the society and economy is anarchic and the military loots and plunders in partnership with dominant civilian players. The three other models of civil-military relations classified by Siddiqa are usually found in the countries where armed forces have played a significant role historically. Here the society is fragmented, economy is pre-capitalist and the state is kleptocratic.[iv] In Kukreja's classification all these three should fall under the Praetorian model.[103] This model is commonly found in most weak regimes and unstable states. Armed forces are more likely to be among the political contenders for political power. It happens because the society is praetorian, the political leadership is ineffective and lack of institutions and structure fails to channelise political support.

Another Pakistani scholar, Saeed Shafqat, classified civil-military relations into two broad models – Military Hegemonic Political System and Party Dominant Political System – in the context of Pakistan.[104] The Military Hegemonic Political System was periodic in Pakistan where the military established its hegemony over the political system. In this system, the military developed its monopoly and control over strategic policy issues and decision-making institutions in the country. The military could manipulate and steer the behavior of political leaders and interest groups in a chosen direction. This model works through political control, political exclusion and by building strategic alliances.[105]

In Shafqat's second model – Dominant Party Political System – the civilian authorities in Pakistan tried to establish the dominance of elected political leadership and civilian political institutions. He traces the origin of this model in the formative years of Pakistan under Liaquat Ali Khan who ventured to establish the Muslim League as the dominant party.[106] Most political parties, especially when in power, showed propensity for a dominant party system as a possible alternative to the military-hegemonic system.

iv. A Kleptocratic government patronage selected few to accumulate personal wealth at the expense of masses. In such a system individuals take advantage of governmental corruption.

Shafqat observes that the dormant tendency of a dominant party system was managed and suppressed under the military-hegemonic system and when the military-hegemonic system showed signs of decay and weakness it has reappeared.

All the military intervention in politics in Pakistan at the initial stage qualifies for the arbitrator military model. General Ayub Khan justified the military's intervention in politics by arguing that the armed forces have entered with great reluctance to fix the political crisis and to bring stability in the country. The armed forces disclaimed any political interest and echoed that they had just entered politics to save the country. They would transfer power to the civilian regime at the earliest. Similarly, General Zia-ul Haq and General Pervez Musharraf, justified their respective interventions in the politics of Pakistan by the "doctrine of necessity." Instead of transfer of power, the military co-opted the civilians to share power. All three referendums and general elections conducted by the military rulers gave them continuation of power rather than transfer of power. Within few years after the military *coup d'état* the face of the regime changed from arbitrator military to the parent-guardian military model. The military civilianised its rule through some constitutional arrangement and a referendum, but the nature of the regime was still military.

Though the military rulers seemed to be dominating and running the show alone, the regimes were in reality oligarchic in nature than personal. The oligarchy included three dominant classes: the indigenous bourgeoisie, the metropolitan bourgeoisie and the landed-feudal class.[107] Under the state/military patronage each class protected the interests of the other group which otherwise should have antagonistic relations in the classical Marxist model argues Alavi.[108] To safeguard its economic interests all three military regimes institutionalised their rule by constitutional arrangements and co-opting political parties. Because the parent-guardian military model evolved from an arbitrator type, therefore some of the characteristics of the former type were likely to be present, such as collaboration with the civil-bureaucracy.

The distribution and sharing of power between bureaucratic-military oligarchy and political parties in Pakistan was not absolute. Even when the military was not in direct control, it often ruled through politicians so long as the latter did not impinge upon its own relative autonomy and power. The view is that when the military would directly become the object of public disaffection, this would lose its mantle of political legitimacy. Therefore, the role of political parties does not necessarily rule out the relative autonomy of bureaucratic-military oligarchies. There is a mediatory role for all, between the competing interests of the three propertied classes. During the second democratic span from 1988 to 1999 the military remained in the background but still played the role of a political arbitrator.

The new role of the military did not bring any significant change in civil-military relations. The military was still in the driver's seat but was dictating the polity from the back channel. The bureaucracy which became the military's primary partner in the first *coup* succeeded in sustaining its influential role during this period also. In fact the military continued to rule the country with the help of the bureaucracy.

Notes

1. Juan J. Linz, "An Authoritarian Regime: Spain," in Erik Allardt and Stein Rokkan (eds.), *Mass Politics: Studies in Political Sociology* (New York: The Free Press, 1970), p. 255.
2. Juan J. Linz, *Totalitarian and Authoritarian Regimes* (Boulder: Lynne Rienner Publishers, 2000), pp. 175-6.
3. Linz, "An Authoritarian Regime: Spain," p. 257.
4. Ibid, p. 264.
5. William A. Darity Jr., *International Encyclopedia of the Social Sciences* (Detroit: McMillan References USA, 2008), p. 214.
6. This type is beyond the scope of this study, hence for an elaborated debate on party authoritarianism see Samuel P. Huntington and Clement H. Moore, *Authoritarian Politics in Modern Society: The Dynamics of Established One-Party Systems* (New York: Basic Books, 1970).
7. Linz, *Totalitarian and Authoritarian Regimes*, p. 184.
8. Ibid, p. 185.
9. Gaetano Mosca, *The Ruling Class*, trans. Hannah D. Kahn (New York: McGraw-Hill Book Company, 1939), p. 223.
10. Samuel Huntington, *The Soldier and the State: The Theory and Politics of Civil-Military Relations* (Dehradun: Natraj Publishers, 2005), pp. 28-31.
11. Ibid, p. 227.
12. Ibid, p. 229.
13. Alexis de Tocqueville, *Democracy in America: Vol.2*, trans. Henry Reeve (New York: Alfred A. Knopf, 1960), p. 265.
14. Ibid, p. 266.
15. Vernon Bogdanor (ed.), *The Blackwell Encyclopaedia of Political Institutions* (Oxford: Blackwell Reference, 1987), 159.

16. Edward Luttwak, *Coup D'état: A Practical Handbook* (New York: Alfred A. Knopf, 1969), p. 12
17. Ibid, p. 4.
18. Ozan O. Varol, "The Democratic *Coup D'état*," *Harvard International Law Journal*, Vol. 53, No. 2, Summer, 2012, p. 356.
19. S. E. Finer, *The Man on the Horseback: The Role of the Military in Politics* (London: Pall Mall Press, 1962), p. 38.
20. Ibid, p. 6.
21. Ibid, pp. 7-9.
22. Cited in Huntington, *The Soldier and the State*, p. 11.
23. Finer, *The Man on the Horseback*, p. 14.
24. Ibid p. 17.
25. Ibid, p. 18.
26. For the detailed explanation of the terms Expertise, Responsibility and Corporateness see Huntington, *The Soldier and The State*, pp. 8-10.
27. Ibid, p. 13.
28. Ibid, p. 20.
29. Ibid, p. 80.
30. Ibid, p. 84.
31. Finer, *The Man on the Horseback*, p. 26.
32. Amos Perlmutter, *The Military and Politics in Modern Times: On Professionals, Praetorians, and Revolutionary Soldiers* (New haven: Yale University Press, 1978), p. 2.
33. Ibid, pp. 2-3.
34. Huntington, *The Soldier and The State*, pp. 83-5.
35. Perlmutter, *The Military and Politics in Modern Times*, p. 4.
36. Ibid, p. 7.
37. Alfred Stepan, *The Military in Politics: Changing Patterns in Brazil* (Princeton: Princeton University Press, 1971), pp. 45-7.
38. Perlmutter, *The Military and Politics in Modern Times*, p. 117.
39. Finer, *The Man on the Horseback*, pp. 28-30.
40. Luttwak, *Coup D'état: A Practical Handbook*, pp. 19-24.
41. Finer, *The Man on the Horseback*, pp. 129-35.
42. Samuel P. Huntington, *Political Order in Changing Societies* (New Haven: Yale University Press, 1976 (1968)), p. 194.
43. Ibid, pp. 194-99.
44. Ibid, p. 212.
45. Linz, "An Authoritarian Regime: Spain," p. 269.
46. Luttwak, *Coup D'état: A Practical Handbook*, pp. 25-6.
47. Ibid, p. 33.
48. Finer, *The Man on the Horseback*, pp. 72-83.
49. Ibid, p. 84.
50. Linz, *Totalitarian and Authoritarian Regimes*, p. 187.
51. Finer, *The Man on the Horseback*, p. 115.

52. Perlmutter, *The Military and Politics in Modern Times*, p. 115.
53. Huntington, *Political Order in Changing Societies*, p. 422.
54. Luttwak, *Coup D'état: A Practical Handbook*, p. 15.
55. Samuel E. Finer, "The Morphology of Military Regimes," in Roman Kolkowitz and Andrzej Korbonski (eds.), *Soldiers, Peasants, and Bureaucrats: Civil-Military Relations in Communist and Modernizing Societies* (London: George Allen and Unwin, 1982), p. 283.
56. Ibid, p. 283.
57. James Burk, " Theories of Democratic Civil-Military Relations," *Armed Forces and Society*, Vol. 29, No. 1, Fall 2002, p. 14.
58. Ibid.
59. Peter D. Feaver, "The Civil-Military Probelmatique: Huntington, Janowitz, and the Question of Civilian Control," *Armed Forces and Society*, Vol. 23, No. 2, Winter 1995, p. 169.
60. Burk, "Theories of Democratic Civil-Military Relations," pp. 20-21.
61. Peter D. Feaver, *Armed Servant: Agency, Oversight, and Civil-Military Relations* (Cambridge: Harvard University Press, 2003), p. 4.
62. Ibid, p. 1.
63. Feaver, "The Civil-Military Probelmatique," p. 153.
64. Ibid, p. 154.
65. Ibid, pp. 154-55.
66. Rebecca L. Schiff, "Civil-Military Relations Reconsidered: A Theory of Concordance," *Armed Forces and Society*, Vol. 22, No. 1, Fall 1995, p. 7.
67. Ibid, p. 12.
68. Ibid, pp. 12-3.
69. Hamza Alavi, "The State in Postcolonial Societies: Pakistan and Bangladesh," *New Left Review*, No. 72, July-August 1972, 145-72.
70. See Ayesha Siddiqa, *Military Inc.: Inside Pakistan's Military Economy* (Karachi: Oxford University Press, 2007), pp.1-23.
71. Hasan Askari Rizvi, *The Military and Politics in Pakistan 1947-1997* (Lahore: Sang-e-Meel Publications, 2000), p. 38.
72. Ibid.
73. Stephen P. Cohen, *The Pakistan Army* (Karachi: Oxford University Press, 1998), pp. 55-74.
74. Pervaiz Iqbal Cheema, *The Armed Forces of Pakistan* (Karachi: Oxford University Press, 2002), p. 55.
75. Cohen, *The Pakistan Army*, p. 63.
76. Ibid, p. 65.
77. Cheema, *The Armed Forces of Pakistan*, p. 81.
78. Stephen P. Cohen, *The Indian Army: Its Contribution to the Development of Nation* (Berkeley: University of California Press, 1971), p. 18.
79. Ibid, pp.22-3.
80. Cohen, *The Pakistan Army*, p. 105.
81. Ibid, pp. 106-7.

82. Ibid, p. 114.
83. Ian Talbot, *Pakistan: A Modern History* (New Delhi: Foundation Books, 2005), p. 126.
84. Cohen, *The Pakistan Army*, p. 115.
85. Tan Tai Yong, *The Garrison State: The Military Government and Society in Colonial Punjab, 1849-1947* (New Delhi: Sage Publication, 2005), pp. 59-60.
86. Ibid, p. 98.
87. Cohen, *The Pakistan*, p. 42.
88. Saeed Shafqat, *Civil-Military Relations in Pakistan: From Zulfikar Ali Bhutto to Benazir Bhutto* (Boulder: Westview Press, 1997), p. 173.
89. Shuja Nawaz, *Crossed Swords: Pakistan, its Army and the Wars Within* (New York: Oxford University Press, 2008), p. 571.
90. The term 'military fraternity' refers to both the serving and retired military personnel, and limited number of civilians who are directly dependent on the military business complex. See Siddiqa, *Military Inc*, p. 1.
91. Anatol Lieven, *Pakistan: A Hard Country* (London: Penguin Books, 2011), p. 163.
92. Ibid.
93. Siddiqa, *Military Inc*, pp. 18-23.
94. Cohen, *The Pakistan Army*, p. 37.
95. Cheema, *The Armed Forces of Pakistan*, p. 82.
96. Zafar Hilaly, "Why Nayyar need not Worry," *The News*, 26 March 2011, URL: http://www.thenews.com.pk/TodaysPrintDetail.aspx?ID=38225&Cat=9 (Accessed on 23 December 2013).
97. Ishtiaq Ahmad, *The Pakistan Army in Politics: Origins, Evolution, Consequences* (New Delhi: Amaryllis, 2013), p. 298.
98. Siddiqa, *Military Inc.*, pp. 30-57.
99. Ibid, p. 47.
100. Ibid, p. 55.
101. Veena Kukreja, *Civil-Military Relations in Developing Countries* (New Delhi: Sage Publication, 1991), pp. 19-21.
102. Ibid, pp. 21-3.
103. Ibid, pp. 23-4.
104. Shafqat, *Civil-Military Relations in Pakistan*, pp. 7-16.
105. Ibid.
106. Ibid.
107. Alavi, "The State in Postcolonial Societies: Pakistan and Bangladesh," pp. 145-72.
108. Ibid.

3. Political Parties in Pakistan: Origin, Evolution and Electoral Participation

> Parties are a necessary evil in free governments.
>
> — Alexis De Tocqueville, 1872[1]
>
> Parties are inevitable. No free large country has been without them.
>
> — James Bryce, 1888[2]

The idea of Pakistan germinated in a political movement championed by the All India Muslim League (AIML) led by Muhammad Ali Jinnah who sought a separate homeland for the Muslims of British India. The demand for a separate state was a reflection of the perceived threat to the interests of the Muslim political elites whose formation can be linked to the colonial state. This was a class of Muslim *Ashraf* – the pre-colonial ruling Muslim elite privileged under the Mughal administration. Hamza Alavi conceptualised this class as the *Salariat* – "section of urban middle class, those with educational qualifications and aspirations for jobs in the state apparatus, the civil bureaucracy and the military."[3] During colonial rule, the *Salariat* was the salaried class mainly dependent on government employment in the British Indian administration – the civil bureaucracy and the military. The *Salariat* realised that after independence the Indian National Congress (INC) would dominate at the national level and their concerns may go unrepresented at the all India level.[4] To protect the interests of the *Salariat* they formed the All India Muslim League in 1906.

The INC's model of democracy was based on universal franchise, one person one vote. This threatened the minority Muslim community and they resorted to "establish their own political order, Pakistan."[5] To attain their own political setup, Jinnah propagated the "two-nation theory"— that India consists of two nations – Hindus and Muslims.[6] Consequently, in 1947 British India was partitioned as India and Pakistan. After its creation,

Pakistan adopted procedural democracy as its governance model in which political parties were supposed to be the instrument of gaining control of the government apparatus on the basis of periodical elections. But as long as, Jinnah, the founder of Pakistan lived, he continued to rule the country on the authoritative viceregal system by appointing himself as the Governor-General of Pakistan. Following his death, the AIML was replaced with a new party founded by Liaquat Ali Khan in 1949.

The renamed Pakistan Muslim League (PML) contested in the first general election for the East Pakistan Legislative Assembly, held in April 1954 but it lost to the United Front (UF) – a coalition of Bengali-nationalist parties.[7] In the house of 309, the UF won 228 seats, including nine seats reserved for women, and the PML managed to win only seven seats. Following this electoral debacle the PML could not revive itself. One of the reasons might have been that the Muslim League represented a popular movement and could not transform itself to a viable political party.[8] The Muslim League which transformed in Pakistan was a top-down movement and the internal structure was deliberately kept weak, as a result when the top leadership was gone they suffered a succession crisis. On the other hand, due to repeated political instability and periodic military rule, the development of political parties also suffered severely.

In the first chapter, the conceptual and practical significance of political parties in a given democracy has been discussed. Political parties have certain roles to play in democracies. They are the linkages between the electorates and their representatives and thus become a link between the government and the citizens. It is the political parties which make a representative government possible in a modern state. Through the political parties people are represented in the organs of democratic governments. Political parties help mobilise people through their programme and form both the ruling and opposition groups. It is only through the political parties people can participate in the polity and governance. But whenever military regimes assumed power they attempted to device their own mechanism to discredit the political parties.

After seizing power in 1958, General Ayub Khan changed the parliamentary system to a presidential system. All the executive powers – selection of the cabinet, appointment and removal of constitutional and administrative positions – were reposed in the hands of the president. General Ayub justified this transition by stating that the parliamentary system of government inherited by Pakistan as a colonial legacy was inadequate for the political requirements of the new state and thus he preferred a presidential setup, which rests upon indirect suffrage.[9] In 1959, he imposed the model of 'Basic Democracy.' Under this scheme Pakistan was divided into two electoral units (East and West Pakistan). Both the units were allotted 40,000 electors to be elected from equal number of administrative divisions units from the respective Units. In total there were 80,000 elected representatives who were called the Basic Democrats, who in turn constituted an electoral college to elect the President.[10]

His *raison d'être* for this new experiment was that Pakistan was not prepared for full democracy. Therefore, he adopted this "scheme of Basic Democracies," which he said, "has been evolved by us after a careful study of the experience of other countries and the special condition prevailing in our own."[11] General Ayub rationalised his experiment stating that the majority was illiterate and had no understanding of the economic and political affairs involved in the 1956 election.[12] Under the proposed scheme, a voter would vote for a person he knows and for the issues of his concern. This move was opposed by the leader of the Awami League representing East Pakistan, Sheikh Mujibur Rahman – who called it undemocratic and demanded a plebiscite to decide on this.[13] This system allowed General Ayub to bypass the political party system as his cabinet drew support from directly elected Basic Democrats, the bureaucracy and above all the military.[14] The system of Basic Democracy was designed to give political basis to the military regime and to undermine the political leaders and to depoliticise the basis of the opposition.[15] A Presidential election was held under this system which civilianised his regime. The system of Basic Democracy isolated the political leaders and parties from the general electorate. The system produced a new political class who were not part of the decision-making process and were dependent and loyal to the centralised command.

After seizing power, through a military coup in 1958, General Ayub banned the political parties. In August 1959, the military government of General Ayub also enacted the Elective Bodies Disqualification Order (EBDO). *De jure* it was enacted to reform public life and public services but *de facto* it served as an institutional tool to keep away the political opposition from the electoral process. Under this order, approximately 6000 persons were 'ebdoed' or disqualified.[16] The EBDO was selectively used to target the interests of the *zamindar*-politicians.[17] Prior to his Presidential referendum General Ayub promulgated the Political Parties Act of 1962 which brought the political parties under regulatory bodies controlled by the military regime.

In 1985, after his long military reign, General Zia-ul Haq decided to conduct a party-less election to gain popular support. To reduce the power of the civilian opposition, he banned political parties and imprisoned many party leaders. He removed Zulfikar Ali Bhutto, the symbol of civilian opposition from the political scene. He set up several disqualification tribunals to inquire into the charges of misconduct, corruption, and misuse of office against the members of national and provincial assemblies. Nearly 180 persons were disqualified to hold any public office for seven years.[18] To further marginalise political parties he introduced the system of separate electorate for Muslims and non-Muslims. This helped him to undercut the Pakistan Peoples Party's (PPP) vote bank. By amending the Political Parties Act of 1962 he left the political parties to the mercy of the Election Commission for the clearance certificate, without which no political party could contest the polls. Most political parties opposed the changes but the military regime conducted the election on a non-party basis and created a rubber-stamp parliament.

After seizing power, like his predecessor, General Pervez Musharraf also attempted to weaken the political parties in Pakistan. He promulgated the Political Parties Order 2002 (PPO), which replaced the Political Parties Act of 1962. Under the order, parties were prohibited to receive funds from private associations thus their financial support was undercut.[19] The PPO mandated that any party which desires to participate in the election, requires to conduct an intra-party election to elect its leader in accordance with the constitution of a political party. In July 2002, General Musharraf issued the Qualification to hold Public Office Order 2002, which established a two-term limit on Prime Ministers. This prevented Benazir Bhutto and Nawaz Sharif for running for office again. Under the Conduct of General Elections Order 2002 candidates were required to have a graduation degree or its equivalent to contest the polls. This in effect disqualified hundreds of party leaders and office holders.[20] General Musharraf tried to marginalise the political parties even at the local government level. During his rule, he held two local body elections on non-party basis. He restricted political campaigns, using party flags, posters or other symbols to mobilise their voters. Any link to political parties could lead to disqualification to contest the polls.[21] Despite the severe constraints imposed by the military regimes, the political parties continued to resist, revive and contest again and again.

Until July 2018 ten general elections have been held in Pakistan. Except for the elections of 1977 and 2013 all the eight general elections were held either directly under the military or in its shadow. In all the elections many political parties participated. Many of them simply withered away and many new parties were formed. For the 2013 general election the Election Commission of Pakistan's showed 216 registered parties.[22] Out of such a large list of political parties, only few of them have shaped the nature of polity and governance. This chapter sketches a brief general mapping of important political parties in Pakistan. The chapter also contextualises the historicity of the conditionality in which these parties have emerged and what their political interests are. This chapter studies the origin and growth of political parties in Pakistan and analyse on which pattern the political parties have developed and how they affect the growth of democratic institutions. It also analyses the origin and growth of selective political parties and their engagement in the electoral process. Further how some of these parties are composed, structured, mobilised and what are their programmatic content is also examined.

Before profiling the political parties, one needs to get an idea of the electoral performance of parties concerned. This comparison is of a quantitative nature but does help to understand the relative significance of political parties with regard to democratic rule. The following tabulation illustrates the number of political parties participated in various general elections held in Pakistan.

Table 3.1: Number of Political Parties Contested in General Elections

Year of Election	1970	1977	1985	1988	1990	1993	1997	2002	2008	2013
No. of Political Parties	22	12	Election without Parties	26	27	40	47	56	36	115

Source: Gilani's Index of Electoral Record, based on data provided by Election Commission of Pakistan (www.gallup.com.pk). Tahir Mehdi et al (eds.), *National Assembly Elections on Pakistan 1970-2008*(Lahore: Church World Service-Pakistan/Afghanistan and Free and Free Election Network, 2010).

The following tables illustrate a comparative seat sharing and popular vote share of main political parties. While drawing comparative analyses of electoral performance in the following sections, the data compiled in these two tables will be referred frequently.

Table 3.2: Election-wise Seat Share of Political Parties in General Elections

Name of Parties	1970	1977	1988	1990	1993	1997	2002	2008	2013
Awami League	167								
PPP	85	155	94	44	88	18	63	89	31
Jamaat-e-Islami	4				3				3
IJI			55	105					
JUI (F)			7	6	3	2			8
PML (N)					73	136	15	68	124
MQM			13	15		12	13	19	18
ANP			2	6	3	10	3	10	1
PTI							1		26
Total No. of seats in the House	313	200	206	206	202	204	272	271	261

Source: Gilani's Index of Electoral Record, based on data provided by Election Commission of Pakistan (www.gallup.com.pk). Tahir Mehdi et al (eds.), *National Assembly Elections on Pakistan 1970-2008* (Lahore: Church World Service-Pakistan/Afghanistan and Free and Free Election Network, 2010).

The first general election was held under the military's watch in 1970 in both the wings of Pakistan. The Pakistan Peoples Party managed to win its seats mostly in the West wing. The next general election was held in 1977 under civilian watch. In this election, major opposition parties formed an electoral alliance called Pakistan National Alliance (PNA). The PNA won only 37 seats. The general elections of 1985 were held on a non-party basis under the control of the military president. In the 1988 elections, the opposition parties formed an electoral alliance called *Islami Jamhoori Ittehad* (IJI) to jointly contest against the PPP but to no avail. The election of 1990 was contested between two alliances, the IJI led by PML (N) and the Pakistan Democratic Alliance (PDA) led by the PPP. In the general election of 2002, the major political parties such as PML (N) and PPP were marginalised by the military government. The military patronised party Pakistan Muslim League (Q) and the Islamist electoral alliance *Muttahida Majlis-e-Amal* (MMA) were major benefactors of this military controlled election. In 2008, Pakistan once again reverted to civilian rule, through the general elections.

Table 3.3: Election-wise Vote Share (in %) of Political Parties in General Elections

Name of Parties	1970	1977	1988	1990	1993	1997	2002	2008	2013
Awami League	39.2								
PPP	18.6	58.6	39	37	38	22	26	31	15
Jamaat-e-Islami	6				3				2
IJI			30	37					
JUI (F)			2	3		2			3
PML (N)					40	46	12	20	33
MQM				6		4	3	7	5
ANP			2	2	2	2	1	2	1
PTI						2	0.8		17

Source: Gilani's Index of Electoral Record, based on data provided by Election Commission of Pakistan (www.gallup.com.pk). Tahir Mehdi et al (eds.), *National Assembly Elections on Pakistan 1970-2008* (Lahore: Church World Service-Pakistan/Afghanistan and Free and Free Election Network, 2010.

Civilian leadership had their opportunities in the three short democratic interludes. In the 25 years of civilian democratic rule, only the PML (N) and the PPP were at the helm of power interchangeably. Other parties enlisted in the above tables also played a pivotal role in shaping the political trajectory of the country. Out of the ten elections in which political parties were allowed, the PPP formed the government five times. In the linear comparison of electoral performance what can be derived from the two tables is that the Pakistan Peoples Party had increased its vote share whenever it stood against the military regime, while its vote share dropped in the subsequent elections following its rule. In the election of 2013, which was fought under the young leadership of Bilawal Bhutto, PPP's vote share dipped to 15 percent, the lowest of all time. Following every PPP government it has been the PML (N) which has increased its vote and seats share and formed governments. Islamic Parties by themselves have never managed to gain substantial vote share. Even during its coalition period, centrist parties like PML (N) under the leadership of Nawaz Sharif had the maximum vote share. MQM and ANP retained their vote share in most of the elections with marginal fluctuation. In the following table and pie chart a comparative performance of the general election of 2013 are shown.

Table 3.4: Party-wise Seat Share in 2013 Election

Party name	No. of Seats
PML (N)	124
PPP	31
PTI	26
MQM	18
Jamaat-e-Islami	3
ANP	1
JUI (F)	8
Total	261

Figure 3.1: Party-wise Vote Share in 2013 Election

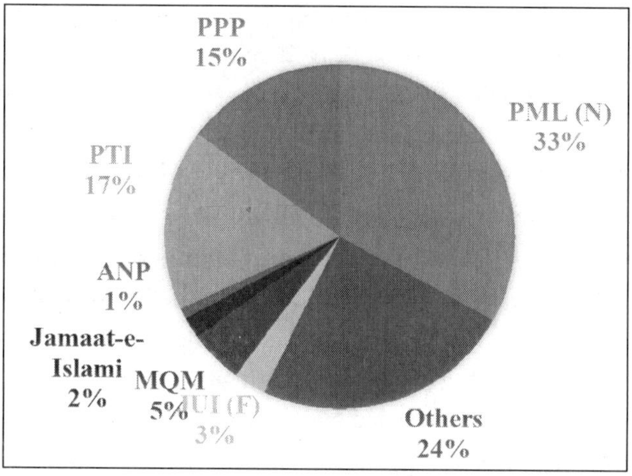

Source: Gilani's Index of Electoral Record, based on Gallup Exit Poll data and ECP data, based on data provided by Election Commission of Pakistan, (www.gallup.com.pk).

The 2013 election through which a civilian government transferred power to another civilian government without the military's intervention, was an extraordinary event in Pakistan's political history. Despite the widespread violence unleashed by the *Tahreek-e-Taliban Pakistan* (TTP) during the election campaign and voting day, the voter's turnout at 53 per cent was high by Pakistani standards. The media played a vital role in deepening the much eroded democracy for which the Chief Election Commission of Pakistan praised it for educating citizenry to realise the importance of their votes.[23] Both electronic and print media had special coverage and debates on elections to emphasise the importance of active participation in elections.[24] One can make a preliminary observation that the electoral process is a growing sign of strengthening democracy, which still needs to have strong roots.

Pakistan Muslim League (Nawaz)

We will change Pakistan

In the contesting claims of being the original political heir of the All India Muslim League, the preamble of the constitution of PML (N) claims it to be "the inheritors of the traditions of Muslim League and its political ideals..."[25]

All India Muslim League is credited for the country's creation. Following the creation of Pakistan it was renamed as Pakistan Muslim League (PML) in 1949. Today there are as many as 20 political parties using the same nomenclature.[26] Following the death of the central leadership the PML could not revive itself. According to Lawrence Ziring, "the inability of the Muslim League to transform itself from a movement to a vibrant unified, and coherent political party...unleashed the divisive forces that... threatened the survival of the young nation."[27] However the PML went through periodic hibernation, transformation, revivalism and co-option. After the death of Jinnah and the assassination of Liaquat Ali Khan, the party went into disarray. It was later co-opted by the first military dictator to civilianise his military rule.

In the 1980s, the PML was led by Pir Pagara, a Sindhi Sufi and political leader. The party was once again co-opted by the third military dictator General Zia, who used it to legitimise his military regime. After the 1985 party-less election the PML's command went to the General Zia's Punjabi protégé, Mia Muhammad Nawaz Sharif. Sharif had enjoyed the military's goodwill. Later he was chosen as Punjab's Chief Minister following the 1985 party-less election. In 1988, Sharif formed a splinter party named Pakistan Muslim League (Nawaz) popularly known as PML (N).

Sharif rose to power under the patronage of the military. He was the poster-boy of the anti-PPP alliance – IJI – in the general election of 1988 after the sudden death of General Zia. Despite all obstacles, the PPP emerged as the largest single party. IJI managed to win only 55 seats out of 206 seats but got a landslide victory in the Punjab provincial election. Instead of sitting in the opposition, Sharif decided to become the Chief Minister of Punjab. Khan Abdul Wali Khan of IJI was nominated as opposition leader. IJI moved a no-confidence motion against the ruling PPP in October 1989 but was defeated at the National Assembly. But the PPP government was dismissed the next year by then President Ghulam Ishaq Khan on the charges of corruption and irregularities.

In the general elections of 1990 IJI won 107 seats under the leadership of Sharif who went on to become Prime Minister for the first time. Sharif embarked on the project of liberalisation, privatisation and industrialisation of the Pakistan economy. In May 1991, the IJI government under Nawaz Sharif passed the 'Enforcement of *Shari'ah* Act of 1991' commonly known as the *Shariat Bill.* Referring to the Objective Resolution which adopted Islam as state religion, the *Shariat Bill* stipulated 'Supremacy of *Shari'ah*' as the law of the land and declared that all laws will be interpreted in the light of *Shari'ah.*[28] The Act directed the state for the Islamisation of education, economy and to ensure that the practices of *Shari'ah* are observed.

Amid these developments, in 1992, the opposition parties led by PPP accused the government of Nawaz Sharif of corruption and rigging in the 1990 elections and began a "Long March" – a series of street protest – across the country. The purpose of the "Long March" was to depose the government of Nawaz Sharif.[29] Mohammad Waseem notes that "it was mainly the military leadership that wanted Sharif to go" and the long march had little to do with the ouster of the IJI government.[30] Nevertheless, the IJI government was dismissed in April 1993 by then President Ghulam Ishaq Khan.

In the 1993 general elections the PML (N) contested on its own platform as the IJI was dissolved. The PML (N) emerged as the second largest party securing 73 seats and sat in the opposition. In 1994, the PML (N) launched *Tehreek-e-Nijat* – movement to get rid of the PPP government. The movement continued to mount pressure till 1996 when Benazir Bhutto's government was dismissed on the charges of corruption by President Farooq Khan Leghari. The general elections were scheduled for February 1997.

The PML (N) formed the government its own for the first time in the centre in 1997, and Nawaz Sharif was sworn in as Prime Minister of Pakistan. The PML (N) won two-third majority in the election securing 136 seats from the 207 general seats. During his second term Sharif conducted nuclear tests (28 May 1998) at Chagai (Baluchistan) followed by India's nuclear test in Pokhran (Rajasthan). This resulted in economic sanctions being imposed on Pakistan by the US and western countries leading to a financial crisis in the country. The PML (N) government also attempted to improve relations with India. In his second term Sharif became vocal against the military's extra-constitutional advances. Through the passage of the Constitution (Thirteenth Amendment) Act of 1997, Sharif repealed the Eighth Amendment promulgated by General Zia in 1985 which empowered the President to dissolve the national assembly and dismiss the Prime Minister. The autonomy of civilian leaders did not augur well for the military establishment. Sharif's government was dislodged in a military coup by

General Musharraf in 1999. Sharif himself was exiled to Saudi Arabia; he subsequently shifted to London.

Two years after the seizure of power through the military coup, General Musharraf did organise a referendum on 30 April 2002. For obvious reasons the referendum was in favour of the military chief. It did legitimise his authority to rule politically. He then held general elections in October 2002 under the Legal Framework Order issued by him as the constitution was put in abeyance. Through the Conduct of General Election Order 2002, he introduced various changes in the electoral process. The order abolished the separate electorate system and after 30 years, elections were to be held on a joint electorate system; the age of voters was now also reduced to 18 years from the previous 21 years.

Like his military predecessors who civilianised their rule through co-opting political parties, General Musharraf also created his own party PML (Q). Benazir Bhutto and Nawaz Sharif, the leaders of the two major political parties were in exile. In the general elections, PML (Q) won 77 general seats and become the largest single party. The PML (N) was reduced to its lowest – 15 seats only. After the election, the PML (Q) formed a coalition government with the support of the MQM, the National Alliance, and independent parties. For the PML (N) it was just a period of political silence.

In 2007, when General Musharraf announced elections due to the pressure from civil-society, political parties and judiciary, Nawaz Sharif decided to come back from exile and lead the electoral campaign of the PML (N). He was allowed to return to Pakistan after the signing of the 'Charter of Democracy' along with Benazir Bhutto.[31] The Charter pledged to abolish the "ban on a 'prime minister' not being eligible for a third term of office" thus clearing the way for Benazir Bhutto and Nawaz Sharif to contest in the election. The Charter further promised to "release all the political prisoners" and allowed "unconditional return of all political exiles" thus paving the way for political parties to participate in the election. Nawaz Sharif returned to Pakistan on 25 November 2007 and led the political campaign for the PML (N) but could not contest in the election due to legal constraints. Nevertheless, the PML (N) participated in the general elections and secured 92 seats. For the first time PML (N) agreed to support the PPP government to keep the common foe, the military away from politics. The party withdrew itself from the coalition government within six months and sat in the opposition.

In the general election of 2013, PML (N) secured a clear majority. For the first time in Pakistan's history a civilian government was able to complete its tenure; the election of 2013 was held under civilian watch. The PML (N) secured 124 seats out of 261 seats which further increased in the by-elections and the addition of proportional seats from reserved seats. The PML (N) released its election manifesto which emphasised its priority to boost-up economic growth, resolution of the energy crisis, and holding up of local body elections if it assume power. It also vowed to reform the tax regime and bring informal economy under the tax system.

On the matter of civil-military relations, the manifesto stated that the Prime Minister will head a Cabinet Committee on Defence and National Security to ensure democratic overview of all aspects of foreign, defence and national security policies; and the party will ensure that all institutions – civil or military – act in accordance with the law and under the instructions and directives of the Federal Cabinet.[32] Chapter Six discusses the politics of PML (N) and tilting balance of civil—military relations. However it needed to be underlined that Sharif, who had suffered at the hands of the military earlier, trod carefully in the fragile corridor of civil-military relations and gradually asserted civilian supremacy in the initial stage of his third term. At the later phase of his tenure the contention between the political and military establishment started to grow on various issues and as result the military managed to get rid of him.

Organisational Structure

The party constitution of PML (N) had also laid out the structure of its Central, Provincial, Local (district), Primary (village) and Overseas organisations. The central organisation was overseen by three central bodies: the Central Council, the Central Working Committee and the Central Parliamentary Board. The Central Working Committee, also known as General Council, was the executive body of the PML (N) organisation and delegates the function of electing the office-bearers, selecting the candidates for election and approving the annual budget. The party's central office had a post of Chairman. The post was largely ceremonial and decisive power rested in the post of the President held by Nawaz Sharif himself. The founder of the PML (N), Fida Mohammad Khan was the first President who served till 1993 till the party was part of the IJI. Sharif was elected as President of the party in 1993 and served till he was ousted in the military coup of 1999. During his exile from Pakistan, the post was rotated amongst the party loyalists. The other party positions were Vice Presidents, Secretary General, Information Secretary, Joint Secretaries and Executive Committee Members.

The Provincial organisation featured the Provincial Council, the Provincial Working Committee, the Provincial Parliamentary Board and the Provincial Election Tribunal. The Provincial Council consisted of members, drawn proportionally from all the provinces, federal administered and autonomous regions. The council members are ex-officio members – all the PML (N) Parliamentarians and members of provincial assemblies were *de facto* ex-officio members. The council members were elected by the subordinate district and city councils. The Provincial Councils were expected to elect provincial office-holders; consider and pass resolution with regard to all matters to implement the objectives of the PML (N); and to affiliate and dissolve local organisations under its purview. The members were elected for three year tenure and required to pay membership fee. There were six positions for the provincial office-bearers. At the top of the hierarchy was a President followed by Vice Presidents, General Secretary, Information Secretary, Finance Secretary and Joint Secretaries. The number of Vice Presidents and joint secretaries were not fixed and the President had the discretion to appoint as many as he deemed necessary.

The Provincial Working Committee (PWC) consisted of members nominated by the President of respective provincial councils. The PWC was the principle executive of the province and tasked to consider and pass all resolution and take necessary steps to execute the passed resolutions. It had the authority to appoint and supervise the activities of affiliate bodies. It could also dissolve the district and city level bodies. It had the power to take disciplinary action against the members and also to approve the annual budget. The Provincial Parliamentary Board (PPB) was a group of upto 12 members nominated by PWC. The PPB had the important task of selecting candidates for provincial assemblies in coordination with the office-holders. Another important body at the provincial organisational structure was the

Provincial Election Tribunal appointed by the PWC. The tribunal was the appellate board that hears appeal against party election at any tier. This structural design was replicated at the local organisational levels – city, town and primary units. The party organisation also consisted of many specialised branches or wings such as: women, youth, lawyers, trade and industry, labour, *Ulema Mashaik*, peasants and minorities.

Pakistan Peoples Party

Islam is our Faith
Democracy is our Policy
Socialism is our Economy
All Powers to the People

The Pakistan Peoples Party is credited for the formation of first elected government in Pakistan. It has ruled the country for 18 years out of 25 years of civilian rule. It is the first political party in Pakistan which has successfully completed a 5-year tenure of civilian government. It is a left to centre party formed in 1967 by Zulfikar Ali Bhutto. Before the formation of the political party, Bhutto was foreign minister in General Ayub's cabinet but resigned due to the difference over the Tashkent Agreement. To oppose General Ayub's military regime he formed his own political organisation. The Pakistan Peoples Party was formed at the Lahore Convention on 30 November 1967. The convention adopted a number of Founding Documents which laid out the ideology and broad programmes of the party.[33] It was at the the same convention that Bhutto was elected as the chairman of the party. The party claimed to bring social and economic justice to all the people of Pakistan on the basis of social-democratic ideas. The convention adopted the following guiding principles for the party: Islam is our Faith, Democracy is our Policy, Socialism is our Economy and, All Powers to the People.[34] In 1970, General Yahya Khan disbanded the One Unit scheme introduced by General Ayub and announced general elections on the basis of universal franchise.

The PPP contested in the first general elections with its populist slogan *Roti, Kapda Aur Makan* (food, clothes and shelter) for all the citizens of Pakistan. The first manifesto of the PPP was a mix of Islamic and Populist aspirations. The manifesto pledged that the party's programme would adhere to the teachings of Islam and "the Party will countenance no laws repugnant to Islam and Qur'an."[35] The party believed that "the equality of Muslims enjoined by Islam can be possible only in an economic and social structure so built as to realise it in practice." To attain that, the manifesto claimed that the party aims "to introduce real democracy in the political field, for which the first condition is the abolition of privileges and the transfer of power to the people. This would be achieved through abolishing "the exploitative capitalist structure of Pakistan." Further the manifesto states that "the ultimate objective of the Party's policy is the attainment of a classless society, which is possible only through socialism in our time."[36]

In its popular sloganeering, the party pledged land reforms and promised to nationalise the industries in popular interest. In the first general elections of 1970, PPP won 81 seats out of 138 seats contested in West Pakistan. It emerged as the second largest party followed by the Awami League led by Sheikh Mujibur Rahman from East Pakistan. Due to the failure of political agreement and reluctance of the military rulers to transfer power to the Awami League there was a great degree of uncertainty. Followed by the military's defeat and eventual dismemberment of Pakistan, Bhutto became the Chief Martial Law Administer. Later he was sworn in as Prime Minister of Pakistan. The new government of PPP initiated various social and economic reform programs. The PPP government framed the 1973 constitution of Pakistan. It also signed the Simla Accord with India to bring back 93,000 Prisoners of War. As pledged in the manifesto that it would eradicate the feudal structure PPP introduced regulation for land reforms. Though it put a cap on maximum land holding but succeeded partially only and land reform is still incomplete in Pakistan.

After the end of the first civilian rule, elections were announced in March 1977. The election resulted in PPP's landslide victory. It won 155 seats in the house of 200. The PNA managed to win 36 seats only. After the election results, PNA alleged that election results were 'rigged' and made a demand for re-election under non-partisan election commission. The opposition announced a boycott of the upcoming provincial elections and also demanded the resignation of the Prime Minster and Chief Election Commissioner.[37] Bhutto paid no heed to the demands of the opposition and declared that results were as expected and PNA's allegations were false. The opposition continued to demand a fresh election; the government arrested some leaders of opposition but not the president of PNA. Even after their release the opposition insisted on Bhutto's resignation and demanded fresh elections; the demands were suppressed. Subsequently PNA's agitation escalated and Punjab witnessed a great deal of violence leading to loss of human lives.

To resolve the impasse with the opposition, Bhutto forwarded a plan known as 'Bakhtiar's Formula' — that "if the PNA won a majority of the aggregate of four assemblies," fresh elections would be conducted for the National Assembly; but Maulana Maududi rejected the formula and said that solution lay only in fresh elections.[38] The agitation continued to mount and the PNA forced Bhutto to come to the negotiation table but to no avail and so the deadlock continued. The PNA intensified its agitation which provided the military its opportunity to intervene and seize political power. The military said that it was intervening because the ruling and opposition parties could not come to a compromise which would throw the country in chaos and crisis "...and this risk could not be taken. The army had, therefore, to act."[39] Martial Law was imposed, the constitution was put in abeyance and Bhutto was arrested on the charges of conspiracy and murder. After spending 21 months in prison he was judicially executed on 4 April 1979.

During martial rule, the PPP under the chairmanship of Benazir Bhutto launched the Movement for Restoration of Democracy (MRD) in 1981 with the objectives of restoring parliamentary democracy and civilian control of the polity. It was a conglomerate of left-oriented parties.[40] Many MRD leaders were arrested in 1983 during the protest movement in Sindh.[41] General Zia-ul Haq appointed himself as President through a referendum in 1984. He banned political parties to function and announced the conducting of non-party based general elections in 1985. The MRD which boycotted the referendum in 1984 also declared that it would boycott the 1985 general elections without parties, but the voters demonstrated their support for the election with a 52 per cent turnout.[42] Only the Pakistan Muslim League, Jamaat-e-Islami, and the Muhajir Quami Movement participated in the election. Muhammad Khan Junejo of PML was appointed as Prime Minister of Pakistan. The MRD saga ended with General Zia's mysterious air crash. Fresh elections were called in 1988 in which PPP decided to contest.

Under Benazir Bhutto's leadership PPP contested the general election of 1988 and secured 94 seats out of 207 seats. Benazir Bhutto became the Prime Minister of Pakistan. It was a short-lived government which ended in two years when President Ghulam Ishaq Khan dismissed it. Two months later elections were held again but this time the PPP lost to the electoral alliance of the *Islami Jamhoori Ittehad* (IJI). PPP sat in the opposition until the next elections were called in 1993 following the pre-mature dismissible of the PML (N) government.

In this election the PPP participated with more energy and new appeal. The 1993 manifesto adopted a "New Social Contract" as its core priority.[43] It asked for "Public-Private-Partnership: An Agenda for Change." The basic idea of it was to redefine the relationship between the Federal-Provincial-and Local "Public-Private-Partnership" in which Public and Private Sectors, the state and people, work together in harmony. It was a clear departure from PPP's founding principle, yet the party won 88 seats in the election and formed the government. As promised in the manifesto that "privatisation policy will be geared to achieve full participation of the forces of production, social development and an end to monopolies" the new PPP government carried out a massive privatisation programme. Once again the government was dismissed in 1997 on the charges of irregularities before its completion of term. Elections were held again but PPP managed to win only 18 seats. The new government of PML (N) was also short-lived as General Musharraf deposed him through a coup. Both Benazir Bhutto and Nawaz Sharif were exiled to London and Saudi Arabia respectively.

After the coup, the general elections were held in 2002 under the Legal Framework Order issued by General Musharraf. Both Sharif and Bhutto were in exile and their parties contested without the top-leadership. This time PPP's performance improved compared to previous elections. However it had to sit in the opposition as the Pakistan Muslim League (Q), created by General Musharraf, formed a coalition government with the MQM, Independent candidates and PPP (Patriot), a defected faction from the PPP. The Pakistan Peoples Party once again rose to power in 2008 when it secured the majority of seats in the general elections. By this time PPP's leadership was replaced due to Benazir Bhutto's assassination.

Following her assassination, her son Bilawal Bhutto and husband Asif Ali Zardari were elected as chairman and co-chairman of the Pakistan Peoples Party. With the new leadership and renewed slogan "*Ilm, Roshni Sab Ko Kaam, Roti Kapda Aur Makaan, Maang Raha Hai Har Insaan*" and new promises the party went to election campaign of 2008. The election manifesto pledged that PPP will reverse the development priorities from market-oriented to social policy-oriented.[44] In this election PPP won 89 seats and formed a coalition government with MQM, ANP and its electoral nemesis PML (N). Yousaf Raza Gilani was elected as Prime Minister. By this time, Pakistan became a quasi-presidential democracy. The President was the repository of all the powers due to the provision of the Eighth Amendment promulgated by General Zia in 1985. The provision of this empowers the president to dismiss the Prime Minister and the cabinet. General Musharraf had revived this provision to reinforce his presidency. In September 2008 presidential election was held and Asif Ali Zardari was elected by defeating the PML (N) candidate.

The period was marred with intensified terror assaults causing scores of civilian and military personnel fatalities. Amid all these turmoil Pakistan Peoples Party completed its term and elections were announced in 2013. The PPP went to the campaign with extended slogan from the previous manifesto: "*Roti, Kapda aur Makaan, Ilm, Sehat Sab Ko Kaam, Dehshat Sai Mehfooz Awam, Ooncha Ho Jamhur Kanaam.*"[45] The manifesto laid out 'seven priorities' to attain its aim. The priorities were: ensuring basic needs, empowerment of all, equitable and inclusive growth, infrastructure for the future, new social contract, protection of people of Pakistan, and engagement with the world. This manifesto reflected PPP's inclination to go back to the populist agenda. With this, there was internal discord within the party, corruption charges against the top leadership with high inflation and long power cuts which reflected in the election results. PPP only won 31 seats, the lowest in its electoral history and sat in the opposition till the 2018 election.

Organisational Structure

During the period of Zulfikar Ali Bhutto, the PPP had laid out its organisational structure through an interim constitution ratified in the founding convention. The 'Preamble' of the interim constitution stated that "to govern the working of the party during the organisational period. It is designed to organise the party throughout the country, promote its growth in the masses and foster collective leadership within its ranks."[46] In its founding convention, Bhutto was elected as Chairman. The executive authority of the party was vested in the institution of chairman. The chairman was authorised to constitute 'Organising' and 'Principles' Committees. The function of Organising Committee was to "undertake the organisation of the party in the country" while Principles committee was supposed to elucidate and propagate the principles of the party.[47] The chairman was empowered to constitute a 'Central Committee' which was supposed to be the highest authority of the party and tasked to elect the other party office-bearers including Vice-Chairman, Secretary-General, Information Secretary and Finance Secretary etc.

After the national level, the chairman would guide the Organising Committee to furnish subordinate 'Organising Committees' at the provincial, zonal, district and city levels. The Central Organising Committee in consultation with the Chairman would elect the chairmen of provincial, zonal, district and city level organising committees. These chairmen would further, in consultation with next higher chairman, constitute their own subordinate organising committees at sub-divisional, ward and primary unit level. In actuality this formal organisational design was never completed as mandated in the interim constitution. The process of setting-up of downward organisational structure was quite slow; members of organising and principles committees were under the chairman's control; in East Pakistan it failed to penetrate and remain limited to West Pakistan only; in Punjab its expansion was higher at bottom than top level; and controlled the most decisions at a personal level.

After the death of its Chairperson, Zulfikar Ali Bhutto in 1979, the party was temporarily dysfunctional due to the imposition of martial rule and the ban on political parties. After Bhutto's death the post of chairman ceded to his widow Nusrat Bhutto. When Benazir Bhutto, the political heir of her father's legacy, assumed the post of chairman of the party, Nusrat Bhutto was honoured as *Rahber* Chairman. The procedure of constituting national level committees were the same and Benazir Bhutto also had the arbitrary discretions. The organisational problems existed more at the *tehsil* and unit levels. These units were formed spontaneously and had to apply to the party for recognition; and there were multiple factions fighting for recognition at the same levels.[48] Pakistan Democratic Forum in its report observed that by 1983 there had been no internal elections since the founding of Pakistan Peoples Party, neither was there a permanent constitution to its conduct (this is applicable to present party functioning too); it is because of this the top leadership is not accountable to the rank and file.[49] After the assassination of Benazir Bhutto in 2007, her son was appointed as the chairman of the party.

Muttahida Quami Movement

Empowering People

Muttahida Quami Movement (MQM), earlier known as the Muhajir Quami Movement, is a secular-ethnic political party which was formed on 18 March 1984 by Altaf Hussain. The MQM originated from a student struggle under the banner of the All Pakistan Muhajir Student Organisation (APMSO) founded on 11 June 1978 in the campus of the University of Karachi by a group of Muhajir students under the leadership of Altaf Hussain to fight against the discriminatory policies of the state and IJT in the universities against the Muhajirs.[50]

The formation of the MQM was a reflection of the collective political aspirations of a community which dominated the state apparatus in the formative phase of Pakistan but was later officially marginalised. In the formative phase of Pakistan, the Muhajirs occupied a hegemonic position in the administrative structure due to two reasons. First, the All India Muslim League was constituted mainly by the Muhajirs, which led the Pakistan movement inherited political power from British India. Second, the Muhajirs, specifically the *Salariat* class, had administrative and bureaucratic experience in the colonial administration. Immediately after partition, Pakistan looked like a migrant state in terms of administration. The political leadership was dominated by the Urdu-speaking Muhajirs. They were only three percent of the total population but appropriated 21 percent of bureaucratic jobs.[51] The Muhajir-led government also discriminated against the majority of the population, the Bengalis, by declaring Urdu as *lingua-franca* which resulted in domination of the Muhajirs in the Pakistani civil service. According to Ayesha Jalal, by 1956, West Pakistanis had occupied 93 percent of official jobs.[52] This situation continued and in 1963, Morrice James, British High Commissioner to Pakistan cabled to the Commonwealth Relation Office and referring to East Pakistan observed that "there were 68 public servants, businessmen, editors etc. – and only seven come from that province."[53] Such political and economic discriminations were contested by the Bengalis but their grievances and dissent were suppressed with coercion. Consequently their agitation transformed into a mass movement and Pakistan lost its East Wing.

The Muhajir dominance began to erode first under General Yahya's regime. In December 1969, under the Removal of Services (Special Provisions) Regulation (known as Martial Law No. 58) 303 Class I civil servants were discharged.[54] Their identities are not clear but it is implied that a majority of them were Muhajirs. The removal was appreciated by the national media as "rooting out of official corruption." Their marginalisation continued under the reformist drive of the elected civilian Prime Minister Bhutto. Due to the nationalisation of industries and financial institutions many Muhajirs lost up to 50 percent of their assets.[55] The Muhajir population increased to 8 percent after the loss of East Wing and they still dominated 33.5 percent of civil service positions. They suffered another blow when Bhutto promulgated the Removal from Services (Special Provisions) Regulation 1972 (known as Martial Law No. 14); this regulation removed 1303 civil servants and gained the title of "purge of 1303."[56] Charles Kennedy concluded that these reforms were a political phenomenon and the consequence of an implicit compromise between politicians and bureaucrats. The marginalisation further accentuated when the Sindh (Teaching, Promotion and Use of Sindhi Language) Bill of 1972 was debated in the provincial assembly and the Muhajirs' demand to give equal status to Urdu was not accepted.[57] It resulted in violence popularly known as the Language Riots.

Under the quota system imposed by the Bhutto government in 1973, Sindh was given a total of 19 percent reservations in the civil services. From this quota, urban Sindh, where Muhajirs were in majority received only 7.6 percent share. Muhajirs though could still compete on the 10 percent general quota on the basis of merit. General Zia revised this system and reserved

10 percent quota for ex-military servicemen.[58] Consequently the armed forces which had a very high percentage of Punjabi officers and soldiers also brought military personnel into the civil-bureaucracy. With these additional 10 per cent lateral entries of Punjabis, along with the already 50 per cent quota and under General Zia's patronage, Punjabis became dominant in the civil-bureaucracy.

The Muhajirs constituted a significant part of the civil-bureaucracy and shared a dominant position with the Punjabis; the Muhajir wing of the bureaucracy used its power to benefit Muhajirs and to disposess the Sindhis.[59] Their dominant position eroded under General Zia's patronage politics and "in ethnic terms the Pushtoons clearly emerged as the junior partners of the Punjabis in the military and bureaucracy."[60] Roedad Khan wrote that during the time of Jinnah and Liaquat Ali Khan, Urdu-speaking people were at the top of the bureaucracy and "after the assassination of Liaquat Ali Khan we saw the rise of the bureaucracy and politicians from Punjab."[61] The Zia period also saw the *Biradariasition* of the bureaucracy and people with certain surnames such as *Tarar*, *Cheema*, and *Araeen* were given preferences due to their *Biradari* affiliation.[62] Thus once mutual partners in the decision-making, the Muhajirs demoralised by Bhutto and Zia, "willingly accepted the position of junior partners."[63]

Following the erosion of their relative authority, the once dominating class of Pakistan, for the first time developed Muhajir-consciousness and began to identify themselves as a minority and a separate nationality. In 1984, they formally created their own political organisation Muhajir Quami Movement (MQM) in order to represent themselves politically.[64] Muhajirs felt that they were denied their collective identity and they were the victim of political hatred and economic angst.[65] The feeling of targeted ethnic victimisation, continuous subjection and treatment as second-class citizenry on the basis of distinct language, culture, interests and lifestyle, propelled the Muhajirs to assert their separate identity.[66]

The party organised its first public meeting on 8 August 1986 at Nishtar Park in Karachi. The MQM decided to form an electoral alliance with *Jeay Sindh Quami Mahaz*, a Sindhi nationalist organisation. To represent the Urdu-speaking Muhajir's grievances politically, the party entered formally in electoral politics and contested in the local bodies' election in Karachi and Hyderabad. Before the general election, the MQM outlined its demands in the founding document known as *Qarardad-i-Maqasid* or 'Charter of Resolution.' The charter blamed the state for the predicament of the Muhajirs and demanded that the Muhajirs should be declared a separate nationality in Pakistan. The other main demands of the charter were: that all Biharis[67] stranded in Bangladesh be brought back as Pakistanis, and Sindh domicile should only be given to those who has been residents of Sindh for at least 20 years, arms licenses were to be issued to Muhajirs and there should be a formation of a joint committee of Muhajirs and Sindhis to see the fair and just implementation of the quota system.[68]

To herald its arrival at the national level the MQM participated in the general elections of 1988, but it fielded its candidates as independents. The party managed to win 13 seats and emerged as the third largest party. It formed the government in alliance with Pakistan Peoples Party on the basis of a 59-point programme known as the 'Karachi Declaration.' The PPP-MQM pact was signed in hope that it "would benefit the Muhajirs, reform the quota system, restore peace and improve Karachi's infrastructure," but the programme was not implemented and both the parties resorted to violence.[69] The marriage of convenience ended in a year when the MQM leaders secretly struck a deal with Nawaz Sharif, resigned from the government and joined the opposition IJI led by him.[70] It then voted against the PPP in a no-confidence motion in the National Assembly, but the PPP government survived.

The MQM went to the general election of 1990 in alliance with the IJI. It improved its tally and secured 15 seats, two more than the previous election. It became part of the new government. In January 1991, the top leadership proposed to change the party's name from Muhajir Quami Movement to Muttahida Quami Movement (Composite Nationalist Movement). The proposal led to internal differences within the party leadership. The fissures resulted in the formation of a breakaway party with the original nomenclature and the suffix *Haqiqi* (real) under the leadership of Afaq Ahmad. In 1992, the military accused the MQM for plotting a separate autonomous state of *Jinnahpur* for the Urdu-speaking Muhajirs. On the pretext of *Jinnahpur-Conspiracy* the military initiated operations called 'Operation Clean-up,' due to which many MQM workers were killed and many leaders either went underground or fled the country. To show its dissent the MQM resigned from the government as well as from the national and provincial assemblies. Altaf Hussain left for London in 1992 even before the army crackdown; he has stayed there since and runs the party from there. In 2009, Altaf Hussain, the self-exiled leader of the MQM, demanded the setting up of a 'truth and reconciliation commission' to enquire about the alleged conspiracy.[71]

The MQM boycotted the general election of 1993 but contested the Sindh provincial election and won 28 seats. The PPP formed the government under the prime minister-ship of Benazir Bhutto which was again dismissed by the President on the charges of extra-judicial executions of MQM workers. General elections were held in 1997 and the MQM participated under the name of *Haq Parast Group* and retained 12 seats. It joined the PML (N) government but quit in September 1998 on the difference over the *Shariat Bill* with the ruling party. The breakaway party MQM (*Haqiqi*) participated in the elections and failed miserably. It did not win a single seat and gathered a mere 0.11 percent votes in total.[72] In July 1997 the MQM changed its name and adopted the new nomenclature —Muttahida Quami Movement, the abbreviation (MQM) was retained. It was a fundamental departure from its founding *raison d'être*. The new MQM attempted to transform itself from an ethnic-militant party to a national party, appealing to all segments of the citizenry by renouncing its identity of a vanguard of Muhajir interests and by associating itself with Sindh identity and interest.[73]

After replacing 'Muhajir' with *Muttahida*, the MQM released its first formal manifesto in 1998. The new manifesto differed in many ways from its 'Charter of Resolution' as it adopted a new philosophy of 'Realism' and 'Practicalism.' It defined 'Realism' as acceptance of reality with an open heart and "based on Realism positive achievement made through ideologically supported pragmatic programs is called Practicalism." The new manifesto attributed the causes of Pakistan's maladies to the feudal lords and elite-bureaucracy which constituted only 2 per cent of people but monopolises the economic and political power structure. It further accused this 2 per cent of occupying the National Assembly by monopolising different political parties.[74] The manifesto appealed to the 98 per cent "poor, oppressed and deprived" masses to get rid of these political parties to save Pakistan from the prevailing political and economic crisis by electing leaders from their own rank represented by MQM. It, however, clarified that it did not aim to make a systematic overhaul but would create a pragmatic mechanism in which all classes of the country would coexist. The manifesto kept some of the demands from the 'Charter of Resolution' but it also added some new demands. It demanded compulsory military training for all citizens, abolition of feudalism through agricultural and land reforms, a parliamentary form of government and more provincial autonomy and privatisation of the economy.

In the 2002 election, MQM contested with its new name and national appeal but performed, as expected, by retaining 13 seats in the national assembly and constituted part of the coalition government led by PML (Q). The MQM withdrew its support to the government on 26 November 2002. It was a period of lull for political parties as all power vested in the institution of the President and parliament acted as rubber stamp only. In the general elections for 2008 MQM improved its seats to 19 and joined the PPP government. Over the difference with the PPP's policies with regard to the spread of Talibanisation in Karachi, and the PPP's failure to maintain law and order in Sindh, the party ministers quit from the government on 27 December 2010 but its support for the coalition continued. The party rejoined the government in May 2011 but it finally quit from the coalition in June 2011 by blaming the government for rigging in the Azad Kashmir election.[75]

In the general elections of 2013, the MQM drafted a new manifesto. Although it was a replication of its previous demands, it tried a populist manifestation by highlighting the party's pledge to bring ordinary people into the realm of the power structure by stopping the entry of feudal families and political dynasties.[76] The merit-based bureaucracy was a recurring theme of MQM's manifesto. The new highlights were the opposition to terrorism and religious extremism. The stress of the manifesto was its demand for devolution of power to the local governments and autonomy of local government institutions. It re-emphasised its philosophy of 'Realism and Practicalism' and eradication of political authoritarianism. In 2013, after decades, the general elections were held under civilian watch. The MQM won 18 seats and sat in the opposition.

Organisational Structure

At times the organisational setup of the MQM appears to be the most secretive among all the political parties. On the other hand it was simplest and hierarchical where everything revolves around its top leadership or Altaf Hussain to be precise. Altaf Hussain is personified as a 'mythical figure' and the first principle to be a MQM member is "blind faith in the leader."[77] Even today young people take oath of "blind trust in him without ever having met him in person."[78] He is addressed as *Quaid-e-Tehreek* (the leader of the movement), or *Pir Saheb* (spiritual guru), or *Bhai* (Big Brother). The importance of reverential reference to supreme leader is appropriately elucidated in the recurring slogan adopted by the MQM workers and voters that "*Humein manzil nahin rehnuma chahiye* (We don't need the destination but the leader)."[79] Every decision is approved in consultation with the founder leader. Nevertheless, it has also developed an organisational structure that observes the political activities of the party.

In the pre-1992 organisational setup when Altaf Hussain was in Karachi, the MQM had the system of office-bearers. It operated from its Central Secretariat at Khursheed Memorial Hall located near Altaf Hussain's home, famously known as *Nine-Zero*. *Nine-Zero* used to be the meeting place of MQM in the early years. From here the office-bearers, chairman, vice-chairman and secretary generals were elected to see the working of the organisation. After the commencement of Operation Clean-up, MQM's organisational arrangement fell into disarray as the leadership had fled and the organisational functioning ceased temporarily. Resultantly MQM did not contest in the very next general elections of 1993. In 2002 a formal restructuring of the command-structure was carried out. However, it still looks like a very top-down structure as illustrated in the following figure.

Figure 3.2: Organisational Structure of Muttahida Quami Movement

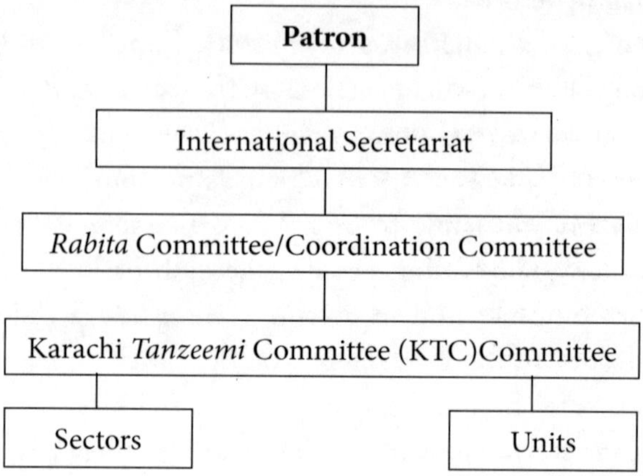

At the top of the decision-making is the chief of the party, usually occupied by the founder of MQM, Altaf Hussain. The post of patron is followed by a *Rabita* Committee or coordination committee, whose members are drawn from Karachi and London. The coordination committee is responsible to oversee the political programme of the party and operates in consultation with the International Secretariat accountable to the chief of the party. Followed by *Rabita* Committee there is the *Tanzeemi* Committee, which was later renamed as the Karachi *Tanzeemi* Committee (KTC). The KTC had responsibility to "mobilise party cadres and the masses, arrange public meetings, rallies, street corner meetings, run election campaigns, organise protest demonstrations and, above all, ensure 'days of mourning'"[80] KTC is accountable to the coordination committee. There are numerous 'Sectors' and 'Units' at the bottom of the organisational hierarchy which works under the direct supervision of KTC. Members of KTC are also drawn from these sectors and units.

Jamaat-e-Islami Pakistan

Sovereignty Belongs to Allah

Jamaat-e-Islami (henceforth Jamaat) or 'Party of Islam' or 'Islamic Assembly' is the oldest of the political parties that is still functioning in Pakistan. It is a right wing and socially conservative party which believes in political Islam and aims to establish an Islamic state by way of gaining state power through elections. The party was founded by Sayyid Abu Ala Maududi, a journalist-Islamist thinker from Hyderabad (India) on 26 August 1941 in Pathankot, a small town near Lahore. Maududi, whose political ideas were shaped from his experience of the colonial political atmosphere and Muslim predicament at that time, was opposed to the idea of Pakistan. He was convinced that the plight of Muslims could only be solved through Islamic revivalism and by the means of political organisation. And the solution could not be attained under the leadership of the Indian National Congress (INC) which was dominated by the Hindus and neither under the Muslim League which was too secular, nor under the *Tabhligi Jamaat* (Missionary Society) which was too religious.[81]

Maududi did not see politics and Islam in seclusion. Rather he believed political power is necessary to the propagation of an Islamic way of life. In the party constitution, Jamaat spelt out its mission and objective i.e to struggle for the establishment of the *Deen* – divine order or Islamic way of life.[82] He considered politics as an "integral and inseparable component of the Islamic faith and Islamic state" through which the problem of the *Ummah*, Muslim community will be resolved.[83] Criticising the inability of the Muslim League to form a solid ideological position to solve the predicament of Muslims, he sought to create a new political party to accomplish the goal of his revivalist movement.[84] After the formation of the Jamaat, Maududi, who was elected as the *Ameer* of the party in the founding meeting, travelled across India between 1941 and 1947 to propagate the ideas of the Jamaat through public meetings and using print materials.

Realising the inevitability of partition, Maududi, who once opposed the idea of Pakistan, migrated to Lahore following that bloody event. The religiously charged milieu of the newly created homeland for Muslim offered fertile soil to cultivate Jamaat's political aspirations. But it did not have much of an impact in the elections. Therefore, on many occasions, Jamaat invested in collective tilling with its electoral alliances such as the Pakistan National Alliance (1977), *Islami Jamhoori Ittehad* (1988 and 1990) and *Muttahida Majlis-e- Amal* (2002). Only on two occasions – once in 1990 and again in 2002 was it a part of the national government and enjoyed a disproportionate share in the government.

Since the creation of Pakistan, Jamaat has acted as a hydra-headed organisation by engaging itself in street protests (such as anti-American protest followed by the US intervention in West Asia and Afghanistan, procession against Salman Rushdie in 1992 and in support of Salman Taseer killers (2011),[85] religious movements (such as *Tehreek-e-Khatm-e-Nabuwwat* in 1953 and *Tehreek-e-Nizam-e-Mustafa* in 1977), covertly supporting the military (in East Pakistan), serving as a socio-cultural NGO and certainly contesting various elections. Despite it being the most under-performing political party, it remained the most influential agency in shaping the national discourse and polity as a whole. The Jamaat was the harbinger of debates in the constituent assembly which shaped the character of the Objective Resolution, the spirit of the constitution that destined the place of religion in Pakistan.

The Jamaat formed its constitution or *Dastoor* in 1952 which was subsequently amended in 1957 and came into force on 1 June of that year. Article 2 of its constitution describes its *Aqida* or creed; *La ilahailla-Allah Muhammad Ur Rasulullah* (there is no God but Allah and Muhammad is the messenger of Allah). It is further elaborated that Allah is the only sovereign and law-giver and all power vested in him, thus no one is accepted as sovereign, king or supreme leader, and Allah's *Sharia* should be the guidance in all matters of economics, politics, social and family life.[86] The second part of the creed asked for acceptance of the authority and teaching of the Prophet. It commanded the acceptance of the guidance and leadership and of the Prophet's *Sunnah* as solution to human problems and accept it as the final argument and reference point.[87]

The Jamaat underwent very challenging initial years in Pakistan. Jamaat, which vocally opposed the Muslim League in pre-partition India, now was under their rule. Amid the party's growing activities and campaign for Islamic constitution and questioning the religiosity of the state many Jamaat leaders including Maududi were sentenced to jail in 1948. Maududi and Jamaat activists were put in prison once again following their agitation against the *Ahmadis* in 1953-1954, which resulted in gruesome violence and death of more than 2000 people. Jamaat was held responsible for the anti-*Ahmadi* riots[88] and Maududi was sentenced to death by a military court, but was later acquitted by the Supreme Court and released in 1954. After the first military coup in 1958 Jamaat was banned under martial law. Maududi's association with prison continued as he was once again imprisoned in 1964 following a crackdown on the Jamaat's office. On 6 July 1964 Jamaat was banned throughout Pakistan and declared an unlawful organisation under the Criminal Law Amendment Act of 1908.[89] Along with 18 other leaders Maududi was arrested under Section 3 of the West Pakistan Maintenance of Public Order Ordinance of 1960. Conspiracy against the government, undermining the loyalty of government and charges of sedition were levied on the Jamaat. The central office and local offices of the Jamaat were sealed.[90] Maududi was released later in the same year.

Jamaat then joined a Combined Opposition Parties (COP),[91] an alliance of five opposition parties to contests the first presidential election, under the basic democracy system, against General Ayub Khan. Fatima Jinnah was nominated as the COP leader. The demand of the COP was the restoration of parliamentary democracy. General Ayub won the election and civilianised his military rule.

After the turbulent years Jamaat announced its participation in the first National Assembly election of 1970. Jamaat manifesto did not propose any radical change from its previous demand of establishing an Islamic way of life. Jamaat's call became peripheral as other issues such as 'Awami League's six point,' 'PPP's call for Islamic socialism,' and 'abolition of one unit scheme' were the central issues of the election.[92] The Jamaat leaders concentrated their attack on Bhutto and Mujibur Rahman. In response, Bhutto evoked Jamaat's anti-Pakistan stance from the pre-partition days.[93] In this election on the basis of universal adult franchise Jamaat fielded 147 candidates for the national assembly of 300 seats, only four of its candidates won and secured a mere 6 per cent votes polled. All seats were won from West Pakistan. Till the next general election it remained a Bhutto-show; however; Jamaat's consistent demand to brand the *Ahmadis* as non-Muslim paid-off when Bhutto declared the *Ahmadis* as non-Muslims against their will in 1974.

After the short experiment with democracy, Bhutto announced the general elections to be held in 1977. The Islamic parties contested from the joint platform of Pakistan National Alliance (PNA), an electoral coalition of nine religious and centrist parties. The alliance was dominated by Jamaat-e-Islami. Jamaat gave its election campaign a religious tone by using a slogan for establishing *Nizam-e-Mustafa* (Islamic system).[94] It "meant different things to different people: to orthodox and fundamentalists it meant a polity which accommodated their religio-political views and guaranteed an effective role for them in the political system."[95] The PNA also replaced PPP's call of Islamic Socialism with *Mussawati-i-Mohammadi* (Islamic egalitarianism).[96] The election produced unsatisfactory results for the PNA as it won only 36 seats out of a total of 200 seats. It branded the election as 'fraud' and 'rigged' and demanded the resignation of Bhutto and fresh elections to be held. Bhutto did not agree to the demands. Consequently PNA mounted street agitations which created a political impasse between the opposition and the ruling PPP. In the absence of political compromise and chaos, the military intervened and martial law was imposed. Bhutto was incarcerated and General Zia occupied the political stage for the coming decade.

Under General Zia, who legitimised his extra-constitutional exercise of political power employing the process of Islamisation, Jamaat enjoyed privileges in the government. "Jamaat leaders occupied important government offices, including cabinet posts, and the party's views were reflected in government programmes."[97] General Zia, who needed political legitimacy to his martial rule, got support from the PNA – the main opposition to the Bhutto regime and the advocate of *Nizam-e-Mustafa* – for his rule and enforcement of Islamisation.[98] In return the Jamaat was permitted "to extend its influence to the bureaucracy, judiciary and public universities" and the party's influence reflected in the Islamisation of legal and educational institutions.[99]

The Zia era ended with his mysterious death in an air crash. Fresh elections were called on a political party basis, which had been banned earlier by the military dictator. The PPP under Benazir Bhutto looked promising by gaining the image of the saviour of democracy after leading the Movement for the Restoration of Democracy (MRD) against General Zia's military rule. As a counterweight to the popularity of the PPP, nine parties, mostly religious, including Jamaat-e-Islami and PML (N) headed by Nawaz Sharif, formed an electoral alliance named *Islami Jamhoori Ittehad* (IJI) or Islamic Democratic Alliance.[100] The IJI, which was created by the military's backing[101], performed well in the election and won 55 seats with 30 per cent vote share. The Jamaat candidates won only six seats from IJI's tally and PML candidates had the majority of seats.

Fresh elections were called in 1990. The nine parties who were part of the IJI in the previous election decided to go with the same alliance. This time around the PPP also formed an alliance, called the Pakistan Democratic Alliance (PDA), with three other parties.[102] In its second stint, the IJI outperformed its electoral nemesis PDA by winning an outright majority. The IJI won 104 seats with 37 per cent vote share. The PDA's vote share was also 37 per cent, but translated into only 44 seats. This time the Jamaat was part of the government. This government also passed the *Shariat Bill.* But after this the Jamaat, at the behest of the military, mounted street agitations against its own coalition partner. The Jamaat's agitation and military's urging caused the dismissal of the IJI government in April 1993.[103] General elections were called once again and held under the direct supervision of the military in October 1993. The alliance-era ended and individual parties contested from their own platforms. Jamaat-e-Islami went solo in this election but with another name, Pakistan Islamic Front. Its performance declined and it won only 3 seats. It remained insignificant and was visible in street protests only. It boycotted the 1997 election and thus lost its voice in the parliament.

In October 2002, General Musharraf conducted controlled elections by manipulating the premises of electoral law. The Islamist parties contested jointly under the banner of *Muttahida Majlis-e-Amal* (MMA). The MMA was composed of six right-wing parties.[104] For the first time in electoral history of Pakistan the religious parties were fortunate, though it was considered "an unnatural alliance" due to the theological differences among the constituents.[105] The roots of differences existed in their belief in distinct schools of thought, sects, and jurisprudence, traditions and revivalist movements. The *Jamiat Ulema-e-Islam* (F) headed by Fazlur Rahman and, *Jamiat Ulema-e-Islam* (Samiul Haq) headed by Samiul Haq represented the Sunni *Deobandi* school of thought; this became the theological nemesis of the *Jamiat Ulema-e-Pakistan* which is ideologically more close to *Barevli Fiqh*, a sect of Sunni jurisprudence; the Jamaat-e-Islami led by the third *Ameer* of the party Qazi Hussain Ahmed was the vanguard of modernist revivalist political Islam; the *Jamiat Ahle Hadith* led by Sajid Mir represented the Wahhabis who claim to be "the people of the Prophet's tradition" and are considered more orthodox and propagate their version of 'puritan' Islam; and the *Islami Tehrik Pakistan* headed by Syed Sajjad Naqvi was the Shia element of the alliance representing the sectarian minority of Pakistan.[106]

After many decades, the religious parties managed to gain in the election results. In the extended house of 272, the MMA won 45 seats, minus the reserved seats, and emerged as third largest party following PML (Q) and PPP. The PML (Q) which is known as 'King's Party', which was created and backed by General Musharraf, won 78 seats and formed the government in alliance. It is believed that the elections were manipulated and rigged by the military[107] to ensure the electoral demise of the PPP and PML (N).[108] Apart from changing the rules of the electoral game, the electoral victory of the PML (Q) was ensured through coercion and persuasion of opposition party workers and politicians to support the military-ruled state agencies.[109] Those who agreed to follow the military's dictate were to be rewarded with profitable posts in the administration and those who declined were bullied and threatened with prosecution on false accusations, and physical intimidation.[110]

To facilitate the religious party, Musharraf promulgated the Conduct of General Elections Order 2002 which warranted a graduation degree or its equivalent to contest the polls, as a result hundreds of party leaders and office holders were disqualified. *Madrasa* certificates were considered equivalent of mainstream degrees by the Election Commission, thus qualifying *Madrasa* graduate candidates of MMA to contest the general elections. Riding on anti-American sentiments the MMA won 29 of 47 seats in Khyber Pakhtunkhwa (KPK) where anti-American feelings were at a high and General Musharraf was identified as the supporter of the US's "War on Terror" which resulted in the suffering of Pakhtuns of this Province. The MMA also won 48 seats in the house of 99 in the provincial election of KPK and formed the government there.

Thereafter Jamaat-e-Islami boycotted the general election of 2008 and once again lost its representation in the National Assembly. After remaining out of the parliament for some time again, Jamaat decided to contest in the 2013 elections. It performed badly and captured only 3 seats, all from KPK. Before the elections, a PEW survey revealed that 84 per cent of Pakistanis prefer *Quranic* law over man-made laws,[111] a position Jamaat had always championed. But the election results were disappointing; this phenomenon was explained by Andrew Wilder who wrote on voting behavior in Punjab. According to Wilder, a Pakistani voter does not vote for a party or candidate who is not supposed to win despite having a belief in their ideas.[112] Irrespective of its poor electoral achievements, Jamaat's ideology has pervasive influence on the Pakistan polity.

Organisational Structure

Jamaat-e-Islami is the most disciplined and organised political party in Pakistan. It is also the most hierarchical and structurally stratified party which has a dedicated cadre-based system similar to the communist party functioning. According to Vali Nasr, the Jamaat, despite based on traditional roots, is a modern party as its structure, procedure and methods reflect modern ideas. It is relatively the most internally democratic party; however, it resembles Lenin's idea of 'democratic-centralisation,' i.e a higher body makes the decision and the rank and file follows with unquestioning obedience.[113]

The party structure consists of members (*arkan*), the affiliate (*muttafiq*) and sympathisers (*hamdard*). The affiliates and sympathisers do not play any official role in the organisation, except that cadres of workers (*karkun*) are drawn from this pool. The members of the party are only eligible to be office-bearers. In the central command structure, the *Ameer,* or executive head, is the highest leader. He is elected by the full members of the Jamaat for a five year tenure. The *Ameer* though enjoys arbitrary discretion and acts in consultation with a *Majlis-e-Shura* (General Council). *Majlis-e-Shura* is elected by all the members. The *Ameer* has the discretion to nominate other office-bearers. This includes the post of *Naib-Ameer* (deputy *Ameer*) and *Qayyim* (Secretary General). The following illustration shows how the organisational structure of the party operates at the national and provincial levels.

Figure 3.3: Organisational Structure of the Jamaat-e-Islami[114]

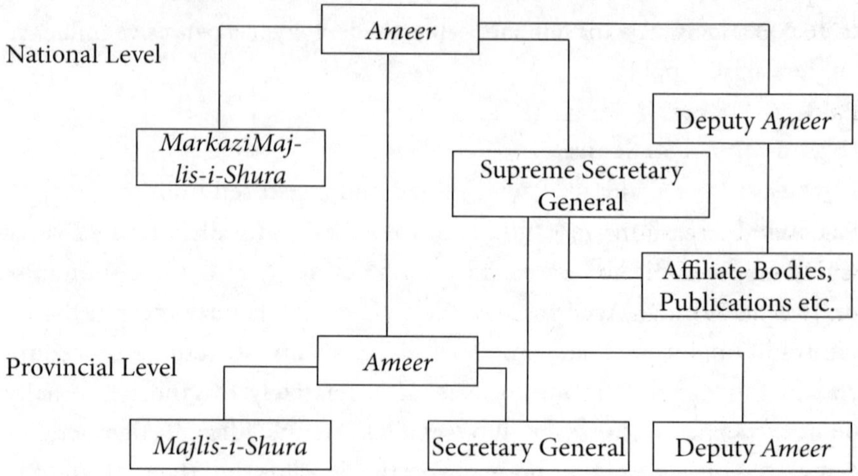

This structure is replicated at every tier from the provincial to the village level. The *Ameer* also has the responsibility to constitute a *Majlis-e-Amila* or Working Committee. Its members are drawn from the *Majlis-e-Shura*. Although the *Ameer* has unchallenged discretionary powers, in the matters of budget and administration he is dependent on the decision of the *Majlis-e-Amila*. Along with such an organisational structure Jamaat has the most stringent membership mechanism. Article 6 of the Jamaat's constitution lays out seven conditions to be fulfilled by the applicant to qualify as a member of the party. The conditions are: oath to the creed of Jamaat, accepting the Jamaat's mission, allegiance to the party's discipline, observing the duties of *Sharia*, abstaining from forbidden deeds, must not posses any illegitimate property/wealth no affiliation with any other party, with this the applicant is only admitted if the concerned cadres deems so.[115] Due to such a complex screening process its membership in the initial years, was insignificant.

At the time of its founding meeting in 1941, only 75 members pledged to the formation of the party. In a conference of only Jamaat members held in February 1957 at Machi Goth its membership stood at 1255 only. This number increased upto 1605 in its 4th All Pakistan Conference at Lahore in October 1963, and the number of sympathisers was 43000.[116] Jamaat maintained membership exclusivity for a very long time. But when it became active in electoral politics the admission procedures were eased-up. Resultantly by 1989, Jamaat's membership rose to 5,723 with 30,792 sympathisers. It swelled manifold by 2003, when its membership increased to 16,033 and number of sympathisers had reached 4.5 million.[117]

Pakistan Tehreek-e-Insaf

Justice, Humanity, Self Esteem

Pakistan Tehreek-e-Insaf (PTI) or Pakistan Movement for Justice, is a centrist and Islamic welfare party founded by cricketer-turned politician, Imran Khan on 25 April 1996. The flamboyant Pakistani cricketer become a philanthropist after retirement and built a charitable cancer hospital named after his mother Shaukat Khanum. He started his party as a socio-political movement after mobilising funds for his hospital. The PTI formed its Central Executive Committee (CEC) in June 1996. The CEC was constituted by the seven founding members including, Imran Khan, Ahsan Rasheed, Naeemul Haque, Mowahid Hussain Syed Hafeez Khan, Nausherwan Burki and Mahmood Awan. Just after its formation in 1996, the party decided to contest in the next general elections of 1997. Imran Khan, the party leader, contested from eight constituencies across Pakistan but did not win a single seat.[118] The party was "touted as an embryo of 'third force' in Pakistani politics" but not taken seriously in the elections and gathered only 2 per cent of the votes polled.

The Central Executive Committee ratified the PTI constitution on 24 January 1999 in Lahore. The constitution in its introduction states its *raison d'être* for entering into Pakistani politics. It says that because the leadership had failed to achieve the ideals of the founding father to create a country free from exploitation, corruption and social injustice rather Pakistan had fallen into the hands of a ruling elite such as "selfish politicians, feudals, civil and military bureaucrats" who plundered the country to the extent that it is at the verge of institutional breakdown. Therefore, the party had decided to enter politics "to mobilise people to extricate Pakistan from its present state of despair and to set it on the path of attaining unity, solidarity, social justice and prosperity."[119] The constitution further laid out 55 objectives of the party to be fulfilled, if it came into power. The Party's main objective is "to make Pakistan an egalitarian, modern, Islamic democratic welfare state which upholds the fundamental rights of the people in which all citizens, regardless of gender, caste, creed or religion can live in peace, harmony and happiness."[120] It then advocates for various reforms, such as more provincial autonomy, decentralisation and devolution of power, free media and police reforms etc. The constitution vowed "to recognise, promote and implement policies that protect the rights of women... and encourage the participation of women in the national and political life."[121] For minorities, the PTI declared its determination to reintroduce and continue the practice of joint electorates and that minorities would be brought into mainstream politics and be given representation at all levels according to their numerical strength.

After the first election the PTI was relatively inactive for a period of time. Formally their representation was not in the parliament and the party was in its formative phase. The PML (N) government which was elected in the 1997 election was dismissed in a military coup within two years. The country fell into the hands of a military dictator who conducted general elections in 2002.This time around, the PTI released its manifesto with detailed policy schemes. The manifesto was presented as "An Agenda for Resurgence." In its preamble, the manifesto emphasised its aspiration for "a modern Islamic republic" based on tolerance and religious plurality.[122] It proclaimed PTI to be a broad-based movement rather than just being a political party.

The PTI manifesto promised to carry out constitutional reform and revive the legislations of 1973 in letter and spirit and abolish amendments, laws and ordinances which empower the President with discretionary powers. However, General Musharraf revived the 8th Amendment which had been introduced by General Zia and was later scrapped by the Nawaz Sharif government. Imran Khan, who supported the military intervention in politics[123] did not say anything about the military rule or reform in civil-military relations in the party manifesto.

With these promises PTI went to the General Elections of 2002 held under the new election laws. This time the PTI chairman Imran Khan managed to win from Mianwali, his home town in KPK. That's how the PTI made an entry to parliament in the second stint, winning just one seat out of 272. The popular vote share reduced from 2 per cent in the previous election to a mere 0.8 per cent. Nevertheless, the PTI sent its first representation to the parliament.

In the controlled political environment under the military's civilianised government the party adopted the path of street protest. Khan in an interview admitted that he was offered Prime Ministership under General Musharraf and Deputy Prime Ministership under the civilian PM Nawaz Sharif and "he refused on both the occasions because he did not want to be tainted by corruption."[124] However General Musharraf rejected his claim on many occasions[125] but admits that he was the best of the lot.[126] However, Imran Khan, who initially supported General Pervez Musharraf, began to question his legitimacy as president and dubbed him as an "American puppet."[127]

His anti-American protest continued in the next year when Imran Khan and his party held a rally against President George W. Bush's visit to Pakistan in 2006. Imran Khan was put under house arrest by the police and many party cadres were arrested.[128] The party activists chanted slogans "Killer Bush Go Back." The PTI was never out of the news and in 2007 when Salman Rushdie was awarded a Knighthood by Queen Elizabeth the PTI condemned the honour and carried out a protest in Peshawar. The PTI supporters chanted "Curse Rushdie, Long Live Osama."[129] In the same year, PTI ran into another controversy when the MQM and the PML (Q) filed dual 'Disqualification References' against the PTI chairman Imran Khan, on the basis of moral misconduct, seeking his disqualification from the National Assembly. However, both the references were rejected by the Election Commission on 5 September 2007.[130] General elections were announced for the same year but were postponed to 2008 following Benazir Bhutto's assassination. The PTI decided to boycott the election and thus were completely out of the National Assembly.

After ending its soul searching in the political wilderness when it stayed away from the parliament, the PTI released its second manifesto for the 10th National Assembly election in 2013. The election was important because for the first time Pakistan witnessed a democratic transition of power. The coalition government, led by PPP, failed to deliver basic civic amenities, especially electricity. Inflation was on a rampant high. The period was also marred with widespread violence and loss of human life. Against this backdrop the new manifesto was released with the slogan "*Naya Pakistan*" (new Pakistan) promising to bring change. The preamble committed to establish a *Naya Pakistan* on "Iqbal's dream and Jinnah's vision encapsulated in an Islamic welfare state."[131] It pledged to fight against injustice and promised to build a just order. The manifesto highlighted the forty thousand people who had lost their lives due to the scourge of terrorism resulting from growing intolerance, therefore the party committed to restore tolerance in the society. The new manifesto stressed that "it is the party of ordinary Pakistanis" and *Naya Pakistan* is hope for the dispossessed and deprived people.

The manifesto blamed the ruling elite, who for their personal aggrandisation exploited Pakistan's resources and made democracy a parody, and the economy dependent on foreign support, thus betraying the nation envisioned by Jinnah. Therefore PTI's *Naya Pakistan*'s objective was to reclaim Jinnah's Pakistan. The foundation of *Naya Pakistan* would be the principles of "justice, peace and prosperity." The manifesto claimed that the PTI derives its vision "from the idea and vision of *Allama* Muhammad Iqbal and Quaid-i-Azam Mohammed Ali Jinnah" and will reclaim Pakistan from those who destroyed it for their personal interest. The manifesto prioritised its mission to build national cohesion, a country free from foreign dictates, a decentralised Pakistan where real power will rest with the grassroots level, and ensure civilian supremacy.

Since PTI has never held power, it had no responsibility to share for the deteriorating condition of the economy, basic amenities, security and American arm-twisting of the Pakistani government. Imran Khan started his political campaign two years in advance in 2011 with highlighting the failures of the incumbent PPP-led government. On 30 October 2011 the party organised its public meeting (which they called PTI *Jalsa*) at Lahore's historic *Minar-i-Pakistan*.[132] Imran Khan called the gathering a sign of a revolution in Pakistan and said that the rulers cannot stop it.[133] He said corruption was the biggest challenge facing Pakistan and his party would strive to resolve this. He "warned politicians to declare their assets or his party would launch a civil disobedience movement against them."[134] One year later, on the same date PTI leaders and workers observed their last meeting day as the Revolution Day.

As the election date approached, PTI accelerated its campaign. The election saw the colossal use of information and communication technologies (ICTs), especially the internet. In the 2013 general election, the PTI emerged as a major gainer of the online campaign. The inclination towards social media for campaigning was the consequence of both the push of the circumstances and pull of the popularity to reach out to large number of *netizens*. The push was the security risk involved in the physical campaign as many party workers died in violent attacks.

The pull was the fact that Pakistan had 8 million Facebook users and around 2-3 million Twitter users who could be reached by using these virtual platforms at any time, day or night. Apart from social networking sites, other platforms like blogs, official party websites and unofficial supporting sites also boosted up the political campaign. Through these platforms voters could evaluate the manifesto, candidates and the party itself. The PTI and the MQM were two political parties which used these new opportunities more efficiently than other parties. Imran Khan's Facebook page *Naya Pakistan* had the largest number of followers compared to other political rivals.

In the elections PTI won 26 general seats and emerged as the third largest party following the PML (N) with 124 seats and the PPP with 31 seats. But PTI become the second largest party as it received 17 per cent of popular vote share, which was 2 per cent more than PPP. PTI won the majority of its seats from Khyber Pakhtunkhwa (KPK), out of the 26 seats it had won 17 in this Province. In KPK, the party also emerged as the single largest party winning 56 seats from a total of 124 seats in the Provincial Assembly elections. Imran Khan decided to sit in the opposition in the National Assembly, but formed a coalition government with the Jamaat-e-Islami and *Awami Jamhuri Ittehad Pakistan* in KPK. After the election, Imran Khan was chosen as "Person of the Year" in a survey conducted by a popular Pakistani news magazine on the basis of jury voting and popular voting. He was chosen "for introducing a vibrant, if raucous, third force in Pakistani politics, for creating waves (if not a tsunami) in the general election."[135] However due to his injury during the election campaign, Khan did not go to the parliament.

A year later year, PTI, which had expected a landslide victory, alleged that the elections were rigged and demanded a judicial commission to be formed to probe the 2013 general elections. Imran Khan then decided to boycott sessions of parliament until the demands were met. He resorted to street protest and launched protest marches. In a public rally at Bhawalpur in June he posed four questions to the government: "Who scripted the victory speech of Nawaz Sharif on May 11, 2013; What was the role of the caretaker Punjab chief minister Najam Sethi; What was the role of the then Chief Justice Iftikhar Muhammad Chaudhry; and lastly why returning officers were not present under the Election Commission of Pakistan."[136] He then issued an ultimatum that "If these demands are not fulfilled within a month, or until July 27, then the government should brace for a 'tsunami march' on August 14."

The government did not agree to the demands and the PTI launched its "*Azadi March*" or (Freedom March) on 14 August 2014 (Independence Day of Pakistan) at *D-Chowk* from where Prime Minister Nawaz Sharif was to hoist the national flag. On the sixth day of the sit-in protest Imran Khan upped the ante by revising his demands. His new demands were: resignation of Prime Minister Nawaz Sharif; dissolution of assemblies and fresh election; electoral reforms; a caretaker government be formed with the consensus of all parties; resignation of all the members of the Election Commission of Pakistan (ECP); Article 6 of the Constitution be invoked against those who helped in the "rigging" of the 2013 general elections.[137] His protest march was joined by another similar march called *Inqilab March* launched by *Pakistan Awami Tehreek*, led by cleric Muhammad Tahir-ul Qadri.

The protests were suppressed with violence and 2520 supporters of the *Azadi March* and *Inqilab March* were arrested and jailed in 27 jails in Punjab.[138] The buzz word of the protest was the slogan "Go-Nawaz-Go", which posed many problems for the PML (N) government. After 126 days of sit-in in the national capital, Imran Khan announced the end of the protest, following the Taliban attack on the Army Public School in Peshawar which killed 148 people. Addressing his supporters he said that "we will have to end the *dharna* due to the present security situation in Pakistan." He also demanded that the Prime Minister setup a judicial commission to investigate the rigging of the last general elections.[139] The government agreed to set-up a judicial commission in April 2015 and Imran Khan and his party returned to parliament after a boycott of eight months.

Organisational Structure

More than 80 per cent of the party's constitution is dedicated to its organisational design. The constitution of the PTI elaborates on formal structures at various tiers. It has respective councils, committees and organisations at national, provincial, district and local levels delegated with specific powers and functions. But for the last 21-odd years since its inception, the party had revolved around its chairman, Imran Khan. He was the lone, but influential voice in the parliament from 2002 to 2007. Khan is the captain of his team who leads from the front and each public meeting and agitation depends on his charismatic personality. At the grassroot level the party's organisational structure is rudimentary. In the last election the PTI made an *ad hoc* arrangement to organise its election campaign with the help of *Tabdeeli Razakar* or Volunteer for Change. They were given crash courses and were motivated through motivational songs such as *Tabdili hum se*. They were addressed as 'PTI Tigers' whose job was to do door to door campaigns and mobilise voters. The strategy seems to have worked for the party as it made inroads in rural areas of Punjab and Sindh.

The working of the formal structure is stipulated in the constitution that the party will have a multi-tier organisational setup. At the top of the organisational pyramid is the National Council (NC) and the Central Executive Committee (CEC) which is accountable to the party chairman. The NC is the supreme body of the party and responsible to consider all matters such as aims, objectives and performance of the organisations. It is also tasked to supervise the works of specialist committees such as women, youth, labour, trade, social media, legal affairs, etc. The NC has the power to approve annual budgets and appoint auditors. The CEC is the executive body of the organisation and is responsible for implementing the decisions of the National Council. It is supposed to monitor and supervise the activities of the Provincial Executive Committees and regional organisations.

At the second tier of organisational hierarchy are Provincial Councils (PC) and Provincial Executive Committees (PEC). The PC is a higher body at the provincial level and responsible for carrying out the party's work at this level. It is responsible for both the CEC and the Provincial President of the party. Its task is to give effect to the decisions taken by the NC and CEC. Its other functions are to monitor and supervise the activities of subordinate organisations under its jurisdiction and approve the annual budget and appoint auditors. The Provincial Executive Committee is accountable to both the CEC and the PC and is responsible for running the everyday functions of the PC. It also acts as an executive authority of the party in the province and is supposed to implement all the decisions of PC. Further the PEC is expected to monitor and supervise the activities of subordinate organisations under its jurisdiction and also constitute sub-committees to carry out specific functions.

At the third level, there are various regional organisations which are supposed to monitor and co-ordinate things with the district organisations. The regional organisations work as a bridge between the district organisation and provincial organisation. They report to the provincial organisation but also have a responsibility to perform on the direction of the national organisation. Followed by regional organisations there are district organisations whose responsibility is to direct and coordinate with lower level organisations such as the Primary, Union Council, *Tehsil/Taluka*/Town organisations. The PEC serves as a link between the higher and subordinate organisations. Its main function is to carry out party objectives within their command areas. At the bottom of the structural hierarchy are the Primary, Union Council, *Tehsil/Taluka*/Town organisations whose primary function is to motivate people to join the party. Another important task these lower-tier organisations are supposed to carry out is to promote and implement party programmes in their areas. The party's organisational structure is illustrated in the following figure.

Figure 3.4: Organisational Structure of the Pakistan Tehreek-e-Insaf

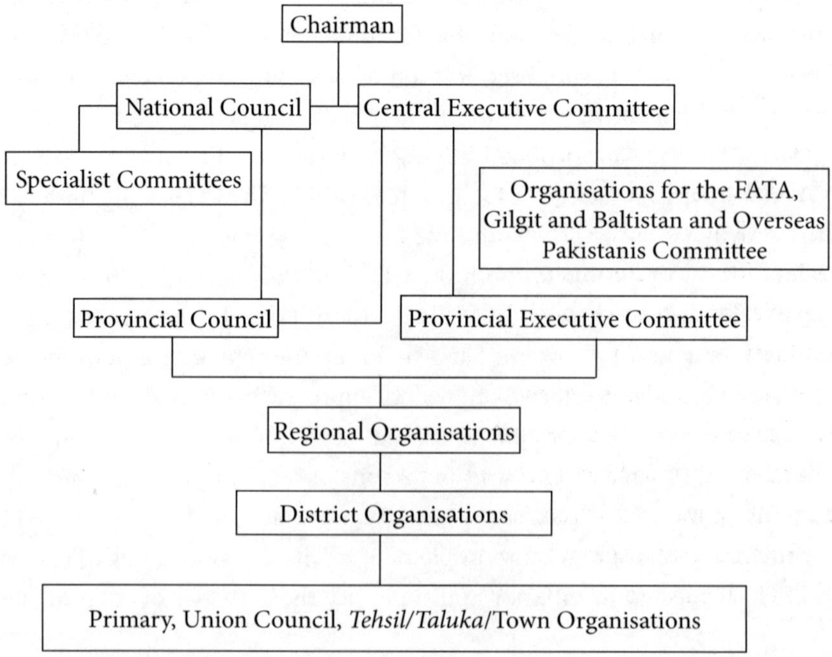

These offices at each level are occupied by office-bearers. Anyone who is an adult and a legitimate citizen of Pakistan can become a member through a simple membership procedure. To be a member of the party, an applicant requires to pay a prescribed fee and is not permitted to have dual party membership. Office-bearers are drawn from these members only. The members are empowered to elect respective office-bearers at different levels. The party Chairman is the top administrative post in the organisation. Following the post of chairman, there are the posts of President, Vice Chairman, Vice Presidents, Secretary General and various posts of subordinate Secretaries to oversee specialist areas. Except for the posts of Chairman and Vice Chairman, the central model of office-bearers is replicated at each tier with minor variations in the number of secretaries. The Chairman is the supreme source of authority and responsible for overseeing all the organisational work in accordance with the party's objectives. He has the authority to delegate any of his powers to the Secretary General or members of the CEC. He possesses all the powers of appointment and suspension, also the powers which the constitution does not specify. Selection of party candidates for the National and Provincial Assemblies are done only in consultation with the Chairman.

The President and Vice Chairman at the central level exercise the power and responsibilities assigned by the Chairman. The Secretary General (SG) is delegated with executive powers and is responsible for directing, supervising and monitoring the organisational work. In consultation with the Chairman, the SG can appoint and remove incumbent in the central office. Other office-holders function as directed by the CEC. Other office-bearers at the subordinate levels are supposed to carry out functions identical to the central office in their respective jurisdiction. Another post in the organisation is of the Central Election Commission appointed by the CEC. The Central Election Commission is responsible for conducting party elections at the central and provincial levels. It further appoints Provincial Election Committees who are entrusted with the functions to hold party elections for all organisations lower than the provincial organisations. To be eligible for elective positions a member needs to have a clear economic background, high moral standard and to not have been involved in any criminal activity.

This chapter attempted to sketch a brief profile of political parties in Pakistan. It explored the socio-political conditions in which these parties took root and how they traversed a complicated trajectory. The discussion also examined how these parties participated in the electoral process and evolved as institutional mechanisms capable of organising and mobilising social and political constituencies. It tried to understand the objectives, *raison d'être*, motivational forces and organisational structures of the parties and how they participated in the electoral process. The exploration found that some parties rose to power and some collapsed. Their course of evolution was determined by two factors. The first being the socio-political conditions in which they had to operate, as discussed in this chapter. The second factor was the political attitude of the leadership which originated from a specific social and political class. The next chapter focuses on the role of the leadership in shaping the outlook of political parties as well as their support base. The synthesised combination of these factors helps in understanding the context which shaped the nature of these parties, which were to shape the political landscape of the country.

Notes

1. Alexis de Tocqueville, *Democracy in America: Vol. 1*, trans. Henry Reeve (New York: Alfred A. Knopf, 1960), p. 174.
2. Quoted in Leon D Epstein, *Political Parties in the American Mold* (Madison: University of Wisconsin Press, 1986), p. 18.
3. See Hamza Alavi, "Nationhood and the Nationalities in Pakistan," *Economic and Political Weekly*, Vol. 24, No. 27, July 1989, p. 1527.
4. Stephen P. Cohen, *The Idea of Pakistan* (New Delhi: Oxford University Press, 2004), p. 24.
5. Ibid, pp. 23-4.
6. Syed Sharifuddin Pirzada, *Foundations of Pakistan: All-India Muslim League Documents, 1906-1947* (Karachi: National Publishing House, 1969), p. 341.
7. The coalition consisted of the *Awami League* led by Maulana Abdul Hamid Khan Bhasani, the *Krishak Praja Party* led by A.K Fazlul Huq, the *Ganatantri Dal* led by Haji Mohammad Danesh and *Nizam-e-Islam* led by Maulana Atahar Ali.
8. Ibid.
9. Discussion with Maya Tudor, New Delhi, 14 December 2014.
10. Mohammad Ayub Khan, "A New Experiment in Democracy in Pakistan," *Annals of the American Academy of Political Science*, Vol. 358, March 1965, p. 109.
11. Mohammad Ayub Khan, *Friends Not Masters: A Political Autobiography* (Lahore: Oxford University Press, 1967), p. 210.
12. Quoted from General Ayub Khan's "Address to a Public Rally in Lyallpur," on 12 October 1959, reprinted in Rais Ahmad Jafri (ed.), *Ayub: Soldier and Statesman, Speeches and Statements (1958-1965) of Field Martial Mohammad Ayub Khan:*

President of Pakistan and Detailed Account of the Indo-Pakistan War 1965 (Lahore: Mohammad Ali Academy,1966), p. 54.

13. Ibid.
14. See excerpts of the Constitutional debate in Badruddin Umar, *The Emergence of Bangladesh: Class Struggle in East Pakistan 1947-1958* (Karachi: Oxford University Press, 2004), pp. 293-300.
15. Hamid Khan, *Constitutional and Political History of Pakistan* (Karachi: Oxford University Press, 2002), pp. 219-21.
16. Ibid, p. 221.
17. Herbert Feldman, *Revolution in Pakistan: A Study of the Martial Law Administration* (Lahore: Oxford University Press, 1967), p. 81.
18. Philip E. Jones, *The Pakistan People's Party: Rise to Power* (Karachi: Oxford University Press, 2003),pp. 30-1.
19. Hasan Askari Rizvi, *The Military and Politics in Pakistan 1947-1997* (Lahore: Sang-e-Meel Publications, 2000), p. 244.
20. "The Political Parties Order, 2002 (Chief Executive's Order No. 18 of 2002),"in *Election Laws Vol. 1*, Election Commission of Pakistan, n. d., pp. 65-6.
21. Over 100 former legislators, 79 of them ex-MNAs and 22 former senators were disqualified by accountability courts to take part in the election. See Ashraf Mumtaz, "Graduation: Record Number of Politicians Out," *Dawn*, 19 July 2002, URL: http://archives.dawn.com/ 2002 /07/19/ top5.htm(accessed on 13 July 2011).
22. Though the polls were nominally on non-party basis, all major parties contested through proxy associations such as PML (Q)'s *Khushal Pakistan*, PPP's *Awam Dost*, PML (N)'s *Jamhooriat Nawaz*, MQM's *Haq Parast* and MMA's *Muttahida Millat-e-Amal.*
23. "ECP registers 216 political parties for upcoming polls," *Pakistan Today*, 14 January 2013, URL: https://www.pakistantoday.com.pk/2013/01/14/ecp-registers-216-political-parties-for-upcoming-polls/ (accessed on 17 March 2014).
24. Qamar Zaman, "Fakhruddin Congratulates Pakistan," *The Express Tribune*, 12 May 2013, URL: http://tribune.com.pk/story/548091/fakhruddin-congratulates-pakistan/ (accessed on 20 October 2013).
25. For the detailed content analysis of various television segments and newspaper articles on 2013 election see Gibran Peshimam, " Media-Powered Democracy: How Media Support has been Pivotal to Pakistan's Latest Democratisation Project," *Reuters Institute Fellowship Paper*, University of Oxford, 2013, pp. 27-38.
26. "The Constitution of Pakistan Muslim League (Nawaz)," URL: http://www.pmln.org/constitution /preamble/ (accessed on 23 July 2014).
27. For the list of Parties with nomenclature of Pakistan Muslim League see Appendix A.
28. Lawrence Ziring, *Pakistan in the Twentieth Century: A Political History* (London: Oxford University Press, 1970), p. 146.
29. It defines *Sharia\'ah* as the Injunctions of Islam as laid down in the Holy *Quran* and *Sunnah*. "Enforcement of *Shari'ah* Act. 1991 (ACT X OF 1991) An Act for the enforcement of *Shari'ah*," pakistan.org, URL: http://www.pakistani.org/pakistan/

legislation/1991/actXof1991.html (accessed on 23 July 2014).

30. "Bhutto Drawing Thousands in Rail Campaign to Oust Government," *The New York Times*, 27 November 1992, URL:http://www.nytimes.com/1992/11/27/world/bhutto-drawing-thousands-in-rail-campaign-to-oust-government.html(accessed on 11 April 2015).
31. Muhammad Mutahir Ali, "The history of Pakistani Street-Politics," *Pakistan Today*, 12 July 2014, URL: http://www.pakistantoday.com.pk/2014/07/12/featured/the-history-of-pakistani-street-politics/ (accessed on 12 April 2015).
32. "Text of the Charter of Democracy," *Dawn*, 16 May 2006, URL:http://www.dawn.com/news/192460/ text-of-the-charter-of-democracy (accessed on 17 November 2013).
33. The 2013 Manifesto of Pakistan Muslim League (Nawaz), URL: http://www.pmln.org/pmln-manifesto-english/ (accessed on 15 March 2015).
34. The Convention adopted ten "Founding Documents" namely: 1: Name of Party; 2: Flag of Party; 3: Why a New Party? 4: Why Socialism is Necessary for Pakistan; 5: Draft Declaration of Principles; 6: The Evolution of the Economy; 7: A Declaration on the Unity of the People; 8: Jammu and Kashmir; 9: The need for Pakistan to have Special Relations with Assam; 10: The Six Points Answered. For detailed text see Verinder Grover and Ranjana Arora (eds.), *Political System of Pakistan Vol. 3: Political Parties, Elections and Regionalism in Pakistan* (New Delhi: Deep and Deep Publications, 1995), pp. 355-420.
35. The Preamble of the Interim Constitution of Pakistan Peoples Party, reprinted Verinder Grover and Ranjana Arora (eds.), Political System of Pakistan Vol. 2: Constitutional Development in Pakistan (New Delhi: Deep and Deep Publications, 1995), p. 421.
36. The 1970 Manifesto of Pakistan Peoples Party, *ppp.org*, URL: http://www.ppp.org.pk/manifestos /manifesto1970.pdf (accessed on 23 March 2015).
37. Ibid.
38. Rafi Raza, *Zulfikar Ali Bhutto and Pakistan 1967-1977* (Karachi: Oxford University Press, 1997), p. 334.
39. Ibid, p. 348.
40. Sahid Javed Burki, *Pakistan under Bhutto 1971-1977* (London: The Macmillan Press, 1980), p. 200.
41. The eight parties of MRD were: Pakistan Peoples Party, Awami National Party, Communist Party of Pakistan, *Jamiat Ulema-e-Islam* (F), *Jeay Sindh Qaumi Mahaj*, National Democratic Party, *Awami Tehreek*, and *Tehreek-e-Istiqlal*.
42. William L. Richter, "Pakistan in 1984: Digging in," *Asian Survey*, Vol. 25, No. 2, February 1985, p. 148.
43. William L. Richter, "Pakistan in 1985: Testing time for the New Order," *Asian Survey*, Vol. 26, No. 2, February 1986, p. 208.
44. The 1993 Manifesto of Pakistan Peoples Party, *ppp.org*, URL: http://www.ppp.org.pk/manifestos /manifesto1993.pdf (accessed on 23 March 2015).
45. The 2008 Manifesto of Pakistan Peoples Party, *ppp.org*, URL: http://www.ppp.org.pk/manifestos /manifesto2008.pdf (accessed on 23 March 2015).

46. The 2013 Manifesto of Pakistan Peoples Party, *ppp.org*, URL: http://www.ppp.org.pk/manifestos /manifesto2013.pdf (accessed on 23 March 2015).
47. Cited in Jones, *The Pakistan People's Party*, p. 207.
48. Ibid, p. 208.
49. Pakistan Democratic Forum, *Pakistan People's Party* (New York: Pakistan Democratic Forum, 1983), p. 9
50. Ibid.
51. The etymological meaning of this Arabic word is "migrant" or "emigrants" which has Islamic connotation as it was used for the Prophet Muhammad and his companions who migrated to Medina from Makka in 622 CE. In the Muslim history refugees or emigrants were addressed as Muhajirs. In the specific context of Pakistan, the term 'Muhajir' was associated with Urdu-speaking people who migrated from India to Pakistan at the time of partition in 1947 and largely settled in urban Sindh. It is a distinct cultural, historical and linguistic group.
52. Mohammad Waseem, *Politics and the State in Pakistan* (Islamabad: National Institute of Historical and Cultural Research, 1994), p. 114.
53. Ayesha Jalal, *The State of Martial Rule: The Origins of Pakistan's Political Economy of Defence* (Cambridge: Cambridge University Press, 1990), p. 223.
54. 06/05/1964, Morrice James to CRO, *East Pakistan – Trends and development*, REF: DO 196/319, DAC. 94/83/1, Dispatch No. 1, PRO cited in Roedad Khan, *The British Papers: Secret and Confidential, India – Pakistan – Bangladesh Documents 1958 – 1969* (Karachi: Oxford University Press, 2002), p. 211.
55. Charles H. Kennedy, *Bureaucracy in Pakistan* (Karachi: Oxford University Press, 1987), p.77.
56. Adeel Khan, *Politics of Identity: Ethnic Nationalism and the State in Pakistan* (New Delhi: Sage Publication, 2006), p. 171.
57. Kennedy, *Bureaucracy in Pakistan*, p. 80.
58. Tariq Rahman, *Language and Politics in Pakistan* (New Delhi: Orient Longman, 1997), pp. 123-25.
59. Hasan Askari Rizvi, *Military, State and Society in Pakistan: 1947-1997*(Lahore: Sang-e-Meel Publications, 2000), p. 258.
60. Feroz Ahmed, *Ethnicity and Politics in Pakistan* (Karachi: Oxford University Press, 1998), p. 102.
61. Feroz Ahmed, "Ethnicity and Politics: The Rise of Muhajir Separatism," *South Asian Bulletin*, Vol. 8 (1988), p. 50.
62. Aurangzaib Khan, "The Whole Roedad: The Journey of a Man, and an Institution through the Decades," *The Herald*, Vol. 48, No. 2, February 2015, p. 61.
63. Sher Ali Khan, Umer Farooq and Mirza Khurram Shahzad, "Dead Weight," *The Herald*, Vol. 48, No. 2, February 2015, p. 53.
64. Ahmed, *Ethnicity and Politics in Pakistan*, p. 118.
65. Moonis Ahmar, "Ethnicity and State Power in Pakistan: The Karachi Crisis," *Asian Survey*, Vol. 35, No. 11, October 1996, p. 1033.
66. Altaf Hussain, *My Life's Journey: The Early Years 1966-1988* (*Safar-i-Zindagi*) trans. Khalid Athar (Karachi: Oxford University Press, 2011), p. 120.

67. Ibid, pp. 137-9.
68. Biharis are the non-Bengali Muslims who migrated from India to then East Pakistan at the time of Partition in 1947. They were the Urdu-speaking West Pakistan loyalists who were stranded in Bangladesh following the 1971 War leading to the creation of Bangladesh. They live in overcrowded camps in Bangladesh and wanted to go to Pakistan.
69. There were altogether 22 demands, for a detailed list of demands of '*The Charter of Resolution*,' see Appendix B.
70. Nichola Khan, *Mohajir Militancy in Pakistan: Violence and Transformation in the Karachi Conflict* (Abingdon: Routledge, 2010), p. 42
71. Ibid.
72. "Retired army officers absolve MQM of Jinnahpur plot: Altaf calls for truth and reconciliation commission" *Dawn*, 25 August 2009, URL: http://www.dawn.com/news/849392/retired-army-officers-absolve-mqm-of-jinnahpur-plot-altaf-calls-for-truth-and-reconciliation-commission(accessed on 27 April 2015).
73. Gilani's Index of Electoral Record, based on Gallup Exit Poll data and ECP data, compiled by Gallup Election Studies Team, 2013.
74. Nichola Khan, *Mohajir Militancy in Pakistan*, p. 33, and Ahmed, *Ethnicity and Politics in Pakistan*, p. 127.
75. The 1998 Manifesto of Muttahida Quami Movement, *mqm.org*, URL: http://www.mqm.org/manifesto /manifesto-contents-1998.htm (accessed on 17 April 2015).
76. Usman Manzoor, "The 22-year history of MQM about-turns," *The News International*, 29 June 2011, URL:http://www.thenews.com.pk/Todays-News-2-54968-The-22-year-history-of-MQM-about-turns(accessed on 11 April 2015).
77. The 2013 Manifesto of Muttahida Quami Movement, *mqm.org*, URL: http://www.mqm.org /manifesto2013 (accessed on 17 April 2015).
78. Abid Hussain, "Big Brother is Watching," *The Herald*, Vol. 18, No.7, July 2014, p. 45.
79. Alizeh Kohari, "The Centre (Still) Holds," *The Herald*, Vol.18, No.7, July 2014, p.52
80. Hussain, "Big Brother is Watching," p. 44.
81. Azfar-ul-Ashfaque, "Spotlight on MQM 'Muscle body'" *Dawn*, 6 September 2014, URL: http://www.dawn.com/news/1130232 (accessed on 28 April 2015).
82. Seyyed Vali Reza Nasr, *The Vanguard of the Islamic Revolution: The Jama`at-i-Islami of Pakistan* (London: I. B. Tauris Publishers, 1994), pp. 5-6 &16.
83. Article 3 of the Constitution of Jamaat-e-Islami, *jamaat.org*, URL: http://jamaat.org/ur/dastoorOrManshoor_detail.php?article_id=1150 (accessed on 1 May 2015).
84. Nasr, *The Vanguard of the Islamic Revolution*, p. 7.
85. Ibid, p. 18.
86. Salman Taseer was a former Governor of Punjab who was murdered in 2011 by his own bodyguard Mumtaz Qadri because of his opposition to the Blasphemy Law.
87. Article 2 of the Constitution of Jamaat-e-Islami.
88. Ibid.
89. M. Munir, *Report of the Court of Inquiry Constituted Under Punjab Act II of 1954 to Enquire Into the Punjab Disturbances of 1953* (Lahore: Government of Punjab, 1954), pp. 253-4.

90. Herbert Feldman, *From Crisis to Crisis: Pakistan 1962-1969* (London: Oxford University Press, 1972), p. 66.
91. Kalim Bahadur, *The Jamaat-i-Islami of Pakistan: Political Thought and Political Action* (New Delhi: Chetna Publication, 1977), p. 105.
92. Combined Opposition Parties was formed against the candidacy of General Ayub Khan, represented by Pakistan Muslim League (Conventional). The COP was composed of five opposition parties namely: Pakistan Muslim League (Council), the Awami League, the National Awami Party, the *Nizam-e-Islam Party*, and the Jamaat-e-Islami.
93. Bahadur, *The Jamaat-i-Islami of Pakistan*, p. 123.
94. Ibid, p. 124.
95. Pakistan Democratic Forum, *Pakistan People's Party*, p. 2.
96. Rizvi, *The Military and Politics in Pakistan 1947-1997*, p. 234.
97. Pakistan Democratic Forum, *Pakistan People's Party*, p. 2.
98. Emad El-Din Shahin (ed.), *The Oxford Encyclopedia of Islam and Politics, Vol.1* (New York: Oxford University Press, 2014), p. 628.
99. Shuja Nawaz, *Crossed Swords: Pakistan, its Army and the Wars Within* (New York: Oxford University Press, 2008), p. 360.
100. ICG, "Islamic Parties in Pakistan," *International Crisis Group*, Asia Report, No. 216, 12 December 2011, p. 4.
101. The Nine Parties of IJI were: Pakistan Muslim League, *Jamiat-i-Islami Pakistan*, National People's party, *Jamiat Ulema-e-Islam*, *Nizam-e-Mustufa* Group, *Markazi Jamiat-e-Ahle-e-Hadith* (Lakhvi Group), *Jamiat-e-Mashaikh Pakistan*, *Azad* Group, and *Hizbullah Jihad.*
102. "Hameed Gul admits he formed IJI," *Daily Times*, 1 February 2008, URL: http://www.thenews.com.pk /TodaysPrintDetail.aspx?ID=24196&Cat=13&dt=8/30/2009(accessed on 29 April 2015).
103. The PDA was composed of: Pakistan Peoples Party, *Tehreek-e-Istaqlal*, *Tehreek-e-Nafaz-e-Fiqah-e-Jafaria*, and Pakistan Muslim League (Malik Qasmi).
104. ICG, "Pakistan: The Mullahs and the Military," *International Crisis Group*, Asia Report, No.49, 20 March 2003, p. 9.
105. The MMA composed of: the Jamaat-e-Islami, the *JamiatUlema-e-Islam* (FazlurRehman), *JamiatUlema-e-Islam* (SamiulHaq), the *JamiatUlema-e-Pakistan*, the *JamiatAhle Hadith Islami Tehrik Pakistan*.
106. ICG, "Pakistan: The Mullahs and the Military," p. 5.
107. For ideological differences among various schools of thought, see Jamal Malik, *Colonisation of Islam: Dissolution of Traditional Institutions in Pakistan* (New Delhi: Manohar Publishers, 1996), pp. 3-6.
108. Hasan Abbas, *Pakistan's Drift into Extremism: Allah, the Army and America's War on Terror* (New York: East Gate Book, 2005), p. 237.
109. Nawaz, *Crossed Swords: Pakistan, its Army, and the Wars Within*, p. 532.
110. Zahid Hussain, "How to Steal an Election," *Newsline*, 13 September 2002, URL: http://www.newsl inemagazine.com/2002/09/how-to-steal-an-election/(accessed on 26 June 2011).

111. Hasan Akbar, "The Rise of the King's Party," *Newsline*, 13 October 2002, URL: http://www.newslinemagazine.com/2002/10/the-rise-of-the-kings-party/(accessed on 28 June 2011).
112. PEW Research Centre, "The World's Muslims: Religion, Politics and Society," 30 April 2013, p.18.
113. Andrew Wilder in a Personal Interaction, New Delhi, 13 August 2014.
114. Nasr, *The Vanguard of the Islamic Revolution*, p. 13.
115. For an in-depth illustration of the organisational structure see Ibid, p. 52.
116. Article 6 of the Constitution of Jamaat-e-Islami.
117. Bahadur, *The Jamaat-i-Islami of Pakistan*, p. 103.
118. Richard C. Martin (ed.), *Encyclopedia of Islam and the Muslim World, Vol. 1* (New York: Macmillan Reference, 2004), p. 371.
119. Ian Talbot, *Pakistan: A Modern History* (London: Hurts and Company, 1998), p. 2.
120. Preamble of the Constitution of *Pakistan-Tehreek-e-Insaf, insaf.org*, URL:http://www.insaf.pk/about-us/know-pti/constitution(accessed on 7 April 2015).
121. Ibid.
122. Ibid.
123. The 2002 Manifesto of *Pakistan-Tehreek-e-Insaf, supprtimrankhan.org*, URL:http://www.support imrankhan.org/downloads/PTImanifesto.pdf(accessed on 9 April 2015).
124. Declan Walsh, "Imran Khan laps up acclaim in Pakistan," *The Guardian*, 31 October 2011, URL: http://www.theguardian.com/world/2011/oct/31/imran-khan-acclaim-pakistan?newsfeed=true(accessed on 17 April 2015).
125. Tim Adams, "The Path of Khan," *The Guardian*, 2 July 2006, URL: http://www.theguardian .com/sport/2006/jul/02/cricket.features3 (accessed on 30 April 2015).
126. "I never ever offered Imran Khan to become Prime Minister, Musharraf deny Imran's claim," *Awaz.tv*, 30 December 2014, URL: http://www.awaztoday.tv/News-Talk-Shows/74621/I-never-ever-offered-Imran-Khan-to-become-Prime-Minister-Musharraf-deny-Imrans-claim.aspx (accessed on 30 April 2015).
127. General Musharraf in an Interview with Indian journalist Barkha Dutt, "Imran Khan is the best of the lot: Musharraf to NDTV," *NDTV 24x7*, 17 November 2011, URL: http://www.ndtv.com/world-news/imran -khan-is-the-best-of-the-lot-musharraf-to-ndtv-566316(accessed on 17 November 2011).
128. Hendrik Hertzberg, "Big News Week," *The New Yorker*, 30 May 2005, URL: http://www.newyorke r.com/magazine/2005/05/30/big-news-week(accessed on 12 April 2015).
129. "Hundreds held in Pakistan to foil protests against Bush visit," *The Hindu*, 5 March 2006.
130. "Pakistanis condemn Rushdie honour," *Al Jazeera*, 27 June 2007, URL: http://www.aljazeera.com/ news/asia/2007/06/200852513144735197.html(accessed on 17 April 2015).
131. Iftikhar A. Khan, "ECP rejects references against Imran," *Dawn*, 6 September 2007, URL: http://www. dawn.com/news/264817/ecp-rejects-references-against-imran (accessed on 1 May 2015).

132. The 2013 Manifesto of the *Pakistan Tehreek-e-Insaf*, *insaf.org*, URL: http://www.insaf.pk/about-us/know-pti/manifesto(accessed on 26 April 2015).
133. *Minar-e-Pakistan* or Tower of Pakistan is the national monument of Pakistan built on the exact location where historic Lahore Resolution was passed on 23 March 1940. The monument symbolises the spirit of Pakistan movement and is situated in Iqbal Park, Lahore.
134. "Imran Khan addresses thousands gathered at Minar-e-Pakistan," *Dawn*, 30 October 2011, URL: http://www.dawn.com/news/670096/thousands-gather-at-the-minar-e-pakistan-ground-for-pti-rally (accessed on 1 May 2015).
135. "Imran Khan's 'tsunami' sweeps Lahore," *The Express Tribune*, 30 October 2011, URL: http://tribune.com.pk/story/285058/pti-rally-in-lahore-live-updates/ (accessed on 1 May 2015).
136. Shayan Naveed and Alizeh Kohari, "Person of the Year," *The Herald*, Annual Issue, January 2014.
137. Kashif Zafar, "Countdown begins: Imran to lead 'tsunami march' on August 14," *The Express Tribune* 28 June 2014, URL: http://tribune.com.pk/story/728176/countdown-begins-imran-to-lead-tsunami-march-on-august-14/ (accessed on 30 April 2015).
138. "Imran lays out 6-point charter of demands," *The Nation*, 21 August 2014, URL: http://nation.com.pk/national/21-Aug-2014/imran-lays-out-6-point-charter-of-demands (accessed on 2 May 2015).
139. Faisal Ali Ghumman, "2,520 PTI, PAT activists in 27 Punjab jails," *Dawn*, 17 August 2014, URL: http://www.dawn.com/news/1125893/2520-pti-pat-activists-in-27-punjab-jails (accessed on 2 May 2015).
140. Habib Ur Rehman , "Imran Khan Announce to End Islamabad Sit-in over Peshawar Attack," *The Pak Media*, 17 December 2014, URL: http://www.thepakmedia.com/imran-khan-announce-ends-islamabad-sit-peshawar-attack/2014/12/17 (accessed on 2 May 2015).

4. Society, Leadership and Social Base of Political Parties

Leadership and party performance are interlinked elements of electoral democracy. A party's performance is mutually correlated to the nature of leadership and social and demographic setting in which it operates. This chapter is divided into three parts. In the first, it discusses how certain social and political determinants are correlated to electoral behaviour in a given demographic setting. In the second the focus is on the party leadership, their social background and roles in shaping the party trajectories. The third part focuses on the social constituencies of the parties. The former is examined in a qualitative framework while the latter is analysed on the quantitative performances in a given support base. To understand the political parties' social base it tries to identify social forces which drive individual or collective behaviour. To comprehend the behavioural pattern of a social constituency *vis-à-vis* a political party, it is necessary to have an overview of a universe within which both are operating. In order to understand why a specific party has particular reach to a particular segment of voters, it is necessary to understand its demographic composition and their political aspirations.

For the purpose of analysis voters can be compartmentalised into age, gender and religious categories. In the context of Pakistan, other social elements such as sect and language become more significant markers which determine their collective electoral behaviour. In the context of South Asia one has to be aware of a peculiar system of caste as well. However, in Pakistan a more close knit *Biradari* system replaces the caste phenomenon. Above all, it is ethnicity which stands out among other markers that determines electoral outcomes. During its first general election of 1970, Pakistan had following major ethnicities: Bengalis, Punjabis, Sindhis, Pakhtun, Muhajirs, Baluch, Kashmiris and other tribal groups. Class could be another crucial prism through which one can interpret the voting pattern. Class is not necessarily an absolute category and might have internal variants. But on occupational terms they can be broadly categorised into the public servants in formal sectors, people engaged in agriculture and related jobs and people engaged in the industrial and the informal and the unorganised sector. In broader terms these segments can be classified through the urban-rural divide. Further, the level of education too plays a role in directing individuals or group behaviour in a given election.

Also something very abstract as ideological orientation of a political party or a leader could help it forge a political constituency in a social base that shares the same ideology. The traditionalists, the patriarchs, the Islamists, the Marxists, the liberals, the feminists and the apolitical masses may vote differently at times. There could be a segment of voters who are loyal and there could be constant vote-banks which may vote for a particular party repeatedly despite knowing the parties' miniscule opportunities of winning. There are also groups of fluid voters who may go by programmatic content and policy vision of a party. Depending on the situations such as mass perception of a party's aspiration, party's position *vis-à-vis* military rule and feudalism, sentimental sloganeering against external forces – anti-Americanism in the frontier region and anti-Indianism in Punjab – might shape a voter's opinion. It was also the populist sloganeering of the Pakistan Peoples Party (PPP) in the past that earned it a mandate in the first two general elections.

There are certain generic socio-political determinants of political behaviour across democracies. From the existing analyses of electoral behaviour as discussed here, an essential conclusion is inferred that caste and *biradari* are a peculiar social organisation that has a decisive impact on electoral outcome, especially in rural Pakistan. Hence it is essential to deliberate on these two concepts prior to discussing the demographic equations in Pakistan. The caste phenomenon in the context of Pakistan is not understood as it is popularly understood in reference to Indian society and Hinduism. The conceptual understanding of caste and *biradari* here has its theoretical bases on the sociological, anthropological and ethnographic works of various scholars of social science.

Caste and *Biradari* in Pakistan

There are two paradigms through which caste can be analysed as a determinant of social stratification that is the positioning of social status and power hierarchy in a given society. The first paradigm traces the genesis of caste in a religio-cultural domain and is largely attributed to the *Manusmirti*, an ancient text of Hinduism on law. The second paradigm is based on the structuralist-functionalist interpretation of caste. The following debate emphasises on the latter paradigm. Some of the seminal conceptual studies of caste-system offer succinct explanations which help to understand this phenomenon. Edward Blunt in his book, *The Caste System of North India*, weaved various attributes found to be common to all castes expanded the definition of caste as:

> A caste is an endogamous group, or collection of endogamous groups, bearing a common name, membership of which is hereditary, arising from birth alone, and imposing on its members certain restrictions in the matter of social intercourse either – (a) Following a common tradition occupation, or (b) Claiming a common origin, or (c) Both following such occupation and claiming such origin, and generally regarded as forming a single homogeneous community.[1]

The characteristics of caste identified by Blunt capture the essential components which together gives a comprehensive meaning minus the concept of 'polluted and pure' added by J. H. Hutton, who was responsible for conducting the 1931 census of British India. In Hutton's definition, caste is endogamous, restricts inter-caste commensality, establishing hierarchical grading, which puts at the top the Brahmin (the pure), who gets polluted by inter-caste dining and marriages with lower caste; caste status is hereditary and culminates into the permanency of division of labour.[2] Prior to Blunt (1931) and Hutton's (1946) formulations, Bhim Rao Ambedkar, the architect of the Indian constitution and the crusader of Dalit emancipation provided a structural-functionalist definition of caste.

In a 1916 anthropological paper titled *"Castes in India: Their Mechanism, Genesis and Development,"* Ambedkar argued that in the pre-caste system, Indian society was made up of classes. This class made itself into a caste by closing itself. As the class became closed, it metamorphosed into a caste-society. Thus, Ambedkar argued that "a Caste is an enclosed class."[3] The caste in Ambedkar's view was an extreme form of class rigidity which sustained and operated through the mechanism of endogamy. He further argued that "*Endogamy is the only characteristic that is peculiar to caste*"[4](emphasis in original), and considered it the genesis and mechanism of caste. Ambedkar was right in his argument, as over a period of time there has been a general acceptance that endogamy is the essential component of the caste system.

Social organisations in Pakistan are much older than the formation of the country itself. Not only this, social formations began much before the arrival of Islam in the region. Thus, according to the structuralist-functionalist paradigm, those who argue that the caste system is not an integral part of Islam cannot deny the practice of caste as a social tradition in Pakistan. However, they do not necessarily call it caste. They call it *Biradari*, a type of kinship institution and principle unit of social organisation. Hamza Alavi found two types of *birdaris* in Punjab and described it as thus (1) *Biraderi* as lineage: here "kinship is based on what is known as the structure of patrilateral parallel cousin marriage," it's kind of a lineage endogamy[5] and (2) *Biraderi* as clan: in this "the biraderi is made up of a number of exogamous patrilineal *gots* (or *gotras*)," and the kinship system is very large.[6] Scholars have used caste and *biradari* interchangeably to connote how the social organisations function in this region.

Zekiye Eglar in his study of a Muslim Punjabi village divided the population into two castes: *zamindars*, who own land or whose ancestors did, and *kammis*, the artisans.[i] Saghir Ahmad argues that Eglar treats *quoms* as caste but stresses its cultural realm. In Ahmad's view the word *quom* is generally employed to connote tribe, sect, people, or nation but villagers do not apply the term in this sense and divide themselves into two *quoms* of *zamindars* and *kammis*.[7] Further both *zamindars* and *kammis* are divided into sub-q*uoms* or say sub-castes. Inayat Ullah found 15 castes (endogamous lineage) of *zamindars* and 11 of *kammis*.[8] Both *zamindars* and *kammis* have internal stratification and the hierarchal status is not contested. Alavi

---

i. Kammis included: barbers, bakers, cobblers, carpenters, potters, blacksmith, *Musallis* (labourers), weavers, tailors, *Mirasis* (bards), *Kashmiris* (got-herders), and *Arains* (vegetable growers). These are the common founded components of village institution and it is not necessary that every village should have all of them. Zekiye Eglar, *A Punjabi Village in Pakistan*(New York: Columbia University Press, 1960) cited in Clarance Malony, *Peoples of South Asia* (New York: Holt, Rinehart and Winston, 1974), p. 375.

juxtaposes another layer, "*zat*" to this stratification. In his study, Alavi found that villagers in Punjab were not clear about the term *zat* but they applied it to identify with certain surnames. "To them the word *zat* did not indicate a position within any ranked social order" and there are no rules or hierarchal order according to which all *zats* could find the social positioning, thus Alavi argued that "essential elements of caste were missing."[9] Nevertheless, all these nomenclatures were used interchangeably and played almost an identical role to what the castes do, generating the "we feeling."

It is important to understand this aspect of caste or *biradari* here for it is a powerful determinant of electoral outcome. Caste is a marker of individual and collective identities. Further these identities transform into associative projection. In an electoral democracy projection of collective association may yield either positive or negative outcomes given the groups' numerical strength. Numerous studies on Indian election exhibit a clear correlation between caste and elections and its subsequent impact on specific groups. Indian sociologist M. N. Srinivas argues that high influence of caste in politics may impede the growth of democracy and considered it as a negative force. Contrary to Srinivas's view Lloyd Rudolf and Sussane Rudolf in their collective work argued that the role of caste in Indian politics has minimised the caste differences and brought oppressed castes closer to political equality.[10] Caste is not only a factor in determining voting behaviour but is also reflected in the choice of candidates by political parties. The parties field their candidates on the basis of calculations of the social compositions of a given constituency.

Among the early studies of elections in Pakistan especially of Basic Democracy elections, Inayat Ullah's study found that "traditional social structure and group identities of family and *biradari* (clan) determined voting behaviour."[11] He further argued in the context of Punjab that a voter "is an inalienable part of multiple groups which completely overshadow his individuality"[12] and it is the family and *biradari* that makes the political decisions. Ahmad had separately argued that class was the shaper of political behaviour rather than traditional caste or kinship ties.[13]Alavi substantiated this finding in his study that voters who are economically dependent on others will vote according to the dictates of those on whom they are dependent, and only those who are economically independent are likely to vote along the lines of kinship or caste.[14] However, Craig Baxter had a contrary opinion as he noted that the results of the 1970 elections broken this myth. He observed that "the influence of major landlords was no longer the dominant factor in Punjab politics and the *biradari* ("brotherhood") of caste and tribal connections controlling the vote had broken down."[15] A caveat is in order here as these studies are not applicable to urban settings in totality and are principally devoted to rural Pakistan.

The second set of analysis of elections begins with the re-emergence of democratic governance followed by the end of the third *junta* regime of General Zia-ul Haq in 1988. In the first comprehensive study of the 1993 elections Mohammad Waseem concluded that:

> Overall, the 1993 voter was a parochial voter, not a national voter. He was bound by considerations of local power structure in terms of caste/*biradari* and tribe, tempered by instant patronage in the form of development funds or money proper. The party voter combined with the patronage voter and the *biradari*/tribal/ethnic/sectarian voter shaped the profile of a Pakistani voter in the 1993 elections.[16]

Waseem however categorically considered social group behavior more important than the individual voting behaviour. He argued that "the basic electoral unit in Pakistani society is not the individual citizen but the leader or spokesman of the local community, be it tribe, sub-caste, sect, sub-sect, faction, trade union, migrant or settler group or women's activist groups."[17] Thus by engaging with a local influential a bulk vote could be ensured. Contrary to this, Andrew Wilder, an American political scientist who studied the voting behaviour in Punjab during the 1993 and 1997 general elections argued slightly differently.

Through his empirical findings, Wilder challenged the common perception that social factors are decisive shapers of voting behaviour. He argued that in urban areas the voting preferences were increasingly getting influenced by political determinants such as party identity and leadership, while in rural areas patronage orientation were determining the voting preferences.[18] He further elaborated, that the "influence of faction and *biradari*" on voting preferences are exaggerated although they continue to be important in the selection of candidates.[19] Wilder is also careful in marking distinction in voting behaviour between parts of Punjab. The next general election was a controlled procedure under the watch of the *junta* regime of General Pervez Musharraf.

Musharraf created his own party which was instrumental in civilianising and legitimising his exercise of political power. Even during the 2002 elections party politics was the central deriving force. Unlike his emphasis on the primacy of *biradari* as the chief determinant in previous elections, Waseem found leadership and ideology as the principle force in that election. Because the election was held to civilianise the military rule and under a military-supervised legal framework, the political and social considerations were subsumed under an anti and pro-military discourse. However, in a personal interview Waseem agreed that *biradari* is still the dominant determinant of voting preferences in rural areas.[20] It must also be admitted that a majority of studies of voting behaviour were carried out within sociological approach which holds groups as a basic unit of analysis rather than rationalist approach which places individuals at the centre of analysis. Secondly, *biradari* on its own is not effective unless it has numerical strength. The demographic equations do correspond to the electoral outcome.

Demography intrinsically is dynamic so is its impact on election outcome. Therefore to understand how election outcomes were related directly or indirectly with fluid demographic equations it is instructive to briefly examine how changes occurred within the elements which explain complexities of a given demography. Along with demography, socio-economic development, rate of urbanisation, literacy, growth of the middle class, development of free media and later of alternative media (internet and specifically social networking) are some variables which are relative shapers of electoral behaviour. Certain shapers are more effective than others and may be instrumental in shaping the end result. Before examining the voting patterns of certain segments *vis-à-vis* political parties, it is important to understand the demographic picture of Pakistan.

The Demography of Pakistan

At the time of the general election of 2013, the population of Pakistan was estimated to be around 180 million,[21] with 86,189,802 electoral rolls[22] marked for a total number of 272 seats allotted for the national assembly. The population rose five times compared to the 33 million counted in 1951, in the first census six decades ago.[23] In the first general election of 1970 the total number of seats allotted to West Pakistan was 138 for 47,918,500 electoral rolls.[24] The first census recorded a gigantic rural-urban divide, skewed sex-ratio and abysmal literacy rate.[ii] Between these two ends Pakistani demography exhibited a torrential and consistent pattern of change. The year 1971 was the historical rupture in Pakistan's history when it lost its majority population, nearly 53 per cent of total Pakistani population following the country's first general election of 1970. Since the separation of East Pakistan, this study remains focused on the present-day Pakistan comprising four major provinces namely Punjab, Sindh, Khyber Pakhtunkhwa (KPK) and Baluchistan.

The second significant change in the demography occurred in 1979 following the Soviet intervention in Afghanistan. The resultant conflict in Afghanistan resulted in a massive influx of Afghans (nearly 3 million) into Pakistan, changing the demographic landscape of the bordering regions.[25] But there was also an outflow of millions of Pakistanis to North America, Europe and West Asia.[iii] This process was quite slow and gradual but it certainly did alter the demography. In addition, the internal demographic variation was brought in by internal displacement due to consistent military operations in the tribal regions and the 2010 floods in the plains. Other common cause of migration – the push and pull of opportunities – resulted in rural to urban migration at a staggering pace. In the period of 1951-1981 the urban population growth was close to 360 per cent compared to the overall population increase at the rate of 164 per cent.[26] It slowed down afterwards but urbanisation outpaced the overall population growth. In the next set of data measured between 1982 and 1997 the urban growth rate was

ii. In 1951 the urban population was a mere 17.8 per cent against 82.2 per cent in the rural count. The 1951 census recorded 53.8 per cent male to 46.2 per cent female population. The condition of education was too poor: according to the 1961 census Pakistan had only 16.7 per cent literate people within which female literacy rate was as low as 6.7 per cent. *50 Years of Pakistan, Volume -1: Population*, pp. 170-3.

iii. Various sources estimate the total number of overseas Pakistanis to be around 8 million, majority of them living in United Arab Emirate (1.6 million), Saudi Arabia (1.5 million), United Kingdom (1.4 million) and the US (Half a million).

4.38 compare to rural growth rate of 2.58.[27] According to a 2013 estimate the urban population stood at 38 per cent of the total population.[28] The impact of such rapid urbanisation reflected on seat allocation between urban and rural divisions. At the time of the first general election the total number of seats allotted to four provincial capitals, considered as urban divisions, were 25.[iv] The number increased by 134 per cent and the total number of combined seats allotted in 2013 stood at 59.[v]

For a closer representation of the correlation between the electorate and the election outcome the examination of the demography is divided into provincial segments instead of a single national unit. These four provinces are distinct ethnic zones with internal variations. In addition there are few relatively autonomous administrative regions commonly referred as Federally Administered Tribal Areas (FATA) located at the Pakistan-Afghanistan border. They are politically insignificant as they collectively send a mere 11 MNAs to the house of 272. Therefore they are not substantially dealt with in the discussion. Other provincial demographic indicators are examined quantitatively to establish a statistical base to substantiate a relative correlation between the social base and political party.

Punjab

At the time of partition, the Muslim majority areas of united Punjab formed the existing province while the Sikh and Hindu dominated areas remained in India. During the country's unified days Punjab's province-status was obliterated to merge it into the One-Unit scheme; Punjab was part of the West Wing. With the dissolution of the One Unit scheme followed by the country's dismemberment, Punjab emerged as the most populace province. The province is divided into three major regions. Northern and Central Punjab is most industrialised region with three major cities: Lahore, Sialkot and Rawalpindi. Western Punjab is highly agrarian and the poverty level is much higher compared to other two regions. Southern Punjab is semi-agrarian with traditional small-scale industries. Ethnically the southwest region has its own native population called Saraikis. Traditionally, they were

iv. In the 1970 election Lahore, Karachi, Peshawar and Quetta were allotted 12, 7, 4 and 2 seats respectively.

v. In the 2013 election Lahore, Karachi, Peshawar and Quetta were allotted 30, 18, 8 and 3 seats respectively.

nomads and now mostly engaged in farming. The Saraikis claim to have their own language and distinct culture and have campaigned to form Saraiki province, Saraikistan. The demand faded during General Zia's time but has resurfaced in recent times.

Another major sub-group of Punjabis is the Potohar people, dispersed over the Potohar Plateau in north Punjab. It is a rugged land surrounded by rivers. The Potohars were traditionally farmers and served as solders in the British imperial army. Today this region is the principle catchment area for military recruitment of the Pakistan Army. Punjabis are the major ethnic group who trace their roots to Indo-European ethnicity. They speak Punjabi and are mainly engaged in agricultural activities. They also dominate military and governmental jobs. According to the 1998 census Punjabis are 55 per cent of the total population. The majority of them are concentrated over the territories of Punjab. A good number of Punjabis (8 to 10 per cent) are also settled in Karachi, the provincial capital of Sindh, and the two districts of KPK, Hazara and Dera Ismail Khan. In the two districts of Baluchistan, Quetta and Loralai, Punjabis constitute no less than 30 per cent of the total population.

When the first population census was carried out, the official count of Muhajirs were over 7 million. The resettlement of Muhajirs or displaced persons, defined by the 1951 Census as "one who has moved into Pakistan as a result of Partition or fear of disturbance connected there with,"[29] had a significant impact on the province's population balance. West Pakistan had the major share of the total refugee influx from various parts of India. Punjab, the most populated province of West Pakistan received 52, 81,000 Muhajirs.[30] The Muhajirs were 25.6 per cent of the total Punjabi population of 206, 36,000. The majority of the migrants who settled in Punjab were from East Punjab which became part of India. The cultural and political assimilation of Punjabi migrants in the new homeland was comparatively easier than other migrants. They settled on the agricultural land abandoned by the outgoing Sikh farmers in the Canal Colony areas and the other urban areas of West Punjab.[31]

According to the 1972 census, Punjab had a total population of 37 million, out of which around 24 per cent were urban.[32] In proportion to its population the province was allotted 82 seats in the general election of 1970 from the total of 138 seats. The seats were divided amongst Southern Punjab (29 seats), Western Punjab (19 seats) and Central and Northern Punjab (34 seats). The first revision of seats after the loss of the eastern wing increased the total number to 200 for the general election of 1977. Punjab's share of seats rose to 116 which was 58 per cent of the total seats exactly proportional to the population share of the province.[33] The Central and Northern Punjab regions had the largest share of 48 seats while Western Punjab had the lowest 28 seats. Southern Punjab alone had a share of 40 seats. Three major urban divisions, Multan, Lahore and Rawalpindi collectively represented 50 seats within it.

According to the last official census, conducted in 1998, the Punjabi population was 73 million – 48 per cent of the country's132 million overall count. It was a steep decline in terms of its percentile share to the total population in previous two decades. However, the seat share had dipped by only 3 per cent. General Musharraf, who seized power in a military coup, revised the number of seats to 272 for the 2002 general election. Punjab was given 150 seats which was 7 per cent higher than its proportional share to the overall population. The three regions of Western, Southern and Central and Northern Punjab received 31, 50 and 69 seats respectively in the new revision. Although the urban population of Punjab was around 32 per cent, the three urban divisions combined had 70 seats in which the Lahore division alone had 30 seats.

Sindh

Sindh was part of the Bombay Presidency and became a separate province in 1936. At the time of Partition, it constituted the part of newly formed Pakistan. Sindh constituted of erstwhile Las-Bela and Kahirpur states and the districts of Karachi. The name of the province originated from the river Sindhu (Indus) flowing through its territory. Sindhis are native to the Indus-Valley civilisation. Sindh has the country's largest urban city, Karachi, which is dominated by the Urdu-speaking Muhajirs and Pakhtuns. The rest are settled in the countryside and engaged in agriculture and related occupation. Clarence Maloney who conducted an ethnographic survey of Sindh noted that Sindhis are landlord farmers and Sindhi social structure is more stratified than in Punjab.[34] He further added: "Sindhis practice the ritual of Islam in more orthodox fashion than do many Punjabis and are proud of their stricter observance of *pardah*."[35] The majority of Sindhis live within the provincial territory with a good number residing in Kalat, now part of the neighbouring province of Baluchistan.

The demography of Sindh began to change due to inward migration of Urdu-speaking Muhajirs from India at the time of Partition. A major portion of Urdu-speaking Muhajirs settled in urban Sindh, specifically in Karachi (the then capital of Pakistan), Hyderabad and Sukkur. The Muhajir influx had a more severe demographic impact in Sindh than Punjab. Sindh had the second major proportion of total migrant population after Punjab and accommodated 11, 67,200 Muhajirs from the total of 66, 09,700 migrants received by West Pakistan as per the 1951 census.[36] The then Federal Capital Area of Karachi (now provincial capital of Sindh) accommodated 6,16,900 migrants along with additional resettlement of 5, 50,300 Muhajirs in Sindh and Khairpur State. In total the Muhajir proportion constituted 19.30 per cent of the total population of Sindh which was 60, 47,000.

The total population of Sindh rose to 14 million according to the 1972 census and proportionally in the general election of 1970 Sindh represented 27 seats in the house of 138. The seats were divided between urban and rural Sindh. Karachi region was allotted 7 seats against 20 seats allotted to interior Sindh. Within interior Sindh, 7 seats each were fixed for Sukkur and Hyderabad divisions which had significant concentration of Muhajir population. The number of seats was revised to 200 for the next election of 1977. Sindh's seats increased to 43 and consequently the seats allotted to Sukkur, Karachi and Hyderabad too increased to 10, 11 and 12 respectively. According to the last official census conducted in 1998, the population of the Sindhis was estimated to have reached 30 million. In the second major seat-revision for 2002 general election Sindh's share was 61 seats in the total of 272 seats. Seats of Sukkur and Hyderabad nominally rose by 1 seat each. Karachi's seats were doubled to 20, proportionally to its estimated 9 million population according to the 1998 census. Karachi's population has doubled in 15 years, and according to 2014 estimate reached 18 million[37] warranting another revision of seat-sharing. The demography of Karachi changed further due to internal migration of Pakhtuns from

Khyber Pakhtunkhwa (KPK) , and Karachi earned the epithet of the largest Pathan city in Pakistan.

Khyber Pakhtunkhwa

Khyber Pakhtunkhwa (KPK), earlier known as North-West Frontier Province (NWFP) is the third most populace province of the country with 17.7 million people.[38] The NWFP was inherited from the Raj at the time of partition. It was an administrative conglomeration of various frontier divisions sharing border with the then frontier regions in the North-West of the empire. It was renamed in 2010, to shed of the colonial connotation attached to it and to give the Pakhtun people a sense of ethnic association with the province. The people of Khyber Pakhtunkhwa prefer to call themselves as Pashtuns or Pakhtuns. They are dispersed over the territories of Afghanistan and Pakistan. Pakhtuns trace their ancestry to Eastern Iran and speak the Pushto language. They are an extremely conservative tribe governed by their own tribal code known as *Pakhtunwali*. Their society is governed through an assembly of tribal elders called *Jirga*. The main principles of *Pakhtunwali* includes *Melmastia* (hospitality), *Nang* (honour), *Nanawatay* (forgiveness) and *Nyaw aw Badal* (justice and revenge). Pakhtuns are proud of their warrior history and of not having been subjugated by outsiders.

Feudalisation was quite a slow process here; however the areas with Pakhtun dominance are the most rural regions of the country.[vi] The Pakhtuns of Pakistan are spread over the foot-hills in the north and in the arid and semi-desert areas of the south-west. The majaority of them are engaged in pastoral life with few engaged in land cultivation.[39] As the Pashtun tribes dispersed far and wide, the clan ties dissolved, and unions of tribes became weak. The population of KPK was altered on two historical occasions. The first occasion was in 1979 during the Soviet intervention, which led to the mass exodus of refugees from Afghanistan through the porous borders into KPK. The second event that had significant impact was Pakistan's military operations in the region

vi. It is the most rural province of the country with 83 per cent people living in rural area which is 16 per cent higher than the national average."Area, Population, Density and Urban/Rural Proportion by Admn. Units," Census of Pakistan 1998, *Pakistan Bureau of Statistics.*

resulting in the internal migration of people.[vii] Pakhtuns have settled in various parts of the country. According to the 1998 census, 30 per cent people in Baluchistan registered Pushto as their mother tongue.[40] In the federal capital, Pushto-speakers are the third largest group following the Punjabi and Urdu-speakers.[41] Similarly Pushto-speakers form the third largest group, around 12 per cent of Karachi's population. Robert Nicholas in his study found half a million Afghans were living in Karachi in 2004 and noted another half to one million urban refugees living in Pakistani cities for various reasons in addition to over one million Afghans living in UNHCR recognised camps.[42]

At the time of the first general election, KPK contributed 12 per cent to the total population but it received 18 per cent seats for the national assembly. The next decade saw 60 per cent growth rate in KPK's population, 3 per cent higher than the national average. The seat-revision was done for the 1977 election before the next census of 1981. The province was allotted 34 seats in the house of 200, which was 3 per cent more than its population share of 14 percent in the national count. The next census recorded the province's population over 17.7 million in the total of 132 million. It was 1 percentile decline of its previous share in the national total but its seat-share remained constant at 17 per cent with 47 seats given in the second revision of 2002.

---

vii. Since 2002 Pakistan Army has undertaken many counter-insurgency operations in the frontier regions bordering Afghanistan. Most of them have been successful. Between 2002 and 2006, a period coinciding with the Global War on Terrorism, the military had undertaken *Operation Al-Mizan* in Federally Administered Tribal Areas (FATA) against the local militants operating from the region. In 2007 the military had to launch a new *Operation Rah-e-Haq* against the Tehreek-e-Nafaz-e-Shariat-e-Mohammadi (TSNM) in the Swat Valley. One year later in 2008,*Operation Sher-e-Dil* was initiated in Bajaur Agency to target the local militants groups. All these operations were undertaken during the military regime of General Musharraf. In the next year, under the civilian government these offensives were intensified. In May 2009 *Operation Rah-e-Rast* in Swat Valley and in October 2009 *Operation Rah-e-Nijaat* in South Wazirstan were launched to combat the growing militancy. In 2014 under the second civilian regime headed by Nawaz Sharif a large scale military *Operation Zarb-e-Azb* was undertaken in North Wazirstan against foreign and local terror groups.

Baluchistan

Baluchistan, literary meaning the land of the Baluch people, is the largest province of Pakistan. It is the least populated province with a populace of 6.5 million which is 5 per cent of the total population.[43] After Pakistan's independence the princely states of Makran, Kharan, Lasbela and Kalat under British suzerainty were made to accede to Pakistan. All these princely states collectively merged to form Baluchistan and became the component of one unit of West Pakistan in 1955. It emerged as a new province following the dissolution of the One Unit system. It shares borders with Afghanistan and Iran and the ethnic Baluchi people are living in all the three countries. It is the most infertile land but is rich with natural gas reserves which have become a major issue between the provincial and federal governments. Ethnically, it has three major constituents: Baluchis, Brahuis and Pakhtuns.

The Baluchis are the largest ethnic group in the province. Ethnographers have divided them into 18 major tribal groups in which Marris and Bugtis are the largest tribal groups.[44] Baluchis have no clear ancestry and said to have Persian ethnicity. Occupationally, they are nomads who travel with their cattle with the changing seasons in search of better grazing lands. The language they speak is derived from Old Persian. Maloney observed that: "Brahuis are firmly nomadic and dislike agriculture, but constantly move about with their black tents, pitching them in villages even in Sindh wherever they can find grazing facilities for their animal."[45] Their language Brahui is Dravidian-based but has Persian, Baluchi and Indo-Aryan vocabulary.[46] Their social structure is similar to their Baluchi co-dwellers. Pakhtuns are the third largest ethnic group in Baluchistan. They are mainly settled in Quetta.

According to the 1998 census, Baluchistan is the least populated, least literate and second most rural province.[viii] Demographically the province never had any decisive say in the national politics or polity as whole. At the time of the first general election the population of Baluchistan was less than

viii. With 6.5 million people and only 18.9 persons per square kilometer density it is the least populated province. The rural population of the province is 76.1 per cent which is 7 per cent lower than the most rural KPK. Its literacy rate is 24 per cent much lower than the national average of 43 per cent. See "Demographic Indicators - 1998 Census," Census of Pakistan -1998, *Pakistan Bureau of Statistics*, URL: http://www.pbs.gov.pk/content/demographic-indicators-1998-census (accessed on 11 September 2014).

4 per cent of the total population but its seat-share was below 3 per cent. The province with 2.4 million people got only 4 seats in which the provincial capital Quetta had half of it. In the first seat revision the seat-share increased by half per cent and the province had a total 7 seats out of 200 seats in the 1977 election. By the second seat revision of 2002 it received 14 seats which were 5 per cent of the total seats exactly proportional to its population. Quetta had 4 seats leaving the rest to the rural divisions. This distribution continued for the last election also. After having this brief understanding of how the social formation and demographic equation determine electoral outcomes in the next section we shall see socio-political sketch of various leaders who had specific personality attributes that also had their own role to play in how their parties advanced. This also helps to examine how they mobilised their support in certain social settings.

Leadership of Pakistan Peoples Party

The Pakistan Peoples Party has given some of the most popular leaders to the country. The party was founded by Zulfikar Ali Bhutto who then became the first elected prime minister of Pakistan. He was the most populist leader Pakistan has ever produced. After his death in 1977 his daughter Benazir Bhutto served the country twice as head of the government. She was one of the rare women who led a major party and a Muslim state. Both the leaders died unnaturally. After Benazir's assassination in 2008, the party was briefly headed by her widower Asif Ali Zardari who later made his son Bilawal Bhutto the chairman of the party. This section only deals with the first two leaders of PPP under whom the party functioned for four decades. The new chairman Bilawal Bhutto has just taken over and has yet to create his own political persona.

Zulfikar Ali Bhutto: A Civilian Dictator

> I was born to make a nation, to serve people,
> to overcome an impending doom….
> I was born to bring emancipation to the people
> and honour them with a self-respecting destiny.[47]

Zulfikar Ali Bhutto thought of himself as a chosen messiah born to emancipate the wretched of Pakistan. His self-image as emancipator is reflected in his writing and politics. Many books have been produced on his personal and political life; however, here the focus is largely limited to his political rise and fall, his political acumen and his political legacy. Zulfikar Ali Bhutto was born in 1928 to a feudal family of Larkana in Sindh, the southernmost province of Pakistan. He was enrolled in Bishop High School in Karachi for his elementary education. In 1934 he had to move to Bombay as his father Sir Shah Nawaz joined Lord Brabourne's cabinet.[48] Bhutto then attended Bombay's Cathedral High School in 1937. He was first married at the age of 13 to his distant cousin who was 10 years older than him. Bhutto called it "typical type of property alliance favoured by feudal Sindhis."[49] He spent a very short period of time with her and married Nusrat Ispahni in 1945.

Shortly after partition, Bhutto went to the University of Southern California to pursue higher education. Bhutto always talked about Jinnah during his California days, often referring to him as "that is my man, that's my idol, the man I respect."[50] His friends from there reflecting on Bhutto said that "this guy really likes power…he enjoyed the thought of being in charge."[51] During his initial California days he spoke of "Islamic heritage" and the need for starting a pan-Islamic movement but by the end of his Berkley years he called himself a "socialist" inspired by the works of Laski, Marx and Engels.[52] By the latter half of 1953 he returned to Karachi to practice law in Dingomal's Chambers. His timing coincided with anti-*Ahmadi* riots that caused mayhem in the city.

He denounced the idea of the One Unit scheme proposed in 1954. He called it "insidious" and argued that "implementation of this notorious proposal will be tantamount to the liquidation of the smaller Unit…thus the land of ancient Sind, which took shape in the civilisation of Mohanjo Daro …will wither into a mere prisoner of the Punjab."[53] His protest against the scheme served as his first step into politics. In the summer of 1958 President Iskander Mirza invited Bhutto to join his cabinet and he obliged. Within a month's time President Mirza dismissed the civilian government and imposed martial law. On 27 October of that year a new cabinet was formed and Bhutto was appointed as Commerce Minister.[54] As Minister of Commerce he brought Pakistan closer to the Soviet Union and China. He had seen Sino-Pakistan friendship as counter to Indian hegemony and "enemy's enemy as potential friend."[55] He deepened the ties with China by signing the Sino-Pakistan Boundary Agreement on 2 March 1963. He was also appointed as minister of "Basic Democracy" with responsibilities to spread awareness about this new system.

His rhetoric of waging a "thousand-year war" against India during the 1965 Indo-Pak war made him an instant hero.[56] His disagreement with General Ayub grew and over the difference on the Tashkent Agreement he resigned in 1966. His detest for General Ayub could be gauged when his foreign secretary reported to him after the death of Lal Bahadur Shastri in Tashkent that "the bastard is dead" — and Bhutto asked "which one?"[57] Bhutto got disenchanted with General Ayub and called his cabinet "mediocre" and his system "half democratic" and "half dictatorial."[58]After his criticism of the military regime he was arrested for a short period. This dramatic arrest gave him the fame he required and in 1967 he formed the Pakistan Peoples Party to oppose the regime organisationally. General elections were held in 1970 on the basis of universal adult franchise. Bhutto won 82 seats and the Awami League led by Sheikh Mujibur Rahman swept the polls in the East Wing by securing 152 seats. The negotiations between Bhutto and Mujibur Rahman failed, leading to political chaos and confusion and thus the military intervened and the rest is history.

Following the dismemberment of the country and the creation of Bangladesh, Bhutto became the Chief Martial Law Administrator and President of the remaining Pakistan and began to consolidate the pieces of scattered Pakistan. He later appointed himself as the first elected Prime Minister of Pakistan. He appointed General Tikka Khan, who earned the notorious title of the "Butcher of Bengal"[59] for his oppression in East Pakistan, as Chief of Army Staff thinking he would be supportive of his civilian government.[60] He framed the 1973 constitution and transformed the presidential system to a parliamentary system. He began to nationalise the basic industries. His nationalisation drive was detrimental to the "twenty-two families" which dominated the economic scene.[61] Bhutto started various reformist drives including structural reorganisation of the military, police and bureaucracy. The bureaucratic reform would reflect on MQM's politics *vis-à-vis* PPP and the military restructuring would take toll of his life.

Bhutto created his own elite force, the Federal Security Force (FSF) which acted as his personal SAVAK[62] till the time he was in power. His practices always contradicted his secular-socialist rhetoric. He gave constitutional legitimacy the Council of Islamic Ideology (CII). He hosted the first Islamic Summit in February 1974 in which delegates of 30 Islamic countries participated. He created Pakistan's first ministry of religious affairs. Bhutto resolved the nineteen-year old dispute with regard to *Ahmadis* by branding them as non-Muslims against their will in 1974. In March 1976 he organised an International *Seerat* Congress. He changed the name of Red Cross to Red Crescent Society. Friday replaced Sunday as the weekly holiday in his time. To neutralise his political opponent Pakistan National Alliance (PNA) which vowed to establish *Nizam-e-Mustafa;* he symbolically banned alcohol and gambling. He made *Islamiyat*, compulsory in primary and secondary schools.

Bhutto at the peak of his power became the sole arbitrator of his country and appointed and dismissed people on his whims. His friends called him a spilt-personality. Bhutto on one side, in their view, was a 'rational, intelligent and responsible' being and 'irrational, impulsive and uncontrollable' on the other . Bhutto did not tolerate an iota of dissent. He got provoked at the slightest of questioning. He punished many of those he branded as treacherous such as the likes of J. A. Rahim and Ahmad Raza Kasuri, and alienated supporters such as Mumtaz Daultana, Mir Rasool Baksh Talpur and Mustafa Khar.

Bhutto decided to hold early elections, one year ahead of the stipulated period. According to Wolpert, he intended to gain the two-third majority and institutionally make the president accountable to the parliament.[63] The PPP had a landslide victory; the PNA rejected the results outright, labeling them rigged and fraudulent. Failing to arrive at any settlement, the PPP and PNA created political anarchy in the country which gave the humiliated military an opportunity to intervene and take charge of the political stage. Prime Minister Bhutto was first taken into protective custody. The military levied charges against Bhutto of electoral rigging, conspiring for civil war and murdering political opponents. Bhutto was held captive incommunicado in solitary confinement in Rawalpindi jail and put in a death cell for more than six month before his execution.

The Washington Post's editorial, following Bhutto's fall, said that "to the extent that his trouble arose from personal hubris than the economic and social conditions."[64] Shahid Javed Burki however argued that his exaggerated pride and self-confidence resulted in retribution and it also cannot be separated from socio-economic conditions.[65] But in his memoir, Bhutto said "he has been made a victim of criminal injustice," lies and prejudice and suffered due to "internal betrayal."[66] He warned that "if I am assassinated through the gallows…there will be turmoil and turbulence, conflict and conflagration."[67] His official biographer Wolpert summed his life as "Few people in Pakistan's history have achieved greater popular power or suffered so ignominious a death as Zulfikar Ali Bhutto"[68]; after his death, the party chairmanship was taken over by his daughter Benazir Bhutto.

Benazir Bhutto: An Inchoate Odyssey

> In Pakistan things are almost never as they seem.
> There are always circles within circles, rarely straight lines.[69]

Born in a feudal Rajput family of Sindh, Benazir Bhutto experienced life in its extremes. Her grandfather, Sir Shah Nawaz, was Prime Minister of Junagarh in British colonial India. Her father, Zulfikar Ali Bhutto, was the first popularly elected Prime Minister of Pakistan. She herself created history by becoming the first ever woman Prime Minister of a Muslim state in modern times. Born in the Bhutto clan, she was privileged to meet personalities like Zhou Enlai, Indira Gandhi, and Henry Kissinger at a very young age. She studied at Harvard and Oxford and married into a big landlord family of Sindh. All these privileges of a princess-like life are overshadowed by her sacrifices and extreme suffering. Her father was imprisoned when she was just a teenager. During her youth her father was executed by the military junta and she was detained and imprisoned for six years along with her mother. Her family lived in exile and her brother was mysteriously murdered. Her husband was imprisoned repeatedly. She lived an exiled life and upon her return she was assassinated.

Benazir Bhutto seemed destined to have such a turbulent and triumphant political career. She was the controversial political heiress of Zulfikar Ali Bhutto's legacy. Born in 1953 to Nusrat and Zulfikar Ali Bhutto, she was the eldest among four siblings. Benazir had two brothers Shah Nawaz and Mir Murtaza and a sister Sanam Bhutto. She completed her 'O Level' education from the Convent of Jesus and Mary in Karachi. Then she went to the US to pursue her higher education and was enrolled in Radcliff College at Harvard University. Benazir completed her under-graduation in Comparative Politics. In her memoir she wrote that it was by studying comparative politics at Harvard, she understood Pakistan better than by living there.[70] Like her father Benazir joined Oxford where she attended Lady Margaret Hall for three years and studied Philosophy, Politics and Economics. Additionally she studied International Law and Diplomacy. In her autobiography she reflected that she had never intended to become a politician, rather she aspired to have a career in Pakistan's Foreign Service.[71] Benazir Bhutto might have become a diplomat if her father was not executed and she was not imprisoned for so many years. In December 1976 she was elected as president of the famous Oxford Union. She was proud of herself being the first Asian woman to be elected as the president of such a prestigious debating club.

After completion of her higher education she returned to Pakistan amid political chaos arising from the political impasse between the PPP and PNA. In 1977, the military intervened and removed her father, Zulfikar Ali Bhutto, from office and held him under protective custody and her family was detained. Her father was hanged in 1979 and she was arrested along with her mother and brother Murtaza. This event had an immense impact on her life and career. She wrote in her last book that "I had been traumatised by my father's arrest, imprisonment, and murder and I know that such mental scars are permanent."[72] Her father was hanged by his own protégé, General Zia under whose rule she was to suffer six years of imprisonment. She recalls her first meeting with her father's "monkey-general" as: "the general standing in front of me was a short, nervous, ineffectual-looking man whose pomaded hair was parted in the middle and lacquered to his head. He looked more like an English cartoon villain..."[73] After her initial detention at their Karachi home she was, along with her mother, transferred to the Larkana Central Jail.

After six years of detention and incarceration she was allowed to travel abroad on medical grounds. After her treatment in London she stayed there for the next two years and resumed her political activities from there. Before leaving for London in 1981 she formed the Movement of Restoration of Democracy (MRD). The MRD was a political alliance formed among the PPP, PNA and other left-oriented parties to mount pressure on General Zia to restore democratic institutions in Pakistan. It remained dormant since its formation till Benazir revived it in 1985. The first major decision MRD took was to boycott the general elections of 1985 to be conducted without political parties. She later admitted that the decision to boycott the elections was a tactical mistake. However, the elections were conducted and General Zia installed his puppet civilian government.

Following General Zia's death the government announced fresh elections in 1988 on party-basis. She threw herself into the election campaign while she was carrying her first child. The party manifesto promised a 'new social contract' and denationalisation and deregulation.

The party won 88 seats and formed the government in alliance with MQM. She created history by becoming the youngest Prime Minister in the world at that time. Her staunch critic, Tariq Ali, wrote a long review on her life titled "Daughter of the West," a cynical reference to her autobiography *Daughter of the East*. Commenting on her first premiership he recalls that she was cornered by the military and president and felt "powerless." He advised her to tell this to the people, instead she felt "satisfied enough" being in power and providing perks to some of her supporters.[74] Anna Suvorova noted that Ali was not evenly fair in his assessment of her work. Benazir Bhutto's biggest achievements were release of political prisoners, reinstating civil-liberties and creating a democratic climate.[75] Moreover, her government was dismissed within two years by the president. But it is also true that no great legislations were passed or any institutional change took place during that time.

Benazir Bhutto was sworn in as Prime Minister for the second time in October 1993. This time her government was marred with charges of graft and financial irregularities. Her husband Asif Ali Zardari, who had earned the pejorative epithet of "Mr. 10 Per Cent", was implicated in corruption charges as well as the murder charge of Murtaza Bhutto. In November 1996 her handpicked President, Farooq Leghari, dismissed her government on charges of corruption and extrajudicial killings.[76] The caretaker government then incarcerated her husband Zardari and their bank accounts were sealed in Switzerland. After conceding defeat in the 1997 general elections she flew to Dubai with her children. In her absentia, the Supreme Court in 1999 held both Benazir and Zardari guilty and sentenced them to five years of jail, fine of 8.6 million US dollars and confiscation of their property.[77] Zardari was already in prison and Benazir was in self-exile in London.

She decided to return to Pakistan after receiving amnesty under the National Reconciliation Order (NRO) promulgated by the President General Musharraf. She was adamant to return to Pakistan on the announced date of 18 October 2007, despite warnings of a attack on her life. She returned to Pakistan on the date she had decided. Her cavalcade was attacked *en route*, she escaped unhurt but around 130 of her supporters died. General Musharraf imposed emergency on 7 November and she was put under house arrest the following day.

Speculation in the media was that her return was a deal brokered by the US between her and General Musharraf. The Western media projected her as a "champion of Pakistani democracy" and "former prime minister" rather than "fugitive politician facing corruption charges in several countries."[78]William Dalrymple who called her "Pakistan's flawed and feudal princess" noted that the "West always had a soft spot for Benazir Bhutto" because she always appeared closer to their ethos with her English language, appearances and liberal ideas.[79]Suvorova also noted that she presented herself in two opposite image before the international community and domestic audience. Her language, appearances, ideas were tailored carefully commensurate to her target audience. For domestic purpose she always presented herself in a "*desi* image."[80]

Benazir Bhutto, who sensed her end was near, left a hand written political testament which urged party members that "I would like my husband Asif Ali Zardari to lead you in this interim period until you and he decide what is best." [81] Later her son Bilawal Bhutto was elected as party chairman. This act of her attracted sharp criticisms. Shashi Tharoor, the then under-secretary to the UN wrote that "She was no great democrat - as her will, naming her 19-year-old son to inherit her party, has confirmed...To her, democracy was a means to power, not a philosophy of politics."[82] As usual Tariq Ali, who despised her, commented that the PPP is being treated as a "family heirloom" and both Pakistan and supporters of PPP "deserve better than this disgusting, medieval charade."[83] Dalrymple who saw Benazir as a "feudal princess with the aristocratic sense" and "far from being natural democrat" holds her responsible for having "brought Pakistan [a] strange variety of democracy, really a form of elective feudalism."[84] Finally she was "a pro-Western feudal leader" and was "as much central part of Pakistan's problems as the solution to them."[85] After her assassination Zardari became the chairman and he named his son Bilawal as co-chairman of the party.

Social Base of Pakistan Peoples Party

Among all the five parties taken in this study, the Pakistan Peoples Party (PPP) is the party that qualifies to be a truly national party. It is national not only in geographic criterion but in all criteria essential for being national. It began as a populist party against an authoritarian regime by mobilising the working and peasant class. In its electoral journey it emerged as an all-encompassing party whose populism attracted cross-classes; whose religious pluralism transcended sectarian divides and minorities as well. In its heyday its appeal neutralised ethnic divisions – a force that determines political outcome today. PPP also established a constituency among women who saw its politics liberating in a conservative society. But the party which formed five civilian governments out of 9 party-based democratic governments is today reduced to mere provincial party. It witnessed a complete transformation of its support base. The following table captures the gradual transition of the PPP's support base viewed through its seat share in the national assembly.

Table 4.1: Provincial wise Seat-Breakdown of Pakistan Peoples Party

Name of Provinces	1970	1977	1988	1990*	1993	1997	2002	2008	2013
Pakistan	85	155	94	44	88	18	63	89	31
Sindh	18	32	31	23	32	18	27	32	29
Punjab	62	108	53	14	50		36	44	1
KPK		8	9	5	6			9	1
Baluchistan		7	1	2	1			4	
Total No. of Seats	138	200	206	206	202	204	272	272	272

* PPP fought elections of 1990 in alliance called Pakistan Democratic Alliance.

Source: Tahir Mehdi et al (eds.), *National Assembly Elections on Pakistan 1970-2008*(Lahore: Church World Service-Pakistan/Afghanistan and Free and Free Election Network, 2010). *Gilani's Index of Electoral Record 1970-2013: Volume 1-9,* based on Gallup Exit Poll data and ECP data, compiled by Gallup Election Studies Team, 2013, URL:www.gallup.com.pk.

All the results tabulated above should be seen in the context of a specific election or combination of elections. These elections did not occur in sequence; rather they came in three interludes followed by periodic junta intervals. A cursory glance of the data suggests that the party in its initial days dominated in Punjab and by the end of the last election held in 2013 was wiped-out from the province. In the context of the first election it should be emphasised that only few parties contested. Moreover, it was a democratic election after a long period of authoritarian rule, thus PPP's populist sloganeering cultivated support among the disenchanted class whose interests had suffered under military rule. Given its Sindhi leadership its good performance in the province was no surprise but in Punjab its performance was unexpected. The party won 75 per cent seats in the first election in Punjab. Its performance in the province was correlated to its local leadership.

In the formative phase the social groups who were interested in PPP were largely from urban settings, 52.9 per cent compared to just 11.8 per cent from the countryside. However, in terms of occupational identity in the Convention Committee, 11 out of 32 were *zamindars* and 3 were from small-scale businesses; lawyers and students were another well represented occupational group.[86] Another segment that had significant presence in the party was that the of anti-feudalist socialist. This group had its political origin in Progressive Group of Punjab Muslim League. Sheikh Muhammad Rashid, an early land reform radical who wanted complete abolition of zamindari and compulsory collective farming, departed from Azad Pakistan Party and joined PPP. The left segment became stronger when socialist politician Taj Muhammad Khan Langah too joined the PPP's left wing in Punjab. The third dominant figure of left politics, Khurshid Hasan Meer of the progressive wing of AIML, also joined it. The top echelon of PPP also had a strong representation of the Muhajir of partition, especially from Punjab.[ix] With this PPP had the service of Muhammad Hanif Ramay, the Islamic Socialist who provided an ideological middle ground and the concept of Islamic Socialism.[87] Student leaders of old Combined Opposition Parties (COP) and

ix. Malik Aslam Hayat, Begum Abad Ahmad Khan, Mubashir Hasan, Mairaj Muhammad Khan and Khurshid Hasan Meer were prominent Partition Muhajirs who occupied powerful positions in the party.

National Student Federation (NSF) too found an influential position in the party.

Pakistan Peoples Party's Punjabi dominance was strongly established in the 1977 election when it won 93 per cent seats in the province. In Baluchistan the party made a clean sweep while in Sindh it won 73 per cent of total seats. Its opposition alliance PNA fared well in KPK but PPP too registered some presence there. This widespread representation suggested that it was a national party with a strong presence in all the provinces and ethnicities. Other than ethnicity and provincial approach there are ideological and class dimensions which too determined the electoral outcome. Shahid Javed Burki argued that there was no political challenge to Bhutto and no viable alternative to his party in 1977.[88] This happened because in the inter-election period Bhutto cultivated a new support base that was sufficient to renew his mandate. His old constituency was a mix of middle class segments who had suffered under Ayub's economic reforms.

In the old constituency Bhutto had the support of left-bent Punjabi and Sindhi intellectuals who were attracted to PPP's socialist leaning. The socialist elements were systematically purged from Bhutto's cabinet in October 1974.[89] The middle class, who supported Bhutto's populist call, suffered severely under his economic, social and administrative reforms. Realising that his urban support was declining Bhutto attempted to build a new constituency in rural Pakistan. Since the two third majorities were living in rural areas and small towns he sacrificed the urban middle class at the altar of election. The space emptied by the left was filled by the landed gentry.[90] The rural constituency was penetrated through landlords who acted as a buffer and channel between themselves and the large bureaucracy. So by the end of the second general elections, PPP's support base had completely transited from a middle-class to a lower and upper class. The socialist elements also left the party and got dominated by bourgeoisie. The party won by an overwhelming majority but couldn't run the government as General Zia staged a *coup d'ëtat* and party politics was banned till 1988 as long as he lived.

After Zulfikar Ali Bhutto was judicially executed, the party leadership passed into the hands of his daughter Benazir Bhutto. With new people in charge its support base in Punjab declined and by 1997 was completely wiped out from the province. PPP also lost its socialist and urban constituency by this time, but it benefited from the anti-military and pro-democracy MRD led by the new leader.

Being a woman, Benazir strived to cultivate a constituency among women. In all the elections campaigns run under her leadership and all the manifestos released under her, promised to repeal all the discriminatory laws against women.[91] She promised to give equal rights and equal opportunities to women. But despite being Prime Minister in 1988 and 1993 she failed to abrogate the *hudud* laws. However, the PPP government under her initiated series of reforms regarding women rights. The party's official website as well as Benazir's last book *Reconciliation* claim that several women were inducted into her cabinet; a Ministry of Women's Development and a Women's Development Bank was established to give credit only to enterprising women. In the universities programmes were created for women's studies ; women's participation in international sports, which had been banned in the years of the Zia's military dictatorship, were legalised.[92] But Anna Suvorova who wrote an excellent biographical sketch of her criticised these achievements as:

> All of this is true, yet the access to bank loans and university programmes, just as the opportunity to participate in Olympic Games once again, could not compensate for the threat looming over ordinary Pakistani women of prison terms, public whipping, and stoning to death as a result of *zina* accusation. Benazir failed to turn the women's liberation movement to her advantage.[93]

Paradoxically the respite came under the military. President General Musharraf in 2006 softened the draconian provisions of *hudud* laws and completely abrogated the 'law of evidence.'[94] The next election was held in 2008 following General Musharraf's departure. Once again the PPP regained some ground in Punjab and rose to power. The party benefited from two reasons. First, that there was civil dissent against the outgoing *junta* regime and prime opposition leader Nawaz Sharif was barred from contesting election. Second, before the election Benazir Bhutto was assassinated and thus the PPP was the beneficiary of a sympathy wave.

In the last election held in 2013, the PPP was reduced largely to interior Sindh. It was the PPP's second worst performance after 1997.

There were various reasons for the limited reach of a once national party. Imran Khan was back after boycotting the previous election. His party secured a majority in KPK and wiped out the PPP from the province. Nawaz Sharif was back and campaigned well against the incumbent party; consequently once a Punjabi-dominated party the PPP won only one seat in the province. The prime reason for the PPP's abysmal electoral performance in the last election is attributed to the image of its new leadership. The new party chairman Bilawal Bhutto is considered naïve in politics and his father Asif Ali Zardari as corrupt. Importantly the party which rose to power by first mobilising the urban middle classes and later rural masses lost both to new political parties. With the emergence of new provincial forces its Punjabi constituency shifted to the PML (N) and its Pakhtun support was captured by the PTI and Karachi was ruled by the MQM. Thus once a national party, which received support across classes, ethnicities, provinces and gender, has today been reduced to a mere rural-Sindhi party. However, political parties go through ups and down and the prospects of revival cannot be completely ruled out.

Leadership of the Jamaat-e-Islami

The Jamaat-e-Islami is the oldest party functioning in the electoral battle and had also gone through several leadership changes.[x] But Jamaat's founding *Ameer*, Sayyid Abul A'la Maududi, who stayed at the helm of power for three decades left a legacy that dwarfs all of its leaders. Jamaat's other leaders remained politically insignificant, as, after Maududi, two decades were consumed by the *junta* regime and one decade was lost due to boycott of two elections by the new *Ameers*. Although Maududi died in 1979 his legacy and philosophy still guides and shapes the Jamaat's political actions. The discussion that follows explains the party's founding *Ameer's* political personality and philosophy that still has a hold over its supporters.

x. The founding *Ameer* Syed Abul A'la Maududi was at the top post from 1940 to 1972. After him the Jamaat elected four *Ameers* who headed the party at various points: Mian Tufail Mohammad (1972 - 1987), Qazi Hussain Ahmad (1987 - 2008), Sayyed Munawer Hassan (2008 - 2014) and Siraj ul Haq (2014–present).

Sayyid Abul A'la Maududi: Reigning the Minds

> I would be proud to serve as a peon under the Islamic system of Jamaat than to acquire the position of president and prime minister in a non-Muslim system.
>
> Sayyid Abul A'la Maududi[95]

Sayyid Abul A'la Maududi was one of the original Islamic thinkers of the last century. Both in the West and East, he is "without doubt the most influential of contemporary Islamic revivalist thinkers."[96] On the originality of his thinking Nadeem Paracha noted that "Abul Ala Maududi is to 'Political Islam' what Karl Marx was to communism."[97] He has influenced thinkers like Sayyid Qutb, Hasan al-Banna and events like the Iranian Revolution.[98] The July 2003 issue of *New Statesman* published a list of "12 Great Thinkers of Our Time" and Maududi was the only Muslim in the list because, according to the magazine, "so influential are Maududi's ideas, and so profound has been his impact on Osama bin Laden and Al-Qaeda as well as moderate Muslims, that we included him even though he died in 1979."[99] Today we know Maududi as a thinker, philosopher, poet, activist, journalist and politician. In this brief profile, the focus is chiefly limited to his political avatar, his party politics and how he envisioned and shaped its course.

Sayyid Abul A'la Maududi was born on 25 September 1903 to Sayyid Ahmad Hasan and Ruqiyah Begum in Aurangabad (Maharashtra), in the erstwhile princely state of Hyderabad. From his paternal side he traces his lineage to Khwaza Moinuddin Chishti of Ajmer, the founder of the *Chishti Sufi Silisila* in South Asia.[100] His mother had an aristocratic Turkish lineage. Maududi's grandmother was related to Sir Sayyid Ahmad Khan, the founder of Anglo Oriental College.[101] Ahmad Hasan attended the college but when his father learned that his son had played cricket, wearing clothes (pant and shirt) worn by *the kaffirs (infidels)*, he was taken out from the college and sent to Allahabad from where he completed his education in law.[102] In 1896 Ahmad Hasan moved to Aurangabad to a relative, Maulvi Muhyu'ddin Khan, who was Chief Justice in the city. In 1900 he embraced Sufism and took *bai'ah* with the same relative who was also a *Chishti Pir* and lived a *fakirana zindagi* (a sage's life).[103] According to Maududi's own account he was born in an ascetic setting. Later Maududi chose his position between the representatives of esoteric and exoteric Islam and rejected "the excessive cult of saints as well as other syncretistic influences" and stressed on in "Islamic law in its pure form."[104]

His father raised him in seclusion, forbidding his meeting with local children, to perfect his Urdu-speaking. He was home-schooled by his father who taught him religious studies, Quran, *Fiqh* (jurisprudence), *Ahadis* (traditions of the Prophet), Arabic, Persian and Urdu.[105] At the age of 11 he was enrolled in Madrasah-i-Fauqaniyah (Oriental High School) of Aurangabad which was affiliated to Osmania University of Hyderabad. In 1915 his father moved to Hyderabad and Maududi was admitted in the local *darul-ulum* (seminary). When he was 15 years old his father died of an illness and Maududi, who therefore could not complete his education, had to look for a job. In 1918 he moved to Bijnore in the United Provinces and joined a journal, *Medinah, (*which was edited by his brother Abul Khayr) as a journalist. Both brothers had to move to Delhi following the closure of the journal after two months of his joining.

In Delhi he restarted his journalistic career with the editorship of *Al-Jamiat*, an organ of the pro-Congress Deobandi *ulema*, the Jamiat Ulema-e-Hind (JUH) which was opposed to British rule. Due to the JUH's pro-Congress stand he resigned from the editorship. In 1932 he launched *Tarjuman al-Quran* which became very popular among Muslims. In 1930 he wrote his seminal work *Al-Jihad Fil Islam*, treatises on the Islamic law of war and peace. This established him as a scholar but he also carved out his niche by writing a multi-volume commentary on the Quran titled as *Tafhim al Quran*. His political interest was nurtured in the Khilafat movement of 1920. After the failure of the Khilafat movement he did not actively participate in politics, rather his engagement remained intellectual. On 26 August 1941, along with 75 supporters, Maududi established his own political party, Jamaat-e-Islami, with the motto of establishing a political order based on divine laws. He was elected as Jamaat's first *Ameer* at its inaugural meeting in 1941 and he held this post till 1972 when due to his deteriorating health he vacated that post. In 1979 he traveled to the US for his kidney treatment and died there.

Vali Nasr has observed that Maududi "was one of the first Islamic thinkers to develop a systematic political reading of Islam and a plan for social action to realise his vision."[106] His political party, Jamaat-e-Islami was the instrument of his "social action" whom Nasr in a separate work titled *The Vanguard of the Islamic Revolution*[107] — a reference to Lenin's "Revolutionary Vanguard Party" whose purpose was to establish the "dictatorship of the proletariat" with the support of the working class to replace the leadership of the bourgeoisie with representatives from the masses.[108] The central objective of Maududi and his party was to establish a complete political and social order based on the Shariah. Maududi's theoretical positioning, *vis-à-vis* the concepts of state, nation, nationalism, sovereignty, democracy and caliphate, has already been discussed in the first chapter. The political origin and growth of the Jamaat has been discussed in the previous chapter. The following section attempts to encapsulate Maududi's reading of Islam and his interpretation of history, and motive forces underlying the germination of his political party.

For Maududi, "only God is the Creator, Sustainer, and Master of the universe and of all that exists in it – organic and inorganic" and the Prophets of Allah are His vicegerents (*khalifa*) on earth.[109] Allah is the only sovereign and Law-Giver. Islam is an enlightened guidance that reached the people through the preaching and practices of the holy Prophet. Before the advent of Islam, men were governed through man-made laws and ignorance – the *Jahiliya*. For Maududi *Jahiliya* is evident in distinct shapes and forms and is antithetical to Islam. He sees other worldviews, belief and practices which do not conform to the divine sovereignty as *Jahiliya,* in perpetual dichotomy with Islam. Maududi's perception of human behaviour was normative. He believed that there are three possible prisms – philosophy, science and Islam – to analyse human problems and their solutions.

The former two are based on *Jahiliya* which leads to the construction of a tyrannical, dishonest, wicked and materialist individual and society.[110] He believed that "sovereignty lies with God" and God has created the state; He alone is the Master and Sole Ruler of this State (*Wahi iska Malik hain aur Wahi iska Hakim hai*).[111] He further holds that: man is a born subject (*paidashi rayaat*) of this divine state; and therefore, possesses no right to invent a way of life or to outline his own duties. Thus in Maududi's view solutions to human problems lie in his subservience to the divine-laws. Now this state, where divine-laws will reign supreme over man-made laws, could not be furnished without a systematic revivalism of Islam through organisational instrumentality. The Islamic state, in his view, will not be limited to political administration only— rather, it will aim to build a system free of exploitation and injustice and promote qualities of purity and virtue.[112]

Abul A'la Maududi believed that there is perpetual conflict between Islam and *Jahaliyat* (ignorance). The *Jahaliyat* includes three metaphysical doctrines of life; *khalis jahalat*, *shirk*, *rehbaniyat* (atheism, polytheism and asceticism).[113] The onslaught of *Jahaliyat* has corrupted Islam which needs a *Tajdid* (revivalist movement) to restore Islam to its original pristine condition. *Tajdid* is nothing but "cleansing Islam of all the un-Godly elements and presenting it and making it flourish more or less in its original form."[114] The corruption occurred due to two reasons; the weakening of the institution of caliphate and rapid expansion of Islamic state. The latter, according to Maududi, resulted in contact with un-Godly communities which embraced Islam but also brought many polytheistic belief and ideas; the ignorance operated under the guise of Islam employing Islamic terminology.[115] Farzana Shaikh captures this tension as "Islam's historical and cultural accommodations with the local environment in India have wrought profound changes in its substance and fundamentally altered the practices and modes of thinking of its local adherents."[116] Therefore, Islam needs a revivalist movement to purge it from the evils and impurities and restore it into its original form and spirit.

The purpose of his 'Islamic Revivalism' was to bring total revolution to oppose *Jahiliya* through *Tajdid* – a continuation of Prophetic mission.[117] The Jamaat was structured to attain this purpose. At the inaugural proceeding of the Jamaat-e-Islami, Maududi said that "Islam itself is a Movement" and the Jamaat's purpose was to move towards "the objective of pristine Islam (*nisbul Islam*)" and to act in accordance with Islam "so its Movement is nothing but an Islamic movement."[118] The objective of launching such an organised movement was to struggle for the establishment of *Hukumat e Ilahya* – the rule of the God.[119] At the foundational proceedings, Maududi said that anyone who believes in the creed of Islam can join the movement but must understand that accepting its mission will mean there was no turning back. Anyone who becomes the part of it will have to work to change the system of the whole world and he "has to bring about a transformation in morality, politics, culture, civilisation, economics, social system and everything else."[120] This ideal Islamic society was to be attained through the systematic implementation of various programmes envisaged by his party, the Jamaat-e-Islami.

Maududi's political prescription was a product of his immediate political and social settings. Nasr noted that he was at one time an Indian nationalist, but succumbed to the lure of Muslim communalism after the failure of the *Khilafat* movement and "his encounter with Hindu revivalism of the *Shuddhi* and *Sangathan* movements and the ever more apparent Hindu domination of the Congress party under Mahatma Gandhi."[121] Until 1936 he remained clean-shaven, watched films and attended music and singing programmes. He married Mahmuda Begum, "who was educated in Delhi's Queen Mary's school, she was quite a modern women, she rode a bicycle and barely observed purdah."[122] Maududi was also dissatisfied with existing Muslim organisations, the Muslim League and JUH, whom he considered too secular and not aiming to establish an Islamic state— rather they were interested only in a state to be governed on the "*ghair Illahi-nizam*" (anti-Godly system) and if the future state will not run on shariah "the future of Pakistan would be *napakistan*, a profane land" and it will be just an "infidelitic (*kafirana*) state of Muslims."[123] To Maududi, the leadership of the league was "trained wholly on the Western pattern" and was bereft of "even an iota of Islamic feeling" , thus he labeled the Muslim League as "*Jamaat-e-Jahiliyat* (Party of Pagans)."[124] In his contempt for modern education he dubbed the Aligarh Muslim University as "*qatalkhana*." While Maududi rejected the creation of Pakistan, but realizing its inevitability, he decided to leave for Pakistan.

During the formative age of Pakistan, because of their opposition to Pakistan movement, their lack of social base in the new homeland and due to the military's intervention in politics the Jamaat's political importance was limited. Nonetheless, it influenced the polity by claiming to represent the vanguard of the Islamic state promised in the slogan for Pakistan. Maududi's aggressive campaign for an Islamic Constitution resulted into the incorporation of the Objective Resolution as the preamble. Thus, in a way, the nature of the constitution was defined in accordance with the Jamaat's view. Maududi was imprisoned four times between 1948 and 1967, spending a total of five years in various jails. Maududi showed his obstinate character by not requesting clemency when he was sentenced to death by the Martial Law court for writing a seditious pamphlet the *Qadiani Masail*, (the *Qadiani* problems). His sentence was later commuted to life imprisonment, but subsequently he was released.

Under his watch, the Jamaat's student wing acted as armed volunteers for the army in East Pakistan. The party never performed well in the elections but had influence across all walks of life and in the minds of many Pakistanis. Though Paracha referred to him as an "Islamic Quack" and observed that the blueprint of his Islamic state "does not exist in the Quran and was only a generation of Maududi's imagination" also admits that "a number of politico-religious forces in Pakistan, as well as many television anchormen, print journalists and publications, are both directly and indirectly influenced by Maududi."[125]

Social Base of the Jamaat-e-Islami

There are two distinct but overlapping elements of a social base that constitute and support the Jamaat-e-Islami as a political party. One of the two elements of Jamaat's social base is made of its core members (*arkan*), affiliates (*muttafiq*) and protectors (*pasban*) who run the organisation, navigate its political trajectories, and formulate its principles and political policies. The second element is made of those who support and vote for the party's political cause. Both these elements have showed intense dynamism and have undergone an intrinsic transformation from the original base. It is therefore important to discuss the pattern of change that occurred within its core and support elements due to various reasons. The discussion tries to establish a correlation between the respective changes.

One way of analysing its social base is to examine its electoral performance which helps to quantify voters' preferences to party's political promise and programmes. Like the Muslim League, which failed to transform itself from a nationalistic movement to a political party, Jamaat too couldn't transform itself from a "holy community" to a viable political party with a programmatic vision. This dilemma existed when the founder of the party, Maududi, was at the helm of power and continued even after his death. Following the abysmal performance in the first general elections and before the next election, Maududi in a party *Shura* of 1975 advocated for total renunciation of electoral politics in the interest of ideological purity.[126] The reason for this concern was the party's defeat in the previous election that gave a mandate to populist Pakistan Peoples Party and a rejection of Jamaat's Islamic ideal. Jamaat as a political party never recovered from that initial tremor. It never achieved substantial representation that could solidify its political stature as illustrated in the following table.

Table 4.2: Provincial wise Seat-Breakdown of Jamaat-e-Islami

Name of Provinces	1970	1977	1985	1988	1990	1993	1997	2002	2008	2013
Sindh	2	2	Elections on non-party basis			1	Boycott	Contested as part of an electoral alliance, MMA	Boycott	
Punjab	1	4		6	7					
KPK	1	3		2	1	2				3
Baluchistan										
Pakistan	4	9		8	8	3				3
Total No. of seats	138	200		206	206	202				272

Source: Mehdi et al (eds.), *National Assembly Elections on Pakistan 1970-2008*. *Gilani's Index of Electoral Record 1970-2013: Volume 3, 4, 5 and 9*. Nasr, *The Vanguard of the Islamic Revolution*, pp. 167 and 185.

To date there were 10 general elections in Pakistan in which the Jamaat contested only thrice on its own. Twice it boycotted the elections in 1997 and 2008. Four times – in 1977 as a part of the PNA, in 1988 and 1990 as a part of the IJI and in 2002 as a part of the *Muttahida Majlis Amal* (MMA) – the party fought in alliance. In 1985 the election was held on a non-party basis under the *junta* government of General Zia. If the election results are analysed in provincial segments there emerges a clear pattern of a constituency shift. In the first general elections the party won 2 seats from the Karachi division, 1 seat each from Dera Ghazi Khan and Dir. The next election of 1977 was fought in alliance under the banner of Pakistan National Alliance in which the Jamaat was the leading partner. The alliance won only 46 seats in which Jamaat's share was only 9 seats. It expanded its reach in Punjab and KPK and successfully defended its Karachi bastion. Following the end of Zia's dictatorship two subsequent elections of 1988 and 1990 were fought in alliance. This time the Jamaat was the junior partner in *Islami Jamhoori*

Ittehad, led by the PML (N). Jamaat's own performance within the alliance was static as it won 8 seats each in the respective polls. However, these two elections culminated in a permanent erosion of its Muhajir stronghold in Karachi. In the next seven general elections the party managed to secure only one seat from Karachi in 1993 when it contested alone and was saturated to 3 seats.

Vali Nasr found in his study that the lower middle-classes, especially the Muhajirs, supported Islamic revivalism and its vanguard Jamaat-e-Islami in Pakistan in the early phase.[xi] There were two reasons for the Muhajirs' distancing themselves from the party. First, there was growing disappointment within the community that the party could not address their grievances. The disenchantment was a result of the realisation of Pakhtun-Punjabi domination of the party's decision-making body. Second, since 1980s there was strong identity mobilisation of the Muhajir community by a new Muhajir-only party, the MQM under Altaf Hussain. MQM contested its first election in 1988 and after that the Jamaat never could win in Sindh. The provincial shift was much clearer in 2002 election when it again participated in alliance after boycotting the 1997 elections. This time the party was a part of a grand alliance of Islamist parties —the Muttahida Majlis Amal (MMA). The new alliance emerged as the largest single winner in KPK and Baluchistan. MMA won 46 seats in total: in KPK the alliance won 29 seats out of 35 while in Baluchistan it secured 6 seats from 14 seats. Its major share of seats (above 75 per cent) shifted to the more rural and tribal regions. The provincial shift was complete when in 2013 the party contested on its own after two decades and was reduced to just 3 seats, all from KPK.

The party's overall electoral failure could be attributed to its tactical faultlines. Jamaat attempted to mobilise the electorate through a literary body of works in a country where the majority of people were illiterate. The party was also firmly grounded in Urdu, thus willingly or unwillingly limited its outreach to the majority grounded in the vernacular by adopting Urdu as its only mode of communication. Apart from this it also had to face the

xi. The Muhajirs associated themselves with Jamaat for two reasons. First, the Muhajirs had no social roots in the new homeland where all other political parties were deeply ethnic in nature and Jamaat promised nationalistic politics. Second, the party workers helped refugees to settle down during the crisis time. Nasr, *The Vanguard of the Islamic Revolution*, p. 81.

local resistance of traditional power dominance of *pirs* and *zamindars* who contained the Jamaat's entry from the countryside and reduced its influence to urban centers only. Thus the party failed to create its own space in the ethno-linguistic domain. However, the party "cultivated votes among the poor through social work, but failed to advocate their cause. The party's services were appreciated, but its politics were irrelevant to the demands of the underprivileged."[127] But the party survived because its ideology found support from important segments of the population.

The core element of its social base, the members and affiliates also exhibited similar tendencies of total constituency shift. Nasr who noted the patterns of changes within the *shura* membership found that membership-distribution shifted from cities to towns and the countryside. The data tabulated in his study showed that in 1957 only six members out of 29 members in Punjab were from small towns. By 1992 there were 28 *shura* members from small towns in the total of 39 members. Similarly KPK had 5 *shura* members in 1957, all of them from Peshawar. In 1992 the provincial share grew to 11 in which Peshawar represented only 2 and the rest came from other small towns. In Sindh the major share was always dominated by Karachi and Hyderabad. The membership distribution also overtly exhibited deep gender disparity. Nasr found that in 1983 there were only 160 women members in a total of 4776. This improved marginally in 1989 when 321 members were women among the 5723 total membership.[128] The second shift was in terms of leadership.

The founder *Ameer*, Maududi, after three decades at the helm of power declined to serve the party further and Mian Tufail Mohammad was elected as the new *Ameer* in 1972. Like his predecessor, Mian Tufail was also a Muhajir, born in Kapurthala (Indian Punjab) and belonged to the Punjabi Arain tribe. So the Muhajirs remained in power till 1987 when Qazi Hussain Ahmad, ethnically a Pakhtun from Nowshera district of KPK, replaced Mian Tufail. Under his leadership the party fought four elections and boycotted two. His period coincided with the rise of the MQM and the loss of the Muhajir constituency. In 2008 once again the leadership went back to a Muhajir *Ameer*, Syed Munawar Hasan, whose family hailed from Delhi but had settled in Karachi at the time of partition. During his period of leadership the Jamaat had no member in the National Assembly as a result of the election boycott. Politically his period was indolent. In 2014 once again the leadership shifted to Pakhtun when Siraj-ul Haq of Dir district was elected by the *shura* in a secret ballot.[129]

Leadership of the Pakistan Muslim League (Nawaz)

The party chairman Mian Muhammad Nawaz Sharif, also known as the "Lion of Punjab," founded the PML (N) in 1988. Thrice he was elected to the top post from the time it was founded. Although he became Prime Minister thrice he could not become a national leader. Coming from a business-family he possesses a pragmatic political acumen. His family is highly active in national and provincial politics and politically controls the largest province, Punjab. He is considered a shy politician with poor oratory but his control over the PML (N) never faced any challenge within. His vocal opposition to the military resulted in a decade long exile during which his political engagement was docile. In the 2013 election he made a triumphant comeback and became Prime Minister for the third time.

Nawaz Sharif: The Politician Industrialist

> Our political philosophy revolves around economic progress,
> If a country is economically strong, it is able to solve all the problems.[130]

Three time Prime Minister of Pakistan and president of PML (N), Mian Muhammad Nawaz Sharif is also the country's wealthiest industrialist being owner of a business conglomerate, the Ittefaq Group. Sharif, a protégé of third *junta* dictator General Zia-ul Haq, and proponent of Sharia law, rose to political prominence with the military's help at various stages. Paradoxically, he was also the victim of the military's excesses in politics due to his vocal opposition to them. Nawaz Sharif who is revered by his supporters as the "Lion of Punjab" and the "Tiger of Pakistan" acquired international fame by conducting a nuclear test which made Pakistan the first Islamic state to possess a nuclear weapon. But Sharif was also put in jail and exiled from his own country.

Nawaz Sharif was born on 25 December 1949 in Lahore. Eldest of three siblings Sharif received his early education along with his brother Shahbaz Sharif from Lahore's Saint Antony School. He was enrolled in Government

College Lahore from where he completed his graduate studies. After the completion of his education he joined the family business. His father Mian Muhammad Sharif was a scrap trader in Lahore before the creation of Pakistan. Sharif's father established a foundry in 1939, which the family lost under Zulfikar Ali Bhutto's nationalisation drive in 1972. This act was to create a long-standing enmity between the Sharifs and the Bhuttos. The business returned to the family hands in 1980 after General Zia's capture of power through a military coup. Sharif became director of the conglomerate and cultivated relations with senior military officers. Raymond Baker noted that this proximity with the military led to his appointment as Punjab's finance and chief minister under the military leader.[131] Because of his political control of Punjab and Pakistan as Prime Minister "Ittefaq Industries grew from its original single foundry into 30 businesses producing steel, sugar, paper, and textiles with combined revenues of $400 million, making it one of the biggest private conglomerates in the nation."[132] These were the 2005 estimate, which might have increased in the last decade.

As Sharif's business flourished under General Zia, so did his political career spurt and took root under his military patron. In 1981 he was appointed as finance minister of the most populace province of the country, Punjab. After the party-less elections of 1985 he was appointed as Chief Minister of Punjab. On 31 May 1988, General Zia dissolved the assemblies and he had to step down. The military then appointed him as Caretaker Chief Minister and he held that position till the next general elections of 1990, in which he was elected as Prime Minister. As Sharif shared the military's right wing tilt he was facilitated by the establishment to form an electoral alliance of conservative parties, the IJI, in 1988 to contest against the PPP. The alliance lost to PPP and Nawaz Sharif chose to run for Punjab instead of sitting in the opposition. After the premature dismissal of the Benazir government, fresh elections were called in November 1990.

The IJI won the election and Nawaz Sharif was elected as Prime Minister for the first time. He revived the nuclear processing programme and defied the US calls for its suspension. Consequently Pakistan was deprived of American financial assistance under the Pressler Law. During his first tenure he initiated privatisation of a range of state-owned enterprises including banking. Sharif constituted a "Privatisation Commission to identify 100 state-owned enterprises that would be sold."[133] He takes credit for building a 367 km multi-lane motorway linking Lahore and Islamabad.[134] He also initiated the "Yellow Cab Scheme" and allowed import of 50,000 vehicles duty free. Baker in his study estimated that both the projects culminated in the loss of state revenues in billions of rupees due to corruption.[135] His position began to erode after Jamaat-e-Islami, the second most important component of the IJI after the PML (N), withdrew its support from the government over the difference of opinion on the participation of the Pakistan army in the First Gulf War of 1991.[136] The second setback was the launching of "Operation Clean-Up", over his head, by the military in Sindh against its coalition partner MQM.[137] But what estranged his ties most with the military were his privatisation initiatives.

Stephen Cohen noted that he had to face the "establishment's wrath" because the military's economic interests were hurt as it "heavily invested in the public sector" and due to new regulations it had to compete with the private sector.[138] So he was dismissed in 1993 by the then President, Ghulam Ishaq Khan, on the charges of corruption and incompetence. He challenged the presidential decision in the Supreme Court. Talbot notes, his challenge created a constitutional crisis but raised Sharif's political stature from "'cowardly businessman' to 'fighter politician.'"[139] The apex court declared the presidential order unconstitutional and reconstituted the National Assembly. But ultimately the establishment succeeded and Sharif was forced to resign though he was reinstated by the Court. Moeen Qureshi was appointed as Caretaker Prime Minister up to the next election held in October 1993, in which Benazir Bhutto was elected as Prime Minister.

After the elections in 1997, Sharif was once again elected as Prime Minister for the second time. After his swearing-in ceremony a columnist wrote that he has the strength in the house that makes him the most powerful premier in the country's history and he can choose to strike down the notorious Eighth Amendment. But "can the tiger roar? Or will Nawaz Sharif prove to be just another paper tiger?"[140] Sharif, who promised in the run-up to the election to ensure the "supremacy of parliament" by "restricting the practices of passing legislation through ordinances,"[141] annulled the provision of Eighth Amendment and shifted the power of appointments of the heads of the armed service to the institution of prime minister, through the passage of the 13th Amendment.[142] During his second term he also fell out with the country's two powerful institutions, the judiciary and military, which culminated in his eventual ouster from premiership.

After the coup in 1999 Nawaz Sharif was arrested and tried on the charges of "kidnapping, attempted murder, hijacking and terrorism and corruption" and a military court sentenced him for life.[143] After 14 months of imprisonment, Sharif's life sentence was commuted to exile after a Saudi brokered agreement in which Sharif "agreed not to take part in politics in Pakistan for 21 years. He has also forfeited property worth $8.3m (£5.7m) and agreed to pay a fine of $500,000."[144] He left the country with his wife, children and brother.

Nawaz Sharif returned to Pakistan in 2007 after signing a 'Charter of Democracy,' a mechanism devised by General Musharraf, that nullifies an electoral law that bans any person to hold prime minister's office more than twice. Under the provision of the said charter political prisoners were freed and political exiles were allowed unconditional return. Sharif returned on 10 September 2007 but was sent back from the airport. He again returned on 25 November 2007. This time he was barred from contesting election but he could lead the party campaign. The PML (N) emerged as the second largest party in the 2008 general elections. On 25 February 2009 he was disqualified by the Supreme Court from holding any public office because of his criminal conviction connected to the 1999 military coup.[145] The verdict was seen as politically motivated under the presidency of his political nemesis Asif Ali Zardari. Three months later the apex court overturned the ban and allowed him to contest.[146] In addition it also dropped the Musharraf-time criminal convictions against him. He contested the last general election of 2013 and in the absence of any other strong political leadership he emerged as the choice of the people. Sharif became head of the government for the third time.

Social Base of the PML (N)

The PML (N) formed three governments at the national level without the help of other parties, so why was it still dubbed as a provincial force? A Pakistani columnist explains this contradiction by using an adage: "if you are absent in Punjab you are out of politics…if you are absent in Pakistan but present in Punjab, you still count for something."[147] It is numerically appropriate because seats from only one province are sufficient to earn the simple majority required. Before the 2002 election the total number of seats in the house was 206, out of which the share for Punjab share was 115, a number more than the simple majority needed to form a government. After a revision the total seats were increased to 272 in which Punjab received 150 which was 5 per cent more than the required majority. The party had fought all the seven elections since its electoral participation in 1988. The first two elections were fought in alliance and after that the PML (N) became a major force in its own right. The party, which has Punjabi origins and leadership, dominated the province whenever it formed governments. Its Punjabi dominance is more evident in the following table which captures its comparative periodic performance in the provinces.

Table 4.3: Provincial wise Seat-Breakdown of PML (N)

Name of Provinces	1988*	1990#	1993	1997	2002	2008	2013
Pakistan	55	104	73	136	15	68	124
Sindh		3	10	9			1
Punjab	45	92	53	109	14	64	117
KPK	8	8	10	15		4	5
Baluchistan	2	1		3	1		1
Total No. of seats	206	206	202	204	272	272	272

* In the election of 1988 PML (N) was part of an electoral alliance IJI
# In 1990 also PML (N) fought as part of IJI and secured a majority to form the government.
Source: Mehdi et al (eds.), *National Assembly Elections on Pakistan 1970-2008.Gilani's Index of Electoral Record 1970-2013: Volume 5-9.*

When provincial electoral performances are compared as shown above, it is established that the PML (N) is predominantly a Punjabi party. The provincial share of Punjab in PML (N)'s overall tally always remained around 90 per cent. The party three times each formed the government and was the main opposition in the house. In 2002 when General Musharraf created his own PML (Q) and Nawaz Sharif was exiled the PML (N) was reduced to an all-time low, 15 seats, out of which 14 were from Punjab. The underlying explanation of the low performance lay in the composition of the PML (Q). The party was popularly called King's party as patronised by then President

Musharraf. Many of the former PML (N) leaders joined the new opportunity and strengthened it. Since the Pakistani army is predominantly Punjabi its political influence in Punjab cannot be separated from PML (Q)'s electoral performance. The PML (Q) won 78 seats of which 68 were contributed by the province. Besides PML (N)'s Punjabi grounding the party relatively fared well in KPK. In the last seven elections in KPK the party won 50 seats which was 18 per cent of the total of 270 seats. Compared to these two provinces, its presence in Sindh is insignificant. In the last seven elections it won just 23 seats out of the total of 361 seats. The party was wiped out at least thrice from the province.

Within Punjab, the party has a high degree of support in Northern and Central regions which were relatively more urban and industrial than other regions. In the poor and agrarian Western Punjab the party has above average support while in semi-agrarian Southern Punjab it has a relatively low support base. There are two identified reasons for the party's relative support in the Southern part. First, some parts of Southern Punjab have geographical proximity with Sindh and PPP had a strong presence in the region. It was Yousaf Raza Gilani, the former Prime Minister and a PPP leader and also is a Saraiki-speaking Punjabi, who helped create a PPP constituency among them. Southern Punjab has a strong presence of the Saraikistan Movement – a movement of identity assertion based on a notion that Saraiki is a distinct language with a rich cultural past and heritage. According to the 1998 Punjab Population Census Report "overall Saraiki speakers constitute 17.4 per cent of Punjab. In rural areas 21.4 per cent and in urban areas 8.4 per cent people speak Saraiki language."[148] Realising that ruling parties are not addressing their grievances Saraiki leaders formed their own political parties.[xii] However, these parties never won a single seat but did have the capacity to influence the outcome. To get their support the PPP government in 2012 passed a resolution in favour of a new province of South Punjab in the

xii. There are eight major Saraiki groups and parties formed in various years and active in South Punjab: Pakistan Sraiki Party (1989), Saraikistan Quami Council (n.d.), Saraiki Quami Movement (1988), Saraikistan Quami Movement (1990), Saraiki National Party (1992), Saraiki Sooba Movement (2002), Saraiki Quami Ittehad (2004), Saraiki Lok Party (2007), enlisted from Hussain Ahmad Khan, *Re-thinking Punjab: The Construction of Siraiki Identity* (Lahore: Research and Publication Centre, National College of Arts, n.d.), pp. 113-15.

National Assembly.[149] Following this the Provincial Assembly of Punjab too passed two separate resolutions in support of the creation of a new province of South Punjab as well as restoration of Bhawalpur province.[150]However, these resolutions are yet to be implemented.

Beside its ethnic and provincial dimension the PML (N) support base has an ideological leaning also. The party is considered a centre-right party with a conservative proclivity. Nawaz Sharif is a political protégé of General Zia-ul Haq who began to Islamise the society and state. The Pakistan Muslim League, from which PML (N) originated, was endorsed by General Zia who appointed Sharif as Chief Minister of Punjab. The first two elections it fought was in alliance with Islamist parties. It formed its first government in 1990 in an alliance. As Prime Minister in his first term Sharif continued the process of Islamisation left incomplete by his political godfather. The PML (N) government introduced the *Shariat* Ordinance and *Bait-ul-Maal*, two Islamic Laws which accelerated the process of Islamisation. To ensure proper implementation of Islamic laws the government established three committees: *Nifaz-e-Shariat* Committee (Sharia Establishment Committee), Islamic Welfare Committee and *Ittehad-e-bain-un-Muslemeen* (Unity of Muslim Bloc). In his second term as Prime Minister he strived to Islamise the legal system of Pakistan by trying to pass a *Shariat Bill*. A detailed discussion of these conservative moves by the Sharif government has been taken-up in the subsequent chapter. One visible correlation of PML (N)'s conservative tilt was also established in the campaign of the 2013 elections when conservative militant forces attacked political workers of many parties but not the PML (N).

Leadership of Muttahida Quami Movement

Muttahida Quami Movement (MQM) can be equated with its leader Altaf Hussain. Once the student leader of Muhajirs, the zenith of Hussain's political career was achieved in 1988 when the MQM was formed under his leadership. Ever since the party members and its supporters have revered him as a *Pir* (preceptor). Hussain had to flee the country in 1992 and did not return to Pakistan thereafter. Despite this, the party continued to remain under his direct or indirect control even in his absence from Pakistan. He alone has been responsible for shaping the party and it is his will that guides the party. Though, there have been internal fissures but in the end it was Hussain who prevailed over all.

Altaf Hussain: An Enigmatic Charisma

Dukhi Dilon ka Charagar, Ghamzadon ka Humnawa,
Jhuka Nahi, Bika Nahin, Altaf Azeem Rehnuma.[xiii]

Altaf Hussain has undoubtedly been the most charismatic leader among his contemporaries in Pakistan. No Pakistani leader of present time is as eloquent as he is. His extraordinary oratory is his charm. His life is a microscopic reflection of a tragic journey of collective aspirations of a migrant community whose ambitions were never realised. He represented the voice of a weary and frustrated community which lost its glory, pride and sense of identity. His followers transformed him into a mystic figure. He earned the title of *Pir* (spiritual guru), *Bhai* (brother), *Quaid-e-Tehreek* (leader of the movement) and above all the *Rahnuma* (the guide). His politics brought the non-elite into an aristocratic parliament made up of *zaminadars*, the business class, tribal *sardars* and ruling dynasties. He was the catalyst of Muhajir politics and even three decades after the foundation of MQM the entire organisational structure and Muhajir politics revolves around his personality cult.

Altaf Hussain was born on 17 September 1953 in Karachi to a Muhajir family which had migrated from Agra at the time of partition.[151] His grandfather Moulana Mufti Ramzan Hussain was a learned scholar and was the Grand Mufti of Agra. Hussain's father Nazir Hussain was in the railways and served as a station master before moving to the new homeland for Muslims. Post partition he worked as office worker in a local mill. Altaf Hussain had ten siblings, six brothers and four sisters. He does not mention his sisters in his memoir. According to Hussain they all lived in a 120sq yds house in Federal B Area in Azizabad, Karachi. This address was to be the

xiii. The healer of the aggrieved, the leader of the bereaved. He didn't bend, he could not be bought, Altaf the great leader. These lines sum-ups the stature of Altaf Hussain among his followers. Cited in Alizeh Kohari, "The Centre (Still) Holds," *The Herald*, Vol.18, No.7, July 2014, p. 52.

future MQM headquarters and today is famously known as 'Nine Zero.'[xiv] He went to the Government Boys School located in a Muhajir-dominated Jail Road area in Karachi. After passing his matriculation he was enrolled in City College of Karachi in 1969 and completed his Intermediate level in the science stream.

He completed B.Sc. from Karachi's Islamia Science College in 1974 and then pursued another bachelor's degree in Pharmacy from the University of Karachi in 1979. After completion of formal education he started his professional career as trainee at the Karachi's Seventh Day Adventist Hospital. Simultaneously, he worked for a multi-national pharmaceutical company. Between 1970 and 1971, politically the most turbulent time of Pakistan, he joined National Cadet Service Scheme and received an year of army training. He was than recruited in the 57th Baluch Regiment and was sent to East Pakistan to fight against the Bengali nationalists. Hussain alleges that after the war, he wanted to join the regular army but was not recruited for being a Muhajir.[152] Thereafter, he resumed his education where he was to discover the 'political' in him.

As graduate student at Karachi University he joined the Islami Jamaat-e-Tulaba, a student wing of the Jamaat-e-Islami. He actively participated in the Jamaat's political activities in and outside the campus. He was appointed as president of the Jamaat's Student Action Committee. Altaf vigorously participated in the PNA's *Nizam-e-Mustafa* against the PPP. He confesses that the Muhajir's participation in PNA was purely for the sake of Islam and Pakistan, as the movement proclaimed, and not due to their hostility to the Bhuttos.[153] Altaf Hussain was disappointed as he was removed from the presidency of Student Action Committee. He realised that rallying behind the Jamaat would not serve the Muhajir cause as it was morphing into a Punjabi-Pakhtun body. He therefore decided to form a student organisation that would address their grievances. In 1978 he, along with Azeem Tariq, co-founded the All Pakistan Muhajir Student Organisation (APMSO) at

xiv. "Nine Zero was never really the MQM headquarters. That was Eight Nine, a small set of rooms in an apartment building in Liaqatabad." Nine Zero was the last two digits of the landline number of the MQM headquarter. But people used to think that it was some sort of code. They developed some kind of nostalgia for it therefore even after losing this place to the Haqiqi faction. The number is used for its symbolic value. *See Kohari, "The Centre (Still) Holds," p. 51.*

Karachi University. The newly formed APMSO was an effective challenge to the older organisations, sometimes even violently countering them.

After being banished from the campus in 1983, the APMSO was restructured into the Muhajir Quami Movement (MQM) in 1984 to formally channelise the Muhajir grievances in the political domain. Altaf Hussain acknowledges in his memoir that his Muhajir consciousness was not a product of his being a Muhajir but shaped by his cumulative life experiences. He felt that Muhajirs were discriminated against in the military recruitment, in the university admissions and all other ethnic communities projected their ethnic identities *vis-à-vis* others. These experiences along with the structural assaults under various military and civilian governments generated a feeling of being a "third class citizen" and consciousness of being a "fifth nationality."[154]

At a later stage he strove to shed the parochial identity politics and tried to broaden MQM's social base and bridge the Sindhi-Muhajir schism. He referred to the Muhajirs as "Urdu-speaking Sindhis" and called himself "the son of Sindh Dharti."[155] In 2001, Hussain married Fazia Gabol, who was of Punjabi ethnicity with a Baluch surname. It was also seen as his attempt to extend his political reach. From his marriage he has a daughter name Afza Altaf. He and Fazia were divorced in 2007. In another liberal gesture the party also replaced the word 'Muhajir' with 'Muttahida' from the name of its student organisation in 2006.

Prior to his exile in the UK, Hussain was arrested and imprisoned several times in his short political career in Karachi. He was first arrested in 1979 for burning the national flag at the mausoleum of Jinnah.[156] In his autobiography, Hussain stated that he was arrested because he demanded the safe repatriation of stranded Bihari Refugees in Bangladesh.[157] However, he was sentenced to nine months prison and five lashes. For the second time, Hussain and few of party supporters were arrested on several criminal charges after his first public address at *Pakka Qila* in Hyderabad on 31 October 1986.[158] They were released later and all the charges were dropped against them. He was also arrested on August 1987 and released five months later. In 1991, he escaped a failed murder attempt. A murder charge was also registered against him. Amidst the crackdown in Karachi on his party in 1992 Hussain fled to London. Thereafter, he never returned to Pakistan but still ran the party from there.

By this time, he had already developed a personality cult amongst his supporters. According to Oskar Verkaaik, at the zenith of his party, the most popular slogan was "*mast Qalandar* Altaf Hussain,"[xv] that in one reading exhibiting his followers' self-effacing commitment to the leader.[159] He was also revered and given the title of *Pir Sahib* who possessed "miraculous power (*barkat*), and because of this he is asked to kiss babies" by his followers who saw him as a possible saviour. During the period when Hussain was present in Pakistan, the new recruits were supposed to take a formal oath (*halafnama*) to exhibit his/her loyalty to Altaf Hussain. The later part of the "Oath", translated by Verkaaik read thus: "I swear that I shall accept Altaf Hussain's decisions, as final in any matter and obey all his decisions. If I disobey any of his decisions, I must be regarded as traitor. I swear that I will have blind trust in party leader Altaf Hussain."[160] The *Quaid-e-Tehreek* – leader of the movement – gradually rose to the status of unquestionable obedience. He was as sacrosanct as a 'holy cow' and "in fact criticising Hussain is akin to committing blasphemy, with guilty deserving death."[161] This is reminded to the people through street graffiti which warns, "*Jo Quaid ka ghaddar hai wo maut ka haqdar hai* (he who betrays the leader deserves death)."[162] Iftikhar Malik denounces Hussain's politics in sophisticated academic vocabulary as: "mafioso-style politicking of venomous tribal chieftain with that of ruthless feudal lord" and thinks that Hussain "controls the city of Karachi like a Mafia godfather figure."[163] In another aspect, Altaf Hussain is considered as a philosopher and writes the party literature himself. Earlier through telephonic conferences, and now through video conference he gives *fikri nashists* (thoughtful sessions) to his followers. These are also available on the party's official website.[164]

Hamza Alavi once described the MQM as a "peripheralised movement of frustrated petty-bourgeois "salariat" classes aspiring to higher employment quotas in a state apparatus held captive by an oligarchy of military-bureaucratic power."[165] As described in the previous chapter Muhajir domination declined to the extent that those who were once the champions

xv. A *Qalandar* is a wandering ascetic in Sufi tradition. Followers of a Sufi saint would revere him as a Qalandar who has risen over the shackles of the material world and has realised hidden wisdom. He will guide the lost to the righteous path and success. It is also conferred as a title on someone in respect and love.

of Pakistan regretted its creation. The level of frustration and pain reflects in two separate statements of Altaf Hussain, whose life in a way is the reflection of the Muhajir nation. In 2004, Hussain in the keynote address of *Hindustan Times Leadership Initiative*, held in New Delhi, said that: "Perhaps the idea of Pakistan was dead at its inception, when the majority of Muslims chose to stay back after partition, a truism reiterated in the creation of Bangladesh in 1971."[166] Two days later, in a formal interview with then Indian Foreign Minister, Natwar Singh, he requested the granting of political asylum to MQM workers facing the establishment's targeted victimisation. The request was politely rejected. In the meeting he recited Muzaffar Razmi's famous Urdu couplet:

Yeh waqt bhi dekha hai taareekh ke safahon ne;
Lamhon ne khata ki thi, sadiyon ne sazaa payee.[167]

Translated as: "Annals of History have witnessed the phenomenon that blunders committed in a short span of time resulted in punishment for centuries" these lines sums up the battered sentiments and their pessimism in the country they created. A few years ago Hussain's regret was much stronger when he declared the two-nation theory as a farce and creation of Pakistan as a "blunder."[168] Recalling the Army Operations of 1992 against the Muhajirs when they were called "offspring of Hindus" and agents of RAW, he described plight of Muhajir in a poetic couplet: "*Na Khuda hi mila na wisal-e-sanam – Na idhar ke rahe na udhar ke rahe ham*" that he summarised as "the two-nation theory rendered the Muslims of the Muslim minority province of undivided India destitute."[169] The Muhajirs struggle for their dignified place in the national narrative and national say is an ongoing struggle

For over the two decades now Hussain has been in self-exile in London. His health has deteriorated. He is the only chief of a major political party in Pakistan, who never contested elections in such a long career. But his charisma did not fade in his absence. People take an oath in his name without even seeing him. After the news of his recent arrest in London on the allegation of money-laundering, the city of Karachi came to a standstill. Abid Hussain, a Karachi-based analyst captures the city's ambience as: "Petrol pumps were cordoned off; market and offices emptied out; panic spread, and fear and anxiety was writ large on the street of Karachi. The city – which has a terrible history of violent protest – seemed like a ticking time bomb, which upon explosion, could destroy everything."[170] Despite all the ups and downs, all success and failures, with all his positive and negative personality attributes, Altaf Hussain remains indispensible for the Muhajir nation and an anathema for many Pakistanis.

Social Base of Muttahida Quami Movement

Muttahida Quami Movement (MQM) was born as Muhajir Quami Mahaj in 1978 as a student organisation to represent the Muhajirs in the educational institutions of Sindh, especially in Karachi. Its genesis coincides with General Zia's *junta* regime when party-based politics was banned in the country. In 1988 General Zia died in a mysterious air crash and the Supreme Court restored party-based electoral politics. In its first election MQM decided to contest independently and fought only from Sindh. The party's first performance was indeed remarkable and it won 13 seats. Within two years it had to face another election due to the premature dismissal of the government. This time it adopted a party name and contested in 24 seats – all from Sindh. It did not try to woo non-Muhajir voters as its 'Charter of Resolution' was limited to Muhajir grievances only. As expected the party did well in the Muhajir-dominated constituencies of Hyderabad and Karachi. The MQM boycotted the election of 1993 as a protest against the military's actions against its members and subsequent exile of its patron Altaf Hussain in 1992. In the intermediate period before the next election it decided to be a catch-all party and go national.

The MQM adopted a new name, Haq Parast Group, for the 1997 general election, in its endeavor to expand its electoral base. For the first time it fielded candidates in other provinces outside of Sindh. Apart from the 28 candidates fighting in Sindh the party fielded 17 candidates in Punjab, 4 each in KPK and Baluchistan. The support of the Muhajirs for Altaf Hussain and his party remained undented. It won 12 seats— 2 from Hyderabad and 10 seats from Karachi. As far as MQM's catch-all attempt is concerned the election established it as Karachi-Hyderabad party. For a detail election record of MQM see the following table.

Table 4.4: Intra-Provincial Seat-Breakdown of MQM

Name of Provinces	1988*	1990	1993	1997#	2002	2008	2013
Sindh	13	15	Boycott	12	13	19	18
Hyderabad	2	2		2	1	2	2
Karachi	11	12		10	12	17	16
Total No. of seats	206	206		206	272	272	272

* Contested as Independent
#Contested with another name, *Haq Parast Group*
Source: Mehdi et al (eds.), *National Assembly Elections on Pakistan 1970-2008. Gilani's Index of Electoral Record 1970-2013: Volume 6-9.*

Not only in terms of seats but also in terms of vote share the MQM's performance is abysmally poor in the other provinces. When in 1997 it tried to go national for the first time its share of votes was 0.09 per cent in Punjab, 0.10 per cent in KPK and 0.19 per cent in Baluchistan. Thus, in the next election of 2002 it fielded 60 candidates in total, of which 52 contested from Sindh. This election also indicated the ideological preferences of the MQM's support base. In this election the major Islamist parties formed an alliance, called the MMA.

The alliance contested from all the seats in Karachi and Hyderabad. MQM, which dominated Karachi in the two previous elections when it won 12 out 13 seats, was now was reduced to 12 out of 20 seats. The MMA won 5 seats in Karachi. For the first time MQM's vote share was as low as 40 per cent, while the MMA had 28 per cent vote share in Karachi.[171] Even in Hyderabad the MQM lost 1 seat— that went to MMA. The impact of the MMA on MQM was clearer in the 2008 elections when the Islamist alliance was dissolve and its constituents contested on their own. This time the MQM captured 17 seats out of 20 and its vote share rose to 69 per cent in Karachi. In Hyderabad it won 2 seats, recapturing its lost seat in the previous election. The situation remained the same in the next election too, with MQM winning 16 seats in Karachi and 2 in Hyderabad. In the previous four elections its combined vote share of three provinces outside Sindh was never more than half a per cent. Two things are clear from the electoral analysis— that the MQM is a purely Karachi-Hyderabad based party. Secondly, it is a Muhajir party, as outside its bastion, voters do not show any interest in its politics. Another thing which continuously affects its support base is the issue of religious identity.

Leadership of Pakistan Tehreek-e-Insaf

Pakistan Tehreek-e-Insaf (PTI) is the newest entry in the electoral arena of Pakistan. The party can be called a one-man show. It is single-handedly founded and nurtured by its founding chairman Imran Khan – a former Pakistani cricket player. Since its inception in 1996 the party has revolved around Khan. Led by the 62 year old politician it is paradoxically called the party of youth. Since the founding of party, it is Khan alone who has remained at its helm. Despite all initial setbacks and popular rejection it was Khan's perseverance that made PTI a crucial political force in Pakistani democratic politics.

Imran Khan: The Warrior Messiah

I Always Believed I Could Win

Once the nation's greatest cricketing hero and philanthropist, Imran Khan today has become Pakistan's most talked-about politician. He has been the most successful cricketer Pakistan has ever produced. As the national captain he won cricket's coveted World Cup of 1992, for which all Pakistanis are proud of him. In his Good Samaritan avatar, after his retirement from sports, he built Pakistan's biggest charitable cancer hospital, Shaukat Khanum Memorial Cancer Hospital, in memory of his mother who died of cancer. In 1993, the Pakistan government honoured him, with *Hilal-i-Imtiaz* (Crescent of Excellence), the second highest civilian honour. His political innings began in 1996 when he launched his political party, *Tehreek-e-Insaf* – movement for justice. For sixteen odd years his party remained politically insignificant until the 2013 general election in which his party emerged as the third largest political force. In 2012 the *Global Post* listed him as the third most influential leader in the world for becoming the "face of the anti-drone movement in his home country."[172] The *Asia Society* recognised him as *Person of the Year* for "shaking up Pakistan's political system"[173] and he also appeared on the cover of the *Time* magazine in the same year.[174] The *Herald*, a Pakistani news magazine, also chose him as its *Person of the Year* in 2014 for "introducing a vibrant, if raucous third force in Pakistani politics."[175] And in 2018 Khan became the Prime Minister of Pakistan.

Imran Khan was born on 25 November 1952 in a landowning Pathan family. His father Ikramullah Khan Niazi belonged to the Niazi Pakhtun tribe which arrived in India when the Lodhis were ruling in the 13th Century; his mother, Shaukat Khanum, was originally from the Burki clan, a Turko-Afghan tribe from Kaniguram, the biggest town in South Waziristan.[176] Khan spent his childhood with his cousins shooting partridge, swimming in the local canal and playing cricket in the surroundings of Zaman Park. He was enrolled in Lahore's famous Aitchison School where speaking Urdu was banned. At the age of sixteen he joined the Lahore Cricket team.

He completed his school education at the Royal Grammar School in Worcester, England. In 1972 he joined the Keble College, Oxford for his graduate studies. In Oxford he befriended Vikram Mehta and Benazir Bhutto. He became the captain of the Oxford University cricket team in 1974. As the captain of the Pakistan team, Imran Khan had good ties with General Zia. It was General Zia who urged him on live television, in 1987, to join the cricket team again for the sake of the country and he obliged. His return proved fruitful for Pakistan as he won the World Cup for his cricket-crazy country.

He married Jemima Goldsmith, a baptised protestant with a Jewish father and Catholic mother. It was at the age of 43 in 1995 that Khan married Jemima, who was half his age. The marriage was criticised by both the English and Pakistani media. While the English criticised her for converting to Islam, the Pakistanis criticised her for being a Jew .[177] From this marriage Khan has two sons, Qasim and Suleman. In 2004 Khan and Jemima got divorced. In 2015 at the age of 62 Khan remarried; this time it was to British-Pakistani journalist Reham Khan who was 20 years younger than him.

He launched his political party in 1996 which became a political force to reckon with; today it rules the country. Imran considers both the PPP and the PML (N) as mafia parties, which used democracy as a cover to plunder the country's resources.[178] It is a moderate branding compared to his view of the MQM which he does not even call a party but a "terrorist organisation." Imran Khan, somewhat in his messiah-complex, says that by involving himself more deeply in Pakistani society he realised that the only way to bring change in the system was to enter in politics himself by forming a political party with decent people to save the country from the corrupt politicians. After analysing the risk of this involvement he decided to launch his own party saying that he "had lost all the fear of dying", as coming to politics meant standing against the "political mafia" who either buy their opponents or eliminate them.[179] Khan launched his party *Tehreek-e-Insaf* on 25 April 1996 and presented it as a "broad based movement" for change with the objective to create a "free society" based on justice and peace.

His formal arrival in politics was viewed as the entry of a "third force in Pakistani politics." Before entering politics, Khan began to distance himself from his old flamboyant life-style that bordered on an aristocratic life. Today we only see him as a politician, who is usually dressed in white *shalwar-kameez,* with red and green (colour of his party flag) scarf tossed over his shoulder. From the very beginning Khan had started 'championing the cause of Islam' by criticising the westernised elite whom he called "brown sahibs" who sustained the colonial legacy. There are three experiences that transformed his attitude to Islam and advocacy for an Islamic welfare state.

The first was his exposure to the Iranian Revolution. In 1974 he visited Iran and believed that Imam Ayatollah Ruhollah *Khomeini* offered a system which was both anti-imperial and Islamic. The second incidence was his meeting with a man named Mian Bashir, whom he called his spiritual guru. Bashir's guidance helped him understand the meaning of suffering and humility; this experience gave Khan a mission in life. The third experience was his encounter with Muhammad Iqbal's philosophy of *Khudi*, the self. Cricket and Iqbal are two most reoccurring words found in his writings, speeches and manifestos. Iqbal's vision and philosophy: "the best weapon against fundamentalism is enlightened Islam" and "back to Quran, forward with *Ijtihad*" i.e. reinterpretation of Quranic principles in the light of new knowledge remains his source of inspiration.[180] What followed from his return to Islam is the criticism of the landed gentry, the military personnel and the civil bureaucracy, whom he called the new ruling elite (the *brown sahib*). The liberal and progressive class then criticised him as "nothing but a hypocrite" and dismissed him as the "biggest brown sahib of them all."[181]

His impatience in this new career was criticised for he was looking for "short cuts."[182] This short cut was his tactical partnership with *Pasban*, an organ of right wing Jamaat-e-Islami, which was behind his fund raising rallies and General Hamid Gul, of the ideological influence on his party.[183] The collaboration did not last long and Khan had to lead solo. A columnist predicted that "there is political naiveté about him which prevents him from being taken seriously as political alternative by serious people."[184]In the first time participation in the 1997 election his party did not win a single seat.

After the election Nawaz Sharif was once again sworn in as Prime Minister of Pakistan. Sharif's government was dismissed in a military coup in 1999. Imran Khan supported the coup. He admitted that he welcomed the coup because it "seemed like an end to the Benazir-Nawaz merry-go-round" and also for a personal reason. According to Khan, to sabotage his political career, the Sharif government tried to implicate Jemima in a false antique-smuggling case. After the coup the cases against her were dropped.[185]

Khan's understanding of Pakistan society has been questioned. An article by him in 1996 came under criticism; his understanding of Pakistani society was dismissed as: "Imran's illiteracy in political theory has prevented him from framing a more thorough, deeper analysis of what is wrong with state and society in Pakistan" and his understanding "did not go beyond identifying the problem areas of Pakistan's politics."[186] Even after three elections his understanding does not seem to be improving, as argued by Rubina Saigol, who assessed Khan's three main discourses – corruption, anti-imperial nationalism and peace. According to Saigol, Khan perceives corruption in normative sense between good and evil, which can be resolved by bringing good and clean individuals; this discourse is "devoid of structural and political understanding of corruption."[187] Khan, the anti-imperial campaigner, who criticises drone attacks and 'war on terror' and is in support of economic policies fully in line with capitalism, is also in favour of making peace with Taliban is akin to compromising democracy.[188] For his pro Taliban stand the liberal call him a "Taliban apologist" and he was afraid that his stand against the Taliban will damage his party's interests.[189] Khan's style of politics also came under severe criticism in 2014 after his series of protests known as the "Azadi March" that created political chaos in the country.

The critics who consider Khan's party as a right-wing party believed that his sit-in did not improve debates within Pakistani politics but helped undermine the idea of democracy.[190] He was also dubbed as "hyper-nationalist" who for easy power shared his "political bed with Jamaat-e-Islami" and for whom "it is not just important that Pakistan changes, but that he be the man to do it."[191] Commenting on his self-obsession, Moeed Yusuf summarised that "his basic message can be reduced to this: I am your man: I will deliver. Period."[192] Despite all his naiveté in politics, his right wing inclinations, his popular rhetoric and messiah-complex, Khan has certainly changed the landscape of Pakistani politics dominated by two feudal/political dynasties.

Social Base of Pakistan Tehreek-e-Insaf

Pakistan Tehreek-e-Insaf's entry in the electoral arena of the country is relatively new. It entered to contest its first election in 1997 when the party's arrival was touted as the entry of a "third force." The new enthusiast contested on 134 seats out of 206 totals. The party leader, Imran Khan, peculiarly, contested from 8 seats in three provinces.[xvi] Khan and his party lost all the seats. The maximum votes he could gather were in his hometown, Mianwali. Here he ended up at third position by securing 17,859 votes from the 101,726 total valid votes polled in the constituency. His worst performance came in Karachi where the national hero of cricket managed to win 911 votes out of 59,078 votes polled. Collectively the party secured 313,673 votes in which Imran Khan's share was 56,542 from all the 8 seats combined. PTI won 2 per cent votes polled in the election. The major share of it came from Punjab (217,169) and KPK (71,042). Thus it was easy to conclude that majority of PTI supporters were concentrated in these two provinces.

Then came the election of 2002, in which electoral rules were revised and the number of seats increased to 272. But the party reduced its candidates and contested only on 94 seats. This time Imran Khan fought from three seats only.[xvii] He managed to win from his home constituency, Mianwali. The voters once again rejected his party. as his collective vote share was less than 1 per cent. More than 85 per cent of its vote share came from Punjab and KPK combined. Its Punjab's vote share was as high as 69 per cent. It was difficult to come to any conclusion about PTI's social base as it won only 1 seat in two elections, but one could perceive the Punjabi-Pakhtun tilt from

xvi. In KPK he fought from Abbottabad and Swat, in Punjab from Mianwali, Dera Ismail Khan, Lahore-3 and Lahore-4, in Sindh from Karachi south and the federal capital Islamabad.

xvii. This time Imran Khan contested only from Mianwali, Swat and Lahore-5 constituencies.

its vote share. The exhausted and demoralised leadership decided to boycott the 2008 election under the military's watch. After a long break the party decided to contest in the 2013 general election, which established the party's political significance as well as its social base.

The PTI returned to national politics with significant impact. The party contested 248 seats and emerged as the second largest party in terms of popular vote share in the polls. It won 26 general seats and was the third largest party following the PML (N) and the PPP. In terms of support base, the result was a pristine statement of its Pakhtun-Punjabi proclivity. All the 26 seats came from Punjab and KPK. The party could not open its account in Sindh and Baluchistan in its third consecutive attempt. Within Punjab and KPK it fared well in certain divisions. The following table shows the intra-provincial concentration of its support base.

Table 4.5: Division-wise Seat-Breakdown in KPK and Punjab

Division – KPK	Seat won	Vote share in %	Division-Punjab	Seat won	Vote share in %
Kohat	3	37	Lahore	1	20
Hazara	2	30	Multan	3	27
Malakand	2	24	Sargodha	2	20
Mardan	3	26	Rawalpindi	3	26
Peshawar	6	41	Total	9	18
FATA	1	11			
Total	17	27			

Source: Gilani's Index of Electoral Record 1970-2013; Volume 9, Pakistan National Election 2013.

The intra-provincial variations showed that the party, which campaigned with populist and Islamist rhetoric, fared well in rural divisions.[xviii] Khan's Islamist rhetoric was well received in KPK, where anti-Americanism was high due to continuous drone-attacks and military operations.[193] PTI fared

xviii. According to the available official data, districts of Hazara, Mardan, Malakand had less than 20 per cent urban population. Kohat was estimated to have 26 per cent urban population while the provincial capital had the highest urban population of 48 per cent. "District at Glance: Khyber Pakhtunkhwa," *Pakistan Bureau of Statistics*, URL: http://www.pbs.gov.pk/pco-kpk-tables (accessed on 20 September 2015).

well in the semi-urban divisions of northern Punjab. Other than rural-urban preferences, surveys showed that more educated people voted for PTI compared to PML (N). This has partly resulted from the party's reach to the educated youth through an online campaign. *Time Magazine* dubbed it as a party of "Social Networkers" due to its popularity among netizens. It captures the magnitude of Khan's online support as: "He is the only politician in the country to have used social media to engage his followers and potential supports on a large scale."[194] Rubina Saigol, who found PTI's support among the conservative Pakhtuns and urban middle class, succinctly summarised that the party is popular "among sections of the middle class in Lahore and Karachi, and among war-weary Pakhtuns in Khyber-Pakhtunkhwa.[195]

But all these equations changed in the 2018 general election, when the PTI emerged as the largest single party, securing 116 seats. It expanded its social and political base in Punjab and Sindh, especially Karachi. In its traditional stronghold KPK it won 30 seats out of 39 while in Punjab it won 60 seats. Compared to its last election tally, when it won 9 seats in the province, it was a quantum leap. PTI was also the gainer of factionalism in MQM. Khan's party did not win a single seat from Karachi in the 2013 election, while in 2018 it won 13 seats out of a total of 20 seats from the Muhajir-dominated Karachi. All this indicates erosion of the political constituency of the old parties while the PTI was now spreading its wings outside its catchment area.

This chapter provided a detailed analysis of the social background and personality traits of the selected political parties and their leaderships. The chapter also outlined a brief social and demographic profile of the country. In this context, the chapter illustrated the possible correlation between the social constituency of political parties and their electoral outcome in a specific demographic condition. The third chapter has already given a understating of how political parties have originated, evolved and participated in the political process. Collectively these two chapters offer a descriptive analysis of socio-political genesis of political parties, their structural functioning as well as characteristics of their leadership. The analyses done has helped in examining how the socio-political universe, in which both the democratic and military regimes operated and shaped their practices which were responsible for the nature of democracy in Pakistan. This fundamental understanding helps in deciphering the correlation between the behaviour of political parties, their leadership and its implications for democracy. This complexity is deliberated in the next two chapters which analyse the attitude and practices of both the democratic and military regimes.

Notes

1. E. A. H. Blunt, *The Caste System of Northern India* (Humphrew Milford: Oxford University Press, 1931), p. 5.
2. J. H. Hutton, *Caste in India* (Cambridge: Cambridge University Press, 1946), p. 49.
3. B. R. Ambedkar, "Castes in India: Their Mechanism, Genesis and Development," Paper presented at an Anthropology Seminar, Columbia University, 9 May 1916. Reprinted in Frances W. Pritchett (ed.), *Dr. Babasaheb Ambedkar: Writings and Speeches, Vol. 1* (Bombay: Education Department, Government of Maharashtra, 1979), pp. 3-22.
4. Ibid.
5. Hamza Alavi, "The Two Biradaris: Kinship in Rural West Punjab," in T. N. Madan (ed.), *Muslim Communities of South Asia: Culture, Society and Power* (New Delhi: Manohar, 1976 reprint 2001), p. 25.
6. Ibid, p. 26.
7. Saghir Ahmad, *Class and Power in a Punjabi Village* (New York: Monthly Review Press, 1977), pp. 72-3.
8. Inayat Ullah, "Caste, Patti and Faction in the Life of Punjabi Village," *Sociolugus,* Vol. 8, No. 2, 1958, pp. 170-86.
9. Alavi, "The Two Biradaris: Kinship in Rural West Punjab," p. 32.
10. For detail argumentations and major works on the subject see Lloyd I. Rudolph and Susanne Hoeber Rudolph, *The Modernity of Tradition: Political Development in India* (Chicago: The University of Chicago Press, 1984), M. N. Srinivas, *Caste in Modern India and Other Essays* (New Delhi: Asia Publishing House, 1962), Rajni Kothari and James Manor (eds.), *Caste in Indian Politics* (New Delhi: Orient Blackswan, 2010), Paul R. Brass, *Caste, Faction and Party in Indian Politics* (New Delhi: Chanakya Publications, 1985).
11. Inayatullah, "Perspective in the Rural Power Structure in West Pakistan", People and Society Series (Karachi: Development Research and Evaluation Group, USAID, 1963), pp. 50-1 cited in Andrew R. Wilder, *The Pakistani Voter: Electoral Politics and Voting Behaviour in the Punjab* (Karachi: Oxford University Press, 1999), p. 6.
12. Ibid.
13. Ahmad, *Class and Power in a Punjabi Village,* pp. 98-9.
14. Hamza Alavi, "Kinship in West Punjab Villages," *Contributions to Indian Sociology,* Vol. 6 No. 1, January 1972.
15. Craig Baxter, "Pakistan Votes - 1970," *Asian Survey,* Vol. 11, No. 3, March 1971, p. 213.
16. Mohammad Waseem, *The 1993 Elections in Pakistan* (Lahore: Vanguard Books, 1994), p. 240.
17. Ibid, p. 235.

18. Wilder, *The Pakistani Voter*, pp. 216-8.
19. Ibid.
20. Discussion with Mohammad Waseem, 18 October 2011, New Delhi.
21. "Pakistan Population 2013," *World Population Statistics*, 14 December 2013, URL: http://www.worldp opulationstatistics.com/pakistan-population-2013/ (accessed on 17 April 2016).
22. ECP, "Electoral Rolls," *Election Commission of Pakistan*, URL: http://elections.com.pk/contents.php? i=12 (accessed on 30 November 2013).
23. *50 Years of Pakistan, Volume - 1: Population* (Karachi: Federal Bureau of Pakistan, Statistical Division, Government of Pakistan, 1998), p. 170.
24. Tahir Mehdi et al (eds.), *National Assembly Elections on Pakistan 1970-2008* (Lahore: Church World Service-Pakistan/Afghanistan and Free and Free Election Network, 2010), p. 30.
25. A large number of Afghan refugees have returned to their country with the help of the United Nations High Commissioner for Refugees (UNHCR). According to a 2006 report, up to 2-4 million Afghan refugees stayed in Pakistan. UNHCR, "Afghan Repatriation Operation 2006: Weekly Statistics Report," *UNHCR.Org*, 31 December 2006, URL: http://www.unhcr.org/cgibin/texis/vtx/search?page=search&docid=47131c6e2&query=unhcr%20statistics(accessed on 30 November 2013).
26. *50 Years of Pakistan, Volume-1: Population*, p. 173.
27. *50 Years of Pakistan in Statistics, Volume-4, 1982-1997: Population*, p. 10.
28. The World Bank, "Urban Population (% of Total)," *The World Bank.Org*, 2013, URL: http://data.world bank.org/indicator/SP.URB.TOTL.IN.ZS (accessed on 2 September 2015).
29. N. Shamsi, "The Integration of Displaced Persons in Pakistan," in *Census of Pakistan 1951: Demographic Miscellany*, Census Bulletin No. 6 (Karachi: Ministry of the Interior, Government of Pakistan, 1957), p. 21.
30. E. H. Slade, *Census of Pakistan 1951: Report and Tables* (Karachi: Ministry of the Interior, Government of Pakistan, 1957), p. 31.
31. Ian Talbot, *Pakistan: A New History* (London: Hurst and Company, 2012), p. 25.
32. *50 Years of Pakistan, Volume-2: Population* (Karachi: Federal Bureau of Pakistan, Statistical Division, Government of Pakistan, 1998), p. 12.
33. In 1972 census, exact population of the country was 65,309,340 in which Punjabis were 37,610,159. See Ibid, p. 13.
34. Clarence Maloney, *Peoples of South Asia* (New York: Holt, Rinehart and Winston, 1974), p. 379.
35. Ibid.
36. Slade, *Census of Pakistan 1951: Report and Tables*, p. 31.
37. Aamna Saiyid, "The Population of Karachi has Doubled in 15 Years," *The Express Tribune*, 13 January 2014, URL: http://tribune.com.pk/story/658394/the-population-of-karachi-has-doubled-in-15-years/ (accessed on 2 October 2015).
38. "Area, Population, Density and Urban/Rural Proportion by Admn. Units," Census of Pakistan 1998, *Pakistan Bureau of Statistics*, URL: http://www.pbs.gov.pk/content/area-population-density-and-urbanrura l-proportion(accessed on 21 November

2014).

39. Yu. V. Gankovsky, *The Peoples of Pakistan: An Ethnic History*, trans. Igor Gavrilov (Lahore: Peoples Publishing House, n.d.), p. 130.
40. "Population by Mother Tongue," *Census of Pakistan 1998*, Pakistan Bureau of Statistics, URL: http://www.pbs.gov.pk/content/population-mother-tongue (accessed on 17 August 2015).
41. In Islamabad, Punjabi-speakers are 71.66 per cent; Urdu-Speakers 10.11 per cent wherein Pushto-speakers constitute 9.52 per cent of the population, Ibid.
42. Robert Nichols, *A History of Pashtun Migration, 1775-2006* (Oxford: Oxford University Press, 2008), p. 51.
43. "Area, Population, Density and Urban/Rural Proportion by Admn. Units," *Census of Pakistan 1998*.
44. Gankovsky, *The Peoples of Pakistan: An Ethnic History*, p. 12.
45. Maloney, *Peoples of South Asia*, p. 380.
46. Ibid.
47. Zulfikar Ali Bhutto, *If I am Assassinated* (New Delhi: Vikas Publishing House, 1979), pp. 142-43.
48. Stanley Wolpert, *Zulfi Bhutto of Pakistan: Life and Times* (New York: Oxford University Press, 1993), p. 21.
49. Salman Taseer, *Bhutto: A Political Biography* (New Delhi: Vikas Publishing House, 1980), p. 19.
50. Wolpert, *Zulfi Bhutto of Pakistan*, p. 29.
51. Ibid.
52. Taseer, *Bhutto: A Political Biography*, pp. 24-5.
53. Wolpert, *Zulfi Bhutto of Pakistan*, pp. 47-8.
54. Taseer, *Bhutto: A Political Biography*, p. 35.
55. Wolpert, *Zulfi Bhutto of Pakistan*, pp. 60 & 66.
56. Rafi Raza, *Zulfikar Ali Bhutto and Pakistan 1967-1977* (Karachi: Oxford University Press, 1997), p. 2.
57. Taseer, *Bhutto: A Political Biography*, p. 68.
58. Wolpert, *Zulfi Bhutto of Pakistan*, p. 117.
59. Willem van Schendel, *A History of Bangladesh* (Cambridge: Cambridge University Press, 2009), p. 161.
60. Shahid Javed Burki, *Pakistan Under Bhutto, 1971-1977* (London: Macmillan Press, 1980), p. 71.
61. Raza, *Zulfikar Ali Bhutto and* Pakistan, p.147.
62. Ayesha Siddiqa, *Military Inc: Inside Pakistan's Military Economy* (London: Pluto Press, 2007), p. 81.
63. Ibid, p. 267.
64. Burki, *Pakistan Under Bhutto*, pp. 171-2.
65. Ibid.
66. Bhutto, *If I am Assassinated*. p. 174.
67. Ibid, p. 160.
68. Wolpert, *Zulfi Bhutto of Pakistan*, p. 1.

69. Benazir Bhutto, *Reconciliation: Islam, Democracy and the West* (New York: Harper Luxe, 2008), p. 23.
70. Benazir Bhutto, *Daughter of Destiny: An Autobiography* (New York: Simon and Schuster, 1989), p. 61.
71. Ibid, p. 81.
72. Bhutto, *Reconciliation*, p. 21.
73. Bhutto, *Daughter of Destiny*, p. 86.
74. Tariq Ali, "Daughter of the West," *London Review of Books*, Vol. 29, No. 24, 13 December 2007.
75. Anna Suvorova, *Benazir Bhutto: A Multidimensional Portrait* (Karachi: Oxford University Press, 2015), p. 182.
76. "President Leghari's Order of November 5, 1996", *pakistani.org*, URL: http://www.pakistani.org/ pakistan/leghari.order.html (accessed on 3 September 2015).
77. Celia W. Dugger, "Pakistan Sentences Bhutto to 5 Years for Corruption," *The New York Times,* 16 April 1999, URL: http://www.nytimes.com/1999/04/16/world/pakistan-sentences-bhutto-to-5-years-for-corruptio n.html (accessed on 3 May 2015).
78. Ibid.
79. William Dalrymple, "Pakistan's flawed and feudal princess," *The Guardian*, 30 December 2007, URL: http://www.theguardian.com/commentisfree/2007/dec/30/pakistan.world (accessed on 1 May 2015).
80. Suvorova, *Benazir Bhutto: A Multidimensional Portrait*, pp. 97-9.
81. For Benazir Bhutto's Will, See Appendix C.
82. Shashi Tharoor, "Bhutto's death has averted a mullah-military Pakistan," *The Guardian*, 4 January 2008, URL: http://www.theguardian.com/commentisfree/2008/jan/04/pakistan.world (accessed on17 May 2015).
83. Tariq Ali, "My heart bleeds for Pakistan. It deserves better than this grotesque feudal charade," *The Independent*, 31 December 2007, URL: http://www.independent.co.uk/news/world/asia/my-heart-bleeds-for-pakistan-it-deserves-better-than-this-grotesque-feudal-charade-767423.html (accessed on 15 May 2015).
84. Dalrymple, "Pakistan's flawed and feudal princess."
85. Ibid.
86. Philip E. Jones, *The Pakistan People's Party: Rise to Power* (Karachi: Oxford University Press, 2003), p. 119.
87. Ibid., p. 125.
88. Burki, *Pakistan Under Bhutto*, p. 173.
89. Ibid, pp. 190-91.
90. Burki noted that for the 1977 election "The Noons and Tiwanas of Sargodha, the Maliks of Mianwali, the Qureshis of Multan, the Hayats of Rawalpindi and Campbellpur, the Legharis and Mazaris of Dera Ghazi Khan were back in political arena as PPP candidates," Ibid, p. 192.
91. The 1993 Manifesto of the Pakistan Peoples Party, *ppp.org*, URL: http://www.ppp.org.pk/manifestos /manifesto1993.pdf (accessed on 23 March 2015).
92. Bhutto, *Reconciliation* p. 200. And "PPP Government's Achievements," *Pakistan*

Peoples Party, *ppp.org*, URL: http://www.ppp.org.pk/achievements.html

93. Suvorova, *Benazir Bhutto: A Multidimensional Portraits*, p. 86.
94. On 15 November 2006 the National Assembly under General Musharraf government passed a Women's Protection Bill that amended the provisions of *Hudud* Ordinance. See Salman Masood, "Pakistan Moves Toward Altering Rape Law," *New York Times*, 16 November 2006, URL: http://www.nytimes.com/ 2006/11/16 /world/ asia/16pakistan.html?_r=0 (accessed on 12 July 2015).
95. Sayyid Abul A'la Maududi expressing his conviction for the cause of Jamaat-e-Islami at the first *Ijtima* of Jamaat held on 25 August 1941. See *Historical Narrative of Jamaat-e-Islami Hind, Vol. 1*(New Delhi: Markazi Maktaba Islami Publishers, 2013), p. 13.
96. Seyyed Vali Reza Nasr, *Mawdudi and the Making of Islamic Revivalism* (New York: Oxford University Press, 1996), p. 3.
97. Nadeem F. Paracha, "Abul Ala Maududi: An Existentialist History," *Dawn*, 1 January 2015, URL: http://www.dawn.com/news/1154419 (accessed on 12 July 2015).
98. Nasr, *Mawdudi and the Making of Islamic Revivalism*, p. 3.
99. Jason Cowely, "12 Great thinkers of our time," *New Statesman*, 14 July 2003, URL: http://mideastweb. org/Middle-East-Encyclopedia/abul-ala-maududi.htm (accessed on 14 August 2015).
100. Syyid Abul Ala Maududi, *Wasa'iq-e-Maududi* (Testimony of Maududi) (Lahore: Idara Ma'arif-i-Islami, 1984), p. 97.
101. Ibid.
102. Nasr, *Mawdudi and the Making of Islamic Revivalism*, pp. 9-10.
103. Maududi, *Wasa'iq-e-Maududi*, p. 97.
104. Jamal Malik, *Colonization of Islam: Dissolution of Traditional Institutions in Pakistan* (New Delhi: Manohar Publishers, 1998), p. 8.
105. Nasr, *Mawdudi and the Making of Islamic Revivalism*, p. 12.
106. Ibid, p. 3.
107. Seyyed Vali Reza Nasr, *The Vanguard of the Islamic Revolution: The Jama`at-i-Islami of Pakistan* (London: I. B. Tauris Publishers, 1994).
108. "The Leninist Concept of the Revolutionary Vanguard Party," *marxist.org*, URL: https://www.marxists. org/history/etol/newspape/socialistvoice/partyPR46.html (accessed on 19 September 2015).
109. Sayyid Abul A'la Maududi, *Islam ka Nizam-e-Hayat* (New Delhi: Markazi Maktaba Islami Publishers, 2013), pp. 29-30.
110. Sayyid Abul A'la Maududi, *Islam Aur Jahalat* (New Delhi: Markazi Maktaba Islami Publishers, 2013), pp. 8-13.
111. Ibid, pp. 21-2.
112. Maududi, *Islam ka Nizam-e-Hayat*, p. 32.
113. Sayyid Abul A'la Maududi, *Tajdeed-O-Ahyaye Deen* (New Delhi: Markazi Maktaba Islami Publishers, 2014), pp. 9-18.
114. Ibid, p. 31.
115. Ibid, pp. 25-7.
116. Farzana Shaikh, *Community and Consensus in Islam: Muslim Representation in*

Colonial India, 1860-1947 (Cambridge: Cambridge University Press, 1989), p. 1.

117. *Rudad-e-Jamaat-e-Islami* (Proceedings of Jamaat-e-Islami) Vol. 1: First Ijtema and Ijtema of Darbhamga-August 1941 to October 1943 (New Delhi: Markazi Maktaba Islami Publishers, 2015), p. 6.
118. Ibid, pp. 6-7.
119. *Rudad-e-Jamaat-e-Islami* (Proceedings of Jamaat-e-Islami) Vol.3: The All India Ijtema of Jamaat-e-Islami, April 1946 – Allahabad (New Delhi: Markazi Maktaba Publishers, 2013), p. 14.
120. *Rudad-e- Jamaat-e-Islami,* Vol. 1, p.8.
121. Nasr, *Mawdudi and the Making of Islamic Revivalism*, p. 5.
122. Abdallah Schleifer, "Mawdudi, Abu al-A'la (1903-79)," in Gerhard Bowering (ed.), *Princeton Encyclopedia of Islamic Political Thought* (Princeton: Princeton University Press, 2013), p. 233.
123. Irfan Ahmad, *Islamism and Democracy in India; The Transformation of Jamaat-e-Islami* (Princeton: Princeton University Press, 2009), p. 62.
124. Ibid.
125. Nadeem F. Paracha, "Maududi's Children," *Dawn*, 11 June 2009, URL: http://www.dawn.com/news/ 812924/maududi%E2%80%99s-children(accessed on 3 October 2015).
126. Nasr, *The Vanguard of the Islamic Revolution*, p. 97.
127. Ibid, p. 82.
128. Ibid, p. 96.
129. "Sirajul Haq replaces Munawar Hassan as chief of Jamaat-e-Islami," *The Express Tribune*, 30 March 2014, URL: http://tribune.com.pk/story/689135/sirajul-haq-replaces-munawar-hassan-as-chief-of-jamaat-e-islami/ (accessed on 7 October 2015).
130. From Nawaz Sharif's pre-election speech in 2013. Jon Boone, "Nawaz Sharif in the Driving Seat in Battle to be Pakistan's PM," *The Guardian*, 19 March 2013, URL: http://www.theguardian.com/world/2013/mar/19/ nawaz-sharif-pakistan-elections-prime-minister (accessed on 25 September 2015).
131. Raymond W. Baker, *Capitalism's Achilles Heel: Dirty Money and How to Renew the Free-Market System* (New Jersey: John Wiley & Sons, Inc., 2005), p. 82.
132. Ibid.
133. Stephen Philip Cohen, *The Idea of Pakistan* (New Delhi: Oxford University Press, 2010). p. 251.
134. "Prime Minister of Pakistan: Mian Muhammad Nawaz Sharif," *Prime Minister's Office, pmo.org,* URL: http://www.pmo.gov.pk/pm_profile.php (accessed on 5 October 2015).
135. Baker, *Capitalism's Achilles Heel*, p. 83.
136. Talbot, *Pakistan: A New History*, pp. 151-2.
137. Ibid.
138. Cohen, *The Idea of Pakistan*, p. 251.
139. Talbot, *Pakistan: A New History*, p. 152.
140. Zaffar Abbas, "Can the Tiger Roar," *The Herald*, Vol. 28, No. 3, March 1997, p. 28.

141. Ibid, p. 29.
142. Shuja Nawaz, *Crossed Swords: Pakistan, Its Army, and the Wars Within* (Karachi: Oxford University Press, 2008), p. 487.
143. Tasgola Karla Bruner, "Sharif may face Death Penalty for Hijacking," *The Independent*, 20 January 2000, URL: https://archive.is/pNT8W#selection-875.0-985.24 (accessed on 7 May 2015).
144. "Pakistan frees Sharif to exile in Saudi Arabia," *The Guardian*, 11 December 2000, URL: http://www.theguardian.com/world/2000/dec/11/pakistan.saudiarabia (accessed on 12 April 2016).
145. Jane Perlez, "Pakistan Court Bars President's Rival from Office," *New York Times*, 25 February 2009,URL: http://www.nytimes.com/2009/02/26/world/asia/26pstan.html (accessed on 28 August 2015).
146. Pakistan Lifts Office Ban on Nawaz Sharif," *The Telegraph*, 26 May 2009, URL: http://www.telegraph. co.uk/news/worldnews/asia/pakistan/5388737/Pakistan-lifts-office-ban-on-Nawaz-Sharif.html(accessed on 7 August 2015).
147. Khaled Ahmad, "Is the PPP Dying?" *Indian Express*, 9 October 2015.
148. Rehana Saeed Hashmi and Gulshan Majeed, "Saraiki Ethnic Identity: Genesis of the Conflict with the State," *Journal of Political Studies*, Vol. 21, No. 1, January 2014, p. 79.
149. Abdul Manan, "Demand for South Punjab," *The Express Tribune*, 5 May 2012, URL: http://tribune.com. pk/story/374354/demand-for-south-punjab/ (accessed on 22 August 2015).
150. Amjad Mahmood, "Assembly backs South Punjab, Bahawalpur Provinces," *Dawn*, 10 May 2012, URL: http://www.dawn.com/news/717071/assembly-backs-south-punjab-bahawalpur-provinces (accessed on 2 September 2015).
151. All personal details are from the preface of his autobiography unless otherwise stated. Altaf Hussain, *My Life's Journey: The Early Years 1966-1988* (*Safar-i-Zindagi*) trans. Khalid Athar (Karachi: Oxford University Press, 2011), pp. xxv-xxvii.
152. "Altaf Hussain: Founder and Leader of MQM," *mqmuk.com*, URL: http://www.mqmuk.com/mainframe /Altaf%20Bhai.htm(accessed on 12 March 2015).
153. Hussain, *My Life's Journey*, p. 25.
154. Ibid, pp. 24-32.
155. Papiya Ghosh, *Partition and the South Asian Diaspora: Extending the Subcontinent* (London: Routledge, 2007), p. 120.
156. Oskar Verkaaik, *Migrants and Militants: Fun and Urban Violence in Pakistan* (New Delhi: Manas Publication in collaboration with Princeton University Press, 2005), p. 68.
157. Hussain, *My Life's Journey*, p. 81.
158. Sabir Shah, "Altaf Hussain arrested for fourth time," *The News*, 4 June 2014, URL: http://www.thenews.com.pk/Todays-News-2-254042-Altaf-Hussain-arrested-for-fourth-time (accessed on 13 September 2015).
159. Verkaaik, *Migrants and Militants*, p. 54.
160. Ibid, p. 72.
161. Abid Hussain, "Big Brother is Watching," *The Herald*, Vol.18, No.7, July 2014, p. 47.

162. Ibid.
163. Iftikhar Malik, *Pakistan: Democracy, Terrorism, and the Building of a Nation* (Northampton: Olive Branch Press, 2010), p. 59.
164. For the text of Fikri Nishist see "Fikri Nishist ," *mqm.org*, URL: http://www.mqm.org/FikriNishist (accessed on 12 March 2015).
165. Cited in Khan, *Mohajir Militancy in Pakistan*, p. 8.
166. Keynote Speech of Altaf Hussain, "India and the World: A Blueprint for Partnership and Growth," *Hindustan Times Leadership Initiative*, New Delhi, 5-6 November 2004, URL: http://www.mqm.org/English-News/Nov-2004/ah-speech-india-061104.htm (accessed on 17 April 2015).
167. Arun Rajnath, "Altaf Hussain Seeks Easier Political Asylum For His Supporters: India Rejects," *South Asia Tribune*, 8 November 2004, URL: http://antisystemic.org/satribune/www.satribune.com/archives /nov04/P1_arun4.htm(accessed on 14 May 2015).
168. Altaf Hussain, "The Slogan of Two-Nation Theory was raised to deceive the one hundred million Muslims of the Subcontinent," 21 June 2000, London, *mqm.org*, URL: http://www.mqm.org/English-News/Jun-2000/twonation-210600.htm (accessed on 8 October 2015).
169. Ibid.
170. Hussain, "Big Brother is Watching," p. 44.
171. *Gilani's Index of Electoral Record 1970-2013: Volume 7, Pakistan National Election 2002.*
172. Talia Ralph, "The Top 9 World Leaders of 2012," *Global Post*,20 December 2012,URL: http://ww w.globalpost.com/dispatch/news/politics/world-leaders/121213/top-9-world-leaders-2012(accessed on 12 May 2015).
173. "Poll: Who Was Asia's Person of the Year in 2012?" *Asia Society*, 20 December 2012, URL: http://asiasociety.org/blog/asia/poll-who-was-asias-person-year-2012 (accessed on 5 May 2015).
174. "The Long Shot," *Time*, Vol. 23, No. 7, 17 December 2012.
175. Shayan Naveed and Alizeh Kohari, "Person of the Year," *The Herald*, Vol. 47, No. 1, January 2014, p. 54.
176. Imran Khan, *All Round View* (London: Chatto and Windus, 1988), p. 1.
177. Khan, *Pakistan: A Personal History*, pp. 204-6.
178. Ibid. p. 208.
179. Ibid, pp. 209-0.
180. Ibid, pp. 363-8
181. Hussain, "Imran's New Innings," p. 27.
182. Khan, "Third Force or Third Farce?" p. 28.
183. Zaigham Khan, "Three's a Crowd," *The Herald*, Vol. 27, No. 5, May 1996, p. 29.
184. Ayaz Amir, "What Does Imran Khan Really Want?" *The Herald*, Vol. 27, No. 5, May 1996, p. 37.
185. Khan, *Pakistan: A Personal History*, p. 241.
186. Rashid Rahman, "Will the Real Imran Khan Please Stand Up?," *Newsline*, Vol. 7, No. 10, April 1996, pp. 31-2.

187. Rubina Saigol, "Three Pillars of Wisdom: A Critical Assessment of Imran Khan and His Politics," *The Herald*, Vol. 47, No. 1, January 2014, p. 60.
188. Ibid, p. 61.
189. Muhammad Amir Rana, "He is Afraid if he takes a Position against Extremism it will Damage his Party's Interest," *Time*, Vol. 23, No. 7, 17 December 2012, p. 23.
190. Sher Ali Khan, "Politics of Disruption," *The Herald*, Vol. 47, No. 11, November, 2014, p. 36.
191. Haseeb Asif, "Striking Success," *The Herald*, Vol. 47, No. 1, January 2014, p. 59.
192. Moeed Yusuf, "Leader/Agitator," *The Herald*, Vol. 48, No. 1, January 2015, p. 77.
193. According to an estimate by New America Foundation the total casualties of drone strikes in Pakistan between 2004 and 2013 were 2851. "Drone Wars Pakistan Analysis," *New America Foundation*, URL: http://securitydata.newamerica.net/drones/pakistan-analysis.html (accessed on 8 October 2015).
194. Rana, "He is Afraid if He Takes a Position against Extremism it will Damage His Party's Interest," p. 23.
195. Saigol, "Three Pillars of Wisdom: A Critical Assessment of Imran Khan and His Politics," p. 60.

5. Political Parties and the Two Civilian Interludes

The germination of Pakistan was complex, because, at its birth its territories were not properly demarcated, its administrative structures were insufficient and its population had no organic bond to its nationalistic project. Thus along with refugee crisis it was faced with the challenges of administration and governance. The issue of political leadership subsided momentarily as Pakistan's founder Muhammad Ali Jinnah, who propagated the idea of the "two-nation theory" that India consists of two nations – Hindus and Muslims[1] and to protect the interest of the *Salariat*, Muslims needed to "establish their own political order, Pakistan,"[2] occupied the leadership of the new country. Jinnah, who promised to develop a democratic order, succumbed to the lure of power and appointed himself as Governor-General of Pakistan. He continued the Viceregal system in which all decisive powers resided in him. In the process, he lost the opportunity to strengthen an institutional mechanism that could have helped resolve the succession issue. He died just a year later and decisive power ceded to Prime Minister Liaquat Ali Khan.

Under his leadership Muslim League, the champion of the Pakistan movement failed to transform itself from a mass movement to a viable party. After Liaquat Ali Khan's assassination in 1951 two members from the Muslim League, Khwaja Nazimuddin and Mohammad Ali Bogra from East Pakistan (now Bangladesh) became Prime Minister. Under Bogra's tenure came the Muslim League's first post-partition electoral challenge in 1954 when it contested in the East Pakistan assembly polls. The provincial election of 1954 was held on the basis of universal adult franchise and separate electorate system. The ruling Muslim League lost decisively to the United Front, a multi-party alliance. The alliance having a clear majority elected Fazlul Haq as chief minister of East Pakistan. Within a month he was dismissed by Prime Minister Bogra on the charges of failure to maintain law and order and for advocating extreme autonomy tantamount to independence.[3] Governor's rule was imposed and Major General Iskander Mirza was given charge of the provincial administration. This behaviour of the members of the Muslim Leaguer was a reflection of the election outcome that severely undermined their political position. The Bengali voters, who were unhappy with the federal government's imposition of Urdu as the national language on them, reduced their numbers to less than ten in the house of 309. This came as a rude shock to the party. As a result the Muslim League became a minority in the second constituent assembly having only 26 members in which only 2 were from East Pakistan.

Thereafter, the rising antagonism between the politicians from the two wings of Pakistan created political confusion and chaos, and their failure to politically resolve it brought the reluctant military into the country's political scene. During its formative phase Pakistan's military, the most developed colonial institution inherited by the country, performed its professional functions of defence and assisted the civil authorities to maintain internal law and order. But civilian failure to come to the political consensus resulted in the expansion of the military's role over the political domain by as early as 1954. Khalid B. Sayeed has observed that "...the military's role had begun to expand in the non-professional field and it was gradually emerging as an important actor in the decision-making process."[4] And once they realised their importance and tasted power there was a natural inclination to hold onto it.

There are two set of arguments attempting to explain why the military moved beyond the military sphere and intervened in the civilian sphere. One set of the arguments explains that because from the beginning Pakistan was mired with institutional and structural weaknesses it could not develop democratic institutions necessary for its operation. Pakistan's leaders consumed a long decade to produce its first constitution which was abrogated within a year by General Ayub Khan in 1958. Other essential institutions of democracy, such as the legislature and the executive were too weak. No direct elections at the national level were held in the first two decades of the formation of the country; consequently legislature was not directly elected. After seizing power in 1958, General Ayub created his own executive accountable to him only. For a long period institutions like the judiciary and the media remained underdeveloped in Pakistan. Though Media was controlled by both civilian and military regimes the judiciary became a reluctant companion of the military.

The second set of arguments explains that beside institutional flaws, it was the military's ambition to play a decisive role in politics that was responsible for their intervention in the civilian sphere. Military officers saw themselves as the saviour of the country and advocated a proactive role for the military to reform society. The military saw itself as the guardian and defender of the idea of Pakistan. From one perspective this rationale was applied to legitimise the military's extra-constitutional cyclic intervention in politics to protect its corporate interests. Over the years, the military has created a vast corporate empire to benefit the military fraternity. When for the first time the military assumed political power, it introduced many policies, whose sustenance is important for the military to make profits. During military rule, its fraternity appropriated vast tracts of land, owned industries, public sector enterprises. Through a quota system, they entered into the civil and foreign services, headed universities and other service sector ventures. To guard its economic interest it was necessary to be in power.

This chapter draws attention to another set of arguments that finds political parties and political leadership at the center of democracy-authoritarianism debate. The party and its leaders which led the movement for creating a new country had no programmatic vision about how the country's institutions would evolve. Unlike India which was a successor state of British India, and had effectively inherited the colonial administrative apparatus – bureaucracy, military and legal system – which were instrumental in developing democratic institutions,[5]Pakistan suffered structural discontinuity. The complex and delicate task of adjusting its people to the alien democratic mechanism was adopted by a stroke of the pen and not by any process of socio-economic changes.[6] Shuja Nawaz also notes that Pakistan tried to build a nation without building institutions that are required for a stable federal structure to evolve in a democratic and pluralistic setting.[7]A decisive factor determining the trajectory of the political system was the preference of the leadership. Sunil Khilnani argues that it was the "intellectual choice"[8]of the leadership that oriented the trajectory of the political system wherein, Maya Tudor argues that, it was the "kind of social class"[9] of the political leadership which championed the freedom movement becoming instrumental in shaping the governance model.

Initially the ruling elite in Pakistan were the Muhajirs, the *Salariat* class, who migrated from India, and started governing its provinces without having any social roots. The problem which arose was that both the politicians and the people of the provinces never belonged to each other, thus creating a kind of mutual trust deficit. On the other hand the native ruling class, feudal and tribal landlords, despised the idea of a democratic government as it could lead to egalitarian distribution of resources and an end to their exploitative practices. They have always manipulated politics in Pakistan and sometime co-opted the military. The military, which itself became landowners, saw feudal lords as partners in exploitation.

The urban elite, especially the Muhajirs, for many years remained indifferent to democratic politics. With this the lack of organisational support, the dearth of leadership after Jinnah and Liaquat Ali, coupled with political malpractices by the politicians, resulted in the weakening of democratic institutions and degeneration of politics. During this period there was not only political confusion but economic conditions also deteriorated to a great extent and as a consequence gave birth to regionalism based on ethnicity and language. Along with this, the spread of violence across Punjab due to the anti-*Ahmadi* riots in 1953, compelled the civilians to impose martial law in Lahore.[i] Martial Law was eventually withdrawn and the city was handed over to the civil administration in two months but it provided the army an experience in civil administration. Hasan Askari Rizvi observed that "the brief period of Martial Law gave the Army a valuable experience of performing the duties of civil governments."[10] It also left a sense among the masses that at a time of crisis the Army could restore peace and offer effective governance.

In March 1958, the parliamentary structure of Pakistan brokedown completely when political conditions became chaotic and political leaders failed to resolve the political crisis arising between the two wings of Pakistan. There was widespread political confusion in the country. In the wake of such a crisis, President Iskander Mirza abrogated the constitution, dissolved the national assembly and dismissed the provincial cabinets. General Ayub Khan who was given the charge of Pakistan's administration imposed Martial Law and became the Martial Law Administrator. It was a very peaceful takeover

i. Martial Law was imposed in Lahore on 6 March 1953. Major General Azam Khan was appointed as the Chief Martial Law Administrator and the city of Lahore was divided into six sectors. Each sector had one Law Administrator.

by the military and no violence took place and no life was lost. The army largely depended on the civil bureaucracy to run the country and set up a unified command of the civil and military administration.

General Ayub civilianised his military government and became the President, drafted a new constitution, formed his own cabinet from the civil and military leadership and executed its programme through the bureaucracy which had an effective implementing mechanism. In the new arrangement, decisive power ceded to the military and the bureaucracy played a subservient role and political leaders acted as puppets at the behest of the military."The Army served as the brain and the civil servants as the hands of the new regime."[11]To undermine the political institutions and political leaders General Ayub designed a system of Basic Democracy, whose purpose was to provide a political basis to his regime and de-politicised the basis of the opposition. Under the new system the legislature was subordinate to the executive as his cabinet drew its support from the Basic Democrats.

The Ayub era ended and was followed, in 1969, by a short spell of the authoritarian regime of General Yahya Khan. His tenure witnessed Pakistan's most difficult period. He was handed over a regime which faced the challenges of restoring order out of political anarchy and widespread violence. Given the burning situation and the lack of a political plan made him dependent on the bureaucracy which had the experience of running the administration. He however, was credited for conducting the country's first free and fair election. He disbanded the 'One Unit' scheme and agreed to hold elections on the basis of universal adult franchise. After holding the successful election, General Yahya failed to transfer power to elected representatives and as a consequence Pakistan lost its Eastern wing. The defeated General Yahya had to quit office, and on 20 December 1971 Zulfikar Ali Bhutto, the leader of Pakistan Peoples Party was sworn in as the new President and Chief Martial Law Administrator of the remaining Pakistan.

The First Democratic Government: A Popular Autocracy

> It is perfectly possible to pervert the Constitution, without changing its form, by merely changing the form of the administration and to make it inconsistent and opposed to the spirit of the Constitution.[12]

These were the cautionary words of B.R. Ambedkar, the architect of the Indian constitution, to the Indian Constitution Assembly. The Politics of Bhutto in Pakistan was an example of how administrative twisting could undermine the constitution, and it did not matter how democratic it was in popular perspective. After picking up the shattered pieces of what remained of post-partition Pakistan, Zulfikar Ali Bhutto, the chairman of Pakistan Peoples Party (PPP) and the first elected Prime Minister of the country, faced with the challenges of constitution drafting, balancing civil-military relations, recalibrating center-province ties and building democratic institutions. He was in a complicated situation as along with legal, administrative, political and social reforms, he also had to control the traditional power elite – political, military, and bureaucratic leadership – and accommodate his electoral constituency which voted him to power. The complexity was that his support base was constituted of groups "modernised" under the Ayub era, an "extreme left," and the elements of a "large land aristocracy."[13]He initiated various policies and programmes which attempted to undercut the power of the traditional elites and create space for new aspirants. In this process, he had to readjust and rearrange economic-structures, civil-military relations and bureaucratic systems. Along with these systemic restructuring he had to satisfy the social aspirations of ideological groups such as the – Islamist, Leftist and Liberals – who were part of Bhutto's composite social base. In his attempt to transit Pakistan from one socio-politico system to another he made certain institutional, legal and social changes that bore implications for democracy in the country. He modified components of administration to the extent that Pakistan virtually lived under an undeclared emergency. The following sections attempts to examine Bhutto's various initiatives and experiments *vis-à-vis* democracy in Pakistan.

Constitution Drafting and Institution Building

Pakistan took nine years to frame its first Constitution which declared it as an Islamic Republic. The constitution decided in favour of a parliamentary form of government in which the executive authority was vested in the Prime Minister and was to be exercised by him in accordance with the Constitution. It characterised a federal structure which clearly laid out the power-sharing provisions between the union and federating units. The

President was to be elected by an Electoral College comprising members of the National Assembly and Provincial Assemblies. The President, on the advice of the Cabinet, was entrusted with multifarious functions. Some of the key appointments, such as those of the Chief Justice of the Supreme Court and judges of the Supreme Court and High Courts, the Governors of the provinces, the Advocate-General, and principal military officers, were made by the President on the advice of the cabinet.

In 1958, just two years after the constitution came into effect it was put in abeyance by the military government of General Ayub. The first military regime introduced its own constitution in 1962 which transferred the parliamentary form to a presidential system, where the President became the repository of all powers. After assuming power Bhutto was faced with the challenge of drafting a new constitution. The initial year of his rule was guided by the Interim Constitution of 1972 that maintained the presidential system. Bhutto must be credited for the drafting of 1973 Constitution that reintroduced a parliamentary system on federal principles.

The constitution of 1973 restored a federal parliamentary system. Within its provision the Prime Minister was to be the chief executive accountable to the National Assembly elected on the basis of universal adult franchise. Heads of the provincial governments were answerable to their respective provincial assemblies. The constitution established a Bicameral Legislature with a lower house called the National Assembly and an upper house called the Senate.[ii] The members of the National Assembly are elected directly, while the Senate members are elected by the provincial assemblies for equal representation of federating units.[iii] The powers of tabling and passing money bills resided with the lower house

ii. In the Senate provinces were given equal representation with tribal areas given certain seats. Senators are elected by joint sittings of National and Provincial Assemblies for a term of six years. Unlike the National Assembly, the Senate cannot be dissolved. But decisive power resides with National Assembly as the Senate can only delay a bill passed by the lower house.

iii. The Senate was established under the provision of Article 59 of the constitution of 1973. At that time it had 64 senators in which 14 each were from four provinces with additional 8 from tribal areas. The numbers were revised many times. The Senate membership was raised to 100 by General Pervez Musharraf through the Legal Framework Order (LFO), 2002. Presently the Senate has 104 senators, in which each province represents 23 senators while 12 come from tribal areas.

and the senate has no say in such matters. The powers of the President, who is to be elected by absolute majority in a joint session of the Senate and the National Assembly, were reduced. The Prime Minister enjoyed a wide range of powers and to move a no-confidence motion against the PM, the mover has to give the successor's name approved by two-thirds majority of the total membership of the National Assembly. The constitution established three legislative lists— federal, provincial and concurrent. The federal government possesses exclusive right to legislate on items enumerated in the federal list, while rights to legislate on common matters have been enumerated in the concurrent list. A striking feature of the 1973 constitution was the insertion of the provision that would hold any act of unconstitutional abrogation of constitution as an act of 'High Treason.' The constitution also laid a provision to establish an independent judiciary and made removal of judges difficult before the end of their term.

Restructuring the Institutions

> From Napoléon I imbibed the politics of power.
> From the Pamphlet [Communist Manifesto] I absorbed the politics of poverty.[14]

The politics of power was reflected in Bhutto's conviction, practice and policies which were introduced in the short period he ruled. Essentially, a feudal, he had always relished the idea of command and ensured that all power flowed from him alone. The systemic revamping of the bureaucracy, the creation of the Federal Security Force, the humiliation and reorganisation of the military and the suppression of critics and political opposition were a reflection of his "politics of power". On the other hand, a populist leader surrounded by socialist politicians, Bhutto also made "politics of poverty" a part of his grand agenda. Measures such as nationalisation of industries, land reforms, agrarian reforms and labour legislations were the important elements of his populist promise. The following sections discuss these two sets of measures primarily motivated by these two variants of politics that shaped Bhutto's politics.

Land Reforms

The landless peasants and tenants participated in the Pakistan movement, hoping that a separate state for Muslims would change the exploitative structure of the landownership primarily dominated by Hindus and exploitative landlords. At the time of partition a few thousand big and medium level landlords owned excessive amount of land in West Pakistan. In 1947 in Sindh only 8 per cent of landlords were holding 54.4 per cent land out of the total of 3, 37,665 land owners in the province.[iv] In Punjab less than 1 per cent big and medium landlords had control over 23.5 per cent land.[v] In real size this one per cent of Punjabi landlords were controlling 6.6 million acres, while 8 per cent of Sindhi landlords had control over only 4.5 million acres land due to the difference in the size of landholding. Partition in turn contributed to the strength of the landlords as dislocation of Hindus and Sikhs enabled the Punjabi Muslim landed gentry to capture the credit and the produce market and to also appropriate the vast tracts of arable lands (abandoned by the Hindus and Sikhs who had migrated to India) by paying off the local and provincial administration and police.[15] In Sindh, according to one estimate, "of the 13, 45,000 acres of land abandoned by Hindus as many as 8, 00,000 acres were seized by Sindhi landlords."[16]

For this apparent reason the landed gentry resisted any form of land reform. They could resist this due to number of reasons and the most decisive factor was their political strength. In 1947 the Central Muslim League Council comprised 50 per cent of council members from Punjab and over 60 per cent of those from Sindh were the big landlords.[17] In the provincial elections of Punjab in 1951, 80 per cent of seats were taken by big landlords while in the 1953 provincial elections in Sindh, 90 per cent of the seats were taken by the *Zamindars*.[18] Added to this "in the National Constituent Assembly in the mid-fifties, about 70 per cent of West Pakistani members

iv. In Sindh 24,064 medium landlords (owning between 100-500 acres land) were controlling 25.3 per cent of total land while 3,045 big landlords (accounting less than 1 per cent and owning 500 acres or above) were controlling 29.1 per cent of the land. S. Akbar Zaidi, *Issues in Pakistan's Economy* (Karachi: Oxford University Press, 1999), table 2.2, p. 19.

v. In Punjab a mere 1,936 big landlords ownined 27, 88,405 acres of land (9.9 per cent) while 19,401 medium landlords were controlling 38,42,986 acres of land (13. 6 per cent). The rest of the land ownership was with 35, 43,300 land owners, Ibid.

were landlords."[19] The second significant share of political leadership apart from local landlords, was that of the Muhajirs, who in the absence of a social-base in the new state realised it was in their interest not to threaten the local feudal structure. In the absence of a sizeable industrial mode of production, land was the paramount asset in this agrarian economy and thus it became an instrument of mediation and political power.[20]Thus, the formulators of the law co-opted civil and military bureaucracy, by giving them "preferential treatment in irrigated land" in the settlement scheme in Punjab and Sindh, which in turn created a "nexus of political power between civil and military bureaucracy and the landlords" that ensured the continuation of status quo.[21] The dominance of the power elite was aptly observed by Mahmood Hasan Khan thus :

> As long as landlords occupied a central place in the balance of power, and their position remained without threat in rural areas, no land reforms could have been implemented. The political system created no new pressures which the landed elite could not successfully resist.[22]

But by 1958 the political situation had drastically changed in Pakistan. The first change came about in the Muslim League in which the landlords who had once had a dominant say were no longer the custodians of power. The second change was due to the merger of all provinces into "One Unit", which made all the provincial assemblies in West Pakistan lose their relative autonomy; the straw that broke the camel's back in this scenario was the military assuming political power through a *coup*. The new *junta* regime had no need of the support of the feudal aristocracy and thus could initiate the much needed land reforms in the country. Hence under the martial law regime, led by General Ayub Khan, West Pakistan saw its first land reform, called the West Pakistan Land Reforms Regulation of 1959, implemented under Martial Law Regulation No. 64. The regulation allowed the landlords ownership of not more than 500 acres of irrigated or 1000 acres of unirrigated land. Under this "about 2.5 million acres were resumed, and 2.3 million acres distributed among nearly 1, 83,371 tenants and small owners. This resumed area constituted 4.5 – 5.0 per cent of the total farm area in Pakistan and the proportion of the beneficiaries in the population was even smaller."[23] This did not bring any substantial change in the agrarian system of Pakistan and the tenants continued to be in stress. Against the backdrop of this situation, Bhutto was able to mobilise the peasants in his populist campaign.

In his election manifesto, Bhutto promised a socialist economy in which the power of the feudals would be reduced stating that: "The breaking up of the large estates to destroy the power of the feudal landowners is a national necessity that will have to be carried through by practical measures, of which a ceiling is only a part."[24] Thus, the much touted land reforms under the populist Prime Minister was introduced in 1972 , replacing the regulation of 1959. The new reform was called the Land Reforms Regulation of 1972 implemented under Martial Law Regulation No. 115. It was distinguished from its earlier form by limiting ceiling on landholdings and also fixing ownership to the individual and not the family.[25] The ceiling was fixed at 150 acres irrigated or 300 acres unirrigated land. It also stopped allowances for resumption of land through the regulation. Despite these radical measures only "0.6 million acres were resumed, far less than the 1959 figure and constituted only 0.001 per cent of the total farm area in the country."[26] Much of the land resumed under the 1972 reforms was never distributed and only 50,548 people benefited from the redistribution and "only 1 per cent of the landless tenants benefited by these measures."[27] The second land reform under Bhutto came five years later in the form of the Land Reform Act of 1977. Its implementation was halted by the military regime; however 1,76,000 acres land was resumed under this from which 88,000 acres land was distributed to some 13,000 beneficiaries.[28]

The tenants, cultivators and small peasants of Pakistan did not benefit much from the redistribution but did so from related measures taken by the popular government. In a popular measure in 1975, Bhutto exempted "small landowners owning upto 12 acres of irrigated land or 25 acres of unirrigated land from the payment of land revenue, local rates development cess and assessment of land revenue" benefiting 7.27 million farmers in the country.[29] With this he "offered 5 marlas of land for building houses to all those who were artisans, farm labourers, or tenants who did not own house" benefitting 7, 00,000 beneficiaries.[30] Thus the combined direct beneficiaries of these two measures were around 8 million in Pakistan. Thus an astute politician like Bhutto did not make as much of a dent in the the power structure of the landlords as he wanted to "use the landlords as his political agents" by keeping the power lever in his hand and could, at any point, fix them by using legal measures.

Although Bhutto strived to cultivate the political support of the diabolically contradictory classes his attempts at land reforms did not bring substantive changes in the feudal structure of the Pakistan society. "In practice his version of socialism turned out to be a mild form of 'democratic socialism' aimed at introducing a mixed economy in the country."[31] The feudal class assumed it as socialist democracy where land – occupied by a selected few – might be redistributed among the have-nots. Gardezi and Rashid have noted that the 'social democracy' adopted by Bhutto did not really attack the class system; instead it helped to maintain the exploitative *status quo*. The attempt at establishing a new socio-economic order by Bhutto did not succeed as the earlier structure of production was not changed by him. His model did "... not succeed in breaking the economic power of the ruling alliances of the big bourgeoisie, the landlords and the military-bureaucratic elite – indeed Bhutto paid with his life for tampering with their political power..."[32] The persistence of the power structure governed through land has remained largely unchallenged and are still alive in their spirit.

Nationalisation

To emancipate the oppressed peasants he initiated land reforms, which did not bring much change to their life and to liberate the exploited working-class he initiated the process of the nationalisation of industries. This process was part of PPP's election promise to establish a new economic order through state intervention in which key industries and financial sectors were to be nationalised. The monopolies of a few elite were to be eradicated.

Nationalisation of key industries and the financial institutions enlisted in the manifesto were carried out in two phases. The first phase was initiated in January 1972, under the influence of the PPP's left-oriented leadership headed by Mubashir Hasan until 1974 when the left elements were purged. In the first phase large-scale industries from the intermediate goods sector were nationalised. During this phase credit policies such as banking and insurance were also restructured. The second phase of nationalisation began in 1974 under the direct control of Bhutto and continued till 1977.

In this period the consumer goods sector and small production units were brought under the remit of nationalisation. The first phase was motivated by "distributional concern"[33] in which monopolies of 22 families due to the excessive wealth accumulation were curbed through state intervention.[34] The measures taken in the second phase was reactionary and driven by Bhutto's wish to "establish his peerless position: having outperformed the rightist on the *Qadiani* issues, he now sought to outdo the left within the party."[35] Both the phases, whether the phase of planned takeover of private sectors units under Mubashir Hasan or the spontaneous action directly under Bhutto, had serious political and economic consequences.

In the initial drive 31 large-scale private sector firms were nationalised in which the management of private sector were brought under the public sector. Instead of ownership the government took-over the management, thus private owners did not have to be compensated; it also banned trading of shares in the stock market; and constituted a 'Worker's Committee' to assist the management run the firm for "maximum social benefit."[36] Bhutto and his ministers held these large-scale private firms responsible for "perceived deterioration of income distribution" and widespread poverty in the country. Therefore they necessitated public acquisition to eliminate poverty and discrimination. However, Shahid Javed Burki has argued that combined share of these industries in the economy of Pakistan was not as big as propagated: "In 1972, the large-scale industrial sector accounted for 12.8 per cent of the gross domestic product and employed only 3.4 per cent of the total labour force. Its contribution to exports was only 8.3 per cent of the total."[37]

The radical and swift measures of the government sent jitters among the corporate class and they reacted sharply. Burki quoted the response of Ahmad Dawood, the second largest industrialist, to put across their point:

> If you kill [a] cow you have meat for one day.
> But if you keep [the] cow, you have milk every day. Pakistan needs milk now.[38]

This was a reflection of ambience of fear of further nationalisation emanating from the first round of public acquisition of private sector firms. It eroded the confidence of the business class to invest in such a hostile environment. To restore their confidence, in May 1972 Bhutto committed to no further nationalisation and emphasised 'harmonious coexistence' of public and private sectors in a newly created mixed economy. This commitment was betrayed first in August 1973 following summer flood that resulted in the price hike of vegetable oil. To control the price, government nationalised the vegetable *ghee* industry in which a good proportion of small and medium-sized entrepreneurs were affected. Subsequently, in the beginning of 1974 the entire credit policy was restructured and the banking and insurance system were nationalised. This resulted in further erosion in the confidence of industrial class. Many of them either moved their assets and business out of Pakistan or invested in trading, deep sea fishing, real estate and construction business, instead of production activities. This had an immense impact on private sector investment, which declined drastically, while the public sector investment grew manifold with the pumping of government money into it. In 1971 the share of public investment of the large manufacturing sector was 5 per cent, which grew to 75 per cent by the end of 1977, while in the same period private sector investment declined to 15 per cent to its 1971 level.[39] The gross fixed capital of large-scale firms in public sector rose from Rs 382.3 million in 1973-74 to Rs 5,436.9 million in 1977-78, while for the same period private sector's assets marginally grew from Rs 697.3 million to Rs 1,188.9 million.[40]

Khalid Bin Sayeed noted that nationalisation measures, initiated under the garb of socialism or mixed economy, did not lead to the creation of socialist society or economy, rather it lead to state capitalism. Sayeed, who called Bhutto's regime "Bonapartist" suggested that the state capitalism created by him enhanced the power of Bonaparte instead of bringing any "structural changes" either in the economy or the society.[41] Bhutto's nationalisation move did not generate any substantial amount of employment, neither material benefit in the economy as expected. By the end of 1976, the combined employment generated by those nationalised heavy industries accounted for just 61,731 at a very high per job investment.[42] The efforts of nationalisation did not bring material changes. Throughout this period inflation was in double digits, agriculture and manufacturing rate were in the negative, the export-import balance was in negative and employment generation was not impressive. In the view of a Pakistani economist, the data does not rationalise the economic predicament of the Bhutto era. In his opinion, the average economic performance of this era was due to a combination of "Bad Luck Factors" , which were beyond the control of Bhutto, and not because of "bad management" of economy[43] considering Bhutto inherited only half of Pakistan after the loss of East Pakistan. In economic logic it was a loss of 50 per cent of the market and a major contributor of export output. Compared to the previous "decade of development," the economic performance of the PPP regime was highly unsatisfactory.

From a political perspective Sayeed noted that Bhutto wanted complete control over all the classes: "Bhutto was primarily motivated by *animus dominandi*, that is, through the aggrandisation of his own power, he wanted to control every major class or interest weakening its power base and making it subservient to his will and policies."[44] By the end of his term he did amass politically unchallengeable power and made others depend on his mercy. But in the process he antagonised several groups. Not merely the big and small businessmen but in the end "entire bazaar became hostile and played a significant part in the 1977 post-election agitation against ZAB."[45] Omar Noman noted that "the antagonism and power of this class were evident in the opposition movement which toppled the PPP government in 1977. It played a critical role in paralysing economic activity during national strikes, thus ensuring the efficacy of the protest."[46] In addition, the workers, who were supposed to be Bhutto's supporters by benefitting from his labour legislation which ensured medical coverage, compensation for injuries and protection against arbitrary termination, turned apathetic to him. This occurred due to the curbing of trade union strikes through coercive measures such as the use of police, paramilitary forces and the Federal Security Forces. Thus the workers did not come out to defend his regime during the onslaught of the massive demonstrations.

Bureaucracy

Pakistan as a postcolonial state also inherited the institutional legacy of its colonial age. The "colonial administrators developed powerful and highly centralised bureaucratic institutions" and weak representative institutions "to help legitimise and strengthen the authority of the bureaucratic state."[47] Consequently military and bureaucracy were the most developed state apparatus inherited along with weak political institutions. The purpose of the colonial bureaucracy was to ensure public order and uninterrupted extraction of taxes that continued with minor modifications even after the colonial retreat. The bureaucratic institutions were so powerful that till 1958 it was a senior partner of the non-elected oligarchy of politicians, military and landed gentry who ruled the country. In the administrative and political disorder in the aftermath of partition the Muhajirs dominated the civil bureaucracy because of their experiences in the colonial administration. With its vast array of delivery systems, the civil service played an important role in decision-making in the political vacuum of the formative years of Pakistan.

Following the 1958 coup, the military occupied the driver's seat and the civil-bureaucracy became the junior partners. But because of its expertise in policy-execution and capacity to penetrate the remotest layer of the social system, its role remained crucial. Due to its lack of know-how in civil administration, the military's reliance on the bureaucracy increased for carrying out programmes that would garner legitimacy for its continuation in power. Simultaneously, the military regime began to replace the old guard with new inductees and reoriented them to the American military doctrine and approach to the problem solving. After assuming power in an internal coup General Yahya Khan was convinced that his predecessor "had been deceived and manipulated by the higher bureaucracy, especially the CSP, which took all the credit for the achievements of the regime and dumped all the blame on the military."[48] Thus the new *junta* regime decided to assume direct control over the bureaucracy, by inducting military officers in supervisory positions in administration and purging the 303 old guards. They were said to be purged for their being close to previous regime rather than abuse of power.[49] General Yahya then further alienated the bureaucracy through his military-style of handling civil servants — and eventually they turned into the regime's passive critics.

The real assault that bruised the back of the bureaucracy – in the name of administrative reform, reorganisation, reorientation and restructuring – came under the elected government of Bhutto. Hell bent on bending the "steel frame"[vi] he criticised the legacy of the civil service for the nation's maladies by asserting:

vi. Shaid Javed Burki in his book borrowed the phrase "the steel frame" from Prime Minister Lloyd George's reference to the Indian Civil Service in a speech to the British Parliament in 1922.

> No institution in the country has so lowered the quality of our national life as to what is called *Naukarshahi* [bureaucratic rule]. It has done so by imposing a caste system on our society. It has created a class of "Brahmins" or mandarins, unrivaled in its snobbery and arrogance, insulated from life of the people and incapable of identifying itself with them.[50]

He was of the view that the dominance of the 'administrative Brahmins' and snobbery of *Naukarshahs* needed to be deflated. He, in an address to the nation, vowed to finish "corruption and maladministration."[51] Thus to fix this ill, the reform began on 12 March 1972 with the collective sacking and demotion of 2000 civil servants, through media announcements, for them being corrupt and inefficient; within a week 500 provincial public servants were sent packing; this was followed by another series of purgings of 24 judicial and 8 Intelligence Bureau officers in April.[52] The purging continued throughout civilian period. This was a clear U-turn of his pledge to the nation that there would be no "vindictiveness" toward any "bureaucrat who has misbehaved with me in the past."[53] Bhutto also went on to fire Roedad Khan (veteran of the Pakistan Civil Service) and ordered the arrest of Altaf Gauhar (principal advisor of Ayub Khan).[vii] In the same address, Bhutto vowed not to indulge in nepotism and favouritism stating: "I am not going to permit my relations to say that we are related to Mr Bhutto. I have no relations, I have no family. My family is the people of Pakistan. My children are the people of Pakistan."[54] This promise also turned-out to be mere words, as in 1974 a prominent Urdu monthly, *Zindagi*, "identified more than 100 senior-level appointees as close relatives and associates of the Ministers in the central Cabinet."[55] Bhutto's official biographer too identified several names who were appointed by him in various ministries and secretariat.[viii]

A second measure employed by Bhutto to curb the power of the civil servants was the abolition of constitutional guarantees that provide security

vii. Other prominent civil servants who were sacked for their past behaviour with Bhutto were: Ghiasuddin Ahmad – Secretary of Defence, Aziz Ahmad – permanent secretary in the Ministry of Foreign Affairs, S. M Yusuf – successor of Aziz Ahmad, Mauzur Elahi– Chief Secretary of Sindh province, and Afzal Agha – Chief Secretary of the Punjab province.

viii. Mumtaz Ali Bhutto, Mir Rasool Baksh Khan Talpur, Jatoi, J. A. Rahim, Mubashir Hasan, Aziz Ahmad, Rafi Raza were some close associates who were given high political and administrative positions.

of tenure to bureaucrats. Under the constitutional guarantees enshrined in 1958 and 1962 constitutions, removal of public servants before their term ended was difficult and could be challenged in the court. The 1973 constitution drafted under Bhutto omitted that provision. Subsequently, through a series of Ordinances and Acts, Bhutto made the civil service accountable to the head of the administration thus leaving public servants to the mercy of the Prime Minister.[56] A scholar has noted that "The new procedure of dismissal accentuated the insecurity of the bureaucrats and further undermined their authority"[57]; the powerful public servants of the past now turned into implementer of policies from 'formulator' of policies since now the decisive power was concentrated in the hands of the political representatives. The third measure was the introduction of a system of "lateral entry" which dismantled the elite structure of the CSP in its entirety.

Under this system, aspirants were not required to go through exams conducted by the Federal Service Commission but were admitted through substandard exams supervised by the Establishment Division headed by a political representative. Along with the closure of the competitive exams the new system also removed the provision of separate training and age limitation and introduced an "egalitarian system" of training. The institution was thoroughly politicised and inducted people supportive of the establishment. Noman noted that "lateral entry system was used ....as instrument for the distribution of political patronage."[58] Under the new system 1374 officers were inducted during 1973-1977, a number three times larger than it would have been possible in the old scheme. In addition, through the lateral entries 5,000 political appointees were recruited into the public service on various grades in the same period.[59] By all these measures by the run-off of the second general election the bureaucracy had been moulded into a docile, timid and obedient party organ as by now the difference between the PPP and the government was quite blurred. A scholar made a telling remark on the bureaucracy's timidity: "So afraid were his servants that in the March 1977 general elections they went out of the way, even beyond Bhutto's instructions, in trying to secure a favourable outcome."[60] The opposition never accepted that result and the first opportunity to build democratic institutions was lost in the hands of old predators of political power, the military, with whom Bhutto had inimical ties.

Civil-Military Relations under Bhutto

When Pakistan was created it was faced with a huge internal crisis; since its borders were not defined clearly it was also faced with the problem of border security. In such circumstances national security, commonly defined as protection of territorial integrity and sovereignty against external aggression, received high priority. The definition was extended to the protection of the country from internal threat and divisive forces. The conflict situation with India allowed the Pakistan Armed Forces to secure top priority in the agenda of the National Assembly and amass half of the budget for itself. The National Assembly could only write a single line to allot such and such amount of budget for defence purposes— no detailing of the expenditure was sought. In 1951, when Ayub Khan became the defence minister he was also the serving C-in-C. He held this position till 1958 until he dislodged the civilian government. From 1958 to 1971 the country was ruled by the military, and decision-making on defence matters became the affair of the military's top brass.

The hardest challenge that arose before the first elected government was to assert and institutionalise civilian supremacy over the military and make it subordinate to the civilian authority. The landed aristocracy was willingly co-opted by the new political dispensation. The traditional political elites were accommodated in the new political system. The bureaucracy was also fixed through various legal orders in the name of administrative reforms. Bhutto employed multiple tactics — from giving constitutional safeguards to civilian supremacy against future military takeovers, creating a parallel paramilitary organisation, and restructuring the command system of Pakistan. To discourage the already humiliated military's role in politics, specific provisions were added in the new constitution. Article 245 enshrined in the constitution clearly prescribed the role of the military to "defend Pakistan against external aggression or threat of war and subject to law, act in aid of civil power when called upon to do so." Article 6 (1) laid out that any subversion of the constitution "by the use of force or show of force or by other unconstitutional means" would qualify as committing 'High Treason' while Article 6 (2) gave parliament the power to make law against the guilty of high treason. The parliament made a law in 1973 that prescribed death penalty for such an attempt, thus giving constitutional protection to civilian supremacy against any possible military takeover. The Third Schedule of the constitution also required members of the armed forces to take an "oath of office" and pledged not to engage in any political activity.

As a political protégé of General Ayub Khan and also someone who had served in his military regime, Bhutto was well aware of the military's institutional strength. Just within two years of assuming power, Bhutto realised the strength of the military's relative autonomy and limitation of his government to command its services. A year after the forming of government Bhutto had to confront "an *abortive* coup plan involving approximately forty officers," and in 1972 friction arose with the armed force "over the refusal of a general to supply troops to quell striking police men engaged in a pay dispute in Punjab."[61] Such experiences compelled him to minimise his reliance on the armed forces to maintain law and order. Thus, he decided to raise his own paramilitary force that would remain under his complete control and in turn reduce the government's dependency on the military not fully subservient to civilian authority.

The outcome was the creation of the Federal Security Force (FSF) in October 1972, with its headquarters in Lahore. In 1974, the total strength of the FSF was 13,875 men and officers and by 1976 the strength rose to 18,563.[62] Bhutto's *raison d'ètre* for creating the FSF was outlined in his note to his chief security advisor. Underpinning his fear of a military takeover the note said:

> The people come out on the streets on the least pretext. They violently defy established authority. Many of them have now become experts in the art of guerilla tactics. Bloody clashes lead to more bloody clashes and the situation deteriorates so much that it becomes necessary to call upon the armed forces to intervene. *Once the armed forces intervene they play according to their own rules. It is necessary for a civilian Government to avoid seeking the assistances of the armed forces in dealing with its responsibilities and problems* (emphasis added). The police force in our country is terribly inadequate and badly equipped...We must make provisions for a first class force.[63]

Though the FSF received legislative sanctions through an act of parliament, the army displayed its displeasure of such a force which was deemed to function parallel to it. The army refused to train the FSF and also blocked the acquisition of tanks and necessary equipment needed by it. The FSF became an instrument of coercion and was "used ruthlessly to bully and intimidate the opposition" and also to disrupt political meetings of opposition parties.[64] During a National Assembly session in 1975, the FSF was brought in and "several protesting opposition members were beaten and physically ejected from the assembly."[65] Bhutto's commentary on the functioning of the FSF was reflective of its failure and degeneration. Noman further argued that it was the coercive use of the FSF to repress civilian leaders that undermined the development of participatory institutions needed to prevent military intervention and contributed to the widespread feeling of betrayal and glued all opposition together against Bhutto.[66]

Besides the constitutional safeguard and creation of the FSF the most crucial element of civil-military relations under Bhutto was the restructuring of the military command-system. Bhutto assumed power at time when the military's reputation was at the lowest. The apex court of the country also pronounced the assumption of power by Yahya Khan as "illegal and unconstitutional."[67] Against this backdrop, along with the restructuring, he also clipped the wings of the military. In an address to the nation he vowed to root out "Bonapartic influences" from the military. During this period, the already disgraced and demoralised military was severely criticised and "described as an anti-people force which supported 'status-quo' forces in the society."[68] The civilian government also constituted a commission to inquire into the debacle of 1971.[ix]The reports of the commission have never been published. In a "cleaning up campaign" Bhutto relieved 43 senior officers associated with Yahya Khan's regime.[69] In March 1972, the top military brass was stunned when the Chief of Army Staff and the Chief of Air Staff were removed on allegations of interfering in the Hamoodur Rehman Commission inquiry.

The restructuring in the military high-command was brought in

ix. Just after the separation of the East Wing in December 1971 Zulfikar Ali Bhutto set-up an inquiry commission under the chairmanship of Justice Hamoodur Rahman, the Chief Justice of the Supreme Court. The commission was tasked to inquire into the facts of the 1971 debacle. The commission questioned total 213 persons including Chiefs of Staff of all the three services, senior commanders and political leaders including Zulfikar Ali Bhutto.

by introducing changes in its administrative arrangement. The Bhutto administration also introduced the country's first 'White Paper' on Higher Defence Organisation (HDO) on 11 May 1976.[70] This was one such effort from the Bhutto government to keep the military subordinate to the civilians. Under the new structure of HDO, the chief responsibility of formulating the defence policy was given to the Defence Committee of the Cabinet (DCC), whereas the Defence Council (DC) and the Joint Chief of Staff Committee (JCSC) only performed advisory roles. It was expected to advice on issues related to the military aspect of national defence. The JCSC was constituted of Chief of Staffs of all the services with an appointed chairman. It was the Ministry of Defence that was supposed to perform the role of implementing actor. The DC was empowered to examine the size, function, and development of the three services and also the budgetary allocation for each. It had the authority to devise guidelines regarding the production, research and defence procurement from foreign states. The DC was accountable to the DCC which was responsible to the PM. The new defence policy arrangement pushed the armed forces into the bottom of the decision-making hierarchy. So for the first time in Pakistan's history, the military was subordinated to civilian power.

The military's reception to these systemic changes was surprisingly not hostile. Despite repeated appeals from the political parties to intervene in politics, the military restrained their activities to the military sphere and followed the civilian leadership. PNA's General Secretary Asghar Khan had written a letter to the Chiefs of Staff requesting to interfere.[71] Mia Tufail, the president of Jamaat-e-Islami too invited the military to step in but the two army generals, who were given charge of armed forces under the Bhutto government, were not influenced by these urgings. General Tikka Khan, infamous as the "Butcher of Bengal" was appointed as Chief of Army Staff in 1972. In return the military commander committed the forces under his control to "loyal execution of the commands of the legally constituted government" and kept the military detached from the civilian sphere.[72] General Zia-ul Haq who was promoted having superseded many seniors in 1976, stressed the need for military professionalism and "advised the troops to adhere to their professional role and paid tribute to the civilian government for maintaining deep interest in modernisation of the military."[73] The military also assisted the civilian government in maintaining law and order over a series of crises erupting in all the four provinces. During 1972-1977, the army was brought in on seven occasions to control the unrest in the country.

On the other hand, with the hostility in the neighbouring countries[x] and the growing arms race with India[xi] Bhutto could not afford to annoy the powerful military. In the process of appeasement, the budgetary allocation for the military in his period grew manifold on the pretext of expansion of modernisation of the military and ordnances. By one estimate Pakistan's defence expenditure during 1972-1977 rose by 218 per cent[74] and per capita spending throughout this period stood at $8.[75] By such efforts Bhutto thoroughly rehabilitated the army and tried to transform it into an instrument of his personal power. In this process, he expanded the national security wing of the bureaucracy – FSF, central intelligence department, the police forces – at the expense of the civic sector. By this process he turned Pakistan into a police state— as Eqbal Ahmad argued: "while in Ayub's time the bureaucracy had played the role of civilianising the military rule, Bhutto played the role of militarising civilian rule by expanding the national security wing of the bureaucracy and rehabilitating the armed forces."[76]Paradoxically it was both the rehabilitation and marginalisation of the military that eventually contributed to the ouster of the civilian government by the military.

---

10. In the east was India which had played a pivotal role in bifurcating Pakistan and by no measure could be called friendly to this country. In the west was Afghanistan in which a communist government under Sardar Muhammad Daud, which was formed following the ouster of King Zahir Shah in 1973. He revived the issue of a separate Pakhtunistan for Pakhtuns, dispersed on and across the Durand Line, which could influence secessionist forces in KPK.

xi. In May 1974, India detonated a nuclear bomb in Pokhran, Rajasthan. This prompted Pakistan to accelerate its nuclear programme started in 1972. This triggered an arms race in South Asia in terms of procurement of conventional weapons. "India's military expenditures in the period 1971-80 exceeded Pakistan's by a ratio of almost four to one ($30.8 billion to $8.2 billion).... Between 1973 and 1982, India's real annual military outlay increased by 53%, Pakistan's by 50%. ...Between 1971 and 1980, India imported foreign arms with a value almost two-and-a-half times greater ($3.76 billion against $1.54 billion) than Pakistan's own arms imports...for the years 1978 to 1982, India stood fourth-accounting for 6.5 % of total Third World arms imports," while Pakistan was below twentieth rank. Statistics from Robert G. Wirsing, "The Arms Race in South Asia: Implications for the United States," *Asian Survey*, Vol. 25, No. 3, March 1985, pp. 269-70.

Party Politics and the Return of the Military

The first elected Prime Minister of Pakistan was voted to power by a popular mandate. But at the end of his tenure, Bhutto's politics was closer to that of a popular autocrat. Not only his policy initiatives and handling of internal affairs but his politics too reflected his dislike for political pluralism. The short democratic interlude under him was characterised by highly autocratic tendencies. His autocratic-style of decision-making was opposed by the collective opposition and from within the party as well.

The first sign of internal fissures came from the party's left-leaning circle. The Left was one of the core components of the PPP's political movement during the military regime. During its transition period from a movement to an organised party, the PPP accommodated the extreme Left as well. Since the ban on the Communist Party in 1951, the direction-less Left also found the PPP as an avenue to carry forward its political programmes. The Left's support base was concentrated in rural KPK where it supported small peasants and sharecroppers in their struggle against the landed aristocracy, while in the urban centres of Punjab, the Left's support base was among the labour unions. During the 1970 election it was the Left's support base that voted PPP to victory in Punjab and gave it a foothold in KPK.[77] The Left component was instrumental in designing the party's populist campaigning.

It was J. A. Rahim – a Bengali communist and Nietzschean theorist – who co-founded the PPP with Bhutto, and shaped the party's political campaign. He was the architect of the party's constitution and slogan. Another Left ideologue was Hanif Ramay, who inserted the phrase "Islamic Socialism" into the party manifesto. A series of articles co-authored by Ramay and Safdar Mir in his left-oriented magazine *Nusrat* attempted to explain the meaning of "Islamic Socialism" which was aspired to by the party.[78]Their explanations of "Islamic Socialism" could be summarised as using the public sector to redistribute the country's resources to the underprivileged. However, the ambiguity also allowed a second interpretation by equating it with Islamic *masawat* (egalitarianism) that appealed to the religious Right. The philosophy of "Islamic Socialism" was a harbinger of the nationalisation drive that saw governmental takeover of private industries and services.

The purging of the Left component from the party saw the expulsion, torture and incarceration of them. Rahim who was a Bengali civil servant and political mentor of Bhutto gave him guidance on managing the civil-bureaucracy. Under Bhutto Rahim assumed various ministries but was sidelined after he had differences over his style of handling internal affairs and purging of the Left-wing. Rahim was tortured by Bhutto's secret police Federal Security Force and later jailed.[79] Like Rahim, Ramay was also given many posts once the party came to power. He first became finance minister and then Chief Minister of Punjab province. Later, he was politically silenced by making him Governor of Punjab, a non-political ceremonial post. Ramay's political successor, Sadiq Husain Qureshi, belonged to the landed gentry with no roots in the party and without any connection with the commoners.[80] Ramay was jailed in 1975. Another founding member Ghulam Mustafa Khar was appointed as Chief Minister of Punjab in 1973. A year later he disagreed with Bhutto's policies and as a consequence was removed and replaced with Ramay. In October 1975 Khar was expelled from the party. Another founding member, a Bhutto loyalist and pro-nationalisation Leftist, Mubashir Hasan resigned from the post of Finance Minister. His resignation was interpreted as a result of his displeasure with Bhutto's announcement of no further nationalisation of the private sector.[81] A few of the party dissenters joined a united opposition that was suppressed by Bhutto.

In popular perception, the PPP was a Left-leaning party with a socialist inclination; however, from the very beginning it was dominated by the landed aristocracy. By one estimate, "70 per cent of those elected on the PPP ticket in 1970 can be classified as capitalists, bankers, businessmen, spiritual leaders, and feudal lords."[82] In the same election, 9 out of 18 Members of National Assembly (MNA) from Sindh were former leaders of Pakistan Muslim League (Convention).[83] But with the departure of the Left, the traditional landlord class, found a way to enter the PPP and were willingly co opted into the party. After the purging of the Leftist elements K. H. Meer observed "the ascendency of the "Islamic" component over the "scientific socialist" wing of the original PPP alliance."[84]A party reorganisation was carried out in 1974. Meraj Khalid, a moderate, was appointed as party organisation president of Punjab province. A conservative landlord from Multan, Nasir Rizvi was appointed as party secretary-general while deputy secretary-general post was given to a radical socialist, Taj Langah.[85] Beside the conservatives, by 1976 *nawabs* and landed aristocrats dominated the provincial governments.

The Punjab governorship was given to *Nawab* of Bhawalpur while *Nawab* of Multan Sadiq Husain Qureshi was appointed as Chief Minister. The son of the former *Nawab* of Junagadh was given the governorship of Sindh while a traditional landlord, Ghulam Mustafa Jatoi, remained Chief Minister of the province. The former *Nawab* of Qalat was appointed as Governor of Baluchistan.

Apart from the internal factionalism within party the biggest challenge came from a united political opposition. The opposition was constituted by a personal and political nemesis created by Bhutto in all the four provinces. His policies toward the non-PPP provincial governments in Baluchistan and KPK were far from democratic and federal. The dismissal of the NAP-JUI government and arrest of their leaders were justified in the name of eradication of separatism. Eqbal Ahmad observed the growing trends of administrative fascism and provincial separatism in the beginning of Bhutto government. Ahmad argued that both the trends of separatism and fascism complemented and justified their existence to each other; separatism drew its sustenance from the excesses of fascist elements instrumentalised through repression of alleged separatist.[86] He further argued that "the complementary enemies, incapable of destroying each other, shall nevertheless damage the society and the people they pretend to serve."[87] The confrontation of both these mutual nemesis sharpened at the last lap of the PPP government resulting in the sacrifice of democracy at the altar of the military.

In the assembly elections, PPP barely managed to win 3 seats in KPK and even failed to open its account in Baluchistan. In KPK, a coalition of National Awami Party (NAP) and Jamitul-ul-Ulema Islam (JUI) secured a majority to form the government while in Baluchistan the NAP-JUI formed the government with the help of independent winners. Before the termination of martial law in April 1971 the PPP and NAP-JUI inked a tri-party agreement. Under the agreement the PPP was to appoint two NAP nominees, Ghaus Bakhsh Bijenjo and Arbab Sikander Khalil, as governors of Baluchistan and KPK respectively; it was also to refrain from using martial law provisions to restrict functioning of the provincial governments. In return NAP-JUI agreed to support the continuance of martial law till August, and not to oppose emergency powers of the federal government.[88] Within a few months Wali Khan realised the excesses of the federal government due to its intervention in provincial autonomy followed by non-procedural removal of civil servants belonging to the provinces.[89] Wali Khan decided to withdraw his support for the continuance of martial law. This move was interpreted as a violation of the tri-party accord.

In pursuit of complete authority Bhutto resorted to petty politics. Bhutto, who dubbed the NAP as disloyal and secessionist for its demand of greater provincial autonomy[90], got the support of Qayyum Khan, a longtime foe of Wali Khan. Qayyum Khan branded the NAP leaders as "traitors, foreign agents, puppet of capitalists and industrialist, and exploiters of Pakistani workers and peasants."[91]In December 1972 a tribal revolt erupted in Baluchistan. To control the uprising, the provincial government raised a private *lashkar* that supposedly besieged the rebellion. The federal government ordered a halt to the operation and sent federal troops to relieve the besieged rebellion. The NAP-JUI government opposed the use of federal forces but it was dismissed in February 1973. The military operation faced an armed resistance from the Baluch rebellion and continued till the imposition of Martial law in 1977.

To mark its protest against the wrongful sacking of the Baluch government, the NAP government resigned in KPK. Within a few months' time all the top NAP leaders from Baluchistan, Ghaus Bakhsh Bizenjo, Ataullah Mengal and Khair Bakhsh Marri were put in jail. A new coalition of PPP, Qayyum Muslim League (QML), independents and Aslam Khattak's party formed the new government in KPK. Khattak was appointed as the new governor and Enayatullah Gandapur as the Chief Minister. To prove its loyalty to Bhutto the new provincial government jailed more than 300 NAP workers, closed down the *Frontier Guardian* (a pro-NAP weekly) and arrested its editor; imposed a ban on the NAP mouthpiece *Shahbaz*. A year later Khattak was replaced with a big landlord of the province Syed Ghawas. In Baluchistan, the tribal *Sardar* Akbar Bugti, who had supported the federal allegations of a secessionist-conspiracy by the NAP leaders, replaced Bizenjo as governor. The first Chief Minister of Baluchistan, also a NAP leader, Ataullah Mengal was replaced with the PPP's Jam Ghulam Qadir Khan, the last ruler of Lasbela.

The final breakup point came with the arrest of Abdul Wali Khan followed by the assassination of Governor Hayat Mohammed Khan

Sherpao in Peshawar. The federal government invoked the Political Parties Act, 1962 and the NAP government was dismissed on the grounds that it was "operating in manner prejudicial to the sovereignty or integrity of Pakistan."[92]The party was banned and all notable leaders, including Wali Khan, were arrested in February 1975. Within two years' of the formation of the provincial governments both were ousted on the charges of secession, the parties were banned and NAP leaders were arrested. The arrest of NAP leaders and dismissal of the provincial governments united the opposition in parliament. A seven-party opposition coalition, the United Democratic Front (UDF)[xii]walked out of an emergency session in the National Assembly and announced a boycott of all assembly elections. However, the JUI assured its participation in the elections. Under pressure, the UDF abandoned its boycott "to resume 'resistance' inside as well as outside the legislature." Besides the NAP the main component of the opposition coalition was from Punjab and Sindh.

The main opposition in Punjab came from the Tehrik-i-Istqlal led by former Air Marshal Asghar Khan who had positioned his party as right-of-centre party and kept it detached from the UDF. Bhutto's response to Tehrik-i-Istqlal was a "news blackout and police harassment, preventing public meetings, denying access to the media, and even (by intimidating the press owners) preventing the party from producing political literature."[93] Asghar Khan in his book wrote that his party had to face the governmental backlash. The Federal Security Force was used to bully and intimidate the opposition and suppress political meetings. The opposition mounted pressure on Bhutto but he succeeded in creating fissures among them. Many QML legislatures defected to the PPP; CML and the JUI too suffered massive defection to the PPP. In 1976 K. H. Meer and Ahmad Raza Kasuri returned to the PPP's fold. The UDF also reversed its boycott stand and agreed to participate in the upcoming election but decided to nominate joint candidates against the PPP. Consequently, after the dissolution of the National Assembly and declaration of the election date, UDF, JUP and Tehrik-i-Istiqlal formed a grand electoral alliance called Pakistan National Alliance (PNA).

---

xii. The UDF was constituted of Pakistan Muslim League, Jamaat-e-Islami, Jamiat-ul-Ulema-e-Islam (Mufti), Pakistan Democratic Party, National Democratic Party (erstwhile NAP), Khaksar, and Azad Jammu and Kashmir Muslim Conference.

In the seat-sharing arrangement, Tehrik-i-Istqlal and JUP were allotted 19 and 17 per cent seats respectively while other alliance partners had to share the remaining 64 per cent seats.[94] To mark its protest against the military's sustained interference in Baluchistan, the PNA decided to give all the seven National Assembly and 40 provincial assembly seats to National Democratic Party (NDP). At a later stage the PNA boycotted the elections in Baluchistan as a mark of protest against the banning of the NAP and arrest of its leaders. Consequently all the seven seats were lost to the PPP. Mufti Mahmood, Maulana Shah Ahmad Noorani, Begum Wali Khan, Professor Ghafoor and Asghar Khan became the face of PNA's electoral campaign. Asghar Khan became *de facto* leader of the opposition, however, *de jure* it was Mufti Mahmood who was heading the alliance. The alliance partners agreed to renounce their distinct associations and release a combined manifesto.

Weinbaum in his analysis of PNA's manifesto found language that was reminiscent of that used in the PPP's first election manifesto; a vague promise of denationalisation and a clearer agenda to further Islamic way of life. The alliances also promised to quit CENTO and disown the Simla Accord. The highlights of the PPP's manifesto discussed in the chapter IV were a repetition of its 1970 campaign promises. The emphasis of the grand campaign was tilted towards a religious tone. Weinbaum who observed two campaigns underscored that, "Increasingly through the campaign, socio-economic issues took a back seat to a competition with the PNA over which party could better serve Islam. The PPP orators dropped nearly all direct references to socialism."[95] During the campaign Bhutto used all state machinery to disrupt and restrict the opposition campaign.

The media coverage was deliberately biased, especially of the *Pakistan Times*, *Associate Press of Pakistan* and the Urdu daily *Jang*. The English daily, the *Dawn* gave limited coverage to the opposition but largely covered pro-government news. The state-owned radio devoted its air time to run pro-Bhutto speeches; however the state television showed some events of the opposition. In his account Asghar Khan noted that opposition candidates were not allowed to file nominations on the seats to be contested by the Prime Minister and Chief Ministers of three provinces. As a result all these, four candidates were elected unopposed. PNA candidates who tried to file nominations from these seats were either detained or abducted.[96] The second general elections were held as scheduled on 7 March 1977. The detailed results are as follows:

Table 5.1: Party-wise Seat Share in 1977 General Election

Parties	Punjab	Sindh	KPK	Baluchistan	Pakistan
Pakistan Peoples Party	108	32	8	7	155
Pakistan National Alliance	8	11	17	–	36
Muslim League (Qayyum)	–	–	1	–	1

Such a massive defeat of the PNA was unacceptable for its leadership which had expected to win. A simple comparison of vote and seat share of two general elections suggests possible discrepancy in the result. In the election of 1970, the opposition parties which had competed with each other secured 57 seats out of 138 seats as against its abysmal performance in the 1977 election when a combined opposition secured a mere 36 seats out of 200 seats. Another paradox of the election results was that in the 1970 elections, vote share of the opposition parties was as high as 61 per cent, at a time when they had contested on their own. These were the same parties which constituted PNA[xiii] and received just 36 per cent votes in the 1977 election. They alleged that the election was rigged and fraudulent and demanded fresh elections. To register its dissent, the PNA announced boycotting the provincial assembly elections scheduled for 10 March. The opposition demanded that the elections should be declared void, resignation of the Prime Minister and replacement of the Chief Election Commissioner.

The PNA agitators started their strikes and demonstrations from 14 March. To control the deteriorating law and order situation the federal government imposed Section 144 of the Pakistan Penal Code and restricted public movement. Bhutto in a radio address on 18 March, rejected the PNA's demands of re-election and his resignation. PNA leaders and the workers were arrested and incarcerated in Kot Lakhpat Jail. By April the opposition had intensified its procession marches, strikes, agitations which halted the public life in the country. Bhutto responded

xiii. The opposition parties vote share in 1970 election as follows : Pakistan Muslim League (Council)11 %, Independent 11%, Markazi Jamiat-ul-Ulema Pakistan 8%, Pakistan Muslim League (Qayyum) 8%, Jamiat Ulema-e-Islam (West Pakistan) 7%, Jamaat-e-Islami Pakistan 6%, Pakistan Muslim League (Convention) 4%, Pakistan National Awami Party (Wali Khan Group) 3% Pakistan Democratic Party 2%.

by using excessive police force and the FSF to contain the unrest. The clash between the agitators and Bhutto's repressive measures culminated in widespread violence and chaos. Failing to control the growing unrest, Bhutto imposed Martial Law in Lahore, Karachi and Hyderabad on 21 April. The armed forces, initailly managed to salvage Bhutto's position, but when the Pakistan army realised that the anti-regime feeling was high and opposition was weak General Muhammad Zia-ul Haq instigated a *coup d'état* and assumed power on 5 July 1977. The PNA welcomed the military's intervention in politics. General Zia, the Chief of Army Staff, extended martial law across the entire country and became the Chief Martial Law Administrator. He dissolved the national and provincial assemblies along with federal and provincial cabinets.

The military returned to the political domain after seven years of civilian interval when General Zia-ul Haq staged the country's third *coup d'état* and dislodged the first elected government. The erosion of democratic institutions in the wake of a mass movement against the PPP regime opened the door for the military once again. During this civilian period, Bhutto managed to undermine the military's overt role in politics. He asserted political leadership over the military and kept them aloof from the political domain. But the mass movement led by an electoral alliance – the Pakistan National Alliance (PNA) – created a political crisis in the country which Bhutto could not resolve. As a result the military, which had been humiliated by the same regime, got its entry to politics again.

Bhutto's era was politically chaotic. It was the most repressive political period in the history of regimes in the country. Eqbal Ahmad who had observed this game of thrones between the civilian and military regimes replacing each other on and off, found the Bhutto period the most repressive of all regimes. In Ahmad's estimation, Bhutto's regime had 30,000-50,000 political prisoners while under Zia's *junta* government the numbers were just around 500.[97]Asghar Khan's figure of political prisoners under Bhutto was 83,825 – much higher than Ahmad's estimation. Although this figure was much higher than the official figure given by the Attorney General in the Supreme Court, which was 1524 people, who were arrested between 14 March and 27 May excluding the 241 people who were killed. Another scholar complied 56 cases of arrests of high profile political leaders and news editors on charges ranging from 'treason, inciting armed revolt, gun-running, attending "seditious" meetings, murder and robbery, abduction, inciting student unrest, inciting labour unrest, criticising Bhutto, complicity in language riot and preventive detention.'[98]Such a brutal repression of citizens by an elected government alienated Bhutto from popular support he received earlier. The cumulative political suffocation of his period brought socialists (his own Leftist faction), democrats (Asghar Khan), religious conservatives (Maududi and Mufti Mahmood), and secularists (Wali Khan) together to oppose him.

He was not only politically alienated but also socially isolated. The Muhajirs despised him for their systemic marginalisation, suppression of Urdu and snatching of administrative privileges. In Karachi where the Muhajirs were dominant, the PPP got only 2 seats out of 11 seats in the election. The Ahmadis who were declared non-Muslims by Bhutto also contributed to his political demise. The peoples' apathy towards him was the biggest reason for his downfall. The people were silent when General Zia seized power in a military coup and arrested Bhutto. His party, which had emerged from a mass movement, made no attempt to organise resistance, though Bhutto expected people to revolt. Bhutto appealed to the people, from his death, about the discriminatory trial against him and possible collapse of Pakistan saying: "More than my life is at stake. Make no mistake about it, the future of Pakistan is at stake."[99] But the people became silent spectators of his unjust execution. In Ahmad's view it happened because there was no one to lead them. He never cultivated any next generation leadership and everything revolved around Chairman Bhutto. Ahmad called him the Perón of Pakistan who had ensured that no popular political force emerged; he did not leave a legacy of political organisation, functioning ideology or of a coherent cadre which could mobilise the public demand.[100] The PPP as a political party, which had the first opportunity to build democratic institutions in Pakistan, acted as a totalitarian party and failed to strengthen any democratic roots. In sum the PPP demoralised and alienated all the institutions –the bureaucracy, the military, political parties, the media – all necessary for building a functioning democracy.

The Third Military Coup: Reversal of Democratic Gain

> Pakistan is like Israel, an ideological state. Take out Judaism from Israel and it will collapse like a house of cards. Take Islam out of Pakistan and make it a secular state: it would collapse.
>
> Zia-ul Haq, 1981[101]

Like the previous two military interventions this intervention that ousted the civilian regime too was non-violent, nonetheless it required rationalisation for being carried out. The apex court rendered it legal legitimacy on the basis of the 'doctrine of necessity' that justified the military's previous "revolution" a need to stabilise Pakistan. The general committed to holding elections within 90 days, but they never took place. "Once the elections were pushed to the background, Islamisation was employed as *raison d'être* of the continuation of martial law."[102] Islamisation provided the much needed social legitimacy to the martial law regime. General Zia who saw himself as the *Ameerul Momineen* – the commander of the faithful – embarked on a programme to enforce his much touted Islamic system (*Nizam-e-Mustafa*) under whose garb the country's popular culture, public policy, economic system and legal structure was Islamised as he understood Islam. Zia issued the *Hudood* Ordinance, instituted a Federal *Shariat* Court, and formed the *Zakat* and *Ushr* Committees. Islamic punishments were prescribed for theft, adultery and drinking, interest-free banking was initiated and 'Jihad' was pursued against the Soviet-backed regime in Afghanistan. But the major emphasis was on how to regulate social behavior, especially of minorities and women.

The founding father, Jinnah had assured, in his speech to the Constituent Assembly in 1947, that the rights of the minorities would be protected.[xiv] In addition, the 1973 Constitution of Pakistan also guaranteed that minorities would be free "to profess, practice and propagate his religion" and "...establish,

xiv. "You may belong to any religion, caste or creed – that has nothing do with the business of the State... we are starting with this fundamental principle that we are all citizens, and equal citizens of one state." Quoted from Muhammad Ali Jinnah, "The President's Address" at Constituent Assembly on 11 August 1947, cited in Z. H. Zaidi (ed.), *Jinnah Papers: Pakistan at Last, 26 July-14 August 1947*, Series 1, Vol. 4 (Islamabad: Qaid-i-Azam Papers Project, 1999), pp. 535-8.

maintain and manage its religious institutions" and ensured equality of all citizens by holding "all citizen are equal before law..."[103] Despite the secular ambition of Jinnah and constitutional safeguards, the religious minorities underwent oppressive experiences under civilian and military regimes alike. However, the worst was to come under General Zia, whose policies inflicted irreversible damage to the rights and progress of minorities and women. To cultivate social legitimacy he revived the discriminatory scheme of separate electorates and made the Blasphemy Law[xv] more stringent. Both the laws made religious minorities second class citizens and pushed the minorities from the mainstream of the country.

Pakistan adopted the scheme of Separate Electorates in 1948 but switched over to the scheme of joint electorates in 1957. Deviating from the scheme of Separate Electorates, termed as a 'colonial heritage', the 1962 constitution maintained the scheme of joint electorates.[104] Following that, general elections were held in 1962, 1965, 1970 and 1977 on the basis of joint electorates. After the revival of the Separate Electorate system by General Zia-ul Haq – through Presidential Order No. 14 in 1985 – the entire society was compartmentalised into five groups, Muslims, Christians, Hindus, Ahmadis, and other smaller religious groups. In the Separate Electorate system a Muslim could vote only for a Muslim and a Christian only for a Christian. Mohammad Waseem observes that General Zia reverted to the Separate Electorates, believing it would prevent religious minorities voting for the Pakistan Peoples Party.[105] He further notes that the whole scheme of Separate Electorates and reservation for minorities has become a farce. Aftab Mughal termed the scheme of Separate Electorates as 'religious apartheid' and believes that it is misused to marginalise the religious minorities.[106] Extending Mughal's proposition Fr. Bonnie Mendes calls it "nothing else but political order apartheid in the name of religion" and used to cut off Christian and other minorities from the Muslim counterparts in the election.[107] The system of Separate Electorates violates the democratic rights not only of minorities but of all Pakistani citizens by denying them the right to elect representatives of their choice.

Apart from imposing the Separate Electorated system, General Zia proclaimed Ordinance XX in 1984, which amended the Pakistan Penal Code.

xv. For the text of Blasphemy Law see Appendix D.

It added two sections 298B and 298C, two provisions specific to Ahmadis – who were already declared non-Muslim by Bhutto – which further restricts their freedom of religion and expression.[xvi]Another section of Blasphemy Law 298A is a Shia-specific provision that prevents Shias from vilifying some companions of the Prophet and other persons considered holy by the Sunnis. Observers believe that official Islam under Gen Zia's Islamisation with its stringent laws did not make people morally good: "In fact, the crime rate for theft, robbery, adultery and drinking increased under the Zia government, reaching its highest point in 1985."[108]With the growing religious intolerance, the cases of blasphemy grew during and after the Zia period even though the death penalty was made mandatory for blasphemy.[xvii] The multiplicity of legal system also poses difficulties for minorities specially the Christians and Ahmadis. Under Article 203-D of the Pakistan Constitution the Federal Shariat Court operates as a parallel judicial system. The Shariat Court has authority to declare defunct any law if it seems to be repugnant to Islam. Moreover non-Muslims[xviii] under Article 203-E (4) are barred to plead as lawyers in the Federal Shariat Court even if a non-Muslim is a party. Women were another group that suffered as severely like minorities under Zia's Islamisation.

---

xvi. The *Ahmadis* are not allowed to have public places of worship, and are thus confined to their homes for worship. They are the only one group which is not allowed to promote their faith as guaranteed by the Constitution of Pakistan. *Ahmadis* are also barred from obtaining a Pakistani passport.

xvii. From 1948-1979, 11 cases of blasphemy were registered. Only three were reported from 1979-1986. Forty-four cases were filed between 1987and 1999. In 2000, 52 cases were registered - 43 against the Muslims and nine against the Non-Muslims. See Mohammad Shahzad, "The Impact of Blasphemy Law," *Dawn*, 18 July 2002, URL: http://www.thepersecution.org/ news/dawn020710.html (accessed on 5 July 2011).

xviii. The constitution also defines the basic belief of a professing Muslim and provides a definition of a non-Muslim. The 1973 Constitution, second amendment, article 260 reads: (a) Muslim means a person who believes in the unity and oneness of Almighty Allah, in the absolute and unqualified finality of the Prophethood of Muhammad (peace be upon him), the last of the prophets, and does not believe in, or recognize as a prophet or religious reformer, any person who claimed or claims to be a prophet, in any sense of the word or of any description whatsoever, after Muhammad (peace be upon him); and (b) non-Muslim means a person who is not a Muslim and includes a person belonging to the Christian, Hindu, Sikh, Buddhist or Parsi community, a person of the Quadiani Group or the Lahori Group who call themselves Ahmadis or by any other name or a Bahai, and a person belonging to any of the Scheduled Castes.

The women of Pakistan, who were already "deprived of many rights on account of customary practices and religious decrees"[109] were further subordinated institutionally through a series of legislations. In 1980, the government issued the first of a series of directives ordering all women government employees to wear Islamic dress. The Government's attempt to Islamise dressing and the conduct of society was directed solely at women. Not satisfied with the progress being made in Islamising women's clothes, the Government issued a new directive on 15 March 1982 that all female staff in schools and colleges will be modestly dressed and will wear a *Chador* over their dress. It created an atmosphere in the country whereby all the males became the judge of women's modesty and status in society.[110] In 1980, the government decided to ban all the women participants from spectator's sports.[111] In January 1983, General Zia passed an executive order barring single women amongst Foreign Service officers from serving abroad.

The concrete step towards Islamisation arrived in the shape of the *Hudood* Ordinance. The Ordinance covers adultery, fornication, rape and prostitution (*Zina*), bearing false testimony (*Qazf*), theft and drinking alcoholic beverages. The punishments were divided between *Hadd* (Quranic) punishments, which include amputations of limbs, flogging, stoning to death and other forms of punishments; and *Taazir* (non-Quranic) punishments for lesser offences, including imprisonment and whipping.[112] The ordinance invoked many discriminatory laws against women which reduced them to second class citizens.

Under the offences of *Zina*, that is, 'sex outside of marriage', justice for women, even in the cases of rape, became near impossible. Under the ordinance a woman is required to produce four Muslims male adults as eye-witness of physical intercourse. A woman who registers a case of rape can by her own admission be prosecuted for adultery while the rapist goes free for the lack of evidence. Women are also open to punishment for adultery, even if they become pregnant, as pregnancy is the proof, while the man involved goes free. The lack of clarity in the law has resulted in discriminatory sentences being given to women. Another provision of the ordinance, the *Qanoon-i-Shahadat* (Law of Evidence), reduced the value of a woman to half of that of a man. According to this "...evidence given by a woman in a court of law will carry half as much weight as that of a man."[113]

Tariq Rahman noted that this law became more detrimental to women who have been raped. As under the evidence of law, a woman's witness is not admissible, thus a rapist could go scot free even if the rape is committed in a girl's hostel.[114]Under the provision of *Qisas* and *Diyat* (the Shariah law for murder) a woman would only receive half the compensation due to a man for the same injury. On the other hand, women guilty of murder, or causing bodily injury, would be liable to get the same punishment as men in a similar situation. The reason given for the reduced *Diyat* for women is that man is the bread winner, therefore, with his death a family loses its provider. It was not only the civil liberties of minorities and women that were suppressed, the free functioning of other essential institutions of democracy was curbed too.

One such institution was the media, an essential element without whose free functioning no democratic country can claim to be a complete democracy. The Zia government severely restricted media freedom by promulgating Martial Law Regulation 49 under which, any publication which breached the "Islamic point of view, national security, national sovereignty, defence, morality, peace or any of the purposes for which martial law has been imposed" could lead to the imprisonment of the media person(s) — read editors/ publishers. General Zia publicly acknowledged that "Democracy means freedom of the press… martial law its very negation."[115] The regulation also gave the martial law regime a free hand to impose pre-censorship and severe restriction on editors and publishers. Copies of published material and printing machines could be confiscated under the regulation.

Like the free media, an impartial judiciary is an essential component of a democratic state. It is expected to uphold the constitution, assure the rule of law, protect a citizen's constitutional and civil rights and prevent arbitrary exercise of power by the states. The judiciary legally validated Zia's unconstitutional assumption of political power, arguing that the army's intervention was necessitated due to the pressing need for political stability. In return, the military regime crippled its ability to function freely. The Zia regime removed the power of judicial review of the "legality and constitutionality of executive decision" and also deprived the judiciary of the authority to protect civil rights— thus the judiciary could not protect the fundamental rights of citizens. General Zia, through the Second Constitutional Amendment Order of 1979, established a system of military courts, parallel to the civilian structure, to try offences under martial law. In 1980 the 'jurisdiction of military tribunals was extended at the expense of the judiciary and by effect of the same order the higher courts were barred from reviewing the actions of military courts.'[116] The following year, the Provisional Constitutional Order of 1981 terminated judicial scrutiny of any politically important executive actions. It declared void all court decisions on the legality of martial law.

The judiciary became so docile that it could not protect constitutional rights of the citizens. The Islamisation of Pakistan's Penal Code, prescribing punishments according to orthodox Islam and the notorious blasphemy law discriminated against the religious and sectarian minority as well against women, and thus breached the fundamental rights of equality and right of non-discrimination guaranteed in the constitution. The higher judiciary is empowered to invalidate such laws that violate the constitution, but it "has failed to do so"[117] The Supreme Court also, rejected repeated challenges to Zia's Eighth Amendment. It is not that all the judges submitted to the military's wrath, individual judges and courts also stood against the authoritarian writ of Zia's military regime. Some courageous judges, such as Supreme Court justices Dorab Patel and Fakhruddin G. Ibrahim, refused to sanctify authoritarian interventions, and preferred to resign rather than undermine constitutionalism and the rule of law.[118] In another instance the Baluchistan High Court stayed a death sentence, passed by a special military court. The same court declared that Zia's measures for curbing the judiciary were illegal.[119]

Despite the judicial legal cover and social legitimacy rendered by *Nizam-e-Mustafa*, General Zia's military regime's political legitimacy was continuously challenged by the political opposition. The gravest political opposition came from the Movement for the Restoration of Democracy (MRD) set up in February 1981. Dominated by the Pakistan Peoples Party, the MRD demanded withdrawal of martial law, elections under the 1973 Constitution, transfer of power to elected representatives and protection of federating units. MRD's politics of agitations resulted in anti-regime strikes by political activists, students, teachers, lawyers and other occupational groups. The martial law regime responded with arrests, detention and a systemic change of the political structure and constitution. Under the new constitutional changes promulgated by General Zia in March 1981, the parties which did not register in 1979 stood defunct. Under the new constitutional order Zia created a 350-member *Majlis-e-Shura* or consultative council.

The council was an appointive body whose members were to be drawn from regular constituencies, *Ulema*, former military personnel, and different occupational groups.[120] Zia described this council as a step towards representative institutions and democracy. However, he despised electoral politics, as in his opinion "elections have given birth only to goons and chaos and confusion" in Pakistan.[121] Amidst these changes political demonstrations continued round the year. During 1982 thousands of political activists, students and teachers were put in lengthy confinement.[122] The *Majlis-e-Shura* took concrete shape in 1982. About 288 members were appointed to the council in which 100 were drawn from political parties in which 60 were from the PPP; 40 members were from the *Ulema* community and the rest had other occupational groups and the military.[123] Despite this, the MRD's political agitation for fresh election continued. Their protest got support from Sindhi nationalists who felt Sindh was being deprived of its legitimate rights under a Punjabi army. The followers of Pir of Hala, the Pir of Ranipur and the Pir of Pagaro, they continued demonstrating throughout the year of 1983. The Sufis who "resented the Zia regime's attempts to introduce the unitarian Sharia structure, since the shrines and other institutions through which they maintained their hold over their followers were anchored in local practices and traditions of the Sufis, who had preached that there was no single uniform way to divine grace," were given organisational support by the PPP and the Sindhi Awam Tehreek led by Rasul Bux Palejo.[124] In Punjab the PPP under the leadership of Begum Bhutto tried to mobilise people for similar protests but failed to generate a positive response from the masses. Nevertheless a series of small scale protests were organised in the province that challenged the legitimacy of the military regime.

To counter his political opposition General Zia decided to civilianise his regime and organised a referendum on 19 December 1984. The referendum asked the question[xix] whether the people of Pakistan approved or disapproved

xix. The question of the referendum reads as follows – "Do you endorse the process initiated by General Zia-ulHaq, the President of Pakistan, for bringing the laws of Pakistan in conformity with injection of Islam laid down in the holy Quran and Sunnah of the Holy Prophet (PBUH) and for the preservation of the Islamic ideology of Pakistan, for the continuation and consolidation of that process, and for smooth and orderly transfer of power to the elected representatives of the people?"

the continuation of the process of Islamisation initiated by General Zia in 1979. An affirmative vote in the referendum meant that people of Pakistan endorsed the Presidency for Zia-ul Haq for a further five years. The official referendum result showed that 98 per cent participants voted in favour of General Zia and extended their confidence in him and as a result, the Chief Martial Law Administrator, General Zia-ul Haq became the President of Pakistan. The referendum alone was insufficient to convince the political parties. Moreover in 1984 the Jamaat-e-Islami, which had supported the military coup and continuation of the martial law regime, and considered it necessary to establish Islamic order, turned critical against it. Following the ban on student political organisations, the suppression of media and declaration of funding of parties as punishable offence, it perceived Zia's rule as "military exploitation of Islam to retain power."[125] In April Mia Tufail, the *Ameer* of Jamaat-e-Islami announced the party's willingness to join the opposition parties to end Zia's rule but was reluctant to go with the MRD.[126] The pressure of political parties continued to mount to hold elections. Amid such a demand General Zia got the Council of Islamic Ideology (CII) to pronounce that "political parties are non-Islamic and only exaggerate political division."[127]

To further neutralise the demands of already defunct parties under the martial law system for election, President Zia conducted General Election in February 1985. The election was held on a non-party basis and system of Separate Electorates was introduced for Muslims and non-Muslims. The MRD, which had boycotted the presidential referendum, also announced a boycott of the party-less General Election and demanded the resignation of President Zia-ul Haq and fresh elections on a party basis. Nevertheless, more than 1200 candidates registered for nearly 200 National Assembly seats and MRD's absence directly benefited the Pakistan Muslim League and Jamaat-e-Islami which had decided to contest in the election.[128] Muhammad Khan Junejo, a Sindhi and PML leader, was appointed as Prime Minister. After the formation of a *de jure* elected government, martial law was lifted in December 1985. The Junejo government began to work to bring political parties into the business of nomocracy and in December passed the Political Parties Bill which laid out new regulations for political parties to function. The MRD constituents once again decided not to be registered with the Election Commission and thus stood defunct. However, the Tehrik-i-Istiklal, which had withdrawn itself from the MRD in October, decided to register itself.[129] All these efforts to move closer to a representative system looked like a farce as the elected government transferred all decisive power to the institution of the President by passing the Eighth Amendment of the constitution.

Amidst the façade of an elected government appointed by the military ruler, the MRD kept demanding fresh elections. The movement, which had been thoroughly suppressed, got a fresh impetus with the arrival of Benazir Bhutto in the summer of 1985. In August she was arrested on the charges of "raising political slogans," "taking out a motorcade," and "holding a political gathering."[130] Later she was released and exiled from the country. In April 1986 Benazir returned to Lahore and organised s series of mass rallies across the country. However, the response of the provincial governments was to detain the opposition leaders using the civil code preventive detention provisions. The PPP also suffered a setback when its senior leader G. M. Jatoi resigned from the party and formed his own National Peoples Party.

By this time General Zia withdrew himself from direct politics but controlled it from behind the curtain. His appointed tutelage parliament under the Prime Ministership of Junejo was given relative autonomy to manage political affairs. Under Junejo's watch began the process of transition to democracy. The Junejo government scheduled a Local Bodies election in November 1987. This time the MRD constituents realised their mistake of not contesting in the previous election. The vacuum created by their absence had helped new political aspirants to consolidate their position. Consequently, mainstream parties found their influence diminished compared to that of newcomers. The chief component of MRD, the Pakistan Peoples Party, therefore, decided to contest and fielded its candidates in 60 per cent of the constituencies in the Local Bodies elections of 1987. A scholar observed that the entire process under Junejo was a success "in restoring free competing politics in the country" and the new political system was perceived as a "bridge to democracy", which in turn weakened the opposition's demand for mid-term party based polls.[131] The next election was scheduled for 1990 but with General Zia's sudden death, the military agreed to prepone the polls in order to fill the political vacuum created due to situation. Fresh elections were held in 1988 in which all major political parties participated and Pakistan once again transited to elected rule from military regime.

Democratic Decay in the Second Democratic Interlude

After a long military interlude, the political scene changed and Pakistan became a democracy again under a new elected prime minister. This heralded an era of complex confrontational politics amongst a range of institutions. The confrontation between President, Prime Minister, military, judiciary and political parties created a crisis of governability in the country. From 1990 to 1999 four elected governments were dismissed by the President on various charges. Although all these governments, headed by Benazir Bhutto and Nawaz Sharif, had an identical fate of premature dismissal they still functioned under distinct operational contexts. The following section attempts to examine how in each term the power tussle of the competing forces determined the growth and decay of democratic institutions and the role the political parties played in this.

Ascent of Benazir Bhutto: An Opportunity Missed

Following the mysterious death of General Zia-ul Haq, general elections scheduled for 1990 were preponed to 1988. The political parties were now allowed to contest in the election. The political parties were still evolving; however, they were all eager to participate in the upcoming election. Pakistan Peoples Party and Jamaat-e-Islami had well developed organisational structures and, above all, experience of participating in a free and fair election. Over the course of time, both the parties lost their founders and were to contest the elections under a new leadership; the MQM led by Altaf Hussain and the PML (N) under Nawaz Sharif were the new entrants in the national competition. The PPP and MQM decided to contest solo under their respective leaders, while the religious parties and PML (N) forged an electoral alliance—*Islami Jamhoori Ittehad* (IJI), to contest collectively. The IJI campaign was targeted at Benazir Bhutto and revolved around the narrative about how a woman could lead an Islamic republic.[132]

The MQM and Awami National Party (ANP) were more concerned about their respective constituencies; however, mild attempts were made to contest beyond their catchment area. The PPP's campaign was relatively much better organised and with some semblance of programmatic promises. What benefited the PPP most was its political legacy inherited by Benazir Bhutto, rather than the campaign as such. She was projected as a victim of

General Zia's tyranny as she suffered years of incarceration and exile from her own motherland. She was also portrayed as crusader of democracy against the '*zulm*' of military's extra-constitutional rule. A segment of people felt silently guilty about her father's execution by General Zia and thus elected his daughter to power as a form of repentance. Benazir Bhutto also won the people's confidence by demonstrating her strong perseverance in fighting back with her skills of mass mobilisation and also leading the MRD after her return.

The general elections were held as scheduled and the PPP emerged as the single largest party. With the support of the MQM and a few independent candidates, the PPP formed the government. Benazir Bhutto created history by becoming the first ever woman Prime Minister of a Muslim state. Expectations were high from her as she assumed power in an ethnically and politically divided country. However, her government failed miserably to perform on the economic front and also mishandled the political scene. Her government was branded as "corrupt and incompetent," and her husband Asif Ali Zardari was labeled as "Mr. 10 Per Cent", being alleged that he was misuing his ties with Benazir to "secure industrial license for clients" who agreed to pay him 10 per cent of the price as fee for his assistance.[133] Her government was not only accused of suffering from policy-paralysis in bringing about new policies and programmes and to pass any significant legislation, but also for mismanaging federal-province relations which resulted in additional pressure on the federal government.

Benazir's management of relations with the political opposition was quite naïve as she created political enemies who would later support the military at the cost of democracy. Firstly she tried to undermine the authority of provincial Chief Ministers. In Punjab, Benazir attempted to appoint provincial official without the consent of Nawaz Sharif, who was Chief Minister of the province. To humiliate her, Sharif sent back her nominees. In a separate attempt Benazir tried to help PPP workers by initiating centrally-funded programmes in provinces with the objective of creating jobs at the district levels for party supporters. The Punjab and Baluchistan governments criticised the initiatives as federal infringement on provincial jurisdiction. The tussle between Benazir and Sharif slipped to a low level when she accused Sharif and his family of "tax fraud" and later asked the railways not to allow carrying of scrap iron from Karachi to Ittefaq foundries.[134] Indeed immature confrontational politics with political opponents was a serious mark of her failure as administrator, but what caused the premature fall of her government were her non-pragmatic relations with the armed forces.

A Pakistani academician observed that the armed forces did not appreciate her assumption of power. They suspected that she would follow her father's operational methods, which had diminished army's power and regularly humiliated them.[135] Saeed Shafqat noted that a kind of "mutual distrust and hostility existed" between the military elites and Benazir, and the armed forces agreed to the 1988 general elections hoping that her party would not win.[136] The Zia period had indoctrinated a generation of military officers hostile to the PPP and both the sides approached each other with suspicion. It is said that there was a tacit agreement between them on certain conditions which would restrain both from interfering in their respective spheres.[137] Benazir did not honour her promise and began to overtly assert her will over military affairs, which began with her formation of a committee to examine the working of intelligence agencies and their relationship with the elected government. On the basis of these findings of the committee she began to state that the Inter-Services Intelligence (ISI) was trying to undermine the functioning of her government and thus chose to control the operations of the ISI.[138] The second point of contention between the civilian government and the military was Benazir's attempt to replace the ISI chief Lieutenant General Hamid Gul against the advice of the COAS.

The ISI under General Gul was said to be the mastermind of the IJI, which pejoratively branded the Bhutto ladies as "gangster in bangles" before the 1988 elections.[139] General Gul was replaced with retired Lieutenant General Shams-ur Rahman Kallu. This act of elected government was interpreted as civilian meddling in the professional matters of the armed forces and a breach of covenant agreed upon by Benazir Bhutto. The issue of appointment continued with the appointment of chairman of Joint Chief of Staffs Committee (JCSC) that not only accentuated the ongoing conflict with the military but also brought in the President in the civil-military matters. This issue at hand was the premature retirement of Admiral Sirohey whose term was to end in November 1988. The President asserted that the appointment of the chairman of the JCSC was his prerogative under Article

243(C), a constitutional amendment made by General Zia-ul Haq. On the other hand, Benazir referred to an executive order passed under Zulfikar Ali Bhutto's term which had fixed the term for services chiefs to three years but not that of the JCSC. Therefore, she stressed that the Prime Minister had the right to decide the tenure of the JCSC as its term was not fixed by the executive order. However, in the end the President's authority prevailed by virtue of the Eighth Amendment. The Sirohey Affair indicated that Benazir strived to deviate from her commitment not to meddle in the military's jurisdiction, which antagonised both the President and the military's top brass.

The third issue of conflict between the elected and military leaders arose due to the casual handling of *Pukka Qila* incident by civilians in May 1990. The source of contention lay in the manner and timing of the operation carried out by the civilian authorities in which 30 Muhajirs were killed and 350 people died in its aftermath. The military's top echelon was not taken on board before the operation. The incident got an ethnic overtone as the Muhajirs interpreted this operation as an ethnic massacre of their community by the Sindhi government and police force. Later the Muhajirs urged the military to "impose martial law and remove Benazir Bhutto" when General Beg visited their area.[140] The COAS and prime minister did not meet for next two month due to the widening gap over this issue. The final significant tussle before her dismissal came in June 1990 when she tried to influence the army's selection board and sought extension for Lieutenant General Alam Jan Mehsud, corps commander of Lahore. The board disagreed with her recommendation and the COAS appointed Lieutenant General Ashraf Janjua to the post. In this situation the military, which perceived Benazir Bhutto as "anti-army and anti-state" but had allowed the election because it was difficult to hold onto power after the sudden death of General Zia, backed the President to dismiss her government.

On 6 August 1990, President Ghulam Ishaq Khan issued a dissolution order under the provision of clause (2) (b) of Article 58 of the Constitution inserted by General Zia-ul Haq that conferred the power on the President to dissolve the National Assembly. By virtue of the presidential order the National Assembly was dissolved on the charges of corruption and nepotism, failure to protect province of Sindh from internal disturbance, attempting to impair superior judiciary's independence and ridiculing its integrity, and undermining the Civil Service of Pakistan.[141] The dissolution order was challenged in all the provincial high courts by writ petitions filed by several PPP leaders. The Lahore High Court upheld the order and thus the final battle was fought in the Supreme Court. The apex court upheld the verdict of the Lahore High Court through a split judgment, although it considered the intention of dissolution order as malafide and targeted to tarnish the image of the PPP. Nonetheless, Pakistan had to undergo fresh election in November 1990 as the Order of Dissolution was upheld by the apex court.

Nawaz Sharif's Assent and the Assault on Democracy

Following the early dismissal of the Benazir Bhutto Government fresh elections were scheduled for November 1990. This time a less confident PPP chose to forge an electoral alliance called Pakistan Democratic Alliance (PDA) to fight against the existing IJI led by PML (N). During the campaign the President, who had dismissed the PPP government, openly appealed to the voters not to vote for Benazir.[142] The IJI projected her as an enemy of Pakistan by repeatedly branding her as an American stooge and friend of Salman Rushdie. To counter the opposition's malicious campaign the PPP took refuge in sloganeering soaked in religious overtones such as: "*Ya Allah Ya Rasool, Benazir Bekasoor*" (O God, O Prophet, bear witness that Benazir is innocent) and "*Sazishon men Ghir gayee bint-e-arz-e-Asia*" (surrounded by conspiracies is she, the daughter of Asia).[143]This rhetoric did not work for her party.

The electoral outcome expectedly was in favour of the IJI and it became the first alliance of parties that secured a two-third majority in the National Assembly. Nawaz Sharif had a clear advantage over the Bhuttos, who had ruled the country twice in the past with a fractured mandate. The new alliance led by PML (N) not only formed government at the national level but unprecedentedly also controlled all the four provincial governments. Despite being the weakest component of the troika, Sharif had better ties with the armed forces having been Zia's protégé.[144]With such strength, the Sharif government looked like a potent political force that would recalibrate the existing power-sharing agreement heavily inclined in favour of the military. He enjoyed the support of other components of the troika and initiated privatisation drives to boost the economy. The economy improved relatively during his term but political confrontation worsened. The central cause behind this was that during IJI's rule, the President and Prime Minister did not meet the opposition leader even once.[145] Instead of gaining strength, democratic institutions during his term decayed *vis-à-vis* the military bureaucratic institutions.

Within the troika, the elected civilian government represented by the Prime Minister surfaced as the weakest component. The President who represented the bureaucratic element of the troika possessed immense power to dismiss the elected government by virtue of the Eighth Amendment. The military, which had absolute command over the coercive apparatus, was the dominant component of the troika, but took a backseat by letting the elected government relative autonomy for a while. In this situation, the infighting of political parties did not strengthen the democratic forces which had remained underdeveloped for decades. During this term, the political parties had no consensus and respect for the rule of the electoral game. The internal fissures opened up within the ruling alliance of IJI when its coalition partners began to break away from it.[xx]However, the PML (N) alone had enough seats to hold onto the helm but lost its two-third majority.

To neutralise the dissenting alliance partners, Sharif announced the amending of the Constitution, which could have ensured the supremacy of Sharia law in Pakistan. Like Zulfikar Ali Bhutto and Zia-ul Haq, Sharif also took refuge in Islam to cover-up his weaknesses. To appease the religious sections he funded the *Deeni Madaris* from the Zia-created *Zakat* funds. Hijab was made compulsory for women news readers on television. The government was harsh in its handling of the media. The non-governmental media houses were charged with sedition for being critical of the government.[146] The issue that made the Sharif government look weak, was the growing violence in Sindh, which compelled him to seek the military's help. He gave a freehand to the military to curb the alleged militant elements of MQM, the PML (N)'s own coalition partner in the province. This move by Sharif dented the political relationship of his party and the MQM, which withdrew its support from the coalition and left the PML (N) government on the verge of collapse.

---

xx. For different reasons the IJI's chief religious constituent Jamaat-e-Islami led by Qazi Hussain Ahmad, its partners in Sindh, the MQM of Alltaf Hussain and the National People's Party led by Ghulam Mustafa Jatoi broke away from it at different phases.

Nawaz Sharif had not only strained his relationship with his own alliance partners and political opposition but also with the President. This was a cardinal sin as the President had the powers to punish him for his disobedience. There were a number of disagreements between them, but two flashpoints annoyed the President. The first tussle was over the choice of the new Chief of Army Staff, a position vacated due to the sudden death of the previous COAS in office. The President, who was empowered by the Eighth Amendment to make this appointment, saw Sharif's attempt to recommend a new COAS as a breach of his authority. He exercised his power and appointed Lieutenant General Abdul Waheed Kakar, a Pakhtun, superseding six senior generals, to the unease of the Punjabi Prime Minister. This move generated the second contention between Sharif and the President. General Kakar's appointment cautioned the Prime Minister and he setup a committee to repeal the powers of the Eighth Amendment by passing a constitutional amendment. He also took this debate outside the parliament to the public and declared: "if we have decided to have a parliamentary system, we will have to give requisite powers to the PM and parliament."[147] In response, the President protested that he would protect the Constitution and prevent its subversion.[148] For Nawaz Sharif, this open confrontation was not an appropriate move, given his fractured relation with his own alliance amidst the non-reconciliatory attitude of the main political opposition.

Benazir Bhutto, who had once opposed the Eighth Amendment, which was used to dismiss her government in 1990, openly supported the President's discretion. She launched a "Long March," a series of protests with the tacit approval of the President.[149] Other opposition parties, including the ex-alliance partners of IJI, joined the Long March to protest against the Sharif government. Amidst this political chaos the President dissolved the National Assembly and the Sharif government on the charges of "misconduct, maladministration, corruption," failure to "discharge its function within the framework of constitution," for "unleashing a reign of terror," against political opponents and for "subverting the authority of the Armed Forces."[150] A caretaker government was installed, headed by Balkh Sher Mazari. The benevolent President returned the favour to those political parties which had opposed the PML (N) by incorporating their representatives in the interim cabinet. Asif Ali Zardari, husband of Benazir, and her close associate

Farooq Leghari were given place in the cabinet with representatives from the Pakistan Muslim League, Jamiat Ulma Pakistan, Jamiat-Ulema-i-Islam and Tehrik-i-Istiqlal.

In response to his dismissal, Sharif filed a petition in the Supreme Court challenging the dissolution order. To the surprise of all, the court reversed the Presidential order arguing that Article 58 2(b) only refers to the dissolution of National Assembly and not of the dismissal of government. The Supreme Court thus declared the dissolution order of President Ghulam Ishaq Khan as illegal by majority of judgment of 10 to 1; the National Assembly was thus restored and Sharif's government was reinstated. The Supreme Court too later rejected the Presidential review petition. Sharif then had to win a vote of confidence in the National Assembly. He urged Benazir to cooperate with him to defeat "the enemies of democracy" in the country.[151] The PPP boycotted the emergency session of parliament called by the PML (N); nonetheless Sharif won the vote of confidence by 120 votes.[152] Following the defeat in Supreme Court, the President urged respective governors of Punjab and KPK to dissolve the Provincial Assemblies. In Punjab, a no-confidence motion was passed against pro-Nawaz, Chief Minister Wyne, who was replaced with a pro-President PML member Manzoor Ahmad Watto. Sensing that the PML (N) would manage a majority in the provincial assembly, Watto dissolved it. In KPK, Mir Afzal Khan, who had been instrumental in establishing a link between Benazir and Ghulam Ishaq Khan, and was therefore partially responsible for Sharif's dismissal, was installed as Chief Minister.[153] The ANP withdrew its support to Mir Afzal for this role but he managed to secure support from the PDA and JUI (F).

Nawaz Sharif and his alliance decided to seek judicial remedy and lodged petitions in respective high courts challenging the dissolution. This act was not taken kindly by the President. On the other hand Benazir was dissatisfied with the judicial decision to reinstate the federal government. She saw this as foul play as her petition in the past to repeal the dissolution order was dismissed by the same court. She persuaded the President to dismiss the Sharif government, but disgruntled by his letdown, she withdrew support from the caretaker government. The PPP further complicated the political situation by announcing a second "Long March" on July 16. The Long March heightened the fear of violent clashes that would have necessitated military's intervention in political matters. Amidst this growing tussle the military brokered a deal between the President and Prime Minister Nawaz Sharif, who agreed to the dissolution of the National Assembly and fresh elections were scheduled for October that year.

Benazir's Comeback and Failure to Govern

Remarkably, Benazir Bhutto who had spoiled her chance to govern the country, returned to power following fresh elections held in October 1993. The party's contestation and electoral outcome underscored two essential changes in the politics of Pakistan. First, it appeared that electoral politics was moving from alliances to a two-party system dominated by the Pakistan Peoples Party and Pakistan Muslim League-Nawaz. The second significant change that became apparent was PPP's losing edge in national politics, especially in Punjab.[xxi] In this election both the PML (N) and PPP decided to contest solo without their former alliance partners. The election outcome exhibited that PPP managed plurality but was short of a securing majority. Nonetheless, the PPP formed a coalition government. Benazir's second term was more dramatic, based on vengeance and lacked commitment to democratic forces. Tahir Amin who observed this period summarised her first year in office as a letdown period in which "the political system suffered from institutional decay, widespread financial corruption, and spiraling ethnic, sectarian and religious violence leading to near-anarchic conditions in certain parts of the country."[154]

This period also witnessed political opposition, especially with the PML (N) indulging in confrontational politics and the adoption of strategies of agitation by the PPP, a party largely weakened by internal factionalism. Benazir's handling of military affairs was not taken positively by the military establishment. A cumulative outcome of all these was loss of democracy once again. Benazir, who learned her political acumen from her father and inherited his party's legacy, appointed herself as chairman of the party. Like her father she never organised any internal election within the party. Pakistan is a typical patriarchal society in which a son is supposed to be the heir of his father. Therefore, when Murtaza Bhutto returned to Pakistan

xxi. For the relative changes of PPP's performance in previous elections, see previous Chapter IV.

after 16 years of exile, his mother Nusrat Bhutto supported him as the true heir of her husband's political legacy. Benazir thought that her mother might declare Murtaza as Bhutto's successor and preempted her by expelling her from the post of PPP's co-chairmanship. The family split grew further when police and Murtaza supporters clashed in January 1994 leaving two persons dead. An accusation of the Benazir government was that there were RAW (Research and Analysis Wing) elements among Murtaza supporters who conspired to create the disturbance.[155]

Benazir behaved as if she was besieged and resorted to the politics of vengeance. The retribution began with the arrest of Imtiaz Gul, an ex-Intelligent Bureau chief during the period of Nawaz Sharif's premiership, for conspiring against her government. Nawaz Sharif and his family were harassed on several charges of tax fraud and financial irregularities and misuse of state authority. Nawaz Sharif resorted to Benazir's old tactic of agitation politics when she was in the opposition. In September 1994, Sharif launched a "train march" from port city of Karachi to the foothill of Peshawar in which he addressed the crowds on the stations. Later in the month, he called for a strike and in October organised a massive "wheel jam" strike. These yielded partial success, but did not impact the government much. The government retaliated and arrested Sharif's father and other opposition leaders.[xxii] The PML (N) responded with disorderliness in the parliament and were beaten up by PPP cadres outside the parliament house. The retribution became overt when Zardari openly expressed to the media "that he wanted the opposition leaders to languish in jails for at least two and half years, exactly the time he himself had spent in jail during the PML (N)'s tenure."[156] In another move, the PPP government replaced top civil servants, who had worked closely with Nawaz Sharif during his first term, with civil servants who earlier worked with Benazir Bhutto.[157] In early 1995, the government impounded passports of business executives who were supporting the opposition. Sharif's properties were also seized. The PML (N), fundamentalist groups and business community responded with street power by shutting down commerce and trade.

xxii. Apart from Nawaz Sharif's father Mian Mohammad Sharif, other prominent opposition leaders arrested were Shaikh Rashid, Chaudhry Shujaat and Nawaz Khokar.

The third year of her government was more erroneous politically, which eventually culminated in Benazir's dismissal. In April 1996, Imran Khan too launched his political party, Pakistan Tehreek-e-Insaf (PTI), which was projected as an alternative to the dominating political dynasties in the country. In June that year the PML (N) called for a nationwide strike against the budget and corruption of the Benazir government. During the strike, violent clashes erupted between the police and political workers which resulted in the death of 3 Jamaat workers. In July nine parties came together for a larger demonstration and strikes that halted the daily life of major cities. In the same month 14 opposition parties, including the main opposition PML (N) formed an alliance that demanded the dissolution of the National Assembly, formation of a caretaker government, independent election commission and independent judicial commission.[158]

That year the ghost of Murtaza Bhutto returned to haunt Benazir, when Murtaza's supporters and the opposition blamed her husband Zardari for his murder. After splitting from the PPP, Murtaza Bhutto had formed a new party with the same nomenclature with a suffix *Shahid* Bhutto (Martyr Bhutto). He was killed outside his house on 20 September 1996. Nusrat Bhutto accused Benazir and Zardari for the murder of her son.[xxiii]Despite the deteriorating political situation, Benazir's government still survived due to her astute handling of civil-military relations this time. Since civilian forces were weak, *vis-à-vis* the military establishment, she was pragmatic enough to show minimal interference in military affairs. The selection of the new Chief of Air and Navy staffs and COAS were made without civilian interference. On the other hand, the military helped the civilian government curb the growing ethnic violence in Karachi.

The Benazir government managed the crisis and happily agreed to the military's withdrawal from Karachi after its Operation Cleanup. In return, the military assisted her in organising paramilitary forces under the command of Major General Mushtaq Malik.[159] Benazir was not only generous in defense allocation but also protected the corporate interest of the armed forces

xxiii.Following Murtaza Bhutto's cold blooded murder Nusrat Bhutto made a public statement that " if I could get justice I will register a case of murder against Benazir Bhutto and her husband Asif Ali Zardari," The statement is reproduced in Fatima Bhutto, *Songs of Blood and Sword: A Daughter's Memoir* (New Delhi: Penguin-Viking, 2010).

by "vigorously campaigning to procure arms from different sources, but especially from the US."[160] Though she managed civil-military relations, by not overstepping, but she committed a cardinal sin by annoying the President.

In November 1996, the President, who was supposed to be close to Benazir, issued a dissolution order by invoking Article 58 2(b) of the Constitution that dissolved her government. Meraj Khaled was appointed as caretaker Prime Minister. The dissolution order by President Farooq Leghari levied a series of charges against Benazir's government.[xxiv]This was also a reflection of ongoing contention between the President and Prime Minister over the issue of appointments of judges. To tame the judiciary's independence, the executive tried to appoint judges of its own choice. The President sought judicial intervention on this issue and referred to the Eighth Constitutional Amendment, which in his opinion empowered the President for the appointment of judges. After a long hearing the apex court gave its verdict that "the President is bound to act in accordance with the said advice of the Prime Minister..."[161]so the annoyed President dissolved Benazir's government, using his constitutional power, and constituted a caretaker government which then put her under "protective custody." Benazir filed a petition in the Supreme Court seeking the reversal of the dissolution order. The Supreme Court rejected the petition calling it "argumentatively irrelevant and scandalous."[162] A second petition was filed —that too was dismissed by the court. Fresh elections were called in February 1997.

Nawaz Sharif's Second Ascent and the Lost Battle with the Military

Within three months of Benazir's dismissal, fresh national and provincial assembly elections were held on 6 February 1997. It was the fourth election in a row, in a less than a decade, followed by the death of General Zia. Such close frequency of elections did not generate popular enthusiasm for polling. The National voting percentage was around 32 per cent, the lowest in Pakistan's electoral history. The election outcome was dramatic for both the PPP, headed by Benazir, and the PML (N), lead by Nawaz Sharif. The PPP which had formed three governments in the past was reduced to the stature

xxiv. Some of the charges were: failure to prevent extrajudicial killings, involvement of state agencies in Murtaza Bhutto's murder conspiracy, undermining the efficiency of judicial organ and violation of fundamental rights.

of a regional party. The PPP managed to win a mere 19 seats from the total of 201 seats, in which 18 seats came from Bhutto's own province Sindh. In provincial elections the PPP's performance was even more abysmal.[xxv] On the other hand, PML (N) won 149 seats, nearly two-thirds of the total. In the Punjab assembly, the PML (N) formed a government by winning a majority while in Sindh and KPK, PML (N) became part of respective coalition governments.

PTI, the new party headed by Imran Khan made a bad start by losing all the seats, including 8 seats contested by Imran Khan himself. The religious parties were reduced to insignificance, although the Jamaat-e-Islami had boycotted the elections. Despite such a humiliating defeat in the polls, the religious parties were unwilling to accept the popular mandate. Both the leaders of JUI and Jamaat declared that "they would launch mass movements to overthrow the present parliamentary system and replace it with a true Islamic government."[163]

The first year of Sharif's second term, saw the past tensions of the previous government resurrecting. First, the sectarian and ethnic violence from under the previous government reached a new high. Meanwhile, the MQM split into two factions, Muhajir Quami Movement headed by Afaq Hasan and Muttahida Quami Movement led by Altaf Hussain. Both the factions overtly indulged in cold-blooded murders of each other's sympathisers. They were virtually engaged in a gang-war. The PML (N) and MQM lead by Altaf Hussain were coalition partners in the Sindh provincial government. The MQM pressed the federal government for the payment of compensation to families of victims "who had been unjustly imprisoned, tortured and killed during the second Benazir Bhutto regime" but the government rejected the demand on the grounds of lack of resources.[164] On the other hand, the sectarian clashes between the Shia and Sunni in the form of "proxy war" between Saudi Arabia and Iran, were fought on Pakistani soil. This resulted in target killings of people from both the communities. All this was leading to an atmosphere of pervasive violence in general.

xxv. The PPP won 2 seats out of 238 in Punjab, 34 seats out of 97 in its home province Sindh and 1 each in NWFP and Baluchistan. In contrast the PML (N) made a clean swipe in the Punjab winning 211 seats, in Sindh it was third largest party after the PPP and the MQM by securing 15 seats. It emerged as the single largest party in NWFP by winning 31 seats out of 76.

The second continuing conflict was the tension between the judiciary and the executive, a start-over from the previous government. Tension arose when Nawaz Sharif rejected the judiciary's nominees for the filling of new vacancies. His defence of the rejection was that the parliament has the right to determine the size of the judiciary and thus he had decided to reduce the number of judges. Sharif's act was interpreted as an assault on the independence of the judiciary and in response the court suspended the 14th Amendment passed by the Sharif government which authorised parties to expel disobeying members. Nawaz Sharif criticised the court verdict, which invited contempt of court charges tantamount to his disqualification as Member of the National Assembly. To prevent this, Sharif agreed to revise the strength of judges of the Supreme Court to 17 and accepted all the nominees of the Chief Justice.[165] The next year was more dramatic in terms of the political tussle between the President, Chief Justice and Prime Minister.

The year began with a courageous move by the government when it passed the Thirteenth Constitutional Amendment that annulled the provision of Article 58 2(b) which had empowered the President to dissolve the National Assembly. In December, Nawaz Sharif managed to get the resignation of President Farooq Leghari and Chief Justice Sajjad Ali Shah. The cumulative result of this tussle was in favour of the Prime Minister. Sharif installed Rafiq Tarar as the new President. The year 1998 began with a growing strain in the centre-provinces relations. The PML (N) alienated its coalition partners by not incorporating them in the decision-making process. The old ally in the then North West Frontier Province(NWFP), the ANP withdrew its support when the federal government refused to rename the province as Khyber Pakhtunkhwa.[166] Another coalition partner in Sindh, the MQM, had a list of demands. When the demands were not met, MQM ministers chose to resign from the National and Provincial Assemblies. On the other hand, ethnic and sectarian violence grew in Sindh and to contain that the federal government imposed governor's rule on the pretext of restoration of law and order in the province.

The event that brought majority of political opponents on a common platform was the construction of the Kalabagh Dam over river Indus. The dam project was opposed by the non-Punjabi provincial governments. To neutralise the collective opposition the right-of-centre party PML (N) responded with an Islamic plank as well as shelved the Kalabagh Dam project. The government introduced the Shariat Bill that could undercut the powers of the Parliament, Judiciary and Provinces and concentrate excessive powers in the hands of the Prime Minister.[167] To counter this move by the federal government, and to protect their provincial interests, these parties called for a collective struggle. Twenty eight parties and ethnic groups got together to form the Pakistan Oppressed Nations Movement (PONM) in October 1998. The Sindhis, Pashtuns, Baluchis and Saraikis were the four major oppressed ethnic groups who joined the common platform to fight the domination of the Punjabis. Paradoxically, ANP and MQM, who had been vocal about ethnic oppression did not join the movement. Their resentment was not new but the product of the imposition of religion-based Pakistani identity, which in their view undermined their linguistic and ethnic identities, as well as their history and cultural heritage. The PONM leaders demanded that in accordance with the Lahore Resolution of 1940, "autonomous and sovereign" loose federations be established on the basis of the ethnic nations of Sindhis, Pashtuns, Baluchis, Saraikis and Punjabis with equal powers.[168] The demands were not met, rather, the opposition was suppressed coercively but "their failure could also be attributed to ideological incoherence, leadership feuds, organisational problems, and mutual jealousies."[169]

In the meantime, PPP opened-up a separate front by forming the 14 parties *Pakistan Awami Ittehad* (Pakistan Peoples Alliance). The alliance was led by Tahirul Qadri, a Sufi cleric and the founder of the *Pakistan Awami Tehrik* (PAT). More than political pressure, ethnic violence and the Executive-Judiciary tussle, it was Sharif's handling of civil-military relations that provoked a direct intervention of military in politics again. By repealing the Eighth Amendment, the Prime Minister acquired the power of appointing the Chiefs of military staffs, a prerogative of the President in the past. Having, acquired this power Sharif could have appointed a new Chief of Army Staff. Further, a conflict between the COAS Jahangir Karamat and Nawaz Sharif appeared on the issue of the nuclear test in May 1998, followed by India's detonation in Pokharan. According to Nawaz Sharif he had not been taken in confidence prior to the test while General Karamat recalled that they all were in agreement.[170] The tussle sharpened when General Karamat expressed his disagreement over Nawaz Sharif's insistence on the army being used in civil administration. There was an array of disagreements between them and Nawaz Sharif, quite strangely, managed to get General Karamat to resign before the completion of his term. This was a first in Pakistan's history — that a civilian authority managed to get a military chief to resign. Thereafter, Nawaz Sharif appointed a new army Chief of Staff— which was an extraordinary achievement after Zulfikar Ali Bhutto. Lieutenant General Pervez Musharraf, an Urdu-speaking Muhajir from Karachi was elevated to the post of COAS by superseding a Pakhtun Lieutenant General Ali Quli Khan and Punjabi Lieutenant General Khaled Nawaz, both senior to him.[xxvi]Sharif expected that being a Muhajir, General Musharraf would be a weak COAS and of no threat to his position *vis-à-vis* a Punjabi-Pakhtun command. According to General Musharraf he was chosen because he was the only one who never approached the Prime Minister for this job.[171]Later the same General Musharraf was to dismiss the Sharif government over many issues, including the disagreement over the battle of Kargil. The fourth military regime took over power in 1999, causing a huge setback to the progression of democracy, however tenuous it might have been.

Notes

1. Syed Sharifuddin Pirzada, *Foundations of Pakistan: All-India Muslim League Documents, 1906-1947* (Karachi: National Publishing House, 1969), p. 341.
2. Ibid, pp. 23-4.
3. Khalid B. Sayeed, *Politics in Pakistan: The Nature and Direction of Change* (New York: Praeger, 1980), p. 73.
4. Ibid, p. 71.
5. Philip Oldenburg, *India, Pakistan, and Democracy: Solving the Puzzle of Divergent Paths* (London: Routledge, 2012), p.1. Also see Sunil Khilnani, "India's Democratic Career," in John Dunn (ed.), *Democracy: The Unfinished Journey: 508 BC AD1993* (Oxford: Oxford University Press), pp. 92-5.
6. G.W., Chaudhry, "Democracy on Trial in Pakistan," *Middle East Journal*, Vol. 17, No. 1/2, Winter-Spring, 1963, p. 1.
7. Shuja Nawaz, *Crossed Swords: Pakistan, its Army, and the Wars Within* (New York: Oxford University Press, 2008), p. xxx.
8. Khilnani, "India's Democratic Career," pp. 97-9.
9. Maya Tudor, *The Promise of Power: The Origins of Democracy in India and Autocracy in Pakistan* (Cambridge: Cambridge University Press, 2013), pp. 3-4.
10. Hasan Askari Rizvi, *The Military and Politics in Pakistan: 1947-86* (Lahore: Sang-e-

xxvi. Lieutenant General Salahuddin Tirmizi was another senior officer overlooked by Sharif.

Meel Publications, 2000), p. 75.

11. Ibid, p. 92.
12. B.R. Ambedkar, the chairman of Indian Constitution Assembly cautioned the Assembly, on 4 November 1948. *Constitution Assembly Debates*, Volume 7, Parliament of India, URL: http://parliamentofindia.nic.in /ls/debates/vol7p1b.htm (accessed on 23 March 2015).
13. Shahid Javed Burki, "Politics of Economic Decision-making during the Bhutto Period," *Asian Survey*, Vol. 14, No. 2, December 1974, pp. 1133-4.
14. Quoted in Stanley Wolpert, *Zulfi Bhutto of Pakistan: Life and Times* (New York: Oxford University Press, 1993), p. 31.
15. Ayesha Jalal, *The State of Martial Rule: The Origins of Pakistan's Political Economy of Defence* (New Delhi: Foundation Books, 1992), p. 79.
16. Ibid, p. 87.
17. S. Akbar Zaidi, *Issues in Pakistan's Economy* (Karachi: Oxford University Press, 1999), p. 27.
18. Mahmood Hasan Khan, *Underdevelopment and Agrarian Structure in Pakistan* (Lahore: Vanguard Publications, 1986), p. 153.
19. Ibid, p. 160, f. n. 45.
20. Ian Talbot, *Pakistan: A Modern History* (New Delhi: Foundation Books, 2005), p. 31.
21. Zaidi, *Issues in Pakistan's Economy*, p. 29.
22. Khan, *Underdevelopment and Agrarian Structure in Pakistan*, p. 156.
23. Syed Nawab Haider Naqvi, Mahmood Hasan Khan and M. Ghaffar Chaudhry (eds.), *Land Reforms in Pakistan: A Historical Perspective* (Islamabad: Pakistan Institute of Development Economics, 1987), p. 26.
24. The 1970 Manifesto of Pakistan Peoples Party, *ppp.org*, URL: http://www.ppp.org.pk/ manifestos /manifesto1970.pdf (accessed on 23 March 2015).
25. Syed Nawab Haider Naqvi, Mahmood Hasan Khan and M. Ghaffar Chaudhry (eds.), *Structural Change in Pakistan's Agriculture* (Islamabad: Pakistan Institute of Development Economics, 1989), p. 87.
26. Zaidi, *Issues in Pakistan's Economy*, p. 31.
27. Ibid.
28. Naqvi et al, *Structural Change in Pakistan's Agriculture*, p. 90.
29. Sayeed, *Politics in Pakistan: The Nature and Direction of Change*, p. 92.
30. Ibid, pp. 92-3.
31. Jamil Rashid and Hasan N. Gardezi, "Independent Pakistan: Its Political Economy," in Jamil Rashid and Hasan N. Gardezi (eds.), *Pakistan: The Roots of Dictatorship* (London: Zed Press, 1983), p. 11.
32. Ibid, p. 14.
33. Omar Noman, *The Political Economy of Pakistan 1947-85* (London: KPI, 1988), p. 75.
34. For concentration of industrial assets of monopoly houses and their comparative loss of value due to nationalisation in West Pakistan see Rashid Amjad, "Industrial Concentration and Economic Power," in Rashid and Gardezi (eds.), *Pakistan: The Roots of Dictatorship*, pp. 255-8.
35. Rafi Raza, *Zulfikar Ali Bhutto and Pakistan 1967-1977* (Karachi: Oxford University

Press, 1997), p. 284.

36. Shahid Javed Burki, *Pakistan Under Bhutto, 1971-1977* (London: Macmillan Press, 1980), p. 114.
37. Ibid.
38. Quoted in Ibid, p. 115.
39. Zaidi, *Issues in Pakistan's Economy*, pp. 100-1.
40. Aijaz Ahmad, "Democracy and Dictatorship," in Rashid and Gardezi (eds.), *Pakistan: The Roots of Dictatorship*, p. 110.
41. Sayeed, *Politics in Pakistan: The Nature and Direction of Change*, p. 97.
42. Ibid, p. 96.
43. Zaidi, *Issues in Pakistan's Economy*, pp. 101-2.
44. Sayeed, *Politics in Pakistan: The Nature and Direction of Change*, p. 91.
45. Raza, *Zulfikar Ali Bhutto and Pakistan 1967-1977*, p. 285.
46. Noman, *The Political Economy of Pakistan 1947-85*, p. 77.
47. Andrew Wilder, "The Politics of Civil Service Reform in Pakistan," *Journal of International Affairs*,Vol. 63, No. 1, Fall/Winter 2009, pp. 19-37. URL: https://jia.sipa.columbia.edu/politics-civil-service-reform-pakistan/ (accessed on 23 March 2015).
48. Ilhan Niaz, *The Culture of Power and Governance of Pakistan 1947-2008* (Karachi: Oxford University Press, 2010), p. 109.
49. Ibid, p. 110.
50. Cited in Wilder, "The Politics of Civil Service Reform in Pakistan."
51. "Z. A. Bhutto, Address to the Nation," 20 December 1971, quoted in Wolpert, *Zulfi Bhutto of Pakistan: Life and Times*, p. 173.
52. Niaz, *The Culture of Power and Governance of Pakistan 1947-2008*, p. 112.
53. Wolpert, *Zulfi Bhutto of Pakistan: Life and Times*, p. 173.
54. Ibid.
55. Burki, *Pakistan Under Bhutto, 1971-1977*, p. 102.
56. For the list of Ordinances and Acts see Lawrence Ziring and Robert LaPorte Jr., "The Pakistan Bureaucracy: Two Views," *Asian Survey*, Vol. 14, No. 12, December 1974, p. 1089.
57. Noman, *The Political Economy of Pakistan 1947-85*, p. 61.
58. Ibid, p. 62.
59. ICG, "Reforming Pakistan's Civil Service," *International Crisis Group*, Asia Report No.185, 16 February 2010, p. 6.
60. Niaz, *The Culture of Power and Governance of Pakistan 1947-2008*, p. 117.
61. Noman, *The Political Economy of Pakistan*, p. 58.
62. Rizvi, *The Military and Politics in Pakistan: 1947-86*, p. 216.
63. Cited in Sayeed, *Politics in Pakistan: The Nature and Direction of Change*, p. 107.
64. Mohammad Asghar Khan, *Generals in Politics: Pakistan 1958-1982* (New Delhi: Vikas Publishing House, 1983), p. 74.
65. Sayeed, *Politics in Pakistan: The Nature and Direction of Change*, p. 107.
66. Noman, *The Political Economy of Pakistan*, p. 59.
67. Jan Mohammad Dawood, *The Role of Superior Judiciary in the Politics of Pakistan*

(Karachi: Royal Book Company, 1984), p. 35.

68. Rizvi, *The Military and Politics in Pakistan: 1947-86*, p. 211.
69. For detail see Ibid, Table XXV, pp. 212-3
70. For detail see Text of the White Paper issued by the Bhutto Government in May 1976 on Higher Defence Organisation in Ibid, Appendix I, pp. 311-19.
71. The letter is reproduced in his book, Khan, *Generals in Politics*, pp. 116-8.
72. Burki, *Pakistan Under Bhutto, 1971-1977*, p. 71.
73. Rizvi, *The Military and Politics in Pakistan: 1947-86*, p. 221.
74. Ibid, Table XXVI, p. 219.
75. Burki, *Pakistan Under Bhutto*, Table 5.2, p. 105.
76. Eqbal Ahmad, "Pakistan in Crisis," an Interview with Nubar Housepian, *Race and Class*, Vol. 22, No. 2, 1980, reproduced in Dohra Ahmad et al (eds.), *Between Past and Future: Selected Essays on South Asia by Eqbal Ahmad* (Karachi: Oxford University Press, 2004), p. 80.
77. Burki, "Politics of Economic Decision making During the Bhutto Period," p. 1134.
78. Nadeem F. Paracha, "Islamic Socialism: A history from left to right," *Dawn,* 21 February 2013, URL: http://www.dawn.com/news/787645/islamic-socialism-a-history-from-left-to-right(accessed on 19 December 2014).
79. Abbas Zaidi, "Whose Pakistan People's Party?" *Gowanus*, n.d., URL: http://www.gowanusbooks. com/party.htm (accessed on 15 January 2016).
80. Raza, *Zulfikar Ali Bhutto and Pakistan 1967-1977*, p. 277.
81. Herbert Feldman, "Pakistan in 1974," *Asian Survey*, Vol. 15, No. 2, February 1975, p. 111.
82. M. G. Weinbaum , "The March 1977 Elections in Pakistan: Where Everyone Lost," *Asian Survey*, Vol. 17, No. 7, July 1977, p. 606.
83. Sharif al Mujahid, "Pakistan: First General Elections," *Asian Survey*, Vol. 11, No. 2, February 1971, p. 119.
84. Richard S. Wheeler, "Pakistan in 1975: The Hydra of Opposition," *Asian Survey*, Vol. 16, No. 2, February 1976, p. 111.
85. Anwar H. Syed, "Pakistan in 1976: Business as Usual," *Asian Survey*, Vol. 17, No. 2, February 1977, p. 184.
86. Eqbal Ahmad, "Pakistan – Signposts to a Police State," *Journal of Contemporary Asia*, Vol. 4, No. 4, November 1974, reproduced in Ahmad et al (eds.), *Between Past and Future*, p. 49.
87. Ibid, p. 50.
88. B. M. Kutty (ed.), *In Search of Solutions: An Autobiography of Mir Ghaus Baksh Bizenjo* (Karachi: Pakistan Study Centre, University of Karachi, 2011), p. 163.
89. Anwar H. Syed, *The Discourse and Politics of Zulfikar Ali Bhutto* (London: Macmillan, 1992), p. 182.
90. Wheeler, "Pakistan in 1975: The Hydra of Opposition," p. 113.
91. Syed, *The Discourse and Politics of Zulfikar Ali Bhutto*, p. 183.
92. Wheeler, "Pakistan in 1975: The Hydra of Opposition," p. 113.
93. Ibid, p. 115.
94. Khan, *Generals in Politics*, p. 102.

95. Weinbaum , "The March 1977 Elections in Pakistan: Where Everyone Lost," p. 609.
96. Khan, *Generals in Politics*, p. 103.
97. Ahmad, "Pakistan in Crisis," p. 68.
98. Syed, *The Discourse and Politics of Zulfikar Ali Bhutto*, pp. 215-8.
99. Zulfikar Ali Bhutto, *If I am Assassinated* (New Delhi: Vikas Publishing House, 1979), p. 196.
100. Ahmad, "Pakistan in Crisis," pp. 73-4.
101. General Zia-ul Haq quoted in "An Engaging Dictator who wants to Stay that Way," *The Economist*, 12 December 1981, p. 48.
102. Rizvi, *The Military and Politics in Pakistan: 1947-86*, p. 249.
103. See Article 20 and 25 of the Constitution of Pakistan 1973 in Verinder Grover and RanjanaArora (eds.), *Political System of Pakistan Vol. 2: Constitutional Development in Pakistan* (New Delhi: Deep and Deep Publications, 1995), pp. 656-8.
104. Mohammad Waseem, "Joint OR Separate Electorate," *Pakistan Christian Voice*, Internet Magazine, October and November 2000, URL: http://www.suffrage-universel.be/res/pkmi03.htm (accessed on 1 July 2011).
105. Ibid.
106. Aftab Mughal, "System of Religious Apartheid," in Ibid.
107. Fr. Bonnie Mendes, "Political Order Apartheid in Pakistan in the Name of Religion," in Ibid.
108. Rubya Mehdi, *The Islamisation of the Law in Pakistan* (Richmond: Curzon Press, 1994), p. 154.
109. Tahmina Rashid, "Empowerment and Subordination of Pakistan Women through Patriarchy, Elitism, Class and Gender Discourse," in Ravi Kalia (ed.), *Pakistan: From the Rhetoric of Democracy to the Rise of Militancy* (New Delhi: Routledge, 2011), p. 85.
110. Khawar Mumtaz and Farida Shaheed, *Women of Pakistan: Two Steps Forward, One Step Back?* (Lahore: Vanguard Books, 1987), pp. 77-89.
111. Ibid, p. 73.
112. Cited in ICG, "Reforming the Judiciary in Pakistan," *International Crisis Group*, Asia Report No. 160, October 2008, p. 10.
113. Hassan N. Gardezi, "Religion, Ethnicity, and State Power in Pakistan: The Question of Class," in Douglas Allen (ed.), *Religion and Political Conflict in South Asia: India, Pakistan and Sri Lanka* (London: Greenwood Press, 1992), p. 81.
114. Tariq Rahman, "The Real Ideology of the Pakistani Male," *tariqrahman.net*, n.d., URL: http://www.tariqrahman.net/newspaper/The%20Surreal%20Face%20of%20Pakistan.htm (accessed on 26 August 2011).
115. Omar Noman, "Pakistan and General Zia: Era and Legacy," *Third World Quarterly*, Vol. 11, No.1, January 1989, p. 35.
116. Ibid, pp. 34-5.
117. ICG, "Reforming the Judiciary in Pakistan," p. 3.
118. Ibid.
119. Noman, "Pakistan and General Zia: Era and Legacy," pp. 34-5.
120. Stephen Philip Cohen and Marvin G. Weinbaum, "Pakistan in 1981: Staying on,"

Asian Survey, Vol. 22, No. 2, February 1982, p. 140.
121. Ibid.
122. Marvin G. Weinbaum and Stephen P. Cohen, "Pakistan in 1982: Holding On," *Asian Survey*, Vol. 23, No. 2, February, 1983, p. 124.
123. Ibid, p. 127.
124. Khalid Bin Sayeed, "Pakistan in 1983: Internal Stresses More Serious than External Problems," *Asian Survey*, Vol. 24, No. 2, February1984, p. 222.
125. William L. Richter, "Pakistan in 1984: Digging in," *Asian Survey*, Vol. 25, No. 2, February 1985, p. 148.
126. Ibid.
127. Lawrence Ziring, "From Islamic Republic to Islamic State in Pakistan," *Asian Survey*, Vol. 24, No. 9 September 1984, p. 932.
128. William L. Richter, "Pakistan in 1985: Testing time for the New Order," *Asian Survey*, Vol. 26, No. 2, February 1986, p. 208.
129. Eliza Van Hollen, "Pakistan in 1986: Trials of Transition," *Asian Survey*, Vol. 27, No. 2, February 1987, p. 145.
130. Richter, "Pakistan in 1985: Testing time for the New Order," p. 212.
131. Rasul B. Rais, "Pakistan in 1987: Transition to Democracy," *Asian Survey*, Vol. 28, No. 2, February 1988, pp. 130-1.
132. Anita M. Weiss, "Benazir Bhutto and the Future of Women in Pakistan," *Asian Survey*, Vol. 30, No. 5 May 1990, p. 434.
133. Anwar H. Syed, "The Pakistan People's Party and the Punjab: National Assembly Elections, 1988 and 1990," *Asian Survey*, Vol. 31, No. 7, July 1991, p. 591.
134. Ibid, p. 594.
135. Ibid, p. 591.
136. Saeed Shafqat, *Civil-Military Relations in Pakistan: From Zulfikar Ali Bhutto to Benazir Bhutto* (Boulder: Westview Press, 1997), pp. 227-8.
137. Syed, "The Pakistan People's Party and the Punjab: National Assembly Elections, 1988 and 1990," p. 591.
138. Shafqat, *Civil-Military Relations in Pakistan*, p. 228.
139. Christina Lamb, *Waiting for Allah: Pakistan's Struggle for Democracy* (New Delhi: Viking, 1991), p. 36.
140. Shafqat, *Civil-Military Relations in Pakistan*, pp. 229-30.
141. Dawood, *The Role of Superior Judiciary in the Politics of Pakistan*, pp. 83-6.
142. Syed, "The Pakistan Peoples Party and the Punjab: National Assembly Elections, 1988 and 1990," p. 594.
143. Ibid, p. 595.
144. Iftikhar Ahmed Sirohey, *Truth Never Retires: An Autobiography of Admiral Iftikhar Ahmed Sirohey* (Jang Publishers, 1995) f. n. 65 in Nawaz, *Crossed Swords*, p. 436.
145. Rais Ahmad Khan, "Pakistan in 1992: Waiting for Change," *Asian Survey*, Vol. 33, No. 2, February 1993, p. 130.
146. Khan, "Pakistan in 1992: Waiting for Change," p. 132.
147. Tahir Amin, "Pakistan in 1993: Some Dramatic Changes," *Asian Survey*, Vol. 34, No. 2, February 1994, p. 192.

148. Ibid.
149. Samina Yasmeen, "Democracy in Pakistan: The Third Dismissal," *Asian Survey*, Vol. 34, No. 6 June 1994, p. 577.
150. Dawood, *The Role of Superior Judiciary in the Politics of Pakistan*, pp. 122-3.
151. Yasmeen, "Democracy in Pakistan: The Third Dismissal," p.585.
152. Nawaz, *Crossed Swords: Pakistan, its Army, and the Wars Within*, p. 471.
153. Yasmeen, "Democracy in Pakistan: The Third Dismissal," pp. 582-3.
154. Tahir Amin, "Pakistan in 1994: The Politics of Confrontation," *Asian Survey*, Vol. 35, No. 2, February 1995, p. 140.
155. Ibid, p. 141.
156. Amin, "Pakistan in 1994: The Politics of Confrontation," p. 143.
157. Robert LaPorte, Jr., "Pakistan in 1995: The Continuing Crises,"*Asian Survey*, Vol. 36, No. 2, February 1996, p. 180.
158. Robert LaPorte, Jr., "Pakistan in 1996: Starting over Again ,"*Asian Survey*, Vol. 37, No. 2, February 1997, p. 120
159. Shafqat, *Civil-Military Relations in Pakistan*, p. 242.
160. Between 1993 and 1995 the defence expenditure was 26 per cent of the entire budget. Ibid.
161. Ibid, pp. 67-70.
162. LaPorte, Jr., "Pakistan in 1996: Starting Over Again," p. 122.
163. Anwar H. Syed, "Pakistan in 1997: Nawaz Sharif's Second Chance to Govern," *Asian Survey*, Vol. 38, No. 2, February 1998, p. 118.
164. Ibid, p. 121.
165. Ibid.
166. Hasan-Askari Rizvi, "Pakistan in 1998: The Polity under Pressure," *Asian Survey*, Vol. 39, No. 1, January-February 1999, p.178.
167. Hassan Abbas, *Pakistan's Drift into Extremism: Allah, the Army, and America's War on Terror* (Armonk-New York: An East Gate Book, 2005), pp. 164-5.
168. Rizvi, "Pakistan in 1998: The Polity under Pressure," p. 180.
169. Hasan-Askari Rizvi, "Pakistan in 1999: Back to Square One," *Asian Survey*, Vol. 40, No. 1, January - February 2000, p. 210.
170. Nawaz, *Crossed Swords: Pakistan, Its Army, and the Wars Within*, p. 493.
171. Pervez Musharraf, *In the Line of Fire: A Memoir* (New York: Free Press, 2006), p. 84.

6. From Military Rule to Democracy: Political Parties' Third Chance to Consolidate

After a decade of unsteady democratic interlude the *junta* regime recaptured its lost power under General Pervez Musharraf in 1999. It was not an extraordinary *coup*, considering Pakistan's political history, and seemed a mundane practice of bloodless alteration of power from one regime type to another.

So when the military regime established itself at the helm of political power it devised many designs to weaken the Pakistan's democratic institutions. This chapter discusses how the military regime of General Pervez Musharraf legitimised his exercise of political power, the process through which political parties were co-opted and weakened. It also looks into the challenge the civilians posed during the military regime and reclaimed the lost space of democracy. The second part of the chapter discusses the present democratic interlude that began with the ouster of General Musharraf in 2008. This part primarily focuses on the politics of political parties in this period. On the basis of political events that occurred in this period it examines the emerging trajectories of political process which is shaping the future course of democracy in Pakistan.

Soldier at the Helm Again: Democratisation Delayed

General Pervez Musharraf in his autobiography wrote that personally he was not in favour of declaring martial law but the corps commanders "were of the view that given the circumstances" it had been forced upon the army to intervene to save the country from drifting into a political crisis.[1] In his first public statement after the *coup* , while suspending the Constitution, he projected the army as the nation's saviour saying:

> The Constitution is but the part of the nation. Therefore, I chose to save the nation…The Constitution has only been temporarily held in abeyance. This is not martial law, only another path toward democracy. The armed forces have no intention to stay in charge any longer than is absolutely necessary to pave the way for true democracy to flourish in Pakistan.[2]

Once again in his memoir Musharraf rationalised the intervention as a response to the people's expectation from the nation's saviour to protect it from corrupt politicians— admitting that: "It is not unusual in Pakistan for the general public and the intelligentsia to approach the Army Chief and ask him to save the nation. In all crises, everyone sees Pakistan's army as the country's saviour."[3] Except for Nawaz Sharif's response, the *coup* was not challenged by the political opposition. Imran Khan, Benazir Bhutto and Altaf Hussain, in fact appreciated the intervention as a means to end a corrupt government.[i] Sharif challenged the dismissal of his government in the Supreme Court. Not surprisingly, the judiciary validated the military takeover of the civilian government on the basis of the doctrine of necessity, but it also instructed General Musharraf to hold elections within three years. General Musharraf wrote of his displeasure with the timeframe set by the judiciary, as before holding to the election he had wanted to restructure the political system of Pakistan for which he needed a minimum of five years.

The assumption of power and nature of his functioning received a mixed response. A Pakistani scholar called this period a "Season of Hope" when the economy, law and order and political system showed signs of improvement.[4] A French scholar called him a "new Ayub Khan" while calling Ayub Khan an "enlightened dictator" for his attempts to modernise the social, economic and legal system while remaining authoritarian politically.[5] Another scholar used more fascinating terms to describe his period as a "Janus-faced-State"a

i. Benazir Bhutto who was campaigning in exile against Sharif responded candidly after the coup saying: "He [Musharraf] was a professional soldier, and I thought that he was very courageous and brave. He'd been a commando, and a person who is a commando can take tremendous risks and think afterward." Quoted in Barbara Crossette, "Coup in Pakistan – Man in the News: A Soldier's Soldier, Not a Political General – Pervez Musharraf," *New York Times*, 13 October 1999. URL: http://www.nytimes.com /1999/10/13/world/coup-pakistan-man-soldier-s-soldier-not-political-general-pervez-musharraf.html (accessed on 4 May 2013).

reference to two-faced mythological Roman god looking at both the past and future. Examining the success and failures of the Musharraf regime the author noted that he lacked legitimacy in securing a popular mandate for his exercise of power and "much was promised but very little was delivered."[6] This section attempts to analyse his period from the framework of democracy – essentially focusing on how political freedom and civil-liberties were treated and how political parties challenged the military rule.

Restructuring the Political System

As the saying goes that 'power corrupts and absolute power corrupts absolutely,' General Musharraf who tasted power decided to hang on longer than the timeframe set by the judiciary. Aware of the fact that he would require to legitimise his longer stay in power, General Musharraf, like his predecessor, civilianised his rule. His method was slightly distinct from the former dictators, who either banned political parties or attempted to create new political system. General Musharraf devised his own mechanism to restructure the existing political system for own convenience. He first alleviated himself to the post of President by conducting a presidential referendum. He became very powerful holding the posts of COAS and President. He then embarked on controlling the legislative organ by holding elections in which his party the PML (Q) managed to form the government. To have complete control over the legislative branch, it was necessary to replace the existing political class with a new class which would also occupy the parliament. For this General Musharraf brought fundamental changes in the political system at the national and local levels.

At the national level, he devised legal-political mechanisms which marginalised and undermined the capacities of political parties necessary for the democratic system. The first impact of this design was to ensure the absence of political leaders of the mainstream opposition parties. Altaf Hussain of the MQM and Benazir Bhutto of the PPP were already in exile while Nawaz Sharif met the same fate after the *coup*. The leaders of the religious parties, those who formed the *Muttahida Majlis-e-Amal* (MMA), did not pose any political opposition to the military regime. Imran Khan of Pakistan Tehreek-e-Insaf (PTI) was not a potent force at that time and also supported the military takeover. Asif Ali Zardari was already in prison on charges of corruption. There was no political opposition to challenge the authority of the military regime even in the controlled election held in 2002.

Before the election General Musharraf made certain changes in the ground rules that clipped the wings of the existing political parties. He replaced the Political Parties Act of 1962 with the Political Parties Order of 2002. The presidential order undercut the financial capacities of political parties by restricting them from receiving private funding. In July, he issued a Qualification to hold Public Office Order of 2002, which fixed a two-term cap on the post of Prime Minister. This ensured that Benazir Bhutto and Nawaz Sharif would not be able to run for office again. He further marginalised the political parties under the Conduct of General Election Order 2002, which made graduation, or an equivalent degree, mandatory for candidates to be eligible to contest the polls. This move disqualified hundreds of political leaders from contesting the elections. On the other hand, the Election Commission recognised *Madrasa* certificates as equivalent to mainstream degrees, thus helping many *Madrasa* graduate candidates of the pro-Musharraf MMA to contest in the polls.

The restructuring of the political system and creation of a new political class supportive of the military regime at the local level started much earlier than on the national stage. In the name of decentralisation of power, General Musharraf promised to devolve powers to the grassroots level and empower the lowest tier of the government at the political and fiscal level. General Musharraf enacted the Local Government Ordinance of 2000 under which local governments were divided into three tiers. At the lowest level, were union councils representing a population of 15,000-20,000; at the mid-tier were *tehsils* or sub-districts councils; at the top of the tier were district councils headed by a *Nazim* or district administrator.[7] A *Nazim* was to be an elected equivalent of a mayor who would become the administrative head of the district. First, local government elections under the new military regime were held in five phases from December 2000 to July 2001.These local body elections were held on a non-party basis and with the exception of the MQM all other parties contested as independent candidates.

Under the new arrangement, the district and sub-district governments were delegated with more administrative and fiscal independence through increased federal grants.The provincial politicians were apprehensive of these newly created local bodies whom they perceived as an alternate power structure which could undermine their hierarchical authority. Their fear and suspicion was not unreasonable, as Ian Talbot noted, that the *Nazims* under the new district administrative system were unsure about how they could utilise their federal allocations bypassing local bureaucrats and provincial legislators.[8] Talbot further remarked that the new *Nazim* system not only failed to improve the efficacy of delivery of service but also weakened the bureaucracy and local governance as a whole.[9] The second round of local government elections were held in October 2005 in three phases. There were some minor modification in the rules, which marginally reduced the power of *Nazims*. By now provinces had new Chief Ministers loyal to General Musharraf. Under the amended Local Government Ordinance the Chief Ministers were empowered to overrule the decisions of district, tehsil and union *Nazims* and also dismiss disobedient *Nazims* if deemed necessary.[10] General Musharraf, in the name of devolution, created a pro-military political class which was politically and financially dependent on the military for its survival.[ii] *International Crisis Group* observed that the rationale for Musharraf's devolution plan was to provide legitimacy to his regime; but to have greater control over the local government he rigged and manipulated the elections and thus distorted his own devolution plan.[iii]Many of the local governments were persuaded or coerced to mobilise their constituents for favourable outcomes for the pro-military politicians.[11] The local governments provided the military its much needed support base to manipulate Pakistan's polity. The military used local governments and

ii. The ultimate controls over devolution scheme remains with the president as it was included in the Sixth Schedule of the Constitution. As a result politicians dare not focus on national or provincial issues which may annoy the President and were thus reduced to focusing on local issues.

iii. The ICG noted in its observation on rigging and manipulation of elections as: "The government's manipulation of the local polls involved gerrymandering of districts to break up support for political opponents of the military; reshuffling of officials to ensure those favourable to the military controlled elections in key areas; rejecting the nominations of opposition candidates; giving direct support to certain candidates in what was supposed to be a non-party election; and direct rigging at the polls, including ballot stuffing, intimidation and seizure of voting stations." See ICG, "Pakistan's Local Polls: Shoring Up Military Rule," *International Crisis Group*, Asia Briefing, No. 43, 22 November 2005, p. 1.

political power to marginalise political parties in the districts. Such schemes undermined the concept of federalism and strengthened regionalism.

In addition to relegating the political parties and banishing political leaders by replacing them with a new political class under the newly devised political arrangement, General Musharraf also attempted to have complete control over the civil administration and economy. Since, the military had directly and indirectly controlled the polity in the past it also nurtured its own internal economic system to support its "military fraternity"[iv] united by a strong sense of *esprit de corps.* Anatol Lieven commented that the military in Pakistan not only views itself as a different breed than society in general, but also inculcates the same feeling in new recruits that they were part of a military fraternity superior to the civil society.[12] The army sees itself both as morally superior to this class, and far more modern, progressive and better educated.[13] The economic system that gave financial autonomy to the military fraternity is called "milbus."[v] It is the system of *milbus* that gives the military a sense of confidence over the civilians. According to Ayesha Siddiqa it was the military's commercial interests that brought changes in the attitude of the military to enhance their influence in the state's decision-making and politics and increase the military's institutional control in the distribution of resources.[14]

The control of the civil administration occurred at two levels. At the first level was the occupation of civilian posts. In 2003, a Pakistani journalist, Nasir Iqbal, tabulated a list of as many as 1,027 military officers who were inducted into senior posts in the civil administration after the *coup*.[15] Iqbal

iv. The term 'military fraternity' refers to both the serving and retired military personnel, and limited number of civilians who are directly dependent on the military business complex. See Ayesha Siddiqa, *Military Inc: Inside Pakistan's Military Economy* (London: Pluto Press, 2007), p. 1.

v. Milbus refers to all activities that transfer resources and opportunities from the public and private sectors to an individual or group within the military, without following the norms of public accountability and for the purpose of personal gratification. See Siddiqa, *Military Inc*, p. 5. There are many profit-making ventures through which the military engages itself into the non-traditional sphere not related to security and exploits national resource. The Fauji Foundation group runs industries like fertiliser, cement and textiles, and Army Welfare Trust has its own farmland, rice and sugar mills. The military is also running businesses like banks, airlines, hotels and financial agencies. The Fauji Foundation also runs hospitals, medical centres, schools, colleges and technical training centres further noted that the induction of military servicemen into civilian positions ranged from the cabinet, the ministries, the foreign services and academia — to the civil service training institutions.[16] The second level of control of civil administration was to institutionalise the "army's role in the state so that the civilians would not be left to rule on their own."[17] The mechanism employed for this purpose was the formation of the National Security Council (NSC). The institution of the NSC was to formalise the representation of both civilian and military leaders in decision-making on issues related to national security, sovereignty, Islamic ideology and the integrity and solidarity of the country.[vi] The NSC was to be headed by the President and comprised the Prime Minister, provincial Chief Ministers, Speakers of the Senate and National Assembly and the leader of the opposition in the National Assembly; the military representation included heads of the three services and Joint Chiefs of Staff Committee. In 2004, the parliament, filled with pro-Musharraf members, passed the National Security Council Act under which a National Security Council was established in the country.

General Musharraf's rationale for setting-up of such an institution was that all the power brokers would be under institutional check under the council and therefore "The army chief can never take over, because he has an institution available to voice his concerns (and the concerns of the worried public) to the Prime Minister and can then allow the constitution and the political process to take their course."[18] However it is argued that the NSC's formation failed to prevent the military's intervention in politics. Hasan-Askari Rizvi in his comparative study of the Turkish and Pakistani model of such a council summarised that the formation of the NSC in Pakistan:

> ...has to be viewed in the context of Pakistan's legacy of military's expanded role in the none professional fields...part of military commanders' efforts to legitimise their role not only in Pakistan's security and defence affairs but also in the major sectors of governance,the economy and society...[19]

vi. The concept of having an institution that would give the impression of civilian control to the decision-making system goes back to the period of the first military regime of General Ayub. He then constituted a National Advisory Council similar to the NSC. Thereafter, General Zia incorporated Article 152-A in the constitution to establish a similar system but instead made amendments in the constitution in 1985 and acquired powers to dissolve the Parliament and Provincial Assemblies.

Rizvi further argued that the NSC was used to ensure the military's strong presence at the highest level in the political system and it never became constraint for General Musharraf in pursuing his political agenda, rather it was never consulted in any political and security issues including the declaration of state of emergency in 2007.[20] The two processes of controlling the decision-making system through the NSC and capturing the civilian administration by occupying civilian positions by servicemen in Jaffrelot's opinion was a kind of "colonisation of the state by the military."[21] The NSC was dissolved in November 2008 by the elected government under Prime Minister Yousaf Raza Gilani. These were the methods General Musharraf adopted to curtail political freedom. Apart from controlling the political system with the above-mentioned mechanisms, the military also gave controlled freedom to a set of civil liberties. The assessment of democracy under General Musharraf will remain incomplete without an understanding of how he managed components of civil liberties.

Managing Civil-Liberties

The international reaction to the military coup by General Pervez Musharraf was neither positive nor negative.[22] General Musharraf made his first appearance with his dogs and tried to project himself as a modern leader intending to fix the problems of Pakistan. After the 9/11 terrorist attacks and Pakistan's willingness to support the American forces against the 'War on Terror,' General Musharraf's popularity rose to its peak.[vii] An American news commentator eulogised him as a "Liberal Autocrat," who was pursuing the "path of radical political, social, educational and economic reform…"[23] The liberal-looking dictator appeared most lenient on media freedom at least in his initial days.[viii] Compared to the past regimes, the state of the media under General Musharraf looked fair and free. In the past, not only under military

vii. General Musharraf revealed in his memoir *In the Line of Fire* that Pakistan was in one sense coerced to join the American forces. According to him, right after the incident of 9/11, he received a call from Colin Powel, the US Secretary of State, who gave him no choice but to join saying: "You are either with us or against us." He further added that the meeting with the US Deputy Secretary of State, Richard Armitage was more threatening, as he candidly threatened that if Pakistan did not side with the US "then we should be prepared to be bombed back to the Stone Age."

viii. Media here includes the traditional print media, electronic media including TV and radio, and the new digital media.

regimes, but even under democratic regimes free expression was invariably muted.

In the past, both the military and civilian regimes had curtailed media freedom by invoking anti-media legislations, cutting-off advertisements or intimidation. Before General Musharraf, the two military dictators General Ayub Khan and General Zia-ul Haq openly controlled and gagged the media critical to them. General Ayub Khan established a Bureau of National Research and Reconstruction (BNR&R), which was later transformed into the Ministry of Information and Broadcasting. One of the key functions of the BNR&R was to promote the regime for which it hired "journalists who were well-known and willing to lend their names to commentaries that were published in national newspapers in support of government policies."[24] It was a subtle way of controlling dissenting voices but General Zia's tactic of restricting them was more ruthless. He publically admitted that "Democracy means freedom of the press… martial law its very negation."[25] Therefore, to regulate the functioning of the media he enacted Martial Law Regulation 49, which gave the martial law regime the powers to confiscate printing machines and published material and also a right to impose pre-censorship. The regulation made it a punishable offence if any publication breached the "Islamic point of view, national security, national sovereignty, defence, morality, peace or any of the purposes for which martial law has been imposed".[26]

After General Zia's death, the elected government of Benazir softened the media restrictions a bit. Though she was severely criticised by the media, Benazir courageously repealed 25 years old Press Publication Ordinance (PPO) under Revised Print and Publication Ordinance (RPPO) in September 1988. Before this, under the PPO of 1962, authorities could legally confiscate newspapers and arrest journalists. She took a progressive step in 1989 by ending the monopoly of the Ministry of Information and Broadcasting to issue permits for import of newsprint by the press. It was an effective legal instrument in the military's disposal to control the supply of newsprint material and thus had considerable leverage in patronising and regulating sections of the media. After her dismissal, Nawaz Sharif on becoming Prime Minister re-equipped the ministry with the same powers. In her second term in 1996, Benazir Bhutto dismantled the National Press Trust under which registration was mandatory to run printing presses and newspapers. Against this backdrop of Pakistan's anti-media history, General Musharraf's ending of the state monopoly over the media by allowing private stakeholders, received appreciation from many quarters.

Comparing the state of the media, a Pakistani scholar found that Musharraf's treatment of the media was less interfering than that of democratic Nawaz Sharif, certainly before he imposed emergency in 2007.[27] But it is further pointed out that because of the media's "middle-class obsession with shopping and celebrity" the once greatly admired press (for its critical and vigorous pursuit) had been trivialised. General Musharraf's appreciable achievement with regard to the promotion of media was the establishment of the Pakistan Electronic Media Regulatory Authority (PEMRA), which controls the functioning of private electronic media. Mohammad Waseem argued that it was a positive step as the PEMRA increased private participation and ended the monopoly of centralised broadcasting.[28] A counter argument against the PEMRA was that it was used by the military regime to silence the broadcast media by either suspending licenses or by threatening to do so.[29] In 2006, the opposition led by the Alliance for Restoration of Democracy (ARD) sought a debate in the Senate over a report which highlighted the increasing incidences of attacks, torture, kidnapping, unknown detention and murders of media persons under the military regime.[30] The worst was yet to come under the emergency in 2007.

The period from May 2007 till Musharraf's ouster in 2008 (including one month of the emergency also) is considered as the most repressive, not only because of the gagging of the press and shutting down of media outlets, but for the scale of physical violence against the journalists. According to an estimation during this period "15 journalists were killed in mysterious circumstances, 357 were arrested or abducted, later to be released (an intimidation measure), 123 were assaulted or injured and 154 were threatened or harassed."[31] A few months before the declaration of emergency PEMRA rules were amended which restricted coverage of the 'Lawyer's Movement' by the private media. Amended provisions of PEMRA were used during the emergency period to censor media coverage.

Independent Judiciary

For the proper functioning of democratic institutions, an independent and non-partisan judicial organ is as essential as free media is. A strong judiciary in an established democracy is supposed to uphold the constitution, protect citizen's civil and fundamental rights and assure rule of law. The judiciary in Pakistan for a long time has not performed these functions, rather, it has sided with the military on many occasions. In the past, the Supreme Court of Pakistan has validated General Ayub Khan's declaration of martial law in 1958; General Zia-ul Haq's capture of power in 1977; and General Musharraf's *coup d'ëtat* in 1999. The judiciary rationalised the military's unconstitutional seizure of political power on the basis of the 'doctrine of necessity' – that the military had intervened just to provide political stability due to political incompetence of civilian leaders to govern the country. Ironically, the supposed protector of the Constitution legitimised each extra-constitutional usurpation of political power by the military and in return, the military clipped the judiciary's ability to function freely.

Aware of the idea that if an independent judiciary plays an impartial role, it can become a nuisance to any non-elected executive, General Zia-ul Haq embarked on making it docile and subservient to his will. The first step he took was to cut off the power of judicial review of the "legality and constitutionality of executive decision."[32] By doing this General Zia ensured that the judiciary was deprived of the power to protect the civil and fundamental rights of Pakistanis if the executive decided to suspend them. The hardest blow to the judiciary's authority came in 1979 under the Second Constitutional Amendment. Under its provision, the martial law regime instituted a structure of military courts. These courts had powers that were parallel to those of the civil courts but were also authorised to try the offences under military laws. The power of the military courts superseded the powers of the civil courts in 1980 when the "jurisdiction of military tribunals was extended at the expense of the judiciary and by effect of the same order the higher courts were barred from reviewing the actions of military courts."[33] The civil courts were turned near impotent in the next year under the Provisional Constitutional Order of 1981. The order made the decisions of the civil court void on the legality of martial law and its power of judicial scrutiny of executive actions was terminated.

The second major setback to the power of civil courts came in 1980, when General Zia Islamised the legal system of Pakistan and instituted a Federal *Shariat* Court under Presidential Order No. 1. The Federal *Shariat* Court exercises original, revisional, appellate and review jurisdictions in *Hudood* cases registered under *Hudood* Laws.[34] The court is backed by constitutional provision and its decisions are binding on High Courts and their subordinate courts. General Zia's Islamisation of the legal system was against the spirit of the 1973 Constitution. The induction of religious laws such as the Islamisation of Pakistan's Penal Code, prescribing punishments according to orthodox Islam and blasphemy laws, discriminations against the religious and sectarian minority as well as against women, breaches the fundamental right of equality and right of non-discrimination guaranteed in the Constitution.

After General Zia the elected governments of Benazir Bhutto and Nawaz Sharif also tried to fiddle with the functioning of the judiciary. Since their own position within the troika was weak they could not interfere with the structure of the judiciary. After a lost decade of elected regimes, the military recaptured power under General Musharraf. The new ruler being a military man attempted to keep the judiciary under complete control from the beginning. The first assault on the functioning of the judicial branch came with the proclamation of martial law that put the Constitution in abeyance under the Provisional Constitutional Order (PCO) No. 1 of 1999. Under the effect of this PCO the President's orders and ordinances were to replace existing legislations and military government's actions could not be challenged before the judiciary.[35] After the *coup*, the courts were reconstituted with judges who bowed down to military's dictate. The judges had to take the Oath of Office under the PCO of 1999 which had removed the reference to judges' responsibility to defend the constitution. The recalcitrant judges who declined to take oath under the PCO were sacked by the martial law regime.[ix] In May 2000, the reconstituted Supreme Court demonstrated its allegiance to the military regime by legally validating General Musharraf's extra-constitutional usurpation of power as well as by punishing the recalcitrant judges by pronouncing that "those judges who had been sacked following the

ix. On 26 January 2000, 13 judges, including chief justice Saiduzzaman Siddiqui, who was appointed by Nawaz Sharif, and four other Supreme Court justices, were removed for refusing to do so.

PCO oath had lost any right to challenge their removal due to the passage of time."[36]

The second interference that caused irreparable injuries to the already lame-duck judiciary came with the passage of the 17thConstitutional Amendment by the titular parliament in 2003. The amendment constitutionally removed the judiciary's power to review acts of the military government. The 17th amendment substituted Article 270AA of the Constitution, a clause which validated all the LFOs, PCOs, Orders and Ordinances enacted, proceeding taken and appointments made by the military regime and made it unquestionable in "any court or forum on any ground whatsoever."[37] But the situation changed in 2007, when the judiciary under Chief Justice – Iftikhar Mohammad Chaudhry – opened up cases of missing persons during General Musharraf's tenure. Taking *Suo Motu* cognisance over the matter the government was questioned by the Supreme Court. General Musharraf whose presidential term was to end in October 2007 was planning a second presidential election to renew his second term as a president. Anticipating that the court might challenge the validity of his presidential election Musharraf forced Justice Chaudhry to resign. Chaudhry's dismissal generated a huge civil society movement led by lawyers which compelled Musharraf to reinstate the Chief Justice. Failing to suppress the agitation, General Musharraf proclaimed emergency in November 2007, but the lawyer's movement continued to mount pressure on him, which ultimately culminated in his departure.

The Lawyer's Movement and Musharraf's Ouster

The main reason for the 'Lawyers' Movement', which resulted in General Musharraf's removal, was rooted in the growing tussle between the executive and judicial organs of the government. The tussle between these two branches came to fore due to the judiciary's initiation of *Suo Motu* proceedings against the intelligence and law enforcing agencies of the government and to the summoning of officials to the court for investigations in the cases of missing persons. Most of the cases of disappearance belonged to the province of Baluchistan, the native province of Iftikhar Mohammad Chaudhry, whom General Musharraf himself elevated to the post of Chief Justice in 2005 superseding other senior judges.[38]

The public perception was that the Chief Justice's judicial activism, especially in the cases of missing persons, was not appreciated as it embarrassed the authorities and antagonised the establishment as some of his decisions posed a challenge to the government.[39] Justice Chaudhry's actions became an irritant when "he demanded investigations into several alleged 400 cases where people had disappeared, mostly from his native Baluchistan, where an insurgency was continuing."[40] It was speculated that security agencies were involved in the disappearances of insurgents who were fighting against the federal forces for greater autonomy. The irked President asked him to resign, which Chaudhry refused to do. The Chief Justice was then dismissed on the charges of abuse of office and misconduct. His case was referred to the Supreme Judicial Council "to investigate allegations of misconduct against him."[41] It is said that General Musharraf anticipated that the Chief Justice would hear a petition challenging the legality of General Musharraf's holding of dual posts of COAS and President simultaneously. Therefore, in a pre-emptive move, Musharraf sacked the Chief Justice.[42]

Following the Chief Justice's dismissal, the lawyer community, especially the bar associations across the country, mobilised behind Chaudhry and launched a massive agitation. On 20 July, Chief Justice's suspension was ruled as "illegal" by invaliding presidential reference and he was reinstated by a 10-3 majority decision.[43] The movement, however, did not end there and continued even after Chaudhry's reinstatement. The agitation got a political impetus in August when political forces joined it. There were two sets of political parties of which one openly was against General Musharraf and the second one sided with the *junta* leader. One group of political parties which included PPP, PML (Q) and MQM, wanted to construct a "transitional" government with Musharraf on top, while second group constituted of the PML (N) and the MMA insisted on complete "transformation" rejecting General Musharraf's political role.[44] The PML (Q) was Musharraf's own creation while the MQM was a Muhajir party without any hostile ties with the Muhajir leader. The PPP's support is said to have been due to its agreement with the military under National Reconciliation Order (NRO). The PML (N) sought complete transformation because under Musharraf's it had lost its political ground and was pushed to the edge. The MMA constituent especially the Jamaat-e-Islami and Jamiat-Ulema-e-Islam, had old differences with the military regime. Apart from seeking a more Islamic foreign policy, the MMA contended General Musharraf's pro-American policies. They also criticised his decision to send Pakistani soldiers to Iraq, and to mark their protest they cooperated with the ARD to resist the LFO.

Amidst the ongoing lawyer movement the coalition of political parties under the banner of All Parties Democratic Movement (APDM) launched a "Go Musharraf Go" campaign on the eve of Pakistan's Independence Day.[x] In September, the lawyers also launched an anti-Musharraf protest by boycotting the courts across the country and demanded his resignation.[45] Unsuccessful in suppressing the movement and anticipating that the judiciary might invalidate his re-election General Musharraf declared a state of emergency on 3 November and lifted it on 15 December after the newly constituted judiciary ratified his re-election. Issuing a fresh PCO he restructured the judiciary by sacking Justice Iftikhar Mohammad Chaudhry along with 13 out of 17 judges of the Supreme Court and deposed more than 50 high court judges.[46] In between the emergency period, he relinquished his post of COAS on 28 November 2007 which was taken over by General Ashfaq Kayani. The national elections were due in January 2008 in which the exiled leaders of PPP and PML (N) were to participate. Benazir Bhutto returned to Pakistan in October 2007 and survived an assassination attempt. She was later assassinated during an election campaign on 27 December therefore the elections were postponed to February 2008. On the other hand, Nawaz Sharif also failed to contest in the election due to legal constraints.[47] It was expected that the parties which supported General Musharraf would form a coalition government. After the election, to the surprise of all, the two historical political nemesis, PPP and PML (N), came together to forge a coalition government. General Musharraf, who was now holding only a civilian post of President, fearing that the government might initiate impeachment proceedings against him, renounced his presidential post and left the country for exile in London in November.

The Third Democratic Interlude: Signs of Hope

By the fag-end of the year 2007, all political parties began to gear-up as they realised the likelihood of fresh elections within few months. The 12th

x. The APDM included 32 parties with leading members of PML (N), MMA and PTI.

National Assembly that was elected in 2002 was to end its term in November 2007. But the next general election was scheduled for January 2008 due to the emergency. The election was further delayed by a month followed by Benazir Bhutto's assassination. Apart from the normal political campaigning two major processes of party politics deserves mention here. The first of these was the silent demise of the MMA, a loose alliance of Islamist parties which rose to power in two provinces in the 2002 elections by opposing pro-American polices of the military government of General Musharraf.[xi] The second, was the formation of the All Parties Democratic Movement (APDM) and its unnoticed collapse.

The MMA, which had in 2002, won the maximum seats ever for a religious pary literally disintegrated prior to the 2008 elections. The alliance, said to have been helped by General Musharraf and the ISI to neutralise other political opposition and which supported the sham parliament under General Musharraf to pass the Seventh Amendment, stood divided on the issue of his re-election by the incumbent parliament.[xii] The alliance was already weakened due to its two major constituents – Jamiat Ulema-e-Pakistan (Sami-ul-Haq) who deserted it in 2005 and Jamiat Ulema-e-Pakistan, whose political significance had been eroded due to the death of its leader Shah Ahmad Noorani in 2003. The internal schism of the alliance was quite apparent in the 2005 Union Council elections in the frontier province. The leading constituents of the alliance, Jamaat led by *Ameer* Qazi Hussain Ahmad also the president of MMA and JUI (F) led by Maulana Fazalur Rahman also the secretary of MMA, joined opposing political alliances and fought against each other. Both the parties were not directly pitched against each other. In certain districts, JUI (F) aligned with the Pakistan Peoples

xi. The MMA won 45 general seats in the 2002 National Assembly elections, an unprecedented notch for any religious party or alliance. The MMA became the third largest party following the ruling PML (Q) and PPP. In the KPK, it won 52 out of 99 seats and formed the government on its own while in Baluchistan it secured 14 seats out of 51 seats and became part of the coalition government.

xii. General Pervez Musharraf's presidential term was ending much before the five year term of the 12th National Assembly that was supposed to end in November 2007. Musharraf, wary of the probability of not having majority support in the upcoming parliament sought to renew his Presidency from the incumbent parliament. He was, t however, re-elected for the next five years ,but had to face resistance from the legal community.

Party (Sherapo) and contested against Jamaat, which joined the ANP-led alliance while in certain districts they contested in alliance.[48] The rift between the two parties grew sharp in 2007 on the issue of General Musharraf's re-election by the outgoing parliament. The Jamaat was not happy with General Musharraf for his *Lal Masjid* military operation[xiii] and thus was not in favour of his second term, while the JUI (F) was not against it.

The fissures grew to the extent that that Jamaat had to explore other political avenues and thus joined the APDM which also included big parties like PML (N), PTI and Pakhtunkhwa Milli Party. The APDM doubted General Musharraf's intention to hold free and fair elections and thus decided to boycott the elections and force him to renounce the presidency to ensure free election under neutral arrangement. In the meanwhile, both the JUI (F) and the Jamaat failed to come to terms with each other and thus fielded their own candidates. On the other hand, the PML (N) retracted its decision of boycott after it could not convince the PPP to do the same. As both Benazir Bhutto and after her, Zardari decided to participate in the election, Nawaz Sharif had no choice but to contest. However, three other constituents of APDM, the PTI led by Imran Khan, Jamaat under its *Ameer*, Qazi Ahmad and Pakhtunkhwa Milli Party headed by Mahmood Achakzai stuck to their boycott plan.[xiv] On the other hand, since the Jamaat was not contesting, the MMA was completely in the control of the JUI (F).

The 13th National Assembly Elections held in February 2008 were fought without stalwarts like Benazir Bhutto, who was assassinated two months before the elections and Nawaz Sharif, who was legally barred from contesting. The PPP was headed by Benazir's widower Asif Ali Zardari. It was expected that the parties supporting General Musharraf would form a

---

xiii. The operation *Lal Masjid* , popularly known as the "Siege of Lal Masjid" , was an armed confrontation between the president Musharraf's government and Islamist fundamentalists militants who had occupied the Mosque at the heart of Islamabad in the summer of 2007. The mosque was said to be associated with hardliner Sunni sectarianism and engaged in the unlawful imposition of their version of Sharia. For a chronological narrative of the incidence see Talbot, *Pakistan: A New History*, pp.193-4

xiv. Apart from APDM, the big parties and leaders in Baluchistan also decided to boycott the election. Political stalwarts like Dr. Abdul Haye Baloch, Mir Hasil Bizenjo, Sardar Akhtar Mengal were not among the contestants. For details of those who boycotted for different reasons see Maqbool Ahmad, "The Nationalists Strike Back, *The Herald*, Vol. 41, No. 2, February 2008, pp. 78-9.

coalition government but the election outcome did not favour the PML (Q). The PML (Q) somehow managed to win only 42 seats and was reduced to the third position followed by the PPP and the PML (N) who won 89 and 68 seats respectively. The MMA only secured 6 seats which were largely won by the JUI (F) candidates. Although, the PPP emerged as the single largest party it fell short of securing the required majority to form the government. After the election, to the surprise of all, the two historical political opponents, the PPP and the PML (N), came together to forge a coalition government. Apart from Nawaz Sharif's party, the MQM headed by Altaf Hussain, which had virtually swept the Karachi Division and the ANP headed by Asfandyar Wali Khan, which had recaptured its bastion from the MMA in KPK, also became part of this grand coalition. The coalition partners backed a senior PPP leader, Yousaf Raza Gilani from Punjab as Prime Minister.

The first notable move from the Gilani government was to convene a National Assembly session to initiate impeachment proceedings against President Musharraf in August. The President who had already shed his uniform had to resign as he had also lost the support of the army.[49] Following General Musharraf's ouster, Asif Ali Zardari was elected as President of Pakistan by the parliament in September of that year. It was expected that he would immediately reinstate the suspended Chief Justice Iftikhar Chaudhry, but he took more than six months to bring him back. By the end of 2009 the unnatural bonhomie between the PML (N) and the PPP came to an end as both developed differences over a number of issues like the judiciary, war on terror and the nationalisation process. Following the PML (N)'s departure a new cabinet was formed in which the ANP, MQM and JUI (F) leaders were incorporated. In December 2010, the MQM withdrew its support from the Gilani government and its ministers resigned due to the government's failure to maintain law and order and contain the rising inflation. The party rejoined the ruling coalition within a months' time. Paradoxically, in 2012 the PML (Q) also joined the new government.

After settling down of the transition from a *junta* to a democratic regime the most progressive step towards democratisation of the system taken by the PPP-led coalition government was the passage of the Seventh National Finance Commission Award and the 18th Amendment in 2010. It was a set of constitutional reforms in which the central feature was the transfer of executive powers from the President to the Prime Minister. It was a historic accomplishment, as for the first time there was a cross-party consensus to stabilise the democratic system by strengthening democratic institutions and governance and keeping the military out of politics. The amendments heralded fundamental changes in the functioning of the state and military relations by redefining the powers of the state organs especially of executive. The key features of the amendment which strengthened the parliamentary system are discussed in the following section.

The 18th Amendment: A Catalyst to Political Transition

In one of his essays on civil-military relations, Charles Kennedy outlined a list of measures employed by the military leaders to reshape, legalise and control the political system after the coup. Among the many measures employed by the military for regime legitimisation and operationalisation one to "avoid legal chaos…, make things legal in the short term…, eliminate political opponents…, arrange to become President…, reinvent local government… and re-write the constitution."[50] Recognising this pattern the elected representatives agreed to reform the constitutional provisions to recalibrate the balance of power. To establish supremacy of the parliamentary system, it was necessary to de-concentrate powers from the military's ambit. To attain this objective the 13th parliament passed a set of constitutional reforms known as the 18th Amendment under President Asif Ali Zardari in 2010. According to a scholar the consensus of the parliament and ease-up of the process to institutionalise a new political framework underscores "the dangers of returning to the politics of the 1990s, where politicians co-opted the army [and vice versa] to undermine their political opponents. Politicians appreciated that short term political gains of army intervention against opponents was outweighed by the weakening of the democratic process."[51] The consensus over the 18th amendment largely was the result of the realisation by the politicians that this provision was instrumental in keeping the military out of power. The job of politicians is to do politics but the political space was arbitrarily occupied by the military.

Under previous military regimes many changes were incorporated in the Constitution which weakened the democratic institutions *vis-à-vis* the military establishment. The 18th Amendment introduced 102 minor and major reforms in the Constitution and thus revitalised the democratic system of Pakistan.[52] Among all these changes few specific set of amendments warrant brief deliberation which recalibrated the role, responsibility and authority of the representative institution. The first major reform to be considered was the reduction of the power of the President. Pakistan's governance system not only oscillated between military and civilian regime but also between parliamentary and presidential forms of governments.[xv]Whenever a military regime ruled Pakistan, it transformed Pakistan's political system into a Presidential system and concentrated all the decisive powers in the post of president. General Musharraf also during his tenure issued numerous LFOs, PCOs, Chief Executive Orders and constitutional amendments that strengthened the Presidency and parliament's survival depended on his will.

One of the major changes under the 18th amendment was the removal of the undemocratic Article 58 2(b) reinstituted by General Musharraf which empowered the President to unilaterally dissolve the national and provincial assemblies under emergency provision. Secondly, the President's power to unilaterally appoint a caretaker government was curtailed under the amended Article 224. Under the new provision, before any such appointment, the President is required to consult the outgoing Prime Minister and the leader of the opposition in the transition period after the dissolution of parliament. Thirdly, the amended Article 48 transferred the power to hold a referendum in important national matters to the prime minister. Lastly, the amended provision of Article 75 of the constitution removed the President's power to keep bills passed by the parliament in abeyance or to have a say on the matter.

The second set of major reforms that brought the political system close to a parliamentary system was the transfer of greater powers and roles to the head of the government, the Prime Minister and the elected parliament. Under the amended provisions of Articles 90 and 99 the

xv. General Ayub's military government transformed the parliamentary form to a presidential system under the 1962 constitution in which the President became the repository of all powers. Zulfikar Ali Bhutto, through the 1973 Constitution, reintroduced a parliamentary system and reduced the post of the President to a ceremonial one. General Zia's military government transformed the parliamentary system into a semi-presidential system. General Musharraf in June 2002 revived the provisions of the 8th Amendment to reinforce his presidency by retaining the power to remove the prime minister and his cabinet.

Prime Minister is recognised as the chief executive, which used to be the role of the President. Secondly, the obligation of the Prime Minister to keep the President "informed" on all policy matters under Article 46 has been removed in the amended version. Thirdly, the new amendment has reduced the powers of the President to unilaterally appoint the Governors of provinces and Chiefs of military staffs. Under the amended Article 101, the President is required to consult the Prime Minister, whose recommendation would be binding, before the appointment of a governor. Similarly, Article 243 obligates the President to appoint the chief of services on the advice of the Prime Minister. Lastly, the amendment to Article 91 also removes the provision introduced by General Musharraf that barred any person to hold office of the Prime Minister more than twice. This provision opened up the possibility of re-election of Nawaz Sharif who could not contest the previous election.

A third set of major reforms in the 18th amendment which promised fundamental changes *vis-à-vis* democratic governance were related to federalism in Pakistan. From its formative phase a power imbalance existed between the provinces and the centre. All the constitutions of Pakistan were centre-heavy which vested disproportionate powers at its disposal. The confrontation over the distribution of resources grew so high that it resulted in the country's dismemberment in 1971. Thereafter many secessionist movements have erupted in the remaining part of Pakistan. Both the military and civilian regimes attempted to suppress them instead of politically resolving these demands. On the other hand, provincial parties have continuously demanded greater autonomy for the provinces. In the beginning, General Musharraf also promised greater devolution of power but these proved to be mere words. The 18th Amendment along with Seventh National Finance Commission Award addresses these grievances to some extent.

According to Stephen P. Cohen the unanimous approval of all four provinces in the passing of the Seventh NFC and 18th Amendment were President Zardari's "accomplishments" which reverses the bearing of the Eighth Amendment and 17th Amendment which had turned Pakistan into a semi-Presidential republic.[53] The PPP-led government called it a "participatory federalism" because of the undisputed endorsement of all political parties to its passage that would usher an improved social contract through meaningful federal reforms.[54] Raza Ahmad outlining the crucial reforms *vis-à-vis* federal arrangements noted that "the eighteenth amendment removed the most glaring obstacle in the path of legislative provincial autonomy, i.e. the vast Concurrent list of legislative subjects. With the deletion of the list, provinces shall enjoy exclusive powers concerning criminal law, contracts, transfer of property, labour welfare, marriage and divorce, among other significant subjects."[55] It should be underlined here that even in the past, governance was based on three lists – federal, concurrent and provincial. But the people at the helm of power at the centre frequently interfered in the functioning of the provincial governments, thus undermining the very basis of federalism. The frequent interference in provincial authority resulted in provincial distrust towards the centre.

The 18th Amendment also tried to address this distrust through a new agreement on the sharing of revenue. Under the amended Article 160, it was agreed upon that "The share of the provinces in each Award of National Finance Commission shall not be less than the share given to the Provinces in the previous Award."[56] This though temporally resolves provincial grievances, but in the future a province whose contribution to the national pool becomes higher than what it receives may lead to fresh conflict. Another important change in balancing of centre-provinces power was brought under Article 101. Under its sub-clause it was made mandatory that a governor who is to be appointed in any province has to be a "registered voter and resident of the province concerned." However, the President retains the right to appoint governors. The new provision restricts any governor to promote the centre's or superior provinces' interests. In another amendment of Article 232, the say of the provincial assembly over emergency provisions was enhanced. Now the consent of the provinces has been made mandatory in case of imposition of emergency in the province concerned. The 18th Amendment also addresses the issue of ethnic grievances of NWFP by renaming it as Khyber Pakhtunkhawa on the demand of its ethnic majority. This was a step forward to create a parity of frontier provinces with the other three provinces. Yunas Samad considered that this amendment has strengthened the drive for ethnic-based provinces; however, it will take a long course to resolve all such demands.[57]

The fourth set of reforms which had significant consequences for the enhancement of democratic accountability was the formation of the National Judicial Commission. The NJC was aimed at enhancing the judiciary's independence and de-politicisation of the judicial institution. Historically, both civilian and military regimes have sacrificed the judiciary at the altar of their political interests. After the political transition in 2008, it was expected that the elected government will free the body from political maneuvering. But President Zardari took two years to bring reform in the appointment system that would enhance judicial efficacy without being partisan. The 18th Amendment substituted Article 175A to constitute a seven member NJC. The NJC was to be chaired by the Chief Justice of the Supreme Court and other members were to comprise of two seniors judges of the Supreme Court, one former CJP, federal law minister, attorney general and a senior advocate of the Supreme Court nominated by the bar council of Pakistan. The commission was delegated with the functioning of appointments of judges to the Supreme Court, High Courts and Federal Shariat Court. This provision renders relative autonomy to the judicial body to function in a non-partisan manner and protect the democratic rights of the citizen.

Apart from these set of reforms, which were to strengthen the democratic setup in the country, Articles 6 and 270 generated huge public and scholarly debate at that time. The amendments to these two articles were considered constitutional safeguards against the possibility of a future military coup. The amended Article 6 revived Clause 1 of the original Article 6 as adopted in the 1973 constitution, which considered the subversion, abrogation or suspension of the constitution by force or show of force as an act of 'high treason.' It further prohibited the judiciary to validate any unlawful arrogation of power by the armed forces. In addition Article 270AA declared the previous authorisation of constitutional changes as unlawful and made them devoid of any legal effect. All these amendments did redefine civil-military relations but were not sufficient in themselves to keep the military subservient to civilian authority. The onus is on the politicians to gradually assert civilian dominance over the military establishment without a direct confrontation.

Civil-Military Relations under President Zardari: A Transformation Unaccomplished

A Pakistani scholar has compartmentalised Pakistan's political system into two theses. One is a "military hegemonic system" in which the "military has a monopoly over strategic policy issues and decision-making institutions" but it never got public legitimacy and evoked civilian resistance; the second is the "dominant political party system", in which the party in power establishes its dominance by weakening the opposition.[58] Because of the tendency to establish dominance, the parties in power did not create the "political space necessary for opposition parties" and pursued confrontational politics and thus failed to build consensus on how to contain the military's role in politics.[59] After the 2008 election, a situation of coalition politics arose because no single party had acquired a majority to form the government. And following the political transition, the coalition government was faced with the old challenge of how to re-establish a paradigm in which the military will possess minimal say in polity.

The political ambience seemed positive for the civilian ascent as the military during this period did not show active interest in political matters. The new army chief, General Ashfaq Kayani, who was appointed by the former President General Musharraf, publically endorsed that armed forces should mind their professional business and have no role in politics.[60] Just a week prior to the general elections of 2008, he recalled more than 300 senior officers working in 23 civil departments. In this apparently positive atmosphere the elected government in its first act of reasserting civilian supremacy attempted to put the intelligence agencies, ISI and IB, under the direct control of the Interior Ministry. Earlier the ISI was under the control of the Prime Minister, but it did not necessarily comply with his orders. With its transfer to the Ministry of Interior, it was expected, at least in principle, that it would be answerable to the full-fledged ministry.[61] The military institution considered it as a civilian overreach to oversee what the military has considered its exclusive sphere of affairs. The civilian government was forced to retract its decision in less than 24 hours due to "immense pressure from the defence circles."[62] In another move to establish its position, the civilian government dissolved the controversial NSC instituted by the previous military ruler. In November 2008, Prime Minister Yousaf Raza

Gilani made a public statement that: "We don't accept Musharraf's NSC. The President and I have discussed the issue and the good news is that we have decided to dissolve it."[63] The military did not oppose the dissolution as the NSC was dormant since its control fell under the civilian president after the political transition.

What infuriated the soldiers most was President Zardari's attempt to redefine the military's monopolistic India-centric policies, including the exclusive Kashmir issue. In one of his interviews with the *Wall Street Journal*, President Zardari attempted to demystify the military's perceived bellicosity towards India by stating "India has never been a threat to Pakistan," and his "democratic government is not scared of Indian influence abroad."[64]To the awe of many, he blatantly called the militants operating in Kashmir as "terrorists" whom General Musharraf had been addressing as "freedom fighters" when he was in power.[65] In the eagerness to improve ties with India, Zardari added insult to injury in the *Hindustan Times Conclave* indicating change in the country's nuclear doctrine of 'first-use' saying Pakistan would not be the first country to use its nuclear arms against India.[66] However, Zardari was "not taken seriously by the Pakistani generals who actually control the Bomb,"[67] neither was his statement received in good taste by the military.

The military's latent confrontation with the civilian government became apparent when it vetoed the civilian leadership's decision to send the ISI chief to India to calm the brewing tensions after the Mumbai terror attacks. According to a *WikiLeaks* document after 2008 Mumbai attacks, US officials persuaded the Pakistani civilian authorities to send the ISI chief, Ahmad Shuja Pasha to India to cooperate with Indian investigation.[68] The civilian government agreed to the proposal and announced his visit but had to reverse its decision as the military overruled it. The major confrontation between the civilian and military institutions surfaced due to the civilian's acceptance of certain provisions of a US bill popularly known as Kerry-Lugar Bill. The bill was passed by the US Congress and became an act in 2010.[69] The Act authorised the release of $7.5 billion non-military aid to Pakistan for the period of 2010-14. The military was displeased with some of the conditions of the bill which it considered objectionable and derogatory. The military not only found its clauses designed to increase civilian scrutiny[xvi] of the military but also its language humiliating and insulting to the nation.[70]

Amidst all these tussles the practical test to show its dominance over the military came in the mid of 2010. By virtue of the 18th Amendment the executive head acquired the power to appoint the chiefs of the services. The new Prime Minister Gilani exercised this authority in July 2010 when he unprecedentedly extended the term of General Kayani (who was to retire in 2011) for three years. In Saeed Shafqat's opinion this act "established civilian supremacy at least in theory and constitutionally."[71] However, Jaffrelot argued that it "reflected Kayani's influence over the civilian government for he was indeed the one who was seeking the deferral."[72] But Shafqat views this short civilian period as the waning of the military's hegemony, as it was no longer managing the country as it did earlier though it still had considerable influence. He aptly captures the essence of this changing scenario as "a system of power sharing seems to be evolving rather than military subordination to civilian supremacy."[73] It is true that the military's power was no longer absolute and civilian engagement with them was pragmatic, but it is also a fact that most of the times it was the military that overruled civilian decisions.

Beside the efforts to develop institutional mechanism to assert supremacy, this period was also marked by a paradox – that the military's popularity was in decline for it was unable to control the deteriorating security situation while the civilian rulers found themselves more dependent on the military to control the increasing homegrown terrorism. Shuja Nawaz noted that during this period, the eastern border against India was calmer but the western front bordering Afghanistan was plagued with insurgency. Therefore, the Pakistan army, after a long time was using its forces within

xvi. Two of its conditions demanded "a detailed description of Pakistan's efforts to prevent proliferation of nuclear-related material and expertise," and "an assessment of the extent to which the Government of Pakistan exercises effective civilian control of the military, including a description of the extent to which civilian executive leaders and parliament exercise oversight and approval of military budgets, the chain of command, the process of promotion for senior military leaders, civilian involvement in strategic guidance and planning, and military involvement in civil administration." See the text of the bill "Text of the Kerry Lugar Bill," *Dawn*, 14 October 2009. URL: http://www.dawn.com/news/913717/text-of-the-kerry-lugar-bill (accessed on 4 May 2015).

its own territory against its own people.[74] More than the external threat the challenge to Pakistan's sovereignty came from within.

The period witnessed ever increasing terror attacks and loss of scores of human lives – civilian and military personnel. From 2007, just prior to General Musharraf's ouster, till 22 July 2011, a series of terror attacks resulted in the loss of 11,726 lives and 23,037 people suffered serious injuries.[75] Some of the spectacular terror attacks which captured considerable airtime of the electronic media and space of the print media were attacks on the Marriott Hotel in Islamabad in September 2008 killing many people.[76] The attack on the Sri Lankan cricket team in Lahore in March 2009 resulted in the isolation of Pakistan in the cricketing world as cricketing countries became reluctant to tour Pakistan. In October 2009, there was an attack on the army's General Headquarters (GHQ) in Rawalpindi by Taliban militants resulting in fatalities on both sides.[77] These events were instrumental in changing people's perception of the army's capabilities to protect Pakistani citizens. With increasing civilian fatalities from U.S. Drone attacks, people become suspicious of the establishment's – armed forces and civilian government – capacities and intentions to protect Pakistani lives and sovereignty. These developments led to the decline in the military's popularity.

In May 2011, Pakistan's armed forces faced serious criticism and its capabilities came under serious questioning following a unilateral surgical operation by US Special Forces within its territory. On 2 May 2011, the world woke up to the shocking news that US special forces had raided Osama bin Laden's hideout in Abbottabad – a garrison town of the Pakistani military – and killed the world's most wanted terrorist. Later allegations were levied that the military institution of Pakistan was not only aware of bin Laden's presence in the country rather it had sheltered him,.[xvii] In a standard

xvii Under pressure the government had to ask the Supreme Court to look into the matter which then constituted a judicial commission called The Abottabad Commission to probe into the circumstantial details of the event leading to bin Laden's liquidation operation. The leaked report of the commission concluded that American operation deep inside Pakistan without its knowledge was a "great humiliation". No one was singled out in the report but the ISI and the security bureaucracy as a whole were held guilty of "incompetence" for their failure to detect both bin Laden and the US operation. For details see Bruce Riedel, "Clueless or Complicit?" *India Today*, 12 July 2013, URL: http://indiatoday.intoday.in/story/osama-bin-laden-pakistan-abbottabad-commission-report-united-states/1/291011.html (accessed on 15 March 2016).

response, the military denied the accusation and showed its displeasure for not being taken into confidence before the operation. On the other hand, the Taliban intensified its attack on the Pakistani forces in retaliation to bin Laden's killing. In one of its fatal attack on Pakistan's naval base, PNS *Mehran*, Taliban militants caused serious fatalities and destruction of aircrafts.[78]

Critics in Pakistan interpreted the raid in Abbottabad as a breach of Pakistan's territorial integrity and questioned the legality of the operation. The failure to either to know about bin Laden's presence or the US operation to liquidate him, raised serious questions on military capabilities to defend the country's sovereignty. The seldom questioned military had to face political scrutiny as the opposition politicians called for the dismissal of the ISI chief. The coalition government had a historic chance to recalibrate power disequilibrium in the existing civil-military relations in favour of the elected government. Instead, the ISI turned the tables by focusing on "how civilian leaders' collaboration had enabled Americans to violate Pakistan's sovereignty."[79] Therefore, giving in to such pressure, the civilian government passed a resolution in the parliament expressing total confidence in the defence forces.[80] The defensive military began to aggressively reassert itself after an incident labeled "memogate" by the media.

The 'Memogate' Issue

In October 2011, an exposé dubbed by the media as the "memogate" scandal revealed that just after one week of bin Laden's death, Pakistan's civilian leadership secretly sought help from the US to save it from a perceived military *coup*. According to a testimony of Pakistani-American businessman Mansoor Ijaz who was the emissary of the 'memo,' Pakistan's Ambassador to the U.S., Hussain Haqqani asked him to pass a secret 'memo' to Admiral Michael Mullen urging Washington's intervention to stop the military establishment from any intervention to bring down the civilian government. The 'memo', which was supposed to be secret and delivered by an unidentified interlocutor said that:

> Civilians cannot withstand much more of the hard pressure being delivered from the Army to succumb to wholesale changes. If civilians are forced from power, Pakistan becomes a sanctuary for UBL's [Osama bin Laden's]

> legacy and potentially the platform for far more rapid spread of al Qaeda's brand of fanaticism and terror. A unique window of opportunity exists for the civilians to gain the upper hand over army and intelligence directorates due to their complicity in the UBL matter.[81]

Stressing the pressing need to protect Pakistan's descent into extremism the memo appealed to the US defence chief Mullen to convey a strong and urgent message to General Ashfaq Kayani, the then army chief and the chief of Inter-Services Intelligence, Ahmad Shuja Pasha to end their plot to topple the civilian government. In response to Washington's assistance the memo offered a direct deal that:

> Should you be willing to do so, Washington's political/military backing would result in a revamp of the civilian government that, while weak at the top echelon in terms of strategic direction and implementation (even though mandated by domestic political forces), in a wholesale manner replaces the national security adviser and other national security officials with trusted advisers that include ex-military and civilian leaders favorably viewed by Washington, each of whom have long and historical ties to the US military, political and intelligence communities.[82]

In addition, the 'memo' made serious commitments including altering of national security leadership in favour of Washington, initiation of formal investigation and fixing the punishment for those who sheltered bin Laden and pledging to hand over Ayman Al Zawahiri, Mullah Omar, and Sirajuddin Haqqani, the Al Qaeda and Taliban terrorists said to be residing in Pakistan. Hussain Haqqani, who was alleged to be the chief architect of the "memo", denied this allegation but rendered his resignation due to the pressure from the military. In a personal interaction Haqqani indicated military sabotage to destabilise the civilian government and called the entire episode a circus in which political and military clowns were pulling each other's legs.[83] According to Jaffrelot, the controversy was reflective of a deeper mutual distrust between the civil and military institutions. In his words it was indicative of a "strong sense of vulnerability" on the part of the civilian authorities if they had generated the memo, or if it was concocted by the ISI it was "evidence of very sophisticated strategy by the Pakistani military to destabilise the civil authorities."[84] President Asif Ali Zardari was also accused of conspiring against the military by giving a tacit nod to the plot, though he denied the allegation.

The Supreme Court of Pakistan took notice of the issue and asked the Ministry of Defence to submit its explanation. In its affidavit, the ministry stated that it had only administrative control over the army and ISI and no operational control over them.[85] On the other hand, the military submitted its reply to the court claiming the 'memo' as real and intended to undermine the military. A judicial commission constituted to probe into the alleged matter called Haqqani "not loyal to the country" and found him guilty of authoring the 'memo.'[86] Alarmed by the Defence Ministry's statement, Prime Minister Gilani spoke against the military in the parliament saying that the military is answerable to the parliament and could not claim being "a state within the state." He further added that: "if some individuals think they are not under the government, they are mistaken. They are under the government and they will remain under the government because we are the elected, chosen representatives of the people of Pakistan."[87] The Prime Minister's words were strengthened by the Chief Justice Iftikhar Mohammad Chaudhry's statement in which he said that now "the system will run according to what the constitution commands," and gone are the days when the judiciary used to validate extra-constitutional acts.[88] This was a radical position to be taken by the judiciary, which had in the past generally rendered legal validation to unconstitutional usurpation of power by the military. On the other hand, the political parties despite their differences, showed a great amount of pragmatism in cementing civilian rule by not offering their allegiance as praetorian agents.

Pragmatic Party Politics or an Antagonistic Contradiction

At the time of political transition there was speculation whether the political parties would cooperate to strengthen democratic institution or would they revert to the confrontational politics of the past. The fear was not unreasonable given past tendencies of the parties to sacrifice democracy at the expense of personal gain. Observation of the political events prior to the final transition led political pundits to conclude that Pakistan was heading towards a "praetorian democracy."[xviii] According to the rumours of the time, Benazir Bhutto had struck a 'deal' under which General Musharraf was to allow her to return and contest election and in return her party was to support his continuation as President for a second term.[xix] In Akbar Zaidi's words: "Pakistan was gearing up for continuity of military rule under the garb of a populist and popular elected coalition led by Benazir Bhutto, the best form of praetorian democracy devised in Pakistan."[89] Others were arguing about the return of the "Troika" system of the past.[90] But completely new dynamics came into operation following the assassination of the protagonist of the script, Benazir Bhutto.

After Benazir's assassination, the PPP led by her widower Asif Ali Zardari campaigned on an emotional slogan "democracy as revenge" to gain sympathy votes. On the other hand a few parties like the Jamaat and PTI called for boycott of the elections to delegitimise the entire electoral exercise. After the election, PPP emerged as the largest single party but was short of a majority to form the government. To the utter amazement of all, the PML (N) supported the PPP to form a coalition government. It was unprecedented cooperation that became a key to give political parties a chance to run the business of governance after almost a decade. The challenge before them was to avoid the lure of "praetorian democracy" by changing allegiance, a common practice of the past.

The initial political atmosphere after the transition was seen to be in favour of the elected representatives. The military was on the retreat and there was a rare consensus across parties to support key constitutional changes in favour of parliamentary arrangements. But the Gilani government, which was trying to follow the politics of reconciliation and collaboration, failed on three essential fronts which included General Musharraf's removal, reinstatement of deposed judges and restoration of the constitution.[91]

---

xviii. A 'praetorian democracy' is an arrangement in which the political parties collaborate with the military and accept the role of a subservient partner and legitimise its otherwise unconstitutional exercise of political authority.

xix. Musharraf enacted the NRO that rendered amnesty to political leaders including Benazir Bhutto who was barred from contesting due to alleged graft charges against them. The PPP which was the second largest party in the National Assembly abstained from voting in parliament in October 2007 and thus allowed General Musharraf to be re-elected as president for a second term.

These were the major issues of contention between the PPP and PML (N) leadership. Dissatisfied with the Gilani government's efforts on these fronts, the PML (N) parted ways from the coalition government in less than three months from its formation but continued its outside support to stabilise the elected government.

In a few months time, the divisions among political parties came to the surface on the issue of the 'War on Terror.' During this time, the entire frontier region bordering Afghanistan, especially the tribal agencies, had been turned into a 'warzone' due to the military's counter-insurgency operations. There were public debates over the war on jihadis and questions were being asked about "whose war it was anyway – America's or Pakistan's?" Against this backdrop there were two sharp divisions. One was led by the left-secularist PPP and supported by the MQM and the ANP which accused Musharraf "for not fighting hard or consistently", while the second faction, led by right-nationalist PML (N) along with Jamaat and PTI, accused Musharraf of "adopting a needlessly aggressive approach at the behest of the Americans."[92] However, in a rare show of consensus all the major parties agreed to the passage of the Swat peace deal between the Taliban militants, represented by the *Tehreek-e-Nifaz-e-Shariat-e-Muhammadi* (TNSM), and the frontier provincial government ruled by the ANP. The deal, officially known as *Nizam-e-Adl Regulation* – Order of Justice – allowed implementation of Shariah law in the Malakand division of the then NWFP.[93] The enactment got the endorsement of the ruling coalition as well as the PML (N) and PML (Q), although MQM abstained from voting. The deal was signed to stabilise the frontier valley following growing humanitarian crisis due to the increasing number of IDPs from the region.

After parting from the coalition, the PML (N) had become the main opposition party and began to mount pressure on the PPP led government to honour its commitments on those three issues. In August, President Musharraf resigned amid fear of impeachment. The PML (N) which supported the impeachment move turned aggressive on the issue of restoration of judges as Nawaz Sharif received support from the lawyers' movement. Unhappy with Zardari's flip-flop to reinstate the unseated judges, then lawyers called for a 'long march' and indefinite agitation in March 2009. Nawaz Sharif also announced his participation in the 'long march', which sent the government into a tizzy. In just three days from the announcement, a three- member bench of the Pakistan Supreme Court, hearing the Sharif brothers' electoral eligibility plea, ruled both ineligible to contest and barred them from holding elected office.[94] On the same day, Presidential rule was imposed in Punjab as the provincial government had been dismissed.[95] Following the court verdict and subsequent imposition of presidential rule, PML (N)'s political workers and leaders took to the street in a show of fierce protest. Weary of the consequence of the coming 'long march' and short of ideas to manage the agitation, the PPP government put Nawaz Sharif under house arrest and imposed a 72 hours preventive restriction on his brother Shahbaz Sharif, Imran Khan and Qazi Ahmad Hussain of Jamaat.[96] However, a resilient Nawaz Sharif defied the order and participated in the 'long march' and addressed his party workers and lawyers. On the next day of the 'long march' Prime Minister Gilani announced that judges would be restored in a week's time and also issued orders to release the political workers and protesters arrested during the 'long march.'[97] Later most of the judges were restored to their position by an executive order by Prime Minister Gilani. In few weeks' time the apex court reversed the disqualification order and both the brothers were back to political business as usual. The PPP government's actions were tantamount to the politics of vengeance.

In April 2011, Pakistan Peoples Party made an alliance with the PML (Q). In return for its supports the PML (Q) politicians were given cabinet posts as well the post of deputy Prime Minister.[98] At first sight it was an absolute turnaround from its ideological commitment to its supporters who backed the party in the fight against the military. A left-oriented commentator called this as an unnatural alliance with the military's *satrap* as "political putrefaction" to cling to power.[99] The PPP rationalised the power-sharing as part of a democratic process. However, this may have been due to the number compulsions as it needed the support of all in the parliament to pass the budget. Given the MQM's past record of unreliability as an alliance partner and its constant confrontation in Sindh, the government needed the support of others to survive the coming years. Firstly, the alliances with its national arch rival PML (N) and provincial political nemesis MQM and lastly with the pro-military PML (Q), made the PPP politically unpopular. The PPP was in the middle of 'antagonistic contradictions' in which it had chosen a partner apparently seen as anti-democratic instrument of the military.

By its fourth year of ruling, the PPP found itself trapped as it was being preyed by three forces. On one front was the military, (desperate to gain its lost ground), who exhibited great bellicosity after the 'memogate' scandal. On the second front, was the belligerent political opposition which too had found its moment of reckoning with the government on the same issue. On the third front was the judiciary under Iftikhar Chaudhry, which was acting as the third autonomous power centre in the country. The military was already in a constant tussle with the Zardari government and had cornered it in a defensive mode ever since the 'memogate' incidence. Amidst the ongoing tug- of- war between the civil government and the military brass, political opposition which was returning to the old-style political vendetta, demanded the resignations of Zardari and Gilani and also an urgent inquiry into the memo issue.[100] In a public gathering, Nawaz Sharif accused the PPP government of selling the country's sovereignty and compromising its self-respect by soliciting American interference in the internal affairs through the memo.[101] He further demanded the initiation of an impartial probe into the alleged matter and threatened to go to the Supreme Court if the government failed to do so. Another threat by the PML (N) was that its MNAs could resign from the National Assembly if an impartial probe was not held. Other PML (N) leaders in rally also called the government a "corrupt Zardari mafia" and dubbed Imran Khan as a "pawn of the establishment" seeking support of the Jewish lobby. In the meantime, the court admitted a petition by the Watan Party seeking a probe into the matter. The court constituted a judicial panel which found both Haqqani and Zardari complicit in its probe. However, the judiciary's clutch on the civil government tightened in the elapsed matter of graft charges against President Zardari.

After surviving multiple crises, the Zardari administration came under a cloud when in the beginning of 2012 the Supreme Court intensified pressure on the Prime Minister to reopen the graft charges against the President. Prime Minister Gilani refused to write a letter to the Swiss authorities to reopen the cases as in his opinion President Zardari had constitutional immunity.[xx] However, the Prime Minister was convicted on contempt of court charges for his defiance to obey the orders. In the meantime, the opposition parties

xx. Article 248 of the Constitution provides immunity to the President stating: "No criminal proceedings whatsoever shall be instituted or continued against the President or a Governor in any Court during his term of office."

also filed a disqualification petition in a loan default case against the premier. After a long defiance, Prime Minister Gilani was disqualified and ousted from the top post in June 2012. After Gilani's disqualification, the PPP nominated Makhdoom Shahabuddin as its candidate for the Prime Ministerial post but due to the issuance of an arrest warrant on the day of nomination his name was withdrawn.[102] Thereafter, Raja Parvez Ashraf, elected as the next Prime Minister, was hard pressed by the Supreme Court to write the letter. After the court's order he finally gave in and wrote the letter to Swiss authorities. A Pakistani observer argued that entire issue was reflective of a partisan attitude of the media and superior judiciary as they only highlighted PPP's corruption and completely overlooked similar situations of corruption in the Punjab and PML (N)'s leadership. In her opinion this was probably "due to the links developed between Chief Justice Iftikhar Muhammad Chaudhry and Mian Nawaz Sharif during the Lawyers' Movement of 2007 and 2008."[103]

The confrontation between the judiciary and the executive is not new to Pakistan and has roots in the past when the judiciary used to act as an instrument of the military. But the recent confrontation was distinct in a way due to the judiciary's act as an autonomous power centre. The judiciary's determination to hold the executive accountable at the expense of parliament, which is the constitutional forum of executive accountability, was indicative of its ulterior motives. The judicial overreach in the guise of judicial activism was impinging on the legislative domain and the working of the executive. For a moment, the judges behaved like generals in black coats by appropriating powers beyond the constitutional prescription. The tussle certainly dented and scarred the face of the civil government.

Without a doubt, it was a period of a fragmented political scene but the Zardari government reached a milestone in its own sense. The formation of a coalition government with the main political rival to keep the military away was in itself a remarkable accomplishment. Mobilisation of a parliamentary consensus to pass the 18th Amendment, that transferred decisive powers to the executive, was unprecedented. All the parties must be credited for their pragmatism to bury their differences temporarily on this issue. Then the efforts to assert civilian supremacy by constantly engaging with the military and not giving chances was reflective of calculated treading on the part of the PPP. By the end of its term, the civilians pulled back some ground from the unilateral arbiter, creating some sort of balance of power. Despite all the assaults inflicted upon the elected government of PPP, it earned the distinction of completing its term. This set into motion a process of peaceful and legitimate transition of power from one elected regime to another.

PML (N)'s Third Chance to Govern: The Plutocracy of the Sharifs

The general election of 2013 was a political milestone created by political parties in Pakistan. Given the fact that democracy remained hostage to political antagonisms, even the mere completion of one civilian term was celebrated as an extraordinary accomplishment. The merit of this election was that it was not arranged under the military or any care-taker government on its behest but under a civilian setup. Unlike the previous election, which was fought as a symbol of democracy's battle against the autocratic *junta* regime, this election had an array of other issues at stake. The main issues in this election campaign were soaring inflation, increasing militancy and acute power shortage across the country. The outgoing government, led by the PPP, must be credited for completing its tenure; however, it faced stark anti-incumbency at the end. On the other hand, its arch rival and conventional alternative political force, the PML (N) faced a serious challenge from Imran Khan's PTI.

Unlike PML (N) which picked issues of governance and economy, Imran Khan, who was dubbed as 'Taliban Khan' and 'Clean-Shaved Mullah'[104] by his opponents campaigned totally on different issues. He blamed the government for the increasing drone attacks in the frontier region and selling Pakistani sovereignty to the Americans.[105] He made anti-Americanism a big issue and projected himself as the saviour of the country. He raised the slogan of '*Naya Pakistan*' and propagated Pakistan is for a changed narrative.[106] He pitched his PTI as an alternative force capable of bringing change from feudalistic and dynastic rule. During the campaign the phrase '*Naya Pakistan*' became the buzzword in both traditional and new media. The defender of the anti-blasphemy law, Imran Khan, projected himself as a right-inclined nationalist, committed to balance Islam and modernism. Therefore, he received tacit support of the Islamist militants who otherwise attacked the PPP, MQM and ANP party workers and leaders.

According to a report compiled by an Islamabad-based think tank, Pakistan witnessed a heightened spree of terrorist attacks and incidences of politically-motivated violence against political leaders, workers and election candidates during the campaigning period of the 2013 elections. The report noted that between 1 January and 15 May there were 148 reported terrorist attacks and 97 cases of political clashes in which 298 people were killed and 885 people were injured.[107] Karachi was the worst affected and most frequently targeted by this; Karachi alone faced 25 attacks in which 60 people lost their lives and 291 people were injured. The report shows that all parties shared the wrath of violent attacks but a party-wise breakup shows that ANP was worst-hit party with as many as 37 attacks by terror groups while the PPP and MQM followed with 12 attacks each. To escape the violent assault, the PPP, MQM and ANP restrained their campaign either to door-to-door campaign or social media platforms.

The election was held as scheduled and produced a predictable outcome. The PML (N) emerged as the single largest party with absolute majority. The incumbent PPP had the third largest vote percentage but occupied the second position with 31 seats. The crusader of 'New Pakistan,' Imran Khan managed to win 26 seats for his PTI and had to settle for third position with the second largest vote percentage. It was an extraordinary ascendancy by a party which had only one seat in the 2002 election since its inception. As the history of Pakistan's election goes back, the political parties levied the charges that the election was rigged and manipulated in constituencies where it lost and free and fair where they won. The PTI hailed the election results in KPK where it formed the government while it raised objections in Lahore and other 25 constituencies in which it lost. On the other hand the PML (N) and PML (Q) jointly questioned the validity of results in rural Sindh where they lost. Official complaints were filed with the Election Commission. The issue of rigging was to create massive protests in the next year and disrupt the government.

The PML (N) could form the government without any support. However as the MQM's history reveals it cannot stay out of power and as such extended unconditional support to the PML (N)'s presidential candidate.[108] Later it was revealed that in exchange for MQM's unconditional support it would be rewarded with a federal cabinet post.[109] The PTI and the PPP became the main opposition parties. The MQM ever since its formation used to be the third largest party because of its stronghold in urban Sindh but now was pushed to insignificance as PTI became the new force. The PML (Q) of General Musharraf who returned to Pakistan from London to lead his party, figured at the bottom of the list with 2 seats, one each from Bhawalpur and Gujranwala. Except for the fact that this election was the first civilian transition of power, nothing was new in terms of party politics. It was indeed a new situation for the PTI as they got such a mandate for the first time. Otherwise every political scene resonated to the politics of the past. The power structure was still a recap of the past traditional, feudalistic, elitist and patronage-based rule.

When Nawaz Sharif rose to the helm for the record third time in 2013 he constituted his cabinet on the basis of personal loyalty overriding merits. The personal preference of Sharif over professionalism was reflected not only in the selection of the cabinet but also in selection of Governors, President and as well as army chief. Mamnoon Hussain, the personal choice of Sharif for the post of President was reflective of the political leader's desire to have a hegemonic control over the polity. In Hasan Askari Rizvi's opinion the new President was chosen for being a "political non-entity within the PML (N) and outside."[110] He never figured in the party's decision-making structure. Similarly the appointment of Punjab governor Muhammad Sarwar from UK was indicative of personal consideration rather than political stature. The personal preferences factor was not limited to the filling of political positions but expanded to the military institution too. The selection of the new army chief was one such move. In the next section this issue is discussed in detail. The make-up of the cabinet, which was full of Punjabis (19 out of 28[111]) and along with three Sharifs (one each in Islamabad, Lahore and GHQ) boosted the public perception of Punjabi rule in Pakistan.

It is no secret that mainstream political parties are dynastic and run as a family syndicate.[xxi] But in 2013 Nawaz Sharif made the Pakistani political system look like family plutocracy of the Sharif clan. Sharif himself was at

xxi. Among powerful dynasties which run mainstream parties are: the Bhuttos of Sindh who are default leaders of PPP, the Sharifs of Punjab who run PML (N), the Bugtis of Baluchistan who have a monopoly over the Jamhoori Watan Party and the Khans of KPK who lead ANP. The MQM and PTI are still led by their founders since their inception and are yet to see leadership transition.

the country's highest post. His brother Shahbaz Sharif was at the top office of Punjab province. The choice of Ishaq Dar as finance minister, who is related to him through his daughter's marriage, extends the claw of the clan.[xxii]Sharif's nephew, Hamza Sharif, also an MNA, was indirectly inducted in the power structure in Punjab.[112] Maryam Nawaz Sharif, the eldest daughter of Nawaz Sharif, who has been active in politics since 2011, and was once described as Sharif's "apparent heir," and "presumed future leader" of his party[113], was given charge of the Prime Minister's Youth Programme in 2013. Sharif's two sons Hasan and Hussain Nawaz Sharif live abroad and ran their businesses. In 2016, they were named in a list of people having offshore accounts which created a huge political crisis for their father in Pakistan. Before this crisis, Nawaz Sharif had to survive a legitimacy challenge created by Imran Khan in 2014.

The Spectre of Azadi-Protest: Typical Pakistani Politics

On the day of Pakistan's 67th Independence Day, the leaders of two political parties organised separate, but simultaneous protests at the federal capital, to bring down the government of Nawaz Sharif. It was a moment of great administrative chaos and political confusion when on 14 August 2014 thousands of agitators assembled at the Central Secretariat area of Islamabad. The agitators were led by Imran Khan, the leader of PTI who projected his protest as *Azadi* march (march for freedom). The other protestors were followers of the Sufi cleric, Tahir-ul Qadri, the chairman of Pakistan Awami Tehreek (PAT), who gathered on his call for the *Inqilab* march (revolution march).[xxiii] The demands

---

xxii. Ishaq Dar is father-in-law of Nawaz Sharif's younger daughter Asma Sharif

xxiii. Punjabi by ethnicity, lawyer by qualification, religious preacher by profession, Dr. Tahir-ul Qadri is a preacher of the *Barelvi Fiqh* – an Islamic school of thought followed by the largest section of Pakistan. He rose to public prominence due to the work of his organisation *Minhajul Quran,* which runs educational centres globally. In 1989, he founded his own political party *Pakistan Awami Tehreek*. He was elected as a MNA in the 2002 election under General Musharraf's military rule. In 2004, Qadri resigned from the National Assembly and settled in Canada. He returned to Pakistan in 2012 to protest against the Zardari government but agreed to withdraw it after the Lahore Declaration. In 2014, he launched a parallel *Inqilab* March alongside Imran Khan's *Azadi* march. For his biographical note see Sher Ali Khan, "The Odd Man Out," *The Herald*, Vol. 47, No. 9, September 2014, pp. 59-63.

of the leaders, which were never agreed to by the government were: the resignation of the Prime Minister, setting-up of a care-taker government and holding of a free and fair snap election. General Musharraf, who was facing a trial for treason, also aligned with the PTI through his party the PML (Q) while agreeing to three points of Imran Khan's demand. A month before the *Azadi* protest both parties in a joint press conference agreed on three points — which were: "May 2013 elections were rigged, the election commission did not play its role and that protest should be held constitutionally and legally for securing rights."[114] The rationale behind these demands was the belief of Imran Khan that the last election was rigged and its outcome was stolen. Addressing the crowds at the launching of the *Azadi* march Imran Khan said that "Nawaz Sharif ... became the Prime Minister in a fixed match with the help of the Election Commission, caretaker government and other major [political] players. Nawaz's victory was unconstitutional as he snatched the public's mandate in a massive rigging."[115] The cleric on the other hand had additional demands: that those responsible for the Model Town massacre in which 17 of his followers were killed by the Punjab police be punished, and also the removal of Punjab Chief Minister Shahbaz Sharif.[116]

On the day of the protest, the cavalcades of the two agitating leaders moved towards Islamabad from Lahore. Their caravans were joined *en route* by the so-called revolutionaries but it was a tiny fraction of boasted "million men march" or "tsunami" of human wave.[117] However, the media's disproportionate coverage made it a spectacular event of the time. The supporters of PAT were largely religious followers of the *Barelvi* cleric and students of his educational institutions. On the other hand the PTI mobilised a section of educated urban youths. Their supporters decided to camp-in in the capital. It was a great spectacle for visual mediums when the 'revolutionaries' sang and danced during their sits-in, which reminded one of the 'Tahrir Square' movement in Egypt. The agitating leaders enthusiastically portrayed the protest as a mass movement reflecting people's will. But after the initial cold response from the government it became clear that leaders of people's will had no roadmap to navigate the progress of the movement. Along with their leaders, the followers decided to camp-out till Nawaz's resignation.

What these leaders did not explain was how the movement would reach its logical conclusion. What if Nawaz Sharif does not resign? Why would the army intervene on their behalf and, why would not the army take power in its hand if it intervened at all? The protest continued to progress without these explanations. On the third day of the protest, Imran Khan called for 'Civil Disobedience', appealing to Pakistanis to refuse to pay taxes and utility bills to the "corrupt government" and issued an ultimatum to Nawaz Sharif to resign within two days, otherwise the protestors would enter the capital's Red Zone area.[118] The call for civil disobedience created panic in the stock market; as a result investors lost billions of rupees in the share market.[119] Two days after the ultimatum the protestors frustrated with the government's delaying tactic entered the Red Zone area of the capital, a high-security zone housing Pakistan's most important buildings, including Parliament, Presidential and Prime Minister Houses and Embassies. The government handed over the security to the army to vacate the area from the agitating crowd.[120] Thereafter the military directed both the conflicting parties to resolve the issue peacefully in a constitutional framework.[121] After a fortnight of protest, the exhausted protestors crossed the threshhold and cordoned off the Prime Minister's house.

As a result of the action by the security forces three protestors died and hundreds got injured.[122] Thereafter, the military had to step-in and once again advised the government to resolve the impasse through dialogue. Prior to this, both Imran Khan and Qadri met the military leaders separately and urged them to act as mediator and claimed that the military had agreed to look into the matter.[123] Their euphoric gesture strengthened the opponents' claim of the protest being orchestrated on behalf of the military. Despite the military's advice to resolve the issue, there was a stalemate as both Imran Khan and Nawaz Sharif did not like to appear as compromising leaders. The protest ended without negotiation when Imran Khan withdrew it following the Peshawar school attack in December. However, the critics believed that the protest had achieved its goal of weakening the Sharif government. Because the military also indicated its willingness to arbitrate during the protest, many opponents of the protest suspected conspiracy of the establishment behind the protest.

Critics branded Imran Khan and Qadri as the military's 'stooges', who had been deployed to weaken the democratically elected government.[124] Some analysts interpreted this crisis as a "soft coup"[125] and "new coup" by the real boss who did not like the civilians to rule their own. But instead of taking power back in their hands the military fixed the civilians through this mechanism.[126] This narrative was corroborated by the synchronised behavioural pattern of the military and agitating parties which unfolded during the period of protest. On 31 August the military issued its third advisory to the government to deal peacefully with the protestors. The statement came after the Corps Commanders' Conference following the violent clash of the previous day in which three protestors died. The statement read thus: "… the conference reviewed with serious concern, the existing political crisis and the violent turn it has taken, resulting in large scale injuries and loss of life," therefore any "further use of force will only aggravate the problem," hence, "…the situation should be resolved politically without wasting any time and without resorting to violent means."[127] The political behaviour before and during the clash indicated that politicians on both sides knew it was coming.

Three days before this advisory, Nawaz Sharif had met General Raheel Sharif and asked him to "facilitate" the resolving of the crisis. After the meeting, General Sharif invited Imran Khan and Qadri to discuss the matter which they happily accepted. A retired military officer Talat Masood expressed his surprise on how eagerly the two leaders agreed to meet the man in khaki "to discuss purely political issues."[128] On the other hand the government rationalised its move to bring the military to arbitrate because of Qadri and Imran Khan's refusal to any other mechanism. The entire episode underlined the weak position of civilian political leadership in the political system of Pakistan. In the words of Mohammad Waseem "The crisis has exposed the incapacity of the Prime Minister to deal with the situation without support of the army."[129] The rationale of his argument lies in the civilian political leadership's meek acceptance of the army's central role in the resolution of the political crisis. By accepting the military's superior role, the political class risked losing the legitimacy of democratic institutions. According to Saeed Shafqat's analysis the crisis was to leave a "problem of legitimacy" to the civilian government and "that is exactly what the crisis aimed at."[130] The incapability to take a decision by Nawaz Sharif was seen as the reason for the army's revival in politics. According to Hasan Askari Rizvi, due to the crisis the government had lost considerable political space and because of the failure of civilian political leaders to manage the crisis effectively the army ascended to national and political prominence.[131] Looking back at the entire episode one cannot deny civilian failure but many saw the military as the architect of the crisis and it had its own reasons.

Many in Pakistan believed that the entire theatrics of crisis was scripted and directed by the military. The sole motive was to weaken the elected government as they increasingly asserted civilian supremacy. Analysts noted that the military did not like Nawaz Sharif's efforts to make peace with India, the trial of General Musharraf, his silence during the Hamid Mir incident and business deals with China without taking the military into confidence.[132]

The next section on civil-military relations discusses these issues in detail. Since Nawaz Sharif had such a massive popular mandate it would have been pertinent on the part of the military to undermine him through his political opponents. When Imran Khan and Tahir-ul Qadri were creating lawlessness in the capital the military was supposed to protect it under the Constitution, either it was ineffective in controlling the situation or deliberately preferred to ignore it.[xxiv] Contrary to its constitutional responsibility to aid the civilian administration the military advised the civilian leadership against using force to stop the protest. The protesting leaders also reciprocated the favour by advising their followers not to confront the army and behave respectfully towards them. During the protest, Imran Khan openly threatened policemen that he would hang them if they dared to stop his march and would drag Nawaz Sharif out of his house.[133] But army did not ask him to behave and why would it when Khan was helping its cause? Even Javed Hashmi – PTI's President – in a public statement said that Khan was working at the behest of the military.[134] In an image control exercise the military's public relation wing issued a statement that the "Army is an apolitical institution" and is not behind the PTI-PAT protest.[135] Later Javed Hashmi was expelled from the PTI.

Ayesha Siddiqa in her sharp criticism of the military's attitude said that indeed the Pakistan army is a professionally structured organisation

xxiv. Under Article 245 of the constitution, the Pakistan army is bound to ensure the security of the federal capital. Despite the government's seeking the army's service to maintain law and order under this constitutional provision, the army allowed the protestors to besiege the Prime Minister house.

but has become "political and politicised" and has dependency in terms of its control over the state which is part of its "psychological architecture."[136] Because of this attitude, the military legitimised the demands of the rabble-rousing duo. The military, instead of being neutral and coming to the aid of the civilians chose to be a referee in the political process, making decisions in favour of the side that rejected to play by the constitutional rule of game.[137] An editorial in a national newspaper captured this behaviour succinctly, writing that when protestors attacked the parliament, the military warned the government against using force instead of restraining the offenders. The editorial stated: "It's as if the army is unaware – rather, unwilling – to acknowledge the constitutional scheme of things: it is the government that is supposed to give orders to the army, not the other way around."[138] All these indicated the military's disregard for the constitutional mechanism to resolve political crises as well as its capacity to undermine elected leaders by using its political opponents.

By the end of the crisis, the military emerged triumphant but there was one positive outcome for the democratic process. Despite the military's ploy to pitch politicians against politicians the larger political class exhibited a high degree of maturity. The mainstream secular parties inducing PML (N)'s arch rival PPP, MQM and ANP along with the religious parties Jamaat-e-Islami and JUF disapproved the demands of dissolution of national and provincial assemblies and resignation of the elected Prime Minister. In a show of support to stabilise the democratic system, the lawmakers from a spectrum of parties asserted their support for Nawaz Sharif in a special session convened by the Prime Minister shortly after the protest.[139] However, despite their collective defence of the democratic system the civilian political leadership became onlookers to their eroding authority. And their position was further weakened because of other issues which brought the government face to face with the military establishment.

Civil-Military Relations: The Tilting Balance

At the time of government formation, Nawaz Sharif's party had a complete majority. Unlike the outgoing coalition government led by the PPP, which was fettered by the alliance partners' whims, the new government was capable of unitary decision-making. Despite its compulsions for coalitions the PPP government appeared to be balancing civil-military relations. The PPP government benefited due to a transition period in which the military restrained itself from open interference in the polity and rebuilt its image as a non-partisan institution committed to national interest. At the end of its tenure the PPP successfully, at least in popular perception, laid out a civil-military framework in which both the actors appeared to be relatively autonomous in their respective spheres. Therefore, the new government which had an absolute majority was expected to tilt the balance in favour of the civilians. The initial year saw the efforts of civilian assertion over certain issues including the choice of a new COAS.

With the change of the head of the government there also came a change of guard as well. General Raheel Sharif was appointed as the army chief by the Prime Minister. The appointment of a new army chief by a civilian government took place after 15 years of gap. Although Nawaz Sharif in a pre-election interview with an Indian journalist had committed that the senior-most General would be appointed as the next army chief,[140] he elevated General Sharif to the post of army chief superseding two senior army officers. Following General Sharif's appointment, Lieutenant General Haroon Aslam, the senior most officer resigned. The election manifesto of the ruling PML (N) promised reforms in civil-military relations. A monitor published by the Pakistan Institute of Legislative Development and Transparency (PILDAT) observed that the new government missed the opportunity to bring reforms in the Higher Defence Organisation (HDO) which is long due since 1976. The monitor also noted that an empowered fulltime defence minister would have been helpful in balancing civil-military relations. Instead the new government has given charge of the defence ministry to the federal water minister.[141] The government also revived the National Security Council (NSC) which was dysfunctional during the previous regime of Zardari. Thereafter, in the next two years the contention between the civilian and military leadership deepened over a range of political and non-political issues.

Even before completing a year in power, the federal government initiated a legal trial of former President General Musharraf. He was to be tried on charges of 'high treason' under Article 6 of the Constitution for his extra-constitutional usurpation of power[142] as well as conspiring the assassination of Benazir Bhutto, murder of Baluch leader Akbar Bugti and murder of *Lal Masjid* cleric Ghazi Abdul Rasheed.[143] In a way, it was a bold move to pursue the case that could have served as a deterrent to servicemen to constrain them into their professional domain. But it was also amounting to fishing in trouble waters as critics saw it as impractical and an act of personal vendetta for Nawaz's ouster in 1999 and removal of the chief justice in 2007. Even General Musharraf pleaded 'not guilty' to the treason charge and earlier called it an act of vendetta.[144] On the other hand, the case of 'high treason' was not in accordance with the law, unlike the 1999 coup in which the Constitution was abrogated. The imposition of emergency in 2007 was under constitutional provisions; therefore, if Musharraf was to be tried it should have been on his action of 1999. Also in the past during his tenure former Prime Minister Yousaf Raza Gilani had told a group of journalists that Article 6 was not applicable in this case. Emphasising the impracticality of the case Gilani stated that:

> Article 6 cannot be applied to one individual ... those who supported him are today in my cabinet and some of them have also joined the PML (N) ... the MMA, the MQM and the PML (Q) supported him ... this is why I have said that it is not doable.[145]

Many in the military also did not like the idea of trial of an army chief by civilians. The decision to impose emergency was not General Musharraf's individual idea, rather it had to be the collective decision of the top brass as well as the political body in power that time. Therefore, General Musharraf's conviction meant reopening of the old wound that could hurt people on both sides. It is unthinkable that the military would have sided with the civilians and sacrificed a member of their own fraternity. The military prevailed and the travel-ban on Musharraf was lifted[146] who avoided many trials. More than the ongoing trial of General Musharraf, what infuriated the military establishment was the federal government's silence on the media's barb against the ISI following an attack on Geo TV journalist Hamid Mir.

On 19 April 2014, Hamid Mir was attacked in Karachi. After the attack his brother openly alleged that the DG (ISI) was involved in the assault. The news channel relentlessly telecast the report and debated the incident in a manner which the army considered degrading and maligning of the institution. What disappointed the military was the federal government's silence during the channel's assault on the ISI and the military. To add insult to injury Nawaz Sharif visited Hamid Mir, which was interpreted as a siding with the accuser. In a damage control mode the military's public relation wing ISPR responded and an official complaint against the channel was filed with PEMRA. In a show of solidarity, General Sharif visited the ISI headquarter and endorsed its plea to PEMRA to ban the transmission of Geo TV as well as suspend its license causing embarrassment to the government.[147] The soldiers who saw a deliberate plot in the silence of the government called it all "orchestrated" while politicians raised questions that if a ruling Prime Minister, a working judge or ordinary citizen can be accused, why could not a general be accused?[148] On the other hand, many political and social organisations staged nationwide rallies in support of the military.[149] While this incident was fading out the divergent approach on counter-insurgency policies by the military and the government made the faultlines of civil-military relations apparent.

In mid-2014, the Pakistan military finally launched an operation named *Zarb-e-Azb* (named after the sword used by the Prophet of Islam) to root out the menace of terrorism from Pakistan.[150] During Zardari's tenure the military had launched similar operations called *Rahe-e-Rast* in which *Tehreek-e-Taliban Pakistan* (TTP) militants were chased out from Swat and Malakand division in 2009. The period under Nawaz Sharif became very volatile as the scale of militant activities and fatalities grew. There was mounting pressure on the federal government to control the militant *tanzeems*, especially the TTP. The military wanted to go hard on the militants operating in the frontier areas. The PML (N) government was in a catch-22 situation due to its broad support base which encompasses large religiously conservative segments sympathetic to justification of the anti-Americanism of the pro-violence *tanzeems*. The religious parties including Jamaat-e-Islami and JUF were openly against the military solution that included attacks on TTP hideouts. On the other hand, secular and left inclined parties such as the PPP, MQM and ANP publicly condemned the spread of violence by terror groups. The PML (N) which never openly opposed militant groups benefitted during the election campaign as they were not targeted and Punjab also remained calm when other provinces were under assault.

Amid the growing militant attacks the PML (N) found itself in tricky situation. On one hand it had risk of losing part of its electoral support, on the other hand the military was determined to take the government on board before launching the military operation. Under pressure, the government proposed peace-talks with the TTP, which they had never asked for.[151] Consequently, the talks never took off but it gave the militants time to relocate their hideouts. After months of waiting without the government's approval, the military launched a military operation called *Zarb-e-Azb* in North Waziristan. After the Peshawar school massacre, in which more than 140 people mostly school children, belonging to the military fraternity were killed,[152] the military hardened its pressure on the civilian government to come on board for the military operation. The Peshawar massacre shaped public opinion in favour of elimination of terrorists to which the political parties also could not disassociate themselves publicly. Even a political leader sympathetic to TTP, such as Imran Khan, had to end his *Azadi* protest and abandon his idea of a peace-dialogue with the Taliban. The federal government in its enthusiasm to show solidarity to popular opinion came up with a National Action Plan (NAP).

The NAP was a 20-point based roadmap to root out terrorism in Pakistan.[153] The action plan was agreed to by all parties in the All Parties Conference chaired by Prime Minister Nawaz Sharif.[154] To implement the NAP two steps were to be taken. First, Provincial Apex Committees in all the provinces were formed to coordinate and implement the NAP.[155] The apex committees comprised both political and military leadership. Second, to combat terrorism by implementing the NAP, special military courts with special powers to try militants accused in terror cases were constituted. To establish military courts, a constitutional amendment needed to be passed, for which political consensus was required. The Jamaat-e-Islami and JUF objected to the use of words "religion and sect" and insisted they be ommited from the amendment bill. Both the parties, along with PTI, abstained from voting — but with support coming in from the PPP and the ANP, the government managed to pass the 21st Amendment to the Constitution and the Pakistan Army Amendment Bill that would empower military courts to try civilians under terror charges.

An editorial in a national daily called the passage of 21st Amendment "A Sad Day" for democracy. It remarked that it would empower the military further and "the 21st constitutional amendment would stand as a monument to the betrayal of the civilian, democratic cause."[156] It was a sad moment, wrote the editorial, to see how meekly the political leadership "has abdicated its democratic responsibilities"[157] and submitted to the generals, allowing them to direct the political process. It pointed out that it was not only the military courts, which undermined civilian institutions, the apex committees too have severely compromised civilian autonomy from the military. A political analyst opined that "the emergence of the apex committee as the focal entity for decision-making pushes the federal and provincial cabinets to the sidelines and brings the army formally into civilian administrative domain."[158] It was a new institutional mechanism through which the military could interfere with provincial autonomy in the name of security.

The government's rationalisation of establishing military courts beyond civilian writ, at the time of civilian rule, exposed two fundamental weaknesses of the elected government. The first was:, the civilian dispensation under PML (N) was not capable of coping with internal security threats and it therefore had to rely on the armed forces. The military which had a coercive edge over civilians did not want to do this 'dirty job' on civilian dictates but on their own terms. Therefore civilians could not resist their demand and had to go along with the military's play. By establishing military courts, the civilians brought the *khaki* into the judicial domain supposedly exclusive sphere of the elected rulers. Secondly, the military's deep penetration in the civilian process reinforces its guardianship of the nation and its 'saviour of Pakistan' attitude. This attitude is a product of the military's long indoctrination of the 'self' imparted through institutional training. The soldiers not only see themselves responsible for the country's security but believe it as their duty to protect the national interest.

The military officers who dislike absolute civilian subordination and adjust to conditional subordination see the military as a "watchdog" of national interest. They believe civilian parties and politicians are incapable of governing and managing national security issues. If the officers perceive that the civilians are not able to manage a "crisis situation" that may dent the "institutional integrity" the military may not hesitate to support a coup for a regime change.[159]Aqil Shah in his study of research papers written at the National Defence University (NDU) between 2000 and 2007 found that the pre-approved subjects on which students were writing had "strong socialisation effects" which had contributed to the watchdog attitude. The subjects ranged from "the inadequacy of the Constitution in forging national integration,"... "elimination of corruption,"..., industrialisation, privatisation, to "development of civil society without compromising national security." These texts in Shah's opinion have "advocated and legitimised a broad military role in governmental affairs."[160] The military periodically has exercised its oversight over civilian authorities and its role and capability of the "ultimate watchdog" remains intact. For the time being it may have preferred not to engage in direct rule but its non-interference in governmental affairs is likely to remain conditional on the behaviour of the elected government that does not undermine national security in the military's view.[161] The 'watchdog' which seemed to be ceding space to the civilians in the post-Musharraf period has now made it clear that it retains a capacity to intervene in the political process. By its interference and attempts to manipulate the political process in the last two years it has amply demonstrated it.

Naya Pakistan: Is There Hope for Democracy?

Today there is a new government in Pakistan led by PTI. It was a historic moment in Pakistan politics when Imran Khan and his party dethroned PML (N) in the July 2018 general election. When the PML (N)-led civilian government completed its tenure and second consecutive civilian term in 2018 it generated hope for the consolidation of democracy. Mere continuation of elected civilian governments has ushered hope that it will stabilise democratic institutions and deepen democratic culture in Pakistan. The PTI rose to power on the promise of creating *Naya Pakistan* to be built on Medina model of Islamic welfare state. This was Imran Khna's promise of change and democratic consolidation. His promise faces an array of challenges. One of the prime challenges, in terms of democratic consolidation, is the rejuvenation of democratic institutions and restoring public faith in them as they had become subject to decay under the previous government.

The government, led by the PPP, passed the ball to a political foe but a partner in democracy, the PML (N) in 2013. Though Nawaz Sharif made a cautious beginning, the circumstances unfolded in an unfavorable but not unexpected manner, which has weakened the case of democracy. In the preceding sections, it's been already discussed how personal preferences of the Prime Minister in the making of the cabinet and other administrative positions undermined the principle of merit. This created the impression of the government being elitist and plutocratic and not democratic. Sharif's government also failed on all crucial fronts, including the management of internal security, managing political crises, improving the economy, delivery of key services (especially supply of electricity) and development of the education and health sector.

In mid-2016 an Islamabad-based think tank published its qualitative and quantitative findings on the quality of democracy for the third year of Nawaz Sharif's government. The report indicated that civilian writ had eroded for the period in consideration. The erosion accelerated even further in the third year, due to military's activism and visibility in framing the country's internal security and foreign policies. More than this, the democratic system atrophied because institutional mechanisms such as parliament and cabinet were circumvented in favour of informal and temporary alternatives to govern the country. The preferences and over-use of *ad hoc* mechanisms such as "all-party conferences," and "apex committees", to formulate policies and as well as to supervise their implementation—also the sacrificing of institutional options, put the government's capabilities to rule in question. According to the report the federal cabinet only met four times in 2015, wherein it is needed to meet 52 times as per the rules.[162] The NSC, which was revived by the Prime Minister after he took charge did not meet even once during this period. Above all, the COAS and the Prime Minister met for a record 78 times ever since Raheel Sharif was appointed army chief in November 2013 till December 2015 — even so for 21% of these meetings the Defence Minsiter was absent.[163]

In the provinces too, the meetings held by the apex committees (constituted to supervise the implementation of the NAP agenda) surpassed the meeting of the provincial cabinets. In Sindh, where rangers were deployed in counter-terrorism operations, the cabinet met six times as against 11 apex committee meetings that were held. In KPK despite the ongoing military operations, the nine apex committee meetings overshadowed the five cabinet sittings. In Baluchistan five cabinet sittings took place as against eight meetings of the apex committees. In the more peaceful (and Sharif's own province) Punjab, the cabinet met only thrice, while apex committees met seven times.[164] On the face of it, the performance of the lawmakers was well below the satisfactory level.

The parliamentarians, whether in the Senate or in the National Assembly, fared average in terms of attendance. The Prime Minister attended only 20 per cent of the sessions in 2015 while Imran Khan was present for two per cent of such sittings.[165] This in a way reflected how seriously they took legislative business. Such an attitude of the elected representative for the democratic system was probably also reflected in public opinion in the assessment of democracy. A separate public opinion survey by the same institute noted that although 64 per cent of the respondents believed that "democratically elected Governments constitute the best system for Pakistan" while the armed forces with 75 per cent approval ratings remained the most trusted institution among all.[166] The worrisome news for the political parties from the survey was that they figured below approval level and one of the least trusted institutions with 36 per cent ratings. It could also be said that civilians collectively failed in their commitment to democracy and were responsible for giving the military a lead in the game. The party in government, PML (N) has to shoulder the larger part of the blame but some in the opposition are to equally blame as their action was in no way helping consolidate democracy. Some remained passive spectators in the hope that they would replace the ruling party in the next election. In this hope the political opposition once again in 2016 attacked the government and in the process weakened the civilian system giving the military another chance to tighten the noose a bit on the civilian administration.

Bruised and compromised, Nawaz Sharif, who had somehow survived the sit-in fiasco of 2014 orchestrated by Imran Khan, conceded considerable civilian space to the military leadership. Through apex committees and military courts, the military institutionally expanded its role in the civilian domain. While in the process of recovering from the sit-in shocks and military's institutional assault, Nawaz Sharif suffered another blow in May 2016 when the International Consortium of Investigative Journalists (ICIJ) made a disclosure about off-shore assets of more than 200 Pakistanis.[167]

Although, the documents released known as the 'Panama Papers' did not name Sharif directly, but they connected him through his three children. A separate category of "Power Players" in the database revealed that Mariam Safdar, daughter of Nawaz Sharif, and his two sons Hussain and Hasan Nawaz Sharif owned off-shore entitlements.[168] Having off-shore entitlements is not illegal in Pakistan but for Nawaz Sharif, being the head of the state, the fallout of the revelations had serious consequences.

The *Panama Leaks* allowed the political opposition to raise the ethical accountability question against him. After the revelation of Sharif family's off-shore holdings the opposition parties demanded "forensic audit by a reputable international firm" as well as probe by the "National Accountability Bureau, the State Bank of Pakistan, the Election Commission of Pakistan and the Federal Board of Revenue" and the setting up of a judicial commission.[169] Upping the ante in a televised speech, the PTI leader demanded Sharif's resignation on ethical grounds saying, "On behalf of the people of Pakistan, I demand your resignation because after the Panama Papers, you have lost the moral authority to run the government."[170] They warned of organising massive protests in case the government does not meet the opposition demands.

In the meantime, the military also played its cards and cornered the civilian government. On 19 April the COAS in an army event called for "across the board accountability" for the betterment of Pakistan which is not possible without uprooting the "menace of corruption."[171] Two days later, the army dismissed six officers on the charges of corruption.[172] In the context of the Panama Papers revelation, it was seen as a calculative decision from the military's side to build pressure on the civilians to act on the matter of corruption which became issue of national debate in Pakistan. Moreover, the politics of the Panama Papers was more about public perception, than legality of having offshore entitlements. Nawaz kept on defending his children rather than addressing the moral and ethical question. To mount more pressure, Imran Khan openly invited the military to take over the country's administration stating that "democracy in Pakistan is threatened by Nawaz's monarchy and the people will celebrate and distribute sweets if the army takes over."[173] Despite the army's symbolic push and political parties' pressure Sharif appeared unmoved. His apparent inaction frustrated the opposition which then organised the *Ehtesab March* in September to demonstrate its street power. The march was led by Imran Khan and his party and supported by the PML (Q), PPP, PAT, and Jamaat-e-Islami.[174] All these political parties had their own reasons to come together on a common platform.

In February 2016, the government angered many religious parties by hanging Mumtaz Qadri – an ex-police guard charged with the murder of former governor of Punjab, Salman Taseer for his opposition to Blasphemy Laws. Qadri's supporters from *Sunni Tehreek* and *Ahle Sunnat* and other political parties held a demonstration against his hanging.[175] What angered the religious parties even more was the passage of The Women's Protection Bill,[176] by the PML (N)'s Punjab government and its resolve to pass similar Acts at the federal level. The agitated Jamaat-e-Islami and JUI (F) in panic convened an all-parties conference of 30 religious parties and called the Act as "un-Islamic" and "against the Constitution of Pakistan and Sharia Law" and made demands to retract it.[177] Within a week, the alarmed religious parties including Jamat-ud-Dawah met again to discuss the scheme of "nationwide movement to bring down the government, put an end to that oh-so-detestable conspiracy of infidels to transform Pakistan into a godless liberal polity."[178] The rationale, critics saw behind the movement was the belief of the religious parties that the sentiment generated in the previous protest could be harnessed to topple the government and by so doing they could revive their political fortune.[179] Therefore, when Imran Khan called for a protest in the wake of the *Panama Leaks* they joined in.

The PML (Q), which had lost its political significance after the 2013 elections was infuriated because its patron, the former President of Pakistan General Musharraf was dragged into legal trials by the government. Thus, whenever it got a chance to weaken the Sharif government in protest, whether it was with the *Azadi* March or the *Ehtesab* March the PML (Q) proactively joined them. The PPP, which was undergoing a leadership transition and needed time to rebuild its organisational structure but would also be happy to see a weak PML (N), smartly supported these movements from outside. The MQM was caught up in a different set of circumstances. Though it did not support such movements, it suffered heavily under the PML (N) government. In September 2013 amid growing cases of violence, the federal governments handed over Karachi's security to the Pakistan Rangers (Sindh). Since then Karachi was *de facto* ruled by the coercive forces than elected representatives. The rangers were conducting raids and crackdowns on hideouts of so-called Muhajir militant elements. With this the media also portrayed the MQM in a negative light which added to the frustration of its leadership. Altaf Hussain, who was crying about targeted victimisation at the hands of federal government, criticised its actions in harsh language, which resulted in his loss of power.

While addressing his followers and protesting against "media bias" Hussain chanted anti-Pakistani slogans, one in which he referred to Pakistan as a "cancer for the entire world" and another one —"down with Pakistan."[180] Following his diatribe MQM supporters attacked the ARY News office in which one person died and several people were injured. The administrative response was to take MQM leaders into custody on the alleged charges of inciting violence in the city; sealed Nine Zero and other zonal offices of the MQM; it also blocked its website.[181] Hussain's remarks on the other hand resulted in public, political and official condemnation and had serious repercussions for both Hussain and the MQM. Cases of treason and spreading terror were filed against him.

The party leaders dissociated themselves from Hussain's slogans, condemned it and expressed patriotism in the social media by raising *Pakistan Zindabad* slogans. The incident turned-out to be a rupture in the power-structure of MQM. Alienated by his own party members, Hussain made the excuse of undergoing "severe mental stress" and begged pardon of the COAS Raheel Sharif and DG Rangers (Sindh) for his anti-Pakistani remarks from and assured them that he would not to repeat such slogans again.[182]Farooque Sattar, the deputy convener and backbone of the party in Pakistan seemed to be not only challenging Hussain's monopoly over the party's decision-making but completely sidelining him. Farooque Sattar in a dramatic statement said Hussain's frequent apologies after such statements ridiculed the entire party and was pushing it into confinement; he added that if this was all a result of "mental stress" it needed to be resolved first, hence, "all the decisions will be made by party members in Pakistan."[183] Such a categorical statement was indicative of a major shift in the methods of functioning of the party. Following such a strong message from MQM leaders within Pakistan Altaf Hussain, now old, sick and isolated handed over "powers of reorganisation, policy-making and decision-making," to the party's coordination committee.[184] Although everything seems settled for the time being, but with the possible departure of Altaf Hussain the MQM will no longer be the force it used to be.

The cumulative result of the infighting amongst political parties was a sign of the weakening of the civilian forces who were supposed to create an alternative system against the military order. The then ruling PML (N), in its over-confidence, alienated almost all the civilian partners in the long term struggle for democracy against the military. The PML (N) government certainly had strength in the National Assembly but its capacity to rule has eroded. Christophe Jaffrelot has succinctly captured the essence of this erosion in a sentence that "the army may be in a position to rule without governing – Nawaz Sharif is offering them a façade of democracy that is most convenient."[185] There is reasoning behind such a strong statement. The army has taken a lead in the internal security matters whether in the frontier regions or Karachi. The civilians had to backtrack on important foreign policy issues such as rapprochement with India or relations with China. Not only have they dominated security and foreign policy but now have also entered the corruption debate within the country, a domain supposed to be purely civilian. So, visibly it was the military that appeared to be ruling the country without taking the responsibility of diurnal issues of governance.

Amid this chaos Imran Khan and his PTI rose to power promising to bring substantial change '*Tabdeeli*' and creating a '*Naya Pakistan*' on the basis of the Medina model. Khan and his party were able to capture power because there was a vacuum of political leadership to which he offered a viable alternative. Thus, in the general election of 2018 PTI emerged as single largest party expanding its social and political base in Punjab and Sindh, especially Karachi. There were two spectrums of arguments which followed from this election outcome. The critics saw the entire electoral exercise as another coming of a deep state in the guise of a constitutional façade. On the other hand the optimists saw it as a pro-democracy step and hoped that it would somehow consolidate the process of democratisation of Pakistan. The positive development for democracy in the last one decade was that functional democracy was in continuation. This very fact can help perpetuate the spread of a democratic culture. Along with this, there is one entire generation which got politicised in this civilian period who might become the carrier of the political system in which they grew up.

Notes

1. Pervez Musharraf, *In the Line of Fire: A Memoir* (New York: Free Press, 2006), p. 144.
2. "Excerpts from General Musharraf's Address," *BBC News*, 17 October 1999, URL: http://news.bbc.co.uk/2/hi/world/monitoring/477829.stm (accessed on 4 May 2013).
3. Musharraf, *In the Line of Fire*, p. 137.
4. Hasan Abbas, *Pakistan's Drift into Extremism: Allah, the Army and America's War on Terror* (New York: East Gate Book, 2005), p. 178.
5. Christophe Jaffrelot, *The Pakistan Paradox: Instability and Resilience* (Gurgaon: Random House India, 2015), pp. 300 &338.
6. Ian Talbot, *Pakistan: A New History* (London: Hurst and Company, 2012), Ibid, p. 196.
7. Musharraf, *In the Line of Fire*, pp. 172-3.
8. Talbot, *Pakistan: A New History*, p. 182.
9. Ibid.
10. ICG, "Reforming the Judiciary in Pakistan," *International Crisis Group*, Asia Report, No. 160, October 2008, pp. 2-3.
11. Massoud Ansari, "How the Referendum was Won," *Newsline*, 15 May 2003, URL: http://www. newslinemagazine.com/2002/05/how-the-referendum-was-won/ (accessed on 4 July 2011). Also see Ajay Darshan Behera, "On The Edge of Metamorphosis," in Ajay Darshan Behera and Mathew Joseph C. (eds.), *Pakistan in a Changing Strategic Context* (New Delhi: Knowledge World, 2004), p. 20.
12. Anatol Lieven, *Pakistan: A Hard Country* (London: Penguin Books, 2011), p. 163.
13. Ibid.
14. Ibid, pp. 18-23.
15. Nasir Iqbal, "1,027 Civilian Posts Occupied by Servicemen," *Dawn*, 3 October 2003, URL: http://www.dawn.com/news/118233/1027-civilian-posts-occupied-by-servicemen (accessed on 29 June 2013).
16. For detailed post-wise inductions see Ibid.
17. Jaffrelot, *The Pakistan Paradox*, p. 341.
18. Musharraf, *In the Line of Fire*, p. 171.
19. Hasan-Askari Rizvi, "National Security Council: A Debate on Institutions and Processes for Decision-Making on Security Issues," *Pakistan Institute for Legislative Development and Transparency*, Discussion Paper. Islamabad, April 2012, p. 29.
20. For the list of major instances of irrelevance of the NSC to policy-making see Ibid, p. 30.
21. Jaffrelot, *The Pakistan Paradox*, p. 344.
22. For a detailed analysis and brief compilation of global and regional responses to the coup and Nawaz Sharif's exit, see Iftikhar H. Malik, "Pakistan in 2000: Starting

Anew or Stalemate?" *Asian Survey*, Vol. 41, No.1, pp. 112-4. Also see Tahir Kamran, *Democracy and Governance in Pakistan* (Lahore: South Asia Partnership-Pakistan, 2008), pp. 176-82.

23. Fareed Zakaria, *The Future of Freedom: Illiberal Democracy at Home and Abroad* (New Delhi: Viking, 2003), pp. 100-1.
24. Shuja Nawaz, *Crossed Swords: Pakistan, its Army, and the Wars Within* (New York: Oxford University Press, 2008), p. 173.
25. Omar Noman, "Pakistan and General Zia: Era and Legacy," *Third World Quarterly*, Vol. 11, No. 1, January 1989, p. 35.
26. Ibid.
27. Tariq Ali, *The Duel: Pakistan in the Flight Path of American Power* (New York: Simon and Schuster, 2008), p.156.
28. Mohammad Waseem, "The Electronic Media Explosion," *Dawn*, 6 November 2006, URL: http://archives. dawn.com/2006/11/06/ed.htm (accessed on 11 July 2011).
29. "Media in Pakistan: Between Radicalisation and Democratisation in an Unfolding Conflict," *International Media Support*, Report, July 2009, p. 14, URL: http://www.i-ms.dk/files/publications/1491 %20Pakistan,final.web.pdf (accessed on 20 June 2011).
30. The report noted that in the first half of 2006 as many as 48 media persons were reported to be undergoing such harassment. "Opposition Seeks Debate in Senate on Media Reports," *Dawn*, 29 July 2006, URL: http://www.dawn.com/news/203609/opposition-seeks-debate-in-senate-on-media-reports (accessed on 2 May 2015).
31. Adnan Rehmat, "Murder and Mayhem: The Worst Year Ever for Pakistani Media," *Intermedia*, 3 May 2008, cited in Jaffrelot, *The Pakistan Paradox*, p. 419.
32. Noman, "Pakistan and General Zia: Era and Legacy," pp. 34-5.
33. Ibid.
34. "Jurisdiction of the Court," *Federal Shariat Court of Pakistan*, n. d., URL: http://www.federals hariatcourt.gov.pk/Jurs.html (accessed on 27 September 2015).
35. See the text of "Provisional Constitution Order 1 of 1999," *Pakistan Constitution Law*, URL: https://pakistanconstitutionlaw.com/provisional-constitution-order-1999/ (accessed on 15 June 2015).
36. Zafar Ali Shah, PLD 2000 Supreme Court, p. 869, cited in ICG, "Reforming Pakistan's Civil Service," *International Crisis Group*,Asia Report, No. 185, 16 February 2010, p. 4.
37. See the text of "The Constitution (Seventeenth Amendment) Act, 2003." *Pakistan Constitution Law*, URL: https://pakistanconstitutionlaw.com/17th-amendment-2003/ (accessed on 15 June 2015).
38. For details see "Profile of Chief Justice and Judges," *Supreme Court of Pakistan*, Annual Report, April 2010- December 2011, URL: http://www.supremecourt.gov.pk/Annual_Rpt/Profile%20of%20the%20Chi ef%20Justice.pdf (accessed on 13 January 2016).
39. Nasir Iqbal, "CJ Suspended, Escorted Home," *Dawn*, 10 March 2007, URL: http://www.dawn.com/news/ 236769/cj-suspended-escorted-home-justice-iftikhar-summoned-by-sjc-on-13th-for-reference-hearing-ex-ju djudges-call-it-a-blow-to-

judiciary-s-independence-minister-defends-decision-whither-judicial-activism (accessed on 15 January 2016).

40. "A general state of disarray," *The Economist*, Vol. 383, No. 8529, 19 May 2007, p. 26.
41. Iqbal, "CJ Suspended, Escorted Home,"
42. The chief justice along with his family was put under house arrest compelled to resign. See the "Text of Chief Justice's affidavit filed in Supreme Court," *Daily Times*, 30 May 2007, URL: http://www.dailytimes. com.pk/default.asp?page=2007%5C05%5C30%5Cstory_30-5-2007pg7_55 (accessed on 7 July 2011).
43. Stephen Graham "Court Restores Pakistan Chief Justice," *Washington Post*, 20 July 2007, URL: http://www.washingtonpost.com/wpdyn/content/article/2007/ 07/20/AR20070 72000562.html (accessed on 12 July 2011).
44. Mathew J. Nelson, "Pakistan 2008: Moving Beyond Musharraf," *Asian Survey*, Vol. 50, No. 1, January-February 2009, p. 19.
45. Mathew Pennington, "Lawyers Relaunch Anti-Musharraf Campaign," *The Washington Post*, 6 September 2007, URL: http://www.washingtonpost.com/wp-dyn/content/article/2007/09/06/AR2007090 600601_pf.html (accessed on 18 August 215).
46. "PCO and its Victim Judges," *Dawn*, 7 January 2008, URL: http://www.dawn.com/news/841674/pco-and-its-victim-judges (accessed on 20 June 2014).
47. For details see Ibid.
48. For detail see Intikhab Amir, "Double Standards," *The Herald*, Vol. 41, No. 10, October 2005, pp. 82-3.
49. Aqil Shah, *The Army and Democracy: Military Politics in Pakistan* (Cambridge: Harvard University Press, 2014), p. 220.
50. Charles H. Kennedy, "A User's Guide to Guided Democracy: Musharraf and the Pakistani Military Governance Paradigm," in Charles H. Kennedy and Cynthia Botteron (eds.), *Pakistan 2005* (Karachi: Oxford University Press, 2006), pp. 123-38.
51. Katherine Adeney, "A Step Towards Inclusive Federalism in Pakistan? The Politics of the 18th Amendment," *The Journal of Federalism*, Vol. 42, No. 4, 23 February 2012, pp. 546-7.
52. For the complete text of the 18th Constitutional Amendment see "Act No. X of 2010," in "Part 1, Acts, Ordinances, Presidents Orders and Regulations," *The Gazette of Pakistan - Extraordinary*, Islamabad, 20 April 2010, pp. 267-316
53. Stephen Philip Cohen, "Pakistan: Arrival and Departure" in Stephen Philip Cohen (ed.), *The Future of Pakistan* (New Delhi: Oxford University Press, 2011), pp. 8-9.
54. Raza Ahmad, "The Endemic Crises of Federalism in Pakistan," *The Lahore Journal of Economics* (Lahore), Vol. 15, September 2010, p. 25.
55. Ibid, p. 26.
56. "Act No. X of 2010," in "Part 1, Acts, Ordinances, Presidents Orders and Regulations," p. 296.
57. Yunas Samad, "Managing Diversity in Pakistan: Going Beyond Federalism," *Sustainable Development Policy Institute* (Islamabad), Working Paper No. 13, March 2013, p. 9.
58. Saeed Shafqat, "Praetorians and the People," in Maleeha Lodhi (ed.), *Pakistan:*

Beyond the Crisis State (New York: Columbia University Press, 2011), pp. 103-4.
59. Ibid, pp. 104-5.
60. "Pak Army Officer Recalled from Civilian Postings," *Times of India*, 12 February 2008.
61. Syed Irfan Raza, "ISI, IB put under Interior Division's Control," *Dawn*, 27 July 2008, URL: http://www.dawn.com/news/313676/isi-ib-put-under-interior-division-s-control (accessed on 12 November 2015).
62. Syed Irfan Raza, "Govt Forced to Withdraw ISI Decision," *Dawn*, 28 July 2008, URL: http://www.dawn.com/news/313820/govt-forced-to-withdraw-isi-decision (accessed on 12 November 2015).
63. Amjad Mahmood, "National Security Council to be dissolved: Gilani," *Dawn*, 29 November 2008, URL: http://www.dawn.com/news/431010/national-security-council-to-be-dissolved-gilani (accessed on 12 November 2015).
64. Bret Stephens, "The Most Difficult Job in the World: Pakistan's President on Terrorism, India and his Late Wife," *Wall Street Journal*, 4 October 2008, URL: http://www.wsj.com/articles/ SB122307507392703831 (accessed on 10 December 2015).
65. Ibid.
66. "HT Leadership Summit 2008, Asif Ali Zardari: How can India and Pakistan Work Together Part 2," *Youtube.com*, 29 October 2009, URL: https://www.youtube.com/watch?v=_fF8cvPoIFs (accessed on 9 April 2014).
67. Christina Otten, "The Mumbai Massacres and Pakistan's New Nightmares," *The Hindu*, 15 December 2008, URL: http://www.thehindu.com/todays-paper/tp-opinion/the-mumbai-massacres-and-pakistans-new-nightmares/article1395432.ece (accessed on 9 April 2014).
68. Nirupama Subramanian, "U.S. Pushed for Pasha's India Visit," *The Hindu*, 19 May 2011.
69. The act is officially known as "Enhanced Partnership with Pakistan Act of 2009."
70. Nirupama Subramanian, "Hue and Cry in Pakistan over Kerry-Lugar Conditions," *The Hindu*, 8 October 2009.
71. Shafqat, "Praetorians and the People," p. 110.
72. Jaffrelot, *The Pakistan Paradox*, p. 265.
73. Shafqat, "Praetorians and the People," p. 112.
74. Shuja Nawaz, "Army and Politics" in Lodhi (ed.), *Pakistan: Beyond the Crisis State*, p. 82.
75. Ishtiaq Ahmad, *The Pakistan Army in Politics: Origins, Evolution, Consequences* (New Delhi: Amaryllis, 2013), p. 422.
76. Nirupama Subramanian, "40 Killed in Islamabad Blast," *The Hindu*, 21 September, 2008.
77. Nirupama Subramanian, "Rawalpindi Attack a Bid to Shatter Army's Confidence," *The Hindu*, 11 October 2009.
78. Jahanzaib Haque, Faraz Khan and Ahmad Jung, "Navy says PNS Base under Control after Attack," *The Express Tribune*, 21 May 2011, URL: http://tribune.com.pk/story/173888/blast-on-dalmia-road/ (accessed on 7 July 2011).
79. Husain Haqqani, *Magnificent Delusions: Pakistan, the United Nations, and an Epic*

History of Misunderstanding (New York: Perseus Books Group, 2014), p. 346.

80. Anita Joshua, “Post-Abottabad: A Failure to see the Faultline,” *The Hindu*, 17 May 2011.
81. Josh Rogin, “Exclusive: Secret Pakistani-U.S. Memo Offering Overthrow of Military Leadership Revealed,” *Foreign Policy*, 17 November 2011, URL: http://foreignpolicy.com/2011/11/17/exclusive-secret-pakistani-u-s-memo-offering-overthrow-of-military-leadership-revealed/ (accessed on 4 January 2014).
82. Ibid.
83. Hussain Haqqani in a personal discussion, 27 February 2013, New Delhi.
84. Jaffrelot, *Pakistan Paradox*, p. 267.
85. “No control over Army, ISI, Pak Defence Min tells SC,” *The Indian Express*, 22 December 2011.
86. “Commission's Report Says Haqqani Behind Controversial Memo,” *Dawn*, 12 June 2012, URL: http://www.dawn.com/news/725930/sc-takes-up-memo-case (accessed on 21 July 2014).
87. “Move Afoot to Bring Own Govt: Gilani,” *Dawn*, 23 December 2011, URL: http://www.dawn.com/ news/82600/no-institution-has-right-to-create-a-state-within-state-pm (accessed on 11 July 2012).
88. “No Validation of Military Takeover, Says Chief Justice,” *Dawn*, 24 December 2011, URL: https://www.dawn.com/news/682874/no-validation-of-military-takeover-says-chief-justice (accessed on 11 July 2012).
89. S. Akbar Zaidi, “Civilian Dictatorship and Praetorian Democracy,” *Economic and Political Weekly*, Vol. 43, No. 37, 13-19 September 2008, p. 8.
90. Haris Gazdar, “Goodbye General Musharraf, Hello Troika,” *Economic and Political Weekly*, Vol. 42, No. 50, 15-21 December 2007, pp. 8-9.
91. S. Akbar Zaidi, “An Incomplete Transition in Pakistan,” *Economic and Political Weekly*, Vol. 43, No. 45, 8-14 November 2008, p. 11.
92. Haris Gazdar, “Find Your War, or Risk Losing It,” *Economic and Political Weekly*, Vol. 43, No. 41, 11-17 October 2008, p. 8.
93. Raja Asghar, “Sharia for Malakand as Zardari Signs Law,” *Dawn*, 14 April 2009 URL: “http://www.dawn.com/news/457187/sharia-for-malakand-as-zardari-signs-law-2 (accessed on 17 August 2016).
94. “SC Makes Public Office out of Bounds for Sharif Brothers,” *Dawn*, 26 February 2009, URL: http://www.dawn.com/news/849139/sc-makes-public-office-out-of-bounds-for-sharif-brothers (accessed on 8 January 2014).
95. “Sharifs Disqualified, Punjab under Governor Rule,” *Dawn*, 26 February 2009, URL: http://www.dawn.com/news/955822/sharifs-disqualified-punjab-under-governor-rule (accessed on 8 January 2014).
96. “Nawaz Put under House Arrest at Model Town Residence,” *The Nation*, 15 March 2009, URL: http://nation.com.pk/lahore/15-Mar-2009/Nawaz-put-under-house-arrest-at-Model-Town-residence (accessed on 8 January 2014).
97. “Gilani Announces Restoration of Deposed Chief Judge,” *Dawn*, 16 March 2009, URL: http://www.dawn.com/news/957245/gilani-announces-restoration-of-deposed -chief-judge (accessed on 8 January 2014).

98. "PML-Q's Demands Fulfilled: Elahi made Deputy PM, 15 Ministries Granted," *Dawn*, 25 June 2012, URL: http://www.dawn.com/news/729424/demands-fulfilled-15-ministries-granted-to-pml-q (accessed on 7 May 2015).
99. Ali Ismail, "Pakistan: Military Sponsored-PML (Q) joins PPP-led Coalition Government," *World Socialist Web Site*, 20 May 2011, URL: https://www.wsws.org/en/articles/2011/05/paki-m20.html (accessed on 13 March 2015).
100. Asad Malik and Owais Jafri, "Memogate: Nawaz Threatens to Move SC if Govt Falls Short," *The Express Tribune*, 20 November 2011, URL: http://tribune.com.pk/story/294687/memogate-nawaz-threatens-to-move-sc-if-govt-falls-short/ (accessed on 17 October 2016).
101. Abdul Manan and Shamsul Islam, "Faisalabad Political Rally: Nawaz Demands Urgent 'Memogate' Inquiry," *The Express Tribune*, 20 November 2011. URL: http://tribune.com.pk/story/294767/PML (N)-all-set-for-faisalabad-rally-today/ (accessed on 17 October 2016).
102. "Arrest Warrant Issued against Makhdoom Shahabuddin," *Dawn*, 21 June 2012, URL: http://www.dawn.com/news/728285/arrest-warrant-issued-against-makhdoom-shahabuddin (accessed on 10 October 2015).
103. Ayesha Siddiqa, "Discovering Democracy: Five Years of Political Rule in Pakistan," *Economic and Political Weekly*, Vol. 4, No. 7, 27 April 2014, p. 23.
104. Jon Boone, "Pakistani Taliban TTP Warns Imran Khan Ahead of Drones March," *The Guardian*, 5 October 2012, https://www.theguardian.com/world/2012/oct/05/pakistan-taliban-ttp-imran-khan (accessed on 28 April 2016).
105. Qaiser Butt, "Govt Complicit in Drone Attacks: Imran Khan," *The Express Tribune*, 23 April 2011, URL: http://tribune.com.pk/story/154987/govt-complicit-in-drone-attacks-imran-khan/ (accessed on 28 April 2016).
106. Sher Khan, "The Coining of the 'Naya Pakistan' Slogan," *The Express Tribune*, 15 May 2013 URL: http://tribune.com.pk/story/549650/the-coining-of-the-naya-pakistan-slogan/ (accessed on 28 April 2016).
107. "Elections 2013: Violence Against Political Parties, Candidates and Voters," Report, *Pakistan Institute for Peace Studies*, Islamabad, May 2013, p. 1. URL: http://san-pips.com/download.php?f=222.pdf (accessed on 12 May 2014).
108. Asif Mahmood, "MQM Pledges 'Unconditional Support' for PML (N) Presidential Nominee," *Dawn*, 27 July 2013, URL: http://www.dawn.com/news/1032084/mqm-pledges-unconditional-support-for-PML (N)-presidential-nominee (accessed on 12 May 2015).
109. "Winds of Change: MQM Warms up to Ruling PML (N)," *The Express Tribune*, 26 November 2014, http://tribune.com.pk/story/797358/winds-of-change-mqm-warms-up-to-ruling-PML (N)/ (accessed on 12 June 2015).
110. Hasan Askari Rizvi, "The Politics of Top Political Offices," *The Express Tribune*, 11 August 2013, URL: http://tribune.com.pk/story/588790/the-politics-of-top-political-offices/ (accessed on 29 September 2015).
111. Hassan Javid "All the King's Men," *The Herald*, Vol. 47, No. 1, January 2014, pp. 44-5.
112. Adnan Adil, "Shahbaz Sharif's Fiefdom," *Newsline*, Vol. 26, No. 2, August 2014, p. 54.
113. Shehrbano Taseer, "The Rebirth of Maryam Nawaz Sharif," *Newsweek*, 23 March

2012, URL: http://newsweekpakistan.com/the-rebirth-of-maryam-nawaz-sharif/ (accessed on 19 January 2014).

114. "Alliance in the Making: PTI, PML-Q Agree on Three Points," *The Express Tribune*, 9 July 2014, URL: http://tribune.com.pk/story/733025/alliance-in-the-making-pti-pml-q-agree-on-three-points/ (accessed on 30 September 2014).
115. Anwer Sumra, "Destination Islamabad: Azadi March Takes Off," *The Express Tribune*, 15 August 2015, URL: http://tribune.com.pk/story/748978/destination-islamabad-azadi-march-takes-off/ (accessed on 28 September 2016).
116. Azam Khan, "Demands Spelled Out: 48-hour Deadline," *The Express Tribune*, 17 August 2014, URL: http://tribune.com.pk/story/749809/demands-spelled-out-48-hour-deadline/ (accessed on 28 September 2016).
117. Earlier Imran Khan called his march a "tsunami march" which was later renamed as "Azadi march." "Imran Warns Nawaz of 'Tsunami March' if Demands not Met," *Dawn*, 28 June 2014, URL: http://www.dawn.com/news/1115509/imran-warns-nawaz-of-tsunami-march-if-demands-not-met (accessed on 29 September 2014).
118. "Pakistan's Khan calls for Civil Disobedience," *Al Jazeera*, 17 August 2014, URL: http://www.aljazeera. com/news/europe/2014/08/pakistan-protests-continue-second-day-2014817142532776182.html (accessed on 8 May 2016).
119. Shahid-ur-Rahman, "The Price of Protest," *Newsline*, Vol. 26, No. 3, September 2014, pp. 25-6.
120. "Red Zone's Security Handed Over to Pakistan Army: Nisar," *Dawn*, 19 August 2014, URL: http://www.dawn.com/news/1126356 (accessed on 12 April 2016).
121. Kamran Yousaf, "On Army Chief's Advice, Govt to Pursue Talks with PTI, PAT Again," *The Express Tribune*, 28 August 2014, URL: http://tribune.com.pk/story/754978/coas-asked-to-help-resolve-political-impasse/ (accessed on 30 May 2016).
122. Sajjad Hussain, "3 Dead in Protests, Pakistan Army Meets, Says Won't Back Off 'Playing its Part," *The Indian Express*, 1 September 20014, URL: http://indianexpress.com/article/world/neighbours/pakistan-showdown-2-dead-over-450-injured-as-police-clash-with-protesters-roads-leading-to-nawaz-sharifs-house-shut/ (accessed on 16 March 2016).
123. "COAS Raheel Sharif Made 'Mediator' to End Political Crisis," *Dawn*, 29 August 2014, URL: http://www.dawn.com/news/1128362/coas-raheel-sharif-made-mediator-to-end-political-crisis (accessed on 12 April 2016).
124. Syed Talat Hussain, "All the General's Men," *Newsline*, Vol. 26, No. 3, September 2014, p. 20. Also see "Catalyst for Change or Military Stooge?," *Dawn*, 13 January 2013, URL: http://www.dawn.com/news /778494/catalyst-for-change-or-military-stooge (accessed on 5 April 2016).
125. Ayesha Siddiqa, "The Elephant in the Room," *Newsline*, Vol. 26, No. 3, September 2014, p. 23.
126. Umair Javed, "Fast Forward to the Past," *The Herald*, Vol. 47, No. 9, September 2014, p. 58.
127. "Pak Military Expresses Serious Concern Over Political Crisis," *The Indian Express*, 1 September 2014, URL: http://indianexpress.com/article/world/neighbours/pak-

military-expresses-serious-concern-over-political-crisis/ (accessed on 15 May 2016).

128. Quoted in Umer Farooq, "Marching Orders," *The Herald*, Vol. 47, No. 9, September 2014, p. 52.
129. Ibid.
130. Ibid, p. 53.
131. Ibid.
132. Hussain, "All the General's Men," p. 21, Siddiqa "The Elephant in the Room," p. 23, and Javed, "Fast Forward to the Past," p. 58.
133. Rubina Saigol "Word Wars," *The Herald*, Vol. 47, No. 9, September 2014, p. 65.
134. Dean Nelson and Javed Siddiq, "Imran Khan 'Plotted with Army to Oust Nawaz Sharif', Colleague Claims," *The Telegraph*, 1 September 2014, URL: http://www.telegraph.co.uk/news/worldnews/asia/pakist an/11068811/Imran-Khan-plotted-with-army-to-oust-Nawaz-Sharif-colleague-claims.html (accessed on 18 May 2016).
135. "Islamabad Stand-off: Army not Backing PTI or PAT, says ISPR," *Dawn*, 1 September 2014, URL: http://www.dawn.com/news/1129011/islamabad-stand-off-army-not-backing-pti-or-pat-says-ispr (accessed on 18 May 2016).
136. Siddiqa "The Elephant in the Room," p. 23.
137. "Blow to Democracy," *Dawn*, 30 August 2014, URL: http://www.dawn.com/news/1128637 (accessed on 27 May 2016).
138. "Army's Questionable Decisions," *Dawn*, 2 September 2014, URL: http://www.dawn.com/news/1129 263 (accessed on 27 May 2016).
139. Azam Khan, "Parliament reposes faith in Nawaz Sharif as Imran, Qadri up the ante," *The Express Tribune*, 20 August 2014, URL: http://tribune.com.pk/story/751325/parliament-reposes-faith-in-nawaz-sharif-as-imran-qardi-up-the-ante/ (accessed on 12 April 2016).
140. Nawaz Sharif's interview with Karan Thapar, "Devil's Advocate," *CNN News 18*, 5 May 2013, URL: https://www.youtube.com/watch?v=EK74wKW3BLU (accessed on 18 July 2014).
141. "Civil-Military Relations in Pakistan," *Pakistan Institute of Legislative Development and Transparency*, Monitor, August –December, 2013, p. 4.
142. "Musharraf Indicted for Treason: Pleads not Guilty to All Charges," *Dawn*, 31 March 2014, URL: http://www.dawn.com/news/1096826 (accessed on 18 December 2015).
143. Jon Boone, "Pervez Musharraf Charged with Benazir Bhutto Murder," *The Guardian*, 20 August 2013, URL:https://www.theguardian.com/world/2013/aug/20/pervez-musharraf-benazir-bhutto-pakistan (accessed on 18 December 2015).
144. "Musharraf Says Army Backs Him over Treason 'Vendetta,'" *The Express Tribune*, 29 December 2013, URL:http://tribune.com.pk/story/652196/musharraf-says-army-backs-him-over-treason-vendetta/ (accessed on 18 December 2015).
145. Zulfiqar Ghuman, "Article 6 Can't Just Apply to One Man: Gilani," *Daily Times*, 17 September 2009, URL:https://web.archive.org/web/20120113101523/http://www.dailytimes.com.pk/default.asp?page=2009%5C09%5C17%5Cstory_17-9-2009_pg1_1 (accessed on 18 December 2015).
146. Jon Boone, "Pervez Musharraf Leaves Pakistan after Three-Year Travel Ban Lifted,"

The Guardian, 18 March 2016, URL: https://www.theguardian.com/world/2016/mar/18/pervez-musharraf-leaves-pakistan-for-treatment-after-travel-ban-lifted (accessed on 8 August 2016).

147. Syed Talat Hussain, "The Clash of Institutions," *Newsline*, Vol. 25, No. 10, May 2014, p. 34.
148. Ibid.
149. Aqil Shah, "Axis of National Security," *The Herald*, Vol. 47, No. 6, June 2014, pp. 35-6.
150. Umer Farooq and Ghulam Dastgeer, "Military Operation," *The Herald*, Vol. 48, No. 7, July 2014, p. 54.
151. "Nawaz Sharif calls for Taliban talks," *Dawn*, 21 May 2013, URL: http://www.dawn.com/news/ 1012539/nawaz-sharif-calls-for-taliban-talks (accessed on 26 July 2014).
152. Jon Boone and Ewen MacAskill, "More than 100 Children Killed in Taliban Attack on Pakistan School," *The Guardian*, 16 December 2014, URL: https://www.theguardian.com/world/2014/dec/16/ taliban-attack-army-public-school-pakistan-peshawar (accessed on 12 November 2015).
153. Abdul Manan, "Fight Against Terrorism: Defining Moment," *The Express Tribune*, 25 December 2014, URL: http://tribune.com.pk/story/811947/fight-against-terrorism-defining-moment/ (accessed on 12 May 2015).
154. "MPC Ends with National Consensus on NAP," *Dawn*, 3 January 2015, URL: http://www.dawn.com/ news/1154662 (accessed on 12 May 2015).
155. "Provincial Apex Committees Formed to Implement NAP," *Geo News*, 3 January 2015, URL: https://www.geo.tv/latest/46-provincial-apex-committees-formed-to-implement-nap (accessed on 17 August 2016).
156. "A Sad Day," *Dawn*,3 January 2015, URL: http://www.dawn.com/news/1154719 (accessed on 27 May 2016).
157. Ibid.
158. Hasan Askari Rizvi, "The Civil-Military Hybrid," *The Express Tribune*, 23 February 2015, URL: http://tribune.com.pk/story/842505/the-civil-military-hybrid/ (accessed on 4 April 2016).
159. Shah, *The Army and Democracy: Military Politics in Pakistan*, p. 20.
160. Ibid, p. 221.
161. Ibid, p. 252.
162. Meeting of the Cabinet should normally be held once a week on a day and time to be specified by the Prime Minister according to Rule 20 (1) of the Rules of Business of the Federal Government.
163. "Assessment of the Quality of Democracy in Pakistan-2015," *Pakistan Institute of Legislative Development And Transparency*, Islamabad, May 2016, p. 17.
164. Ibid, p. 18.
165. Ibid, p. 48.
166. "Public Opinion on Quality of Democracy in Pakistan: At the End of the Second Year of Federal and Provincial Governments June 2014 – May 2015," *Pakistan Institute of Legislative Development and Transparency*, Islamabad, October 2015, p. 225.
167. Marina Walker Guevara "ICIJ Releases Database Revealing Thousands of Secret Offshore Companies," *ICIJ*, 9 May 2016, URL: https://panamapapers.icij.org/

blog/20160509-offshore-database release.html? utm_content=buffercee67&utm_medium=social&utm_source=twitter.com&utm_campaign=buffer (accessed on 12 September 2016).

168. "Panama Papers: The Power Players," *ICIJ*, URL: https://panamapapers.icij.org/the_power_players/ (accessed on 12 September 2016).
169. Raza Khan, "Opposition Demands 'Forensic Audit Firm' Probe Panama Papers Revelations," *Dawn*, 8 April 2016, URL: http://www.dawn.com/news/1250754 (accessed on 14 September 2016).
170. Khawar Ghuman, "Imran Calls for PM's Resignation," *Dawn*, 11 April 2016, URL: http://www.dawn.com/news/1251383 (accessed on 14 September 2016).
171. "'Across the Board Accountability' Essential for Prosperous Pakistan: Gen Raheel," *Dawn*, 19 April 2016, http://www.dawn.com/news/1253087 (accessed on 14 September 2016).
172. Mateen Haider, "Gen Raheel Dismisses 6 Army Officers from Service over 'Corruption,'" *Dawn*, 22 April 2016, URL: http://www.dawn.com/news/1253497 (accessed on 17 September 2016).
173. Zaigham Khan, "Who Will Celebrate Martial Law?," *The News*, 15 July 2016, URL: https://www.thenews.com.pk/print/137412-Who-will-celebrate-martial-law (accessed on 17 September 2016).
174. "PTI, Allies Launch Ehtesab March Today," *The News*, 3 September 2016, URL: https://www.thenews. com.pk/print/147324-PTI-allies-launch-Ehtesab-march-today (accessed on 17 September 2016).
175. "Religious Activists out Against Qadri's Hanging," *Pakistan Today*, 1 March 2016, URL: http://www.pakistantoday.com.pk/2016/03/01/city/karachi/religious-activists-out-against-qadris-hanging/ (accessed on 2 August 2016).
176. The Women's Protection Bill, passed by Punjab Assembly in February 2016, gives legal protection to women from domestic, psychological and sexual violence.
177. "Women Protection Act against Pakistani Constitution, Sharia: Siraj-ul-Haq," *The Nation*, 15 March 2016, URL: http://nation.com.pk/national/15-Mar-2016/women-protection-bill-against-pakistani-constituti on -sharia-siraj-ul-haq (accessed on 12 August 2016).
178. Farrukh Khan Pitafi, "Reminiscing 1977," *The Express Tribune*, 25 March 2016, URL: http://tribune. com.pk/story/1072846/reminiscing-1977/ (accessed on 12 August 2016).
179. Ibid.
180. "What Altaf Said...," *Dawn*, 23 August 2016, URL: http://www.dawn.com/news/1279393 (accessed on 23 August 2016).
181. "Rangers Take MQM Leaders into Custody, Seal Party Headquarters Nine Zero," *Dawn*, 23 August 2016, URL: http://www.dawn.com/news/1279250/rangers-take-mqm-leaders-into-custody-seal-party-headquarters -nine-zero (accessed on 23 August 2016).
182. "I Was Under Severe Mental Stress: Altaf Apologises to Military for Anti-Pakistan Remarks," *Dawn*, 23 August 2016, URL: http://www.dawn.com/news/1279430/i-

was-under-severe-mental-stress-altaf-apologise s-to-military-for-anti-pakistan-remarks (accessed on 23 August 2016).

183. "Farooq Sattar Sidelines Altaf: 'MQM will Operate Only From Pakistan," *Dawn*, 24 August 2016, URL: http://www.dawn.com/news/1279446/farooq-sattar-sidelines-altaf-mqm-will-operate-only-from-pakistan (accessed on 24 August 2016).
184. "Altaf 'Hands Over' party affairs to Rabita Committee After Statements by Farooq Sattar," *Dawn*, 24 August 2016, URL: http://www.dawn.com/news/1279656/altaf-hands-over-party-affairs-to-rabita-commit tee-after-statements-by-farooq-sattar (accessed on 24 August 2016).
185. Christophe Jaffrelot, "The Façade of Democracy," *The Indian Express*, 1 April 2016.

7. Conclusion

For most of its political history Pakistan has oscillated between democratic and military regimes. For half of the last seven decades, since its creation, Pakistan has remained under direct military domination and for the rest under its indirect shadow. Many scholarly studies have pointed out to the different sources of motivation behind the military's interventions in Pakistan. The prevalence of minimal political culture – a social pre-condition for military's political ambition was one such motivation and reason for military's intervention in Pakistan. Hamza Alavi's thesis of the over-developed state apparatus and weak political institutions, as a result of colonial inheritance, was one such pre-condition for the military's political role. Contemporary scholars like Ayesha Siddiqa, Anatol Lieven and Aqil Shah in their separate works established a strong correlation between military professionalism which inculcates the feeling of "fraternity," *esprit de corps* and soldiers being superior than civilians to the military interventions. Siddiqa in her seminal work *Military Inc.* established the correlation between military corporatism, which she called "milbus", and military intervention in Pakistan. In sum, the presence of 'minimal political culture,' 'inheritance of strong military organisation,' 'military professionalism,' and 'military corporatism,' had played a relative role in the marginalisation of the democratic process in Pakistan. However, this study argues that political parties had a definitive correlation to the growth and diminution of the democratic institutions in Pakistan.

A political party system is a modern phenomenon specifically associated with the modern nation-state. In the case of postcolonial states, it is not older than a century. Both in theory and practice a political party means an organised body of people striving to attain political power through agreed constitutional principles. A political party is an organised group seeking political power whether by democratic elections or by revolution. Political parties have roles to play in democracies. They connect the linkages between the electorates and their representatives, thus becoming a link between the government and citizen. It is the political parties which make a representative government possible in modern state. Through the political parties, people are represented in the organs of democratic government. Political parties help mobilise people through their programme and form both the ruling and opposition groups. Above all, through them people can participate in the polity and governance.

In the last seven decades, the political parties in Pakistan got repeated opportunities to rule the country and strengthen democratic institutions. This study argues that the political parties were the central force which was needed for the legitimisation and stabilisation of the political process and system. And for this reason, even the military regimes created their own political parties or patronised some parties. In this framework, this study explored this intriguing paradox that in Pakistan where the political parties found their opportunities to consolidate democratic institutions and how they could not seize those moments. To understand why the political parties behaved the way they did, this study raised few research questions. To what extent the political parties are responsible for the deepening of authoritarianism and consolidation of democracy in Pakistan? Why have the political parties showed authoritarian tendencies? What was the role of authoritarian tactics and policies of political parties in de-politicising the masses which had implications for democratisation in Pakistan?

To examine these correlations in Pakistan, this study has explored the practices of political parties – whether in power or in the opposition – during three democratic interludes and as well as under military regimes. The study focused on a descriptive analysis of genesis, growth and electoral participation of the political parties. It also studied the personality traits of the leadership, their social background and their political attitude and practices to correlate their contribution to the consolidation of democracy and yet also the persistence of authoritarian regimes.

In the formative phase, political parties experienced severe restrictions that prevented their growth. Periodically, political parties were completely banned under military regimes. However, the political parties had their own short interludes to exercise political power. The first democratic interlude began with the formation of a first elected government under Zulfikar Ali Bhutto in 1971. Zulfikar Ali Bhutto, the leader of the Pakistan Peoples Party (PPP) and first elected Prime Minister of the country, had a historic chance to consolidate democracy in Pakistan. When Bhutto formed the first democratic government after two decades of Pakistan's creation, he was faced with the challenge of reviving essential institutions. The first reform taken to task was the drafting of the constitution. The constitution written under him facilitated the restoration of a political system from Presidential to a federal parliamentary order. It transferred decisive powers into the hands of elected representatives. Thereafter, Bhutto embarked on his politics of poverty and power through administrative measures.

Bhutto's politics of poverty began with the initiation of the nationalisation drive of industries and land reforms to emancipate the wretched of Pakistan. The nationalisation drive did not bring change in the life of the exploited working class, neither did it create an equitable socialist society, rather it sealed the open society into state capitalism. The biggest promise of change he made to the peasants and tenants of Pakistan was the revolutionary land reforms and abolishing the power of feudal landlords. The land reform measures carried out under Bhutto did not benefit the cultivators as such, and because the landed gentry had occupied a major part of the legislature, they successfully resisted any form of official land reform.

So two of Bhutto's mega-projects – nationalisation and land reform – did not bring any change in the life of the common citizens who voted him to power. On the other hand, Bhutto amassed incontrovertible political power and pursued the politics of power. His politics of power was apparent when he revamped the bureaucracy, reorganised the military and created his own secret paramilitary force. The restructuring of the bureaucracy began with the drafting of the new constitution which clipped off its legal safeguards through constitutional measures. However, his reforms turned out as an ethnic vendetta directed at the Muhajirs who comprised a large portion of the bureaucratic system. He purged most of them and cultivated a new official class loyal and obedient to him. Through nepotism he inducted his relatives and friends in the system. By employing these measures, he metamorphosed the civil bureaucracy into a docile and obedient party organ.

The opacity of his autocratic politics was at an extreme level when he dealt with the military. Through constitutional measures, Bhutto confined the role of the military as a subordinate organ of the elected government. In a democratic framework, it was an appropriate repositioning of the military to its deserved place. But what angered the military was the method of civilian leadership in doing so. First, he reorganised the military's command structure by introducing white papers on it, and to undermine its coercive hegemony created his own paramilitary force, the Federal Security Force (FSF). In practice, the FSF worked as a parallel coercive institution under Bhutto's authority. Simultaneously, he militarised civilian rule by using the FSF.

The militarisation of the civilian regime using the secret force was more evident and apparent when he dealt with political opponents and critics from within and outside the PPP. Within the party, anyone who exhibited, or even indicated any difference with Bhutto's autocratic method of decision-making, was either purged or physically tortured. His period was far from democratic in culture, rather it could be characterised as popular autocracy. In the pursuit of complete control he alienated the bureaucracy, military, political parties and even friends in the party. He was so insecure that he never nurtured the next generation leadership outside his dynasty. As a result, when General Zia-ul Haq, with the support of the united political opposition seized power in 1977, his party failed to organise any resistance. With this, the PPP, the first party to rise to power, ruined its opportunity to consolidate democracy in Pakistan. The question arises here as to why did Bhutto – who was popularly elected – exhibit such extreme authoritarian tendencies and not build democratic institutions during his tenure.

This study falls back on two important reasons for an explanation. The first apparent reason was Bhutto's personality traits and social background which was reflected in his political attitude. Coming from a political and feudal family Bhutto had made inroads into the power elites at a very young age. He developed a liking for power and disliked his critics. So when he rose to power, he ruled like a feudal lord who despised plurality of views. Bhutto purged his critics within the party and eliminated his political opponents outside the party using legal and coercive measures. A feudal and a Sindhi, Bhutto won in the national election, but significantly lost in the provincial elections that followed thereafter. Therefore, he disliked the federal mode of power-sharing and in pursuit of amassing more power undermined provincial leaders by weakening the federal arrangement.

The second apparent reason was the transformation of the PPP as Bhutto's personal enterprise. The PPP was founded as a popular movement by anti-military political groups to collectively challenge the authoritarian government. At the beginning, it had a dense party organisation as well as a collective body of decision-making. After the PPP came to power, Chairman Bhutto rid the party of any form of inner democracy. The system of decision-making was never institutionalised and it revolved around Chairman Bhutto. Within the party, any challenge was neutralised forcefully. To have absolute control over the party, Bhutto ostracised all his party fellows who helped to build the party. The PPP under Bhutto attempted to evolve as a hegemonic party and establish a hegemonic party-system. In this process, he tried to cultivate a climate in which the opposition parties were denied any possibilities of winning elections. By projecting an aura of electoral invincibility, the PPP tried to prevent the other parties the possibility of power alteration – a necessity in democracy. In the garb of building democratic order, Bhutto militarised the state and choked the breathing space for organic growth of political parties. The distrust between Bhutto and other political parties became so deep-rooted that they were not willing to compromise; rather the opposition parties welcomed the military's intervention in 1977. Once the military General became the administrator of Pakistan he altered the political process of the country which resulted in the weakening of the role of political parties and democratic politics as a whole.

After a brief repressive democratic interlude from 1971 to 1977 under the PPP, Pakistan came under the longest martial law regime under General Zia. The new dictator who perceived himself as *Ameer-ul-Momeen* was interested in moulding the social order more than the political system. All political activities were frozen and a new era of Islamic order was initiated. The foundation of his version of Islamic utopia was built on numerous legal and social measures. The issuance of the *Hudood* ordinance, instituting of *Shariat* Court and formation of *Zakat* and *Ushr* committees changed the legal and social way of life in the country. He brought substantive change in the status of minorities by reviving the scheme of separate electorates and applying stringent provisions of blasphemy law. Under the provisions of *Hudood* laws, which covered the issues of *Zina*, *Qazf* and *Qanoon-e Shahadat*, the value of women was reduced to half of their male counterparts. In this way minorities and women, ostensibly equal citizens in a democratic system, were stripped of their rights of political freedom and civil liberties.

Although all military regimes have systematically marginalised the growth of political parties, General Zia's source of motivation was rooted in the strand of Islamic scholarship that viewed the Quran as didactic as well as a book of political and social guidance and not people as the source of sovereignty. Sayyid Abul A'la Maududi, the ideologue of Jamaat-e-Islami, which supported the military regime of General Zia, saw the synthesis of political order and social order in an Islamic state. Similarly, Mohammad Iqbal also argued that Islam does not bifurcate between worldly affairs and private affairs and the state and the church are organic to each other. Maududi further argued that only God has sovereignty to make laws and therefore human-made legislations cannot coexist with the laws of God. And the rulers are chosen to enforce the laws of God and people who possess authority in whatever capacity among the Muslims should be followed. He did not question the source of authority because in his understanding power of the state is required to bring reforms that Islam wants to introduce. Interestingly, Maududi founded a political party and strived to attain political power, but paradoxically rejected the need of political parties and differences of opinion in an Islamic state.

So General Zia, who used the plank of establishing an Islamic order to legitimise his extra-constitutional stay in power, successfully delegitimised the necessity of political parties by creating a new political system. First, he put the political process in a long hibernation by banning all political parties and activities in the country. Thereafter, he cultivated a political process devoid of political parties by conducting party-less elections at various tiers of the government. By doing this, he replaced the traditional power elites with a new class of political elites who were dependent on the regime for their survival. On the other hand, he also marginalised women and religious minorities through legal measures to cultivate support among the conservative class. Collectively these classes helped in entrenching the regime's political role. Exploiting the roots of the origin of the "idea of Pakistan" based on religion, General Zia tried to justify the creation of a theocratic polity. Under this he shaped a narrative that projected political parties as evil. But political parties also consistently fought back his regime through mass mobilisation and after his death in 1988 made a political comeback.

The regime change, after General Zia's death in 1988, generated great hope for democracy and political parties which came to political prominence after a decade. But this period could be considered as a decade of democratic decay for various reasons. The disdain for democracy occurred both in public perception and practice. The larger portion of the onus rests on political parties which were the central forces responsible for building democratic institutions. At the beginning of the second democratic interlude civilian leaders, especially Benazir Bhutto and after her Nawaz Sharif, who were free of a negative historical baggage, had the opportunity to create a new democratic legacy, but failed to do so. Mainstream political parties, whether new or old, especially PPP and PML (N), which switched power between themselves, played a very detrimental role in the process of democratisation.

During this short and crisis-ridden democratic interlude four elected governments were formed but none of them could complete their tenure. The assessment of this period shows that political parties indulged in politics of vengeance, confrontation and agitation. Their methods included Long March, Train March, Wheel Jam and other forms of general strikes. Their protest created unmanageable chaos and sometimes led to violent clashes creating immense pressure on the ruling party. Against this backdrop, the President, equipped with the power of dissolving the government, dismissed three civilian regimes on various charges. The charges ranged from corruption, nepotism, misconduct, maladministration, failure to maintain law and order, interference in the judicial process and so on. Beside these fronts, what civilian regimes could not manage was civil-military relations as well as institutional balance. This entire period could be characterised as an era of confrontational politics among institutions which claimed state power.

The confrontational politics of political parties created a crisis of governability. This resulted in degradation of democratic institutions as well as democracy as a form of governance in public perception. It was evident in the gradual downslide in voter turnout in subsequent elections. There was a loss of enthusiasm in democratic politics and people turned indifferent to party politics. In another way, the political parties, which were new at the helm of administration and were uncertain of their own place, did not allow democratic institutions to grow. Both the PPP and PML (N) which rose to power twice tried to undermine the media through various legal measures. They also attempted to make the judiciary weak and reduce the power of the President. On the other hand, the President and judiciary which were enjoying their positions as autonomous power centres disliked civilian attempt to make them subservient to the elected government. So, when due to the infighting and weakness of political parties, the military created its opportunity to intervene in the civilian sphere in 1999, the judiciary validated it. There was no popular resistance to the coup and even the media remained silent. The change of regime did not mean much for common citizens as civilian rule was full of chaos and confusion and did not bring any substantive change in their life standard. So it was a peaceful and bloodless regime change which brought the military once again to the helm of power.

This time, the new dictator General Pervez Musharraf did not create a new political system but decided to function within the existing system by creating his own political party Pakistan Muslim League (Quaid). His period is also considered as a "benevolent autocracy" as civil liberties, especially growth of media was unprecedented. But he, being an unelected dictator despised political parties; he therefore designed a legal framework in which his patronised parties could capture political power. Since these parties owed their survival to the new framework they remained loyal to their patron. He successfully marginalised the existing political parties by crafting new arrangements within which they were supposed to operate. The new electoral framework and rules and the state machinery collectively facilitated the PML (Q) – patronised by the military and right wing parties – to manage electoral victory. In return, these parties helped the civilianisation of the military rule and prolonging of its exercise of political power. Many politicians sensing the winnability of the PML (Q), defected from their old parties and joined it.

During his long rule, General Musharraf also tampered with and modulated the rules of the political process to de-legitimise the need of political parties' independent role. To some extent political parties were demonised for Pakistan's political ailments. But due to the eruption of public agitation, especially of civil society led by lawyers, General Musharraf had to step down in 2008. After his ouster, the mainstream parties had the opportunity to contest and win elections. In the election, these parties found that, barring a few exceptions, their electoral support base was reduced to their ethnic and traditional constituencies. This happened because these parties had been out of power for so long that their capacity to distribute patronage in exchange of support in elections had eroded. Due to this reason their old constituencies shifted to other regional parties which were active during this period. But because there was an anti-military regime sentiment running high in the campaign, PPP and PML (N) could regain their lost toehold

The decade of marginalisation, absence of core leadership and erosion of organisational penetration, weakened the political parties. With fragmented organisational structures PPP and PML (N) contested unprepared. Both the parties could not secure a majority as voters gave a split mandate. But to keep the military away from the polity, the traditional nemesis formed a grand coalition government led by the PPP which effectively opened up the possibilities for democratic consolidation. It was a historic and exemplary example of party cooperation in Pakistan. The most remarkable accomplishment of the coalition government lead by the PPP was the passage of the 18th constitutional amendment in 2010. The amendment reversed many constitutional provisions brought about by the military regime and transferred decisive powers to the institution of the parliament. This way it revived the democratic spirit of the political system in Pakistan.

For democracy, the positive of this multi-party coalition government was that at least for the time-being it buried the propensity of confrontational politics, which had been responsible for allowing space to the military to play a role in politics. The majority of the parties showed a consensus on developing a paradigm in which the military's interference in the civilian sphere could be minimised. Because it was a transition period and the new military chief publicly announced not to interfere in the civilian domain, it appeared that the military's hegemony was waning. In addition the discovery and neutralisation of Osama bin Laden within Pakistan's territory cast apprehensions on the military's capacity and also its competence as an institution came under question. Thus, at least for the time-being the military did not overtly resist the new power-sharing system and subordination to civilian supremacy. But this equation changed, when it was revealed that the civilian regime was seeking US intervention in balancing civil-military ties through a 'memo.' The 'memogate' incidence put the civilian regime under immense pressure. But surprisingly political parties across the spectrum stood with the civilian regime.

This cooperation of political parties was reflective of their contradictory pragmatism. On one hand, if they did not cooperate they risked losing an opportunity to consolidate democracy and consequently strengthening the military. On the other hand, the continuation of civilian government would lead to the empowerment of their political rivals. The approach they devised was to support the government minimally, so that it did not collapse and opposed it on issues that would nurture their own constituencies. The opposition parties protested and organised marches against the PPP for its failure to reinstate the deposed judges. The PPP responded by detaining the opposition leaders. This episode exposed the faultlines of the coalition and there being a united force against the military appeared superficial. When the PML (N) left the coalition, the PPP joined hands with the military-backed PML (Q) and the unreliable MQM. Despite all shortcomings and multipronged onslaught by the judiciary, political parties and the military, the civilian government still managed to complete a first ever full term. It did assert civilian supremacy over the military establishment, at least periodically, and after completing its tenure in 2013 transferred power to another party democratically. This historic accomplishment was the result of pragmatic bonhomie of the political archrivals which revived the ventilated democracy.

The transition was accomplished under a civilian regime and thus generated immense hopes for democracy to be consolidated. Nawaz Sharif, who became Prime Minister for the third time after the 2013 election, began to tread the corridors of power calculatedly. Since the leadership in Pakistan is democratic only in outlook and not in conviction, personal loyalties override merits when it comes to distribution of office. Sharif was no different from the others and constituted his cabinet on nepotism and inducted his relatives, friends and loyalists. While choosing his cabinet and allocating public offices, Sharif overrode merit and displayed bare favouritism. It reminded of the era of patronage distribution that prefers loyalists at the expense of institutions. His style of governance had faced criticism from all quarters as his period was mired with political crises emanating from political opponents supported by the military.

Imran Khan who hoped to win the election did not accept the election outcome. Accusing the result of being fraudulent and rigged, he held a massive sit-in protest in 2014. His protest was projected as *Azadi March* which attempted to seize the capital. Khan was joined by the Pakistan Awami Tehreek (PAT) chief Tahir-ul Qadri who also organised a parallel protest called *Inquilab March*. During the protest, the call for civil disobedience by Imran Khan was a serious blow to the economy. In addition, the law and order situation also deteriorated. In the end, the protests created a crisis of regime legitimacy as the chaos became unmanageable and political parties sought the military's referral giving it the role of a referee. This again revealed the incapacity of political parties and portrayed them as the producer of nuisance and chaos and military as the ultimate saviour in a crisis situation. This also exposed the military's capacity to pitch politicians against politicians and use political parties as their proxies. During this period the positive for democracy was that mainstream parties did not become part of the military's gameplan and supported the elected regime. Somehow the Nawaz Sharif government survived the crisis. But the real challenge before him was how to balance civil-military ties.

Nawaz's relation with the military sank to the lowest on issues realted to the trial of General Musharraf, initiating rapprochement with India, media trial of the ISI, the launch of operation *Zarb-e Azb* and establishment of military courts. The industrialist-politician Nawaz Sharif is considered a seasoned politician but paradoxically his tenure beginning in 2013 consolidated the military institutionally. Amidst the deteriorating security situation, the military pressurised the government to establish constitutional mechanisms to try the militants. The government which had a majority in the parliament amended the constitution to establish military courts which were also given the powers to try civilians. This was an institutional mechanism with political legitimacy through which the military could intervene in internal political matters in the domain of the elected government. The military, which detests civilian subordination, now could dictate to the civilians in the name of security.

On the other hand, civilians themselves undermined institutional and constitutional mechanisms and platforms to device policy. The excessive dependence on *ad hoc* platforms such as all-party conferences and apex committees outside the parliament eroded their writ on issues purely related to the civilian domain. Public surveys of this period found that people trusted the military more than the government represented by political parties. It seems that political parties still could not change their attitude and as a result ended up strengthening the military as exhibited during *Azadi*

March protest crisis. After that PML(N) had to face a succession crisis when Nawaz Sharif was disqualified by the Supreme Court in July 2017, one year prior to the completion of his tenure. He was found guilty of dishonesty and concealing his source of income thus barred from holding public office. A week before the national election in 2018 Nawaz Sharif was arrested in Lahore after being convicted in a corruption case. However, with the help of other mainstream parties especially PPP, the PML(N) government survived that crisis. Some of the parties appeared to have realised that their growth is related to the survival of democracy. The limited change in their political attitude could be the product of internal transformation as well as the arrival of new political competitors.

The relative transformation of political parties and limited stability of democracy in Pakistan was not easy. While making an assessment of evolution of democracy and political parties one has to consider the following facts. The emergence of political parties in Pakistan was a superimposition due to the peculiar colonial history of the subcontinent. Unlike the European countries where traditional feudal structures transformed due to the processes of industrialisation and urbanisation into new social formations and reorganised political parties as power structures, South Asian countries had distinct evolutionary trajectories. The reorganisation of the political power structure in South Asia was not organic but was interrupted and redesigned by colonial intervention. The political parties which inherited political power at the time of colonial retreat were the creation of colonial powers for the purpose of handling over power. They acted as agency to the superior authority instead of governing themselves.

In many provinces of erstwhile British India, a particular class, caste, race, ethnicity or religious group were dominating irrespective of their numerical strength. The colonial intervention reversed such existing ruling elites with new ruling elites. The colonial powers created a class loyal to their interest. This was done by replacing the traditional ruling class with a new ruling class which agreed to submit their allegiance to them. This created social and political strains between the competing factions. Once their patronage eroded, social fragmentation intensified giving birth to new conflicts. At the time of decolonisation, the transfer of power in South Asia did not happen in a vacuum. It required an institutional arrangement. The British had already set in place governing structures but power had to be transferred to political parties. And power was transferred to political parties despite their limited social base in the areas they were supposed to rule. In the case of India, it was the Indian National Congress which to some extent had a legitimate claim on power. Wherein in Sri Lanka, power was transferred to the United National Party (UNP) formed in 1946 and explicitly set up to transfer power only two years before its independence. In the case of Pakistan, power was transferred to the All India Muslim League (AIML) which claimed to represent the Muslims of united India. The Muslim League had no social roots in the areas on whose behalf it negotiated power.

Another historical process which Pakistan did not traverse was the advancement of suffrage to the masses in a gradual process. The Pakistani citizenry had the rights of universal adult franchise at the time of its inception without having been much involved in the electoral processes. The areas which formed Pakistan had experience of colonial parliamentarianism but were not exposed to competitive party politics as they were ruled by the political agents. The democracy in Pakistan was not a bottom-up evolution but an accidental revolution from above in which the elite class found legitimate methods to be in power; a classic case of "circulation of elite mass." The democratisation of Pakistan was always an elitist project to which the masses were never associated. The nature of Pakistani democracy could be better explained by Joseph Schumpeter's idea that it is an institutional arrangement in which individuals attain decisive power through the competitive procedure of voting. The struggle is for exercise of power rather than for the good of its people. However, the nature of this power struggle has shown signs of fluidity in recent times.

The historical analysis of the trajectories of democracy in Pakistan has shown that in the course of time some old parties collapsed completely. Some of them though revived under a new leadership and structure. Many new parties were formed with new modes of mobilisation under changed social and political context. The old ruling parties were side-lined as new players occupied the centre stage. While classifying the political parties in Pakistan one has to be very cautious in applying any broad generalisation to them. Their social background is different, their ideologies vary and structures have distinct qualities.

The current National Assembly is not full of elites. Leadership from the Khyber Pakhtunkhwa is more of traditional tribal Sardars. They are not necessarily rich but very powerful. The leadership from Sindh and Southern Punjab is largely feudal. The central Punjab produces middle-scale business class. The very rich business class, comprising very few families is not in politics. Now, this heterogeneous lot has different interests and there has been erosion in the culture of the feudal elements. The leadership of political parties is frozen and needs to be broken. The upper tip of the pyramid is determined by elites and dynasties. It is very personality-centric. However, urban-based parties such as MQM have brought non-elite leadership into the Parliament although they represent a particular ethnic community. PTI which consists of many old leaders from other parties has also channelled new leadership to the house.

All the selective parties under consideration except the Jamaat-e-Islami showed fluidity in their ideology, organisational restructuring and programmatic commitments. Their social base has also shifted in the course of time. PPP, which began as a populist left-oriented party with pan-national social base, shifted to more conservative economic policies under Benazir Bhutto. It was once a mass-based party but now has been reduced to rural Sindh. The Jamaat started as a religious fundamentalist party with cadre-based structure did not compromise on its core ideology but has eased-up its membership procedures. Its social base was among the Muhajirs and conservative middle classes. After the formation of MQM, Jamaat has lost its support base to it.

The Muhajir Quami Movement started as an ethnic-based party and had limited social base among the Muhajirs. It is structurally a cadre-based party. In its second avatar as Muttahida Quami Movement it transformed itself from an ethnic-based party to a catch-all party. This shift was visible in its programmatic commitments but its electoral performance did not show any major gain. The PML (N) began as a counter-force to the PPP and as the religious right with fiscal conservatism. Today it is a mass-based party with major support in Punjab. PTI began as both a personalistic party and movement party. Structurally it is open-ended but its support base lies with the educated urban youth active in the alternative media. The party support base has increased ethnically in the province of Khyber Pakhtunkhwa. PTI heavily relies on the charismatic attributes of its leader.

Historically, the All India Muslim League in united India originated parallel to the Indian National Congress on the basis of religion, while the Awami League in Pakistan represented ethnic aspiration of the Bengalis against the apparently non-Bengali Muslim League. Thereafter electoral mechanism including overall political system fell and developed under the military's clutches. Therefore Pakistan did not get the opportunity in which political parties developed while competing against each other under a legitimate institutional system. And when political parties got opportunities to create a credible political order and consolidate democracy, they failed miserably. Instead of representing voters' preference in the government, political parties functioned as patronage networks through which their supporters benefited. Barring one or two mainstream parties, a residual feature of most political parties is that they are elitist, dynastic, clientelist and ethnic-based. A cumulative impact of these features on democratic consolidation was negative. Since most parties in Pakistan are mass-based rather than cadre-based, internal democracy is not possible. However, they are neither oligarchic nor autocratic but decision-making lies with the top leadership and people place low trust on them.

It has to be recognised that, political parties despite their being not fully developed are the central political force serving as an instrument for public contestation by representing voters' preferences through institutional mechanism. Like democracy, political parties are also a recent import to Pakistan and despite their being in a formative phase they have contributed to solidify participatory democracy providing a legitimate system of presenting public choice. Political parties are indispensible to the functioning of democracy in Pakistan. They are the legitimate institutions which represent the public choice and collective interests of the masses in the political process and play a key role in consolidation of democracy. Currently, political parties are at the helm of power for the second consecutive term and have showed signs of maturity in continuing civilian rule. The very continuation of a civilian regime has generated hope for democratic consolidation, but political parties sometimes play foul and harm their own cause. Political parties still show tendencies to seek arbitration from the military in times of crisis, which exhibits the weakness of their belief in the democratic system.

Unless, political parties agree to the rules of the game and show patience and allow legitimate elected regimes to function, parties would remain vulnerable to the military's dictates.

Glossary

Adl	Justice
Ahadis	Plural of '*Hadis*,' *see below*
Ahle Sunnat	Those who follow traditions, the term denotes orthodoxy
Ahmadis	Followers of Mirza Ghulam Ahmad of Qadian, a sect in Islam founded in 1889. They were declared as non-Muslims in 1974 by PPP Government in Pakistan
Al-assabiah	Group-feeling, kinship, tribal ties
Alim	A person educated in Islamic law and capable of giving opinion in religious matters
Al-mulk	Royal authority
Ameer	Leader/commander
Ameer-ul-Momineen	Leader/commander of the faithful
Aqida	Creed
Arkan	Member of a party
Ashraf	Literally meaning Nobles. People claimed to be the descendent of Prophet Muhammad, upper caste Muslims who are racially superior to fellow converted Muslims
Azadi	Freedom
Bhai	Brother
Biradari	A type of kinship institution and social organisation in South Asian communities, tribal lineage endogamy or kinship ties
Chowk	Square/an open market area in a city at the junction of two roads
Coup d'état	A French word, literally meaning 'stroke of the state.' In the context of this study it means capturing political power by the military by

	overthrowing a civilian regime
Darul ulum	Seminary, an institution of advanced religious learning
Deen	Literally meaning religion
Deeni-Madaris	Plural of Madrasa, see below
De-facto	In-fact
De-jure	Holding a specified position by rightful entitlement
Deobandi	A revivalist movement within Sunni Islam, especially among the followers of *Hanafi* Jurisprudence. The movement started in 1869 in Deoband, India, from where it derived its name. Its primary argument is that Muslims have fallen behind the West because they deviated from the pristine teaching of the Prophet
Desi	Native
Diyat	An Islamic law under which compensation should be paid to the victim or heirs of the victim in cases of murder. It is part of *Hudood* laws in Pakistan
Ehtesab	Accountability
Fakirana Zindagi	A Sage's life
Fikri Nashist	Thoughtful sessions, series of inspirational speeches by Altaf Hussain to his followers
Fiqh	Jurisprudence
Ghadir Khumm	Hadith of the Pond of Khumm. According to Shia belief the Prophet of Islam had delivered a speech at Khadir Khumm, near the city of al-Juhfah, according to which he had chosen Hazrat Ali as his heir in 632 CE
Ghair Illahi-Nizam	Anti-Godly system
Gotras	Clan. In Hinduism it refers to the people of same patrilineal ancestors
Hadd	Singular of '*Hudood*,' *see below*

Hadis	The saying of Prophet Muhammad
Hamdard	Sympathiser
Haqiqi	The real
Hijb-i-Allah	The party of God
Hilal-i-Imtiaz	Literally, Crescent of Excellence. Second highest civilian award given to both civilians and military officers in Pakistan
Hudood	Literally, limit, Punishments, plural of *Hadd*. These are punishments for crimes clearly prescribed in *Qu'ran* and *Sunnah*
Hukumat-e-Ilahiya	Divine government
Ijtihad	Individual inquiry conducted by an '*alim*,'to determine the ruling of Islamic law
Inqilab	Revolution
Islami Jamhoori Ittehad	Islamic Democratic Alliance
Islami Riyasat	Islamic State
Islami	Islamic
Islamiyat	Islamic Studies
Jahiliya	Literally, ignorance, pre-Islamic Arabia which was deprived of divine guidance
Jamaat	Party, Organisation, Group
Jamaat-e-Islami	Literally, party or society of Islam. It is a conservative political organisation founded by Sayyed Abul A'la Maududi in 1941 in undivided India to restore the pristine principles of Islam
Jamaat-e-Jahiliyat	Literally, the party of ignorant or pagans. Sayyed Abul A'la Maududi branded AIML as such a party
Jamiat Ahle Hadith	A religio-political party in Pakistan promoting the *Ahle Hadees* religious movement
Junta	A group of military personnel which rules a country by taking power using force
Kafir	Infidel
Kafirana	of Infidels

Kammis	The community which serves the villagers with labour and craft occupation traditionally associated with their ancestors
Karkun	Political party-workers
Khalifa	The Caliph
Kharijite	They were the people who rebelled against the Umayyad Caliphate in the seventh century CE. They were the first traceable sect of Islam which deviated from the ideal norms of behaviour prescribed in Islam. Majority of the Muslims rejected their position
Khatm-e-Nabuwwat	Finality of Prophet. It was also a campaign to declare *Ahmadis* as non-Muslims in Pakistan in 1974
Khilafat	The Caliphate
Khudi	The concept of the self. It was a philosophical concept of the self, propounded by Muhammad Iqbal in his book *Asrar-i-Khudi*, The Secrets of the Self
Lutf	The Grace
Madrasa	A centre of learning or school to impart Islamic teachings and train *ulema*
Majlis	Assembly/Council
Majlis-e-Amila	Executive Council
Majlis-e-Shura	Consultative Assembly
Markaz	Centre/Head office
Markazi	Central
Masawat	Egalitarianism
Mashaik	Plural of *Shaikh*, a learned Sufi master
Masjid	Mosque
Maulana	A title given to graduates from religious seminaries
Millat	Religious community/Nation/composite
Mu'tazilite	They were the people who followed a school of theological thought called *Mu'tazili* in

	the 8th Century Arabia. They could be called illuminati of their time who deserted the accepted interpretation of *Qu'ran* and had their own reading of it
Muhajir	Literally, Migrants. Historically these were the people who migrated with Prophet Muhammad from Makkah to Madina in 622 CE. In the context of this study *Muhajirs* were those who migrated to Pakistan from India in 1947
Mussawati-i-Muhammadi	The Islamic egalitarianism
Muttafiq	Affiliates
Muttahida Majlis-e-Amal	United Council of Action. It was political alliances of mainstream religious parties in Pakistan which collectively opposed the US 'War on Terror' in Afghanistan, campaigned to enforce *Shariah* law and contested together in the general elections of 2002
Muttahida	Composite
Naib-Ameer	Deputy leader
Naukarshah	Bureaucrat.
Naya Pakistan	New Pakistan. A political slogan of PTI during election campaign of 2013
Nazim	An elected administrator of district or administrative unit
Nifaz	Enforcement/imposition or act of enforcement
Nisbul	Pristine
Nizam al-kufr	Order of Infidelity
Nizam	Order/system
Nizam-e-Adl	Order of Justice
Nizam-e-Mustafa	Order of the Prophet/ Islamic system of governance
Pakhtunwali	A set of tribal code practiced among Pakhtuns
Pardah	Literally, curtain. A practice of male-female separation among Muslims

Pasban	Sentinel
Pir	Sufi spiritual guru
Qadiani Masail	The Qadiani Question. A pamphlet written by SayyedAbul A'la Maududi
Qanoon-i-Shahadat	Law of evidence, part of *Hudood* laws
Qarardad-i-Maqasid	Charter of Resolution. It is a Sindhi-Muhajir accord of 1988
Qazf	Bearing false testimony, a crime under *Hudood* laws
Qisas	*Shariah* law for murder that makes testimony of two Muslim male witnesses necessary as proof. It is part of *Hudood* laws
Quaid	Leader
Quaid-i-Azam	Supreme Leader, a title given to Muhammad Ali Jinnah
Quaid-i-Tehreek	Leader of the movement, a title given to Altaf Hussain
Quami	Of nation/community
Quom	Nation/community/kinship
Qurashite	Descendent of the Prophet Muhammad's clan called *Quraish*
Rabita	Contact
Rah-e-Rast	Also known as the Second Battle of Swat. It was an armed operation launched by the Pakistan military in Swat Valley in 2009 to root out the militants from the region
Rahnuma	The guide – one who leads to the righteous path
Risalat	Message or revelation to the Prophets of Islam
Risalat-as-Saqifah	The doctrine of *Imamate* from a Shi'a perspective
Salariat	The salaried class mainly dependent on government employment in the British Indian administration – the civil bureaucracy and the military

Sangathan	Literally, organisation. It was a socio-political movement also known as *Hindu Sabha* movement aimed at uniting different sections of the Hindus into one consolidated organisation
Sardar	Title of tribal/clan leader in KPK and Baluchistan
Shariat	A body of laws which govern Muslim personal and social life
Shirk	Polytheism.
Shuddhi	Literally, purification. It was early 20th Century socio-political movement founded by the *Arya Samaj*. It aimed at converting outcaste people into the fold of mainstream Hindu practice through the ancient rite of *Shuddhikaran*
Sunnah	Tradition, following the example of the practices of the Prophet Muhammad
Suo Moto	A Latin legal term meaning 'on its own motion,' the term is used in legal phrase where government agency acts on its own cognizance
Tabdeeli Razakar	The volunteer of change
Tabligh	Missionary activity, propagation of Islamic teachings
Tablighi Jamaat	Missionary society, it is an organisation of Sunni Muslims who believe that Muslim should return to the pristine principles of the Prophet. And like his companion must travel and spread the teachings of Islam.
Tahfim al-quran	The Meaning of the *Qu'ran*. It was Maududi's interpretation of the *Qu'ran*
Tajdid	Renewal, a revivalist movement in Islam during the first millennia
Tamasha	A fuss/grand show
Tanzeem	Organisation
Tarjuma al-quran	The Translation of the *Qu'ran*. It was Maududi's translation of the *Qu'ran*.

Tawheed	Oneness of God, Unity of God
Tehreek-e-Nizam-e-Mustafa	Movement to establish the order of the Prophet
Tehreek-e-Taliban	Movement of the students/a socio-political organisation that originated in Afghanistan in early 1990s and took over the government in 1996
Tehreek-e-Nifaz-e-Shariah	Movement for the Enforcement of Islamic Law. It is a group of militants with the objective to impose Shariah law in Pakistan
Tehsil	Administrative division in some of the South Asian countries
Troika	A group of three people working together.
Ulema	Plural of '*alim*'
Ummah	A nation of Muslims
Zamindar	A landowning community, traditionally linked with cultivation as the parentage occupation
Zarb-e-Azb	Joint military operations by the Pakistan Armed Forces against militant groups
Zina	Sex outside marriage, a crime in Hudood laws that covers adultery, fornication, rape and prostitution
Zindabad	Long live, slogan used to cheer or encourage
Zulm	Tyranny

Interviewees

Andrew Wilder, Vice President, Asia Programmes, United States Institute of Peace, Washington, D.C., (New Delhi, 13 August 2014.)

Arbab Tahir, General Secretary, Awami National Party, Khyber Pakhtunkhawa, (New Delhi, 15 July 2013).

Babar Sattar, AJURIS, Advocates & Corporate Counsel, Islamabad, (New Delhi, 22 March 2013).

Husain Haqqani, Professor of the Practice of International Relations, Boston University and former Ambassador of Pakistan to the United States, (27 February 2013, New Delhi).

Ishtiaq Ahmad, Professor Emeritus of Political Science, Stockholm University, Stockholm, (New Delhi, 22 March 2013).

Kalim Bahadur, Former Professor, School of International Studies, JNU, (New Delhi, 16 March 2012).

Karamat Ali, Executive Director, Pakistan Institute of Labour Education and Research, (New Delhi, 11 August 2013).

Maya Tudor, University Lecturer in Government and Public Policy, Blavatnik School of Government, Oxford University, UK, (New Delhi, 13 December 2013).

Moeed Yusuf, Director, South Asia Programmes, United States Institute of Peace, Washington, D.C., (New Delhi 6 August 2014).

Mohammad Waseem, Professor of Political Science, Department of Social Sciences, Lahore University of Management Sciences, Lahore, (New Delhi, 18 October 2011).

Nukhbah Langah, Assistant Professor, Forman Christian College, Lahore, (New Delhi, 16 March 2012).

Philip K. Oldenburg, Professor, University of Columbia, New York, (New Delhi, 3 November 2012).

Salim Raza, Former Governor, State Bank of Pakistan, (New Delhi, 25 November 2011).

Sherry Rehman, Former Ambassador of Pakistan to the United States & Former Federal Minister of Information & Broadcasting, (New Delhi, 13 July 2013).

Syed Savail Hussain, Independent Economist, Lahore, (New Delhi, 22 March 2013).

Yaqoob Bangash, Assistant Professor of History, Forman Christian College, Lahore, (New Delhi, 17 March 2012).

Bibliography

Primary Sources

Manifestos, Constitutions and Proceedings of Political Parties

Rudad-e-Jamaat-e-Islami (Proceedings of Jamaat-e-Islami) Vol. 1: First Ijtema and Ijtema of Jamaat-e-Islami, Darbhanga, August 1941 to October 1943 (New Delhi: MarkaziMaktabaIslami Publishers, 2015).

Rudad-e-Jamaat-e-Islami (Proceedings of Jamaat-e-Islami) Vol.3: The All India Ijtema of Jamaat e Islami, Allahabad, April 1946 (New Delhi: MarkaziMaktabaIslami Publishers, 2013).

The 1970 Manifesto of Pakistan Peoples Party, *ppp.org*, URL: http://www.ppp.org.pk/manifestos/manifesto1970.pdf (accessed on 23 March 2015).

The 1993 Manifesto of Pakistan Peoples Party, *ppp.org*, URL: http://www.ppp.org.pk / manifestos/manifesto1993.pdf (accessed on 23 March 2015).

The 1998 Manifesto of MuttahidaQuami Movement, *mqm.org*, URL: http://www.mqm.org/manifesto/manifesto-contents-1998.htm (accessed on 17 April 2015). http://www.mqm.org/manifesto/manifesto-contents-1998.htm

The 2002 Manifesto of Pakistan-Tehreek-e-Insaf, *supportimrankhan.org*, URL: http://www.supportimrankhan.org/downloads/PTImanifesto.pdf(accessed on 9 April 2015).

The 2008 Manifesto of Pakistan Peoples Party, *ppp.org*, URL: http://www.ppp.org.pk / manifestos/manifesto2008.pdf (accessed on 23 March 2015). https://pppp.org.pk/final/wp-content/uploads/2018/12/manifesto2008.pdf

The 2013 Manifesto of MuttahidaQuami Movement, *mqm.org*, URL: http://www.mqm.org/manifesto2013 (accessed on 17 April 2015).

The 2013 Manifesto of Pakistan Muslim League (Nawaz), *pmln.org*, URL: http://www.pmln.org/pmln-manifesto-english/ (accessed on 15 March 2015). http://voiceofpmln.blogspot.com/2013/03/pmln-manifesto-2013.html

The 2013 Manifesto of Pakistan Peoples Party, *ppp.org*, URL: http://www.ppp.org.pk / manifestos/manifesto2013.pdf (accessed on 23 March 2015). http://www.pppp.org.pk/manifestos/manifesto2013.pdf

The 2013 Manifesto of Pakistan Tehreek-e-Insaf, *insaf.pk*, URL: http://www.insaf.pk/about-us/know-pti/manifesto(accessed on 26 April 2015) https://www.scribd.com/document/134950996/PTI-Manifesto-2013

The Constitution of Jamaat-e-Islami, *jamaat.org*, URL: http://jamaat.org/ur/dastoorOrManshoor_detail.php?article_id=1150(accessed on 1 May 2015)

The Constitution ofPakistan Muslim League (Nawaz), *pmln.org*, URL: http://www.pmln.org/constitution/preamble/ (accessed on 23 July 2014). http://www.pmln.us/constitution/

The Constitution of *Pakistan-Tehreek-e-Insaf*, *insaf.pk*, URL:http://www.insaf.pk/about-us/know-pti/constitution (accessed on 7 April 2015).

Speeches and Statements

Iqbal, Mohammad, *Speeches, Writings and Statements of Iqbal* complied by Latif Ahmad Sherwani (Lahore: Iqbal Academy Pakistan, 1944).

Iqbal, Muhammad, *Speeches and Statements* compiled by Shamloo (Lahore: Al-Manar Academy, 1944).

Jafri, Rais Ahmad (ed.), *Ayub: Soldier and Statesman, Speeches and Statements (1958-1965) of Field Martial Mohammad Ayub Khan: President of Pakistan and Detailed Account of the Indo-Pakistan War 1965* (Lahore: Mohammad Ali Academy, 1966).

Khan, Roedad, *The British Papers: Secret and Confidential, India – Pakistan – Bangladesh Documents 1958–1969* (Karachi: Oxford University Press, 2002).

Lincoln, Abraham, *Lincoln: Speeches and Writings 1859-1865* (New York: The Library of America, 1989).

Zaidi, Z. H. (ed.), *Jinnah Papers: Pakistan at Last, 26 July-14 August 1947, Series 1, Vol. 4* (Islamabad: Qaid-i-Azam Papers Project, 1999).

Autobiographies/Biographies

Bhutto, Benazir, *Daughter of Destiny: An Autobiography* (New York: Simon and Schuster, 1989).

Bhutto, Fatima, *Songs of Blood and Sword: A Daughter's Memoir* (New Delhi: Penguin-Viking, 2010).

Bhutto, Zulfikar Ali, *If I am Assassinated* (New Delhi: Vikas Publishing House, 1979).

Hussain, Altaf, *My Life's Journey: The Early Years 1966-1988* (*Safar-i-Zindagi*), trans. Khalid Athar (Karachi: Oxford University Press, 2011).

Khan, Mohammad Ayub, *Friends Not Masters: A Political Autobiography* (Lahore: Oxford University Press, 1967).

Kutty, B. M. (ed.), *In Search of Solutions: An Autobiography of Mir Ghaus Baksh Bizenjo* (Karachi: Pakistan Study Centre, University of Karachi, 2011).

Maududi, Syyid Abul Ala, *Wasa'iq-e-Maududi* (Testimony of Maududi) (Lahore: Idara Ma'arif-i-Islami, 1984).

Pervez Musharraf, *In the Line of Fire: A Memoir* (New York: Free Press, 2006).

Wolport, Stanley, *Zulfi Bhutto of Pakistan: Life and Times* (New York: Oxford University Press, 1993).

Official Statistics on Populations

"Area, Population, Density and Urban/Rural Proportion by Admn. Units," Census of Pakistan 1998, *Pakistan Bureau of Statistics*, URL: http://www.pbs.gov.pk/content/area-population-density-and-urbanrural-proportion (accessed on 21 November 2014).

"Demographic Indicators – 1998 Census," Census of Pakistan 1998, *Pakistan Bureau of Statistics*, URL: http://www.pbs.gov.pk/content/demographic-indicators-1998-census (accessed on 11 September 2014).

"District at Glance: Khyber Pakhtunkhwa," *Pakistan Bureau of Statistics*, URL: http://www.pbs.gov.pk/pco-kpk-tables (accessed on 20 September 2015).

"Pakistan Population 2013," *World Population Statistics*, 14 December 2013, URL: http:/

/www.worldpopulationstatistics.com/pakistan-population-2013/(accessed on 17 April 2016).

"Population by Mother Tongue," Census of Pakistan 1998, *Pakistan Bureau of Statistics*, URL: http://www.pbs.gov.pk/content/population-mother-tongue (accessed on 17 August 2015).

50 Years of Pakistan in Statistics, Volume-4, 1982-1997: Population (Karachi: Federal Bureau of Pakistan, Statistical Division, Government of Pakistan, 1998).

50 Years of Pakistan, Volume-1: Population (Karachi: Federal Bureau of Pakistan, Statistical Division, Government of Pakistan, 1998).

50 Years of Pakistan, Volume-2: Population (Karachi: Federal Bureau of Pakistan, Statistical Division, Government of Pakistan, 1998).

Shamsi, N., "The Integration of Displaced Persons in Pakistan," in *Census of Pakistan 1951: Demographic Miscellany*, Census Bulletin No. 6 (Karachi: Ministry of the Interior, Government of Pakistan, 1957).

Slade, E. H., *Census of Pakistan 1951: Report and Tables* (Karachi: Ministry of the Interior, Government of Pakistan, 1957).

The World Bank, "Urban Population (% of Total), *worldbank.org*, 2013, URL: http://data.worldbank.org/indicator/SP.URB.TOTL.IN.ZS(accessed on 2 September 2015).

UNHCR, "Afghan Repatriation Operation 2006: Weekly Statistics Report," *unhcr.org*, 31 December 2006, URL: http://www.unhcr.org/cgibin/texis/vtx/ search?page=search& docid =47131c6e2& query=unhcr%20statistics(accessed on 30 November 2013).

Acts, Laws and Ordinances

"Enforcement of Shari'ah Act. 1991 (ACT X OF 1991) An Act for the enforcement of Shari'ah," *pakistani.org*, URL: http://www.pakistani.org/pakistan/legislation/1991/actX of1991.html(accessed on 23 July 2014).

"Provisional Constitution Order 1 of 1999," *Pakistan Constitution Law*, URL: https://pakistanconstitutionlaw.com/provisional-constitution-order-1999/(accessed on 12 August 2015).

"The Constitution (Seventeenth Amendment) Act, 2003," *Pakistan Constitution Law*, URL: https://pakistanconstitutionlaw.com/17th-amendment-2003/ (accessed on 12 August 2015).

Pakistan Penal Code (Act XLV of 1860), *pakistani.org*, URL: http://www.pakistani.org/pakistan/legislation/1860/actXLVof1860.html(accessed on 15 November 2014).

The Constitution (Eighteenth Amendment) Act, 2008, "Act No. X of 2010," in "Part 1, Acts, Ordinances, Presidents Orders and Regulations," *The Gazette of Pakistan-Extraordinary*, Islamabad, 20 April 2010, pp. 267-316.

The Constitution of the Islamic Republic of Pakistan: As Amended by the Constitution (Nineteenth Amdt.) Act, 2010 (Act No. I of 2011), corrected and modified by Zaka Ali (Karachi: The Ideal Publishers, 2011).

Electoral Data

Gilani's Index of Electoral Record 1970-2013: Volume 1-9, based on Gallup Exit Poll data and ECP data, compiled by Gallup Election Studies Team, 2013, URL: www.gallup.com.pk (accessed on 4 May 2014).

ECP, "Electoral Rolls," *Election Commission of Pakistan*, URL: http://elections.com.pk/contents.php?i=12 (accessed on 30 November 2013).

Mehdi, Tahir et al (eds.), *National Assembly Elections on Pakistan 1970-2008: A Compendium of Elections Related Facts and Statistics* (Lahore: Church World Service-Pakistan/Afghanistan and Free and Free Election Network, 2010).

Report, Briefings and Surveys

PEW Research Centre, "The World's Muslims: Religion, Politics and Society," 30 April 2013, URL: https://muslimstatistics.files.wordpress.com/2015/03/worlds-muslims-religi on-politics-society-full-report.pdf (accessed on 22 May 2014).

Munir, M., *Report of the Court of Inquiry Constituted Under Punjab Act II of 1954 to Enquire Into the Punjab Disturbances of 1953* (Lahore: Government of Punjab, 1954).

"Public Opinion on Quality of Democracy in Pakistan: At the end of the Second Year of Federal and Provincial Governments, June 2014 - May 2015," *Pakistan Institute of Legislative Development And Transparency*, Islamabad, October 2015, pp. 1-400.

"Assessment of the Quality of Democracy in Pakistan -2015," *Pakistan Institute of Legislative Development And Transparency*, Islamabad, May 2016, pp. 1-82.

TV Interviews

"HT Leadership Summit 2008, Asif Ali Zardari: How can India and Pakistan Work Together part 2," *Youtube.com*, 29 October 2009, URL: https://www.youtube.com/watch?v=_fF8cvPoIFs (accessed on 9 April 2014).

"I never ever offered Imran Khan to become Prime Minister, Musharraf deny Imran's claim," *Awaz.tv*, 30 December 2014, URL: http://www.awaztoday.tv/News-Talk-Shows/74621/I-never-ever-offered-Imran-Khan-to-become-Prime-Minister-Musharraf-deny-Imrans-claim.aspx (accessed on 30 April 2015).

General Musharraf in an Interview with Indian journalist Barkha Dutt, "Imran Khan is the best of the lot: Musharraf to NDTV," *NDTV 24x7*, 17 November 2011, URL: http://www.ndtv.com/world-news/imran-khan-is-the-best-of-the-lot-musharraf-to-ndtv-566316(accessed on 17 November 2011).

Nawaz Sharif's interview with Karan Thapar, "Devil's Advocate," *CNN News 18*, 5 May 2013, URL: https://www.youtube.com/watch?v=EK74wKW3BLU (accessed on 18 July 2014).

Nawaz Sharif's interview with Karan Thapar, *CNN IBN*, 6 May 2013, URL:https://www.youtube.com/watch?v=PY66ks783VA (accessed on 12 December 2013).

Secondary Sources

Books

Abbas, Hasan, *Pakistan's Drift into Extremism: Allah, the Army and America's War on Terror* (New York: East Gate Book, 2005).

Ahmad, Dohra, Iftikhar Ahmad and Zia Mian (eds.), *Between Past and Future: Selected Essays on South Asia by Eqbal Ahmad* (Karachi: Oxford University Press, 2004).

Ahmad, Irfan, *Islamism and Democracy in India; The Transformation of Jamaat-e-Islami* (Princeton: Princeton University Press, 2009).

Ahmad, Ishtiaq, *The Pakistan Army in Politics: Origins, Evolution, Consequences* (New Delhi: Amaryllis, 2013).

Ahmad, Saghir, *Class and Power in a Punjabi Village* (New York: Monthly Review Press, 1977).

Ahmed, Feroz, *Ethnicity and Politics in Pakistan* (Karachi: Oxford University Press, 1998).

Aldrich, John H., *Why Parties?: The Origin and Transformation of Political Parties in America* (Chicago: University of Chicago Press, 1995).

Ali, Tariq, *The Clash of Fundamentalisms: Crusades, Jihads and Modernity* (London: Verso, 2002).

____________, *The Duel: Pakistan on the Flight Path of American Power* (New York: Simon and Schuster, 2008).

Allardt, Erik and Stein Rokkan (eds.), *Mass Politics: Studies in Political Sociology* (New York: The Free Press, 1970).

Allen, Douglas (ed.), *Religion and Political Conflict in South Asia: India, Pakistan and Sri Lanka* (London: Greenwood Press, 1992).

Anderson, Benedict, *Imagined Communities: On the Origin and Spread of Nationalism* (London: Vesro, 1995).

Bahadur, Kalim, *The Jamat-i-Islami of Pakistan: Political Thought and Political Action* (New Delhi: Chetna Publication, 1977).

Baker, Raymond W., *Capitalism's Achilles Heel: Dirty Money and How to Renew the Free-Market System* (New Jersey: John Wiley & Sons, Inc., 2005).

Baxter, Craig and Charles Kennedy, *Pakistan: 1997* (New Delhi: Harper Collins, 1998).

Behera, Ajay Darshan and Mathew Joseph C. (eds.), *Pakistan in a Changing Strategic Context* (New Delhi: Knowledge World, 2004).

Bhutto, Benazir, *Reconciliation: Islam, Democracy and the West* (New York: Harper Luxe, 2008).

Blood, Peter R. (ed.), *Pakistan: A Country Study* (Washington DC: Federal Research Division, Library of Congress, 1995).

Blunt, E. A. H., *The Caste System of Northern India* (Humphrew Milford: Oxford University Press, 1931).

Bogdanor, Vernon (ed.), *The Blackwell Encyclopaedia of Political Institutions* (Oxford: Blackwell Reference, 1987).

Bowering, Gerhard (ed.), *Princeton Encyclopedia of Islamic Political Thought* (Princeton: Princeton University Press, 2013).

Brass, Paul R., *Caste, Faction and Party in Indian Politics* (New Delhi: Chanakya Publications, 1985).

Burki, Sahid Javed, *Pakistan under Bhutto 1971-1977* (London: Macmillan Press, 1980).

Caramani, Daniele (ed.), *Comparative Politics*, (New York: Oxford University Press, 2011).

Cohen, Stephen P., (ed.), *The Future of Pakistan* (New Delhi: Oxford University Press, 2011).

____________, *The Idea of Pakistan* (New Delhi: Oxford University Press, 2004).

Dahl, Robert A., *A Preface to Democratic Theory* (Chicago: The University of Chicago Press, 2006).

____________, *Democracy and Its Critics* (New Delhi: Orient Longman, 1989).

Darity Jr., William A., *International Encyclopedia of the Social Sciences* (Detroit: McMillan References USA, 2008).

Dawood, Jan Mohammad, *The Role of Superior Judiciary in the Politics of Pakistan* (Karachi: Royal Book Company, 1994).

Donohue, John J. and John L. Esposito, *Islam in Transition: Muslim Perspectives* (New York: Oxford University Press).

Dunn, John (ed.), *Democracy: The Unfinished Journey: 508 BC-AD 1993* (Oxford: Oxford University Press, 1992).

Duverger, Maurice, *Political Parties: Their Organization and Activity in the Modern State*, trans. Barbara and Robert North (New York: John Wiley and Sons, 1963).

Epstein, Leon D., *Political Parties in the American Mold* (Madison: University of Wisconsin Press, 1986).

Feaver, Peter D., *Armed Servant: Agency, Oversight, and Civil-Military Relations* (Cambridge: Harvard University Press, 2003).

Feldman, Herbert, *From Crisis to Crisis: Pakistan 1962-1969* (London: Oxford University Press, 1972).

Feldman, Herbert, *Revolution in Pakistan: A Study of the Martial Law Administration* (Lahore: Oxford University Press, 1967).

Finer, S. E., *The Man on the Horseback: The Role of the Military in Politics* (London: Pall Mall Press, 1962).

Gankovsky, Yu. V., *The Peoples of Pakistan: An Ethnic History*, trans. Igor Gavrilov (Lahore: Peoples Publishing House, n.d.).

Gellner, Ernest, *Nations and Nationalism* (New Delhi: Select Book Service Syndicate, 1986).

Ghosh, Papiya, *Partition and the South Asian Diaspora: Extending the Subcontinent* (London: Routledge, 2007).

Grover, Verinder and Ranjana Arora (eds.), *Political System of Pakistan Vol. 2: Constitutional Development in Pakistan* (New Delhi: Deep and Deep Publications, 1995).

_______________ (eds.), *Political System of Pakistan Vol. 3: Political Parties, Elections and Regionalism in Pakistan* (New Delhi: Deep and Deep Publications, 1995).

Hajari, Nisid, *Midnight's Furies: The Deadly Legacy of India's Partition* (Gurgaon: PenguinViking, 2015).

Hamlin, Alan and Philip Pettit (eds.), *The Good Polity* (Oxford: Blackwell, 1989).

Haqqani, Husain, *Magnificent Delusions: Pakistan, the United Nations, and an Epic History of Misunderstanding* (New York: Perseus Books Group, 2014).

Hobsbawm, Eric J. *Nations and Nationalism Since 1780: Programme, Myth, Realty* (Cambridge: Cambridge University Press 1992).

Huntington, Samuel P. and Clement H. Moore, *Authoritarian Politics in Modern Society: The Dynamics of Established One-Party Systems* (New York: Basic Books, 1970).

Huntington, Samuel P., *Political Order in Changing Societies* (New Haven: Yale University Press, 1976 (1968).

_____________, *The Soldier and the State: The Theory and Politics of Civil-Military Relations* (Dehradun: Natraj Publishers, 2005).

Hutchinson, John and Anthony D. Smith (eds.), *Nationalism* (Oxford: Oxford University Press, 1994).

Hutton, J. H., *Caste in India* (Cambridge: Cambridge University Press, 1946).

Jaffrelot, Christophe, *The Pakistan Paradox: Instability and Resilience* (Gurgaon: Random House India, 2015).

Jalal, Ayesha, *The State of Martial Rule: The Origins of Pakistan's Political Economy of Defence* (Cambridge: Cambridge University Press, 1990).

Jones, Philip E., *The Pakistan People's Party: Rise to Power* (Karachi: Oxford University Press, 2003).

Kalia, Ravi (ed.), *Pakistan: From the Rhetoric of Democracy to the Rise of Militancy* (New Delhi: Routledge, 2011).

Kamran, Tahir, *Democracy and Governance in Pakistan* (Lahore: South Asia Partnership-Pakistan, 2008).

Katz, Richard S and William Crotty (eds.), *Handbook of Party Politics* (London: Sage Publication, 2006).

Kennedy, Charles H. and Cynthia Botteron (eds.), *Pakistan 2005* (Karachi: Oxford University Press, 2006).

Kennedy, Charles H., *Bureaucracy in Pakistan* (Karachi: Oxford University Press, 1987).

Key, V. O., *Politics, Parties, and Pressure Groups* (New York: Thomas Y. Crowell, 1958).

Khaldun, Ibn, *The Muqaddimah: An Introduction to History, Vol. 1-3*, trans. Franz Rosenthal (New York: Pantheon Books, 1958).

Khan, Adeel, *Politics of Identity: Ethnic Nationalism and the State in Pakistan* (New Delhi: Sage Publication, 2006).

Khan, Hamid, *Constitutional and Political History of Pakistan* (Karachi: Oxford University Press, 2002).

Khan, Hussain Ahmad, *Re-thinking Punjab: The Construction of Siraiki Identity* (Lahore: Research and Publication Centre, National College of Arts, n.d.).

Khan, Imran, *All Round View* (London: Chatto and Windus, 1988).

____________, *Pakistan: A Personal History* (London: Bantam Books, 2012).

Khan, Mahmood Hasan, *Underdevelopment and Agrarian Structure in Pakistan* (Lahore: Vanguard Publications, 1986).

Khan, Mohammad Asghar (ed.), *Islam, Politics and the State: The Pakistan Experience* (New Delhi: Select Book Service Syndicate, 1985).

____________, *Generals in Politics: Pakistan 1958-1982* (New Delhi: Vikas Publishing House, 1983).

Khan, Nichola, *Mohajir Militancy in Pakistan: Violence and Transformation in the Karachi Conflict* (Abingdon: Routledge, 2010).

Khan, Qamaruddin, *Al-Mawardi's Theory of the State* (Lahore: Islamic Book Foundation, 1983).

____________, *The Political Thought of Ibn Taymiyah* (Islamabad: Islamic Research Institute, 1985).

Kolkowitz, Roman and Andrzej Korbonski (eds.), *Soldiers, Peasants, and Bureaucrats: Civil-Military Relations in Communist and Modernizing Societies* (London: George Allen and Unwin, 1982).

Kothari, Rajni and James Manor (eds.), *Caste in Indian Politics* (New Delhi: Orient Blackswan, 2010).

Kukreja, Veena, *Civil-Military Relations in Developing Countries* (New Delhi: Sage Publication, 1991).

Lamb, Chirstina, *Waiting for Allah: Pakistan's Struggle for Democracy* (New Delhi: Viking, 1991).

LaPlombara, Joseph and Myron Weiner (eds.), *Political Parties and Political Development* (Princeton: Princeton University Press, 1966).

Lieven, Anatol, *Pakistan: A Hard Country* (London: Penguin Books, 2011).

Lijphart, Arend, *Patterns of Democracy: Government Forms and Performance in Thirty-Six Countries* (New Haven: Yale University Press, 1999).

Linz, Juan J., *Totalitarian and Authoritarian Regimes* (Boulder: Lynne Rienner Publishers, 2000).

Lodhi, Maliha (ed.), *Pakistan: Beyond the Crisis State* (New York: Columbia University Press, 2011).

Luttwak, Edward, *Coup D'etat: A Practical Handbook* (New York: Alfred A. Knopf, 1969).

Macpherson, C. B., *The Life and Times of Liberal Democracy* (Oxford: Oxford University Press, 1977).

Madan, T. N. (ed.), *Muslim Communities of South Asia: Culture, Society and Power* (New Delhi: Manohar, 2001).

Madani, Hussain Ahmad, *Composite Nationalism and Islam*, trans. Mohammad Anwar Hussain and Hasan Imam (New Delhi: Manohar, 2006).

Malik, Iftikhar, *Pakistan: Democracy, Terrorism, and the Building of a Nation* (Northampton: Olive Branch Press, 2010).

Malik, Jamal, *Colonisation of Islam: Dissolution of Traditional Institutions in Pakistan* (New Delhi: Manohar Publishers, 1998).

Maloney, Clarence, *Peoples of South Asia* (New York: Holt, Rinehart and Winston, 1974).

Martin, Richard C. (ed.), *Encyclopedia of Islam and the Muslim World, Vol. 1* (New York: Macmillan Reference, 2004).

Maudoodi, Sayyid Abulala, *Nationalism and India*, trans. Qammaruddin Khan (Lahore: Tarjuman-Ul-Quran, 1941).

Maududi, Sayyed Abul'ala, *Islam Aur Jahalat* (Islam and Ignorance) (New Delhi: Markazi Maktaba Islami Publishers, 2013).

____________, *Islam ka Nizam-e-Hayat* (Islamic Way of life) (New Delhi: Markazi Maktaba Islami Publishers, 2013).

____________, *Tajdeed-O-Ahyaye Deen* (Revivalist Movement in Islam) (New Delhi: Markazi Maktaba Islami Publishers, 2014).

____________, *First Principles of Islamic State*,trans. Khurshid Ahmad(Lahore: Islamic Publication Limited, 1967).

____________, *Political Theory of Islam* (New Delhi: Markazi Maktaba Islami Publishers, 2003).

Mehdi, Rubya, *The Islamisation of the Law in Pakistan*(Richmond: Curzon Press, 1994).

Mernissi, Fatema, *Islam and Democracy: Fear of the Modern World*, trans. Marry Jo Lakeland (Cambridge: Perseus Publishing, 2002).

Mosca, Gaetano, *The Ruling Class*, trans. Hannah D. Kahn (New York: McGraw-Hill Book Company, 1939).

Mumtaz, Khawar and Farida Shaheed, *Women of Pakistan: Two Steps Forward, One Step Back?* (Lahore: Vanguard Books,1987).

Naqvi, Syed Nawab Haider, Mahmood Hasan Khan and M. Ghaffar Chaudhry (eds.), *Land Reforms in Pakistan: A Historical Perspective* (Islamabad: Pakistan Institute of Development Economics, 1987).

____________, (eds.), *Structural Change in Pakistan's Agriculture* (Islamabad: Pakistan Institute of Development Economics, 1989).

Nasr, Seyyed Vali Reza, *Mawdudi and the Making of Islamic Revivalism* (New York: Oxford University Press, 1996).

____________, *The Vanguard of the Islamic Revolution: The Jama`at-i-Islami of Pakistan* (London: I. B. Tauris Publishers, 1994).

Nawaz, Shuja, *Crossed Swords: Pakistan, its Army and the Wars Within* (New York: Oxford University Press, 2008).

Niaz, Ilhan, *The Culture of Power and Governance of Pakistan 1947-2008* (Karachi: Oxford University Press, 2010).

Nichols, Robert, *History of Pashtun Migration, 1775-2006* (Oxford: Oxford University Press, 2008).

Oldenburg, Philip, *India, Pakistan, and Democracy: Solving the Puzzle of Divergent Paths* (London: Routledge, 2012).

Pakistan Democratic Forum, *Pakistan People's Party* (New York: Pakistan Democratic Forum, 1983).

Perlmutter, Amos, *The Military and Politics in Modern Times: On Professionals, Praetorians, and Revolutionary Soldiers* (New Haven: Yale University Press, 1978).

Pirzada, Syed Sharifuddin, *Foundations of Pakistan: All-India Muslim League Documents, 1906-1947* (Karachi: National Publishing House, 1969).

Pritchett, Frances W. (ed.), *Dr. Babasaheb Ambedkar: Writings and Speeches, Vol. 1* (Bombay: Education Department, Government of Maharashtra, 1979).

Rahman, Tariq, *Language and Politics in Pakistan* (New Delhi: Orient Longman, 1997).

Rashid, Jamil and Hasan N. Gardezi (eds.), *Pakistan: The Roots of Dictatorship* (London: Zed Press, 1983).

Raza, Rafi, *Zulfikar Ali Bhutto and Pakistan 1967-1977* (Karachi: Oxford University Press, 1997).

Rizvi, Hasan Askari, *Military, State and Society in Pakistan: 1947-1997*(Lahore: Sang-e-Meel Publications, 2000).

____________, *The Military and Politics in Pakistan: 1947-86* (Lahore: Sang-e-Meel Publications, 2000).

Rudolph, Lloyd I. and Susanne Hoeber Rudolph, *The Modernity of Tradition: Political Development in India* (Chicago: The University of Chicago Press, 1984).

Sartori, Giovanni, *Parties and Party System: a Framework for Analysis* (London: ECPR Press, 2005).

Sayeed, Khalid B., *Politics in Pakistan: The Nature and Direction of Change* (New York: Praeger, 1980).

____________, *The Political System of Pakistan* (Boston: Houghton Mifflin Company, 1967).

Schendel, Willem van, *A History of Bangladesh* (Cambridge: Cambridge University Press, 2009).

Schumpeter, Joseph A., *Capitalism, Socialism and Democracy* (New Delhi: Adarsh Books, 2011).

Shafqat, Saeed, *Civil-Military Relations in Pakistan: From Zulfikar Ali Bhutto to Benazir Bhutto* (Boulder: Westview Press, 1997).

Shah, Aqil, *The Army and Democracy: Military Politics in Pakistan* (Cambridge: Harvard University Press, 2014).

Shahin, Emad El-Din (ed.), *The Oxford Encyclopedia of Islam and Politics, Vol.1* (New York: Oxford University Press, 2014).

Shaikh, Farzana, *Community and Consensus in Islam: Muslim Representation in Colonial India, 1860-1947* (Cambridge: Cambridge University Press, 1989).

Siddiqa, Ayesha, *Military Inc.: Inside Pakistan's Military Economy* (Karachi: Oxford University Press, 2007).

Smith, Anthony D., *Nationalism: Theory, Ideology, History* (Cambridge: Polity Press, 2001).

Sourosh, Abdolkarim, *Reason, Freedom, and Democracy in Islam: Essential Writings of 'Abdolkarim Sourosh*, trans. Mahmoud Sadri and Ahmad Sadri (New York: Oxford University Press, 2000).

Srinivas, M. N., *Caste in Modern India and Other Essays* (New Delhi: Asia Publishing House, 1962).

Stepan, Alfred, *The Military in Politics: Changing Patterns in Brazil* (Princeton: Princeton University Press, 1971).

Suvorova, Anna, *Benazir Bhutto: A Multidimensional Portraits* (Karachi: Oxford University Press, 2015).

Syed, Anwar H., *The Discourse and Politics of Zulfikar Ali Bhutto* (London: Macmillan, 1992).

Talbot, Ian, *Pakistan: A Modern History* (London: Hurts and Company, 1998).

____________, *Pakistan: A New History* (London: Hurst and Company, 2012).

Taseer, Salman, *Bhutto: A Political Biography* (New Delhi: Vikas Publishing House, 1980).

Tocqueville, Alexis de, *Democracy in America: Vol. 1and 2*, trans. Henry Reeve (New York: Alfred A. Knopf, 1960).

Tudor, Maya, *The Promise of Power: The Origins of Democracy in India and Autocracy in Pakistan* (Cambridge: Cambridge University Press, 2013).

Umar, Badruddin, *The Emergence of Bangladesh: Class Struggle in East Pakistan 1947-1958* (Karachi: Oxford University Press, 2004).

Verkaaik, Oskar, *Migrants and Militants: Fun and Urban Violence in Pakistan* (New Delhi: Manas Publication in collaboration with Princeton University Press, 2005).

Waseem, Mohammad, *Politics and the State in Pakistan* (Islamabad: National Institute of Historical and Cultural Research, 1994).

____________, *The 1993 Elections in Pakistan*(Lahore: Vanguard Books, 1994).

Wilder, Andrew R., *The Pakistani Voter: Electoral Politics and Voting Behaviour in the Punjab* (Karachi: Oxford University Press, 1999).

Zakaria, Fareed, *The Future of Freedom: Illiberal Democracy at Home and Abroad* (New Delhi: Viking, 2003).

Ziring, Lawrence, *Pakistan in the Twentieth Century: A Political History* (London: Oxford University Press, 1970).

Articles from Journals

"A General State of Disarray," *The Economist*, Vol. 383, No. 8529, 19 May 2007, p. 26.
"An Engaging Dictator Who Wants to Stay That Way," *The Economist*, 12 December 1981, p. 48.
"The Long Shot," *Time*, Vol. 23, No. 7, 17 December 2012.
Abbas, Zaffar, "Can the Tiger Roar," *The Herald*, Vol. 28, No. 3, March 1997, pp. 27-31.
Adeney, Kathrine, "A Step Towards Inclusive Federalism in Pakistan? The Politics of the 18th Amendment," *The Journal of Federalism*, Vol. 42, No. 4, 23 February 2012, pp. 539-65.
Adil, Adnan, "Shahbaz Sharif's Fiefdom," *Newsline*, Vol. 26, No. 2, August 2014, pp. 53-6.
Ahmad, Maqbool, "The Nationalists Strike Back," *The Herald*, Vol.41, No. 2, February 2008, pp. 78-9.
Ahmad, Raza, "The Endemic Crises of Federalism in Pakistan," *The Lahore Journal of* Economics, Vol. 15, September 2010 pp. 15-31.
Ahmar, Moonis, "Ethnicity and State Power in Pakistan: The Karachi Crisis," *Asian Survey,* Vol. 35, No. 11, October 1996, pp. 1031-48.
Ahmed, Feroz, "Ethnicity and Politics: The Rise of Muhajir Separatism," *South Asian Bulletin*, Vol. 8, No. 1-2, 1988, p. 48-60.
____________, "Kinship in West Punjab Villages," *Contributions to Indian Sociology*, Vol. 6, No. 1, January 1972, pp. 1-27.
____________, "Nationhood and the Nationalities in Pakistan," *Economic and Political Weekly*, Vol. 24, No. 27, July 1989, pp. 1527- 34.
Alavi, Hamza, "The State in Postcolonial Societies: Pakistan and Bangladesh," *New Left Review*, No. 72, July-August 1972, pp.145-72.
Ali, Tariq, "Daughter of the West," *London Review of Books*, Vol. 29, No. 24, 13 December 2007, pp.3-9.
Amin, Tahir, "Pakistan in 1993: Some Dramatic Changes," *Asian Survey*, Vol. 34, No. 2, February 1994, pp. 191-99.
____________, "Pakistan in 1994: The Politics of Confrontation," *Asian Survey*, Vol. 35, No. 2, February 1995, pp. 140-46
Amir, Ayaz, "What Does Imran Khan Really Want?," *The Herald*, Vol. 27, No. 5, May 1996, pp. 36-7.
Amir, Intikhab, "Double Standards," *The Herald*, Vol. 41, No. 10, October 2005, pp. 82-3.
Asif, Haseeb, "Striking Success," *The Herald*, Vol. 47, No. 1, January 2014, pp. 58-60.
Baxter, Craig, "Pakistan Votes-1970," *Asian Survey*, Vol.11, No. 3, March 1971, pp. 197-218.
Burk, James, "Theories of Democratic Civil-Military Relations," *Armed Forces and Society*, Vol. 29, No. 1, Fall 2002, pp. 7-29.
Burki, Shahid Javed, "Politics of Economic Decision-making During the Bhutto Period," *Asian Survey*, Vol.14, No.2, December 1974, pp. 1126-40.
Chaudhry, G.W., "Democracy on Trial in Pakistan,"*Middle East Journal*, Vol. 17, No. 1/2,

Winter-Spring, 1963, pp. 1-13.

Cohen, Stephen Philip and Marvin G. Weinbaum, "Pakistan in 1981: Staying on," *Asian Survey*, Vol. 22, No. 2, February 1982, pp. 136-46.

Farooq, Umer, "Marching Orders," *The Herald*, Vol. 47, No. 9, September 2014, pp. 51-4.

Farooq, Umer, and Ghulam Dastgeer, "Military Operation," *The Herald*, Vol. 48, No. 7, July 2014, pp. 54-62.

Feaver, Peter D., "The Civil-Military Probelmatique: Huntington, Janowitz, and the Question of Civilian Control," *Armed Forces and Society*, Vol. 23, No. 2, Winter 1995, pp. 149-78.

Feldman, Herbert, "Pakistan in 1974," *Asian Survey*, Vol. 15, No. 2, February 1975, pp. 110-16.

Gazdar, Haris "Goodbye General Musharraf, Hello Troika," *Economic and Political Weekly*, Vol. 42, No.50, 15-21 December 2007, pp. 8-9.

___________, "Find Your War, or Risk Losing It," *Economic and Political Weekly*, Vol. 43, No.41, 11-17 October 2008, pp. 8-9.

Gunther, Richard and Larry Diamond, "Species of Political Parties: A New Typology," *Party Politics*, Vol. 9, No. 2, pp. 167-99.

Haque, Nazil Jamil, "Wanting to become Prime Minister is a small Ambition," *Newsline*, Vol. 7, No. 10, April 1996, pp. 35-37.

Hashmi, Rehana Saeed and Gulshan Majeed, "Saraiki Ethnic Identity: Genesis of the Conflict with the State," *Journal of Political Studies*, Vol. 21, No. 1, January 2014, pp. 79-101.

Hollen, Eliza van, "Pakistan in 1986: Trials of Transition," *Asian Survey*, Vol. 27, No. 2, February 1987, pp. 143-54.

Hussain, Abid, "Big Brother is Watching," *The Herald*, Vol.18, No.7, July 2014, pp. 44-9.

Hussain, Syed Talat, "All the General's Men," *Newsline*, Vol. 26, No. 3, September 2014, pp. 16-21.

___________, "The Clash of Institutions," *Newsline*, Vol. 25, No. 10, May 2014, pp. 33-4.

Hussain, Zahid, "Imran's New Innings," *Newsline*, Vol. 7, No. 10, April 1996, pp. 24-30.

ICG, "Reforming Pakistan's Civil Service," *International Crisis Group*,Asia Report, No. 185, 16 February 2010, pp. 1-27.

___________, "Authoritarianism and Political Party Reform in Pakistan," *International Crisis Group*, Asia Report, No.102, 28 September 2005, pp. 1-28.

___________, "Islamic Parties in Pakistan," *International Crisis Group*, Asia Report, No.216, 12 December 2011, pp. 1-36.

___________, "Pakistan: The Mullahs and the Military," *International Crisis Group*, Asia Report, No.49, 20 March 2003, pp. 1-35.

___________, "Pakistan's Local Polls: Shoring Up Military Rule," *International Crisis Group*, Asia Briefing, No. 43, 22 November, 2005, pp. 1-16.

___________, "Reforming the Judiciary in Pakistan," *International Crisis Group*, Asia Report, No. 160, October 2008,pp. 1-36.

Ignazi, Piero, "The Crisis of Parties and the Rise of New Political Parties," *Party Politics*, Vol. 2, October 1996, pp. 569-85.

Javed, Umair, "Fast Forward to the Past," *The Herald*, Vol. 47, No. 9, September 2014, pp.

55-8.
Javid, Hassan, "All the King's Men," *The Herald*, Vol. 47, No. 1, January 2014, pp. 43-5.
Khan, Aamer Ahmed, "Third Force or Third Farce?," *The Herald*, Vol. 27, No. 5, May 1996, pp. 25-8.
Khan, Aurangzaib, "The Whole Roedad: The Journey of a Man and an Institution through the Decades," *The Herald*, Vol. 48, No. 2, February 2015, pp. 59-65.
Khan, Mohammad Ayub, "A New Experiment in Democracy in Pakistan," *Annals of the American Academy of Political Science*, Vol. 358, March 1965, pp. 109-113.
Khan, Rais Ahmad, "Pakistan in 1992: Waiting for Change," *Asian Survey*, Vol. 33, No. 2, February 1993, pp. 129-40.
Khan, Sher Ali, "Politics of Disruption," *The Herald*, Vol. 47, No. 11, November, 2014, pp. 36-8.
Khan, Sher Ali, "The Odd Man Out," *The Herald*, Vol. 47, No. 9, September 2014, pp. 59-63.
Khan, Sher Ali, Umer Farooq and Mirza Khurram Shahzad, "Dead Weight," *The Herald*, Vol. 48, No. 2, February 2015, pp. 49-58.
Khan, Zaigham, "Three's a Crowd," *The Herald*, Vol. 27, No. 5, May 1996, pp. 29-32.
Kohari, Alizeh, "The Centre (still) Holds," *The Herald*, Vol.18, No.7, July 2014, pp. 50-52.
LaPorte Jr., Robert, "Pakistan in 1995: The Continuing Crises," *Asian Survey*, Vol. 36, No. 2, February 1996, pp. 179-89.
__________, "Pakistan in 1996: Starting Over Again," *Asian Survey*, Vol. 37, No. 2, February 1997, pp. 118-25.
Malik, Iftikhar H., "Pakistan in 2000: Starting Anew or Stalemate?" *Asian Survey*, Vol. 41, No.1, pp. 104-15.
Mujahid, Sharif al, "Pakistan: First General Elections," *Asian Survey*, Vol. 11, No. 2, February 1971, pp. 159-71.
Naveed, Shayan and Alizeh Kohari, "Person of the Year," *The Herald*, Annual Issue, January 2014, pp. 53-7.
Nelson, Mathew J., "Pakistan 2008: Moving Beyond Musharraf," *Asian Survey*, Vol. 50, No. 1, January-February 2009, pp. 16-27.
Noman, Omar, "Pakistan and General Zia: Era and Legacy," *Third World Quarterly*, Vol. 11, No.1, January 1989, pp. 28-54.
Peshimam, Gibran, "Media-Powered Democracy: How Media Support has been Pivotal to Pakistan's Latest Democratization Project," *Reuters Institute Fellowship Paper*, University of Oxford, 2013, pp. 1-46.
Rahman, Rashid, "Will the Real Imran Khan Please Stand Up?," *Newsline*, Vol. 7, No. 10, April 1996, pp. 31-2.
Rais, Rasul B., "Pakistan in 1987: Transition to Democracy," *Asian Survey*, Vol. 28, No. 2, February 1988, pp. 126-36.
Rana, Muhammad Amir, "He is Afraid if He Takes a Position Against Extremism it will Damage His Party's Interest," *Time*, Vol. 23, No. 7, 17 December 2012, p. 23.
Rehman, Sherry," A Khan for all Seasons," *The Herald*, Vol. 27, No. 5, May 1996, pp. 33-5.
Richter, William L., "Pakistan in 1984: Digging in," *Asian Survey*, Vol. 25, No. 2, February 1985, pp. 145-154.
__________, "Pakistan in 1985: Testing time for the New Order," *Asian Survey*, Vol. 26,

No. 2, February 1986, pp. 207-18.

Rizvi, Hasan Askari, "National Security Council: A Debate on Institutions and Processes for Decisions-Making on Security Issues," *Pakistan Institute for Legislative Development and Transparency*, Discussion Paper, Islamabad, April 2012, pp. 1-34.

____________, "Pakistan in 1998: The Polity under Pressure," *Asian Survey*, Vol. 39, No. 1, January-February 1999, pp. 177-84.

____________, "Pakistan in 1999: Back to Square One," *Asian Survey*, Vol. 40, No. 1, January-February 2000, pp. 208-18.

Saigol, Rubina, "Three Pillars of Wisdom: A Critical Assessment of Imran Khan and His Politics," *The Herald*, Vol. 47, No. 1, January 2014, pp. 60-2.

Saigol, Rubina, "Word Wars," *The Herald*, Vol. 47, No. 9, September 2014, pp. 64-6.

Samad, Yunas, "Managing Diversity in Pakistan: Going Beyond Federalism," *Sustainable Development Policy Institute* (Islamabad), Working Paper No. 13, March 2013, pp. 1-15.

Sayeed, Khalid Bin, "Pakistan in 1983: Internal Stresses More Serious than External Problems," *Asian Survey*, Vol. 24, No. 2, February1984, pp. 219-28.

Schedler, Andreas, "What is Democratic Consolidation?" *Journal of Democracy*, Vol. 9, No. 2, April 1998, pp. 91-108.

Schiff, Rebecca L., "Civil-Military Relations Reconsidered: A Theory of Concordance," *Armed Forces and Society*, Vol. 22, No. 1, Fall 1995, pp. 7-24.

Shah, Aqil, "Axis of National Security," *The Herald*, Vol. 47, No. 6, June 2014, pp. 35-8.

Shahid-ur-Rahman, "The Price of Protest," *Newsline*, Vol. 26, No. 3, September 2014, pp. 25-6.

Siddiqa, Ayesha, "Discovering Democracy: Five Years of Political Rule in Pakistan," *Economic and Political Weekly*, Vol. 4, No. 7, 27 April 2014, pp. 23-5.

____________, "The Elephant in the Room," *Newsline*, Vol. 26, No. 3, September 2014, pp. 22-4.

Syed, Anwar H., "Pakistan in 1976: Business as Usual," *Asian Survey*, Vol. 17, No. 2, February 1977, pp. 181-90.

____________, "Pakistan in 1997: Nawaz Sharif's Second Chance to Govern," *Asian Survey*, Vol. 38, No. 2, February 1998, pp. 116-25.

____________, "The Pakistan People's Party and the Punjab: National Assembly Elections, 1988 and 1990," *Asian Survey*, Vol. 31, No. 7 July 1991, pp. 581-97.

Varol, Ozan O., "The Democratic Coup D'etat," *Harvard International Law Journal*, Vol. 53, No. 2, Summer, 2012, pp. 292-356.

Waseem, Mohammad, "Causes of Democratic Downslide," *Economic and Political Weekly*, Vol. 37, No. 44/45, 2-15 November 2002, pp. 4532-38.

Weinbaum, M. G., "The March 1977 Elections in Pakistan: Where Everyone Lost," *Asian Survey*, Vol. 17, No. 7, July 1977, pp. 599-618.

Weinbaum, Marvin G. and Stephen P. Cohen, "Pakistan in 1982: Holding On," *Asian Survey*, Vol. 23, No. 2, February 1983, pp. 123-32.

Weiss, Anita M., "Benazir Bhutto and the Future of Women in Pakistan," *Asian Survey*, Vol. 30, No. 5, May 1990, pp. 433-45.

Wheeler, Richard S., "Pakistan in 1975: The Hydra of Opposition," *Asian Survey*, Vol. 16,

No. 2, February 1976, pp. 111-18.

Wirsing, Robert G., "The Arms Race in South Asia: Implications for the United States," *Asian Survey*, Vol. 25, No. 3, March 1985, pp. 265-91.

Yasmeen, Samina, "Democracy in Pakistan: The Third Dismissal," *Asian Survey*, Vol. 34, No. 6, June 1994, pp. 572-88.

Yusuf, Moeed, "Leader/Agitator," *The Herald*, Vol. 48, No. 1, January 2015, pp. 76-7.

Zaidi, S. Akbar, "Civilian Dictatorship and Praetorian Democracy," Economic *and Political Weekly*, Vol. 43, No.37, 13-19 September 2008, pp. 8-9.

____________, "An Incomplete Transition in Pakistan," *Economic and Political Weekly*, Vol. 43, No.45, 8-14 November 2008, pp. 10-11.

Ziring, Lawrence and Robert LaPorte Jr., "The Pakistan Bureaucracy: Two Views," *Asian Survey*, Vol. 14, No. 12, December 1974, pp. 1086-1103.

Ziring, Lawrence, "From Islamic Republic to Islamic State in Pakistan," *Asian Survey*, Vol. 24, No. 9, September 1984, pp. 931-46.

Online Sources

"'Across the Board Accountability' Essential for Prosperous Pakistan: Gen Raheel," *Dawn*, 19 April 2016, URL: http://www.dawn.com/news/1253087 (accessed on 14 September 2016).

"A Sad Day," *Dawn*, 3 January 2015, URL: http://www.dawn.com/news/1154719 (accessed on 27 May 2016).

"Alliance in the making: PTI, PML-Q agree on three points," *The Express Tribune*, 9 July 2014, URL: http://tribune.com.pk/story/733025/alliance-in-the-making-pti-pml-q-agree-on-three-points/ (accessed on 30 September 2014).

"Altaf 'hands over' party affairs to Rabita Committee after statements by Farooq Sattar," *Dawn*, 24 August 2016, URL: http://www.dawn.com/news/1279656/altaf-hands-over-party-affairs-to-rabita-committee-after-statements-by-farooq-sattar (accessed on 24 August 2016).

"Altaf Hussain: Founder and Leader of MQM," *mqm.org*, URL: https://mqmuk.com/altaf-hussain/ (accessed on 12 March 2015).

"Apex Court Clears NRO," *Dawn*, 28 February 2008, URL: http://www.dawn.com/news /291403/apex-court-clears-nro (accessed on 19 September 2012).

"Army's questionable decisions," *Dawn*, 2 September 2014, URL: http://www.dawn.com/news/1129263 (accessed on 27 May 2016).

"Arrest warrant issued against Makhdoom Shahabuddin," *Dawn*, 21 June 2012, URL: http://www.dawn.com/news/728285/arrest-warrant-issued-against-makhdoomshahabuddin (accessed on 10 October 2015).

"Bhutto Drawing Thousands in Rail Campaign to Oust Government," *New York Times*, 27 November 1992, URL:http://www.nytimes.com/1992/11/27/world/bhutto-drawing-thousands-in-rail-campaign-to-oust-government.html(accessed on 11 April 2015).

"Blow to Democracy," *Dawn*, 30 August 2014, URL: http://www.dawn.com/ news/1128637 (accessed on 27 May 2016).

"Catalyst for change or military stooge?" *Dawn*, 13 January 2013, URL: http://www.dawn.com/news/778494/catalyst-for-change-or-military-stooge (accessed on 5 April 2016).

"Civil-Military Relations in Pakistan," Monitor, *Pakistan Institute of Legislative Development and Transparency*, August-December, 2013, p. 1, URL: http://www.pildat.org/publications/publication/CMR/MonitorOnCivilMilitaryRelationsinPakistan_August012013_December152013.pdf (accessed on 12 July 2014).

"COAS Raheel Sharif made 'mediator' to end political crisis," *Dawn*, 29 August 2014, URL: http://www.dawn.com/news/1128362/coas-raheel-sharif-made-mediator-to-end-pol itical-crisis (accessed on 12 April 2016).

"Commission's report says Haqqani behind controversial memo," *Dawn*, 12 June 2012, URL: http://www.dawn.com/news/725930/sc-takes-up-memo-case (accessed on 21 July 2014).

"Constitution Assembly Debates," Volume 7, *Parliament of India*, URL: http://loksabhaph.nic.in/Debates/cadebatefiles/C04111948.html (accessed on 23 March 2015).

"Drone Wars Pakistan Analysis," *New America Foundation*, URL: http://securitydata.newamerica.net/drones/pakistan-analysis.html (accessed on 8 October 2015).

"Excerpts from General Musharraf's address," *BBC News*, 17 October 1999, URL: http://news.bbc.co.uk/2/hi/world/monitoring/477829.stm (accessed on 4 May 2013).

"Farooq Sattar sidelines Altaf: 'MQM will operate only from Pakistan," *Dawn*, 24 August 2016, URL: http://www.dawn.com/news/1279446/farooq-sattar-sidelines-altaf-mqm-will-operate-only-from-pakistan(accessed on 24 August 2016).

"Fikri Nishist," *mqm.org*, URL: http://www.mqm.org/FikriNishist (accessed on 12 March 2015).

"Gilani announces restoration of deposed chief judge," *Dawn*, 16 March 2009, URL: http://www.dawn.com/news/957245/gilani-announces-restoration-of-deposed-chief-judge (accessed on 8 January 2014).

"Hameed Gul admits he formed IJI," *Daily Times*, 1 February 2008, URL: http://www.thenews.com.pk/TodaysPrintDetail.aspx?ID=24196&Cat=13&dt=8/30/2009(accessed on 29 April 2015).

"I was under Severe Mental Stress: Altaf Apologises to Military for anti-Pakistan Remarks," *Dawn*, 23 August 2016, URL: http://www.dawn.com/news/1279430/i-was-under-severe-mental-stress-altaf-apologises-to-military-for-anti-pakistan-remarks(accessed on 23 August 2016).

"Imran Khan's 'tsunami' sweeps Lahore," *The Express Tribune*, 30 October 2011, URL: http://tribune.com.pk/story/285058/pti-rally-in-lahore-live-updates/ (accessed on 1 May 2015).

"Imran lays out 6-point charter of demands," *The Nation*, 21 August 2014, URL: http://nation.com.pk/national/21-Aug-2014/imran-lays-out-6-point-charter-of-demands (accessed on 2 May 2015).

"Imran vows to be truthful, loyal with masses after assuming powers," *The Nation*, 23 March 2013, URL: http://nation.com.pk/national/23-Mar-2013/imran-vows-to-be-truthfu l-loyal-with-masses-after-assuming-powers (accessed on 1 May 2015).

"Imran warns Nawaz of 'tsunami march' if demands not met," *Dawn*, 28 June 2014, URL: http://www.dawn.com/news/1115509/imran-warns-nawaz-of-tsunami-march-if-demands-not-met(accessed on 29 September 2014).

"Islamabad stand-off: Army not backing PTI or PAT, says ISPR," *Dawn*, 1 September 2014, URL: http://www.dawn.com/news/1129011/islamabad-stand-off-army-not-backing -pti-or-pat-says-ispr (accessed on 18 May 2016).

"Jurisdiction of the Court," *Federal Shariat Court of Pakistan*, n. d., URL: http://www.federalshariatcourt.gov.pk/Jurs.html(accessed on 27 September 2015).

"Media in Pakistan: Between Radicalisation and Democratisation in an Unfolding Conflict," *International Media Support*, Report, July 2009, URL: http://www.i-ms.dk/files/publications/1491 %20Pakistan,final.web.pdf (accessed on 20 June 2011).

"Move afoot to bring down govt.: Gilani," *Dawn*, 23 December 2011, URL: http://www.dawn.com/news/682600/no-institution-has-right-to-create-a-state-within-state-pm (accessed on 11 July 2012).

"MPC ends with national consensus on NAP," *Dawn*, 3 January 2015, URL: http://www.dawn.com/news/1154662 (accessed on 12 May 2015).

"Musharraf indicted for treason; pleads not, guilty to all charges," *Dawn*, 31 March 2014, URL: http://www.dawn.com/news/1096826(accessed on 18 December 2015).

"Musharraf says army backs him over treason 'vendetta,'" *The Express Tribune*, 29 December 2013, URL: http://tribune.com.pk/story/652196/musharraf-says-army-backs-him-over-treason-vendetta/(accessed on 18 December 2015).

"Nawaz put under house arrest at Model Town residence, *The Nation*, 15 March 2009, URL: http://nation.com.pk/lahore/15-Mar-2009/Nawaz-put-under-house-arrest-at-Model-Town-residence (accessed on 8 January 2014).

"Nawaz Sharif calls for Taliban talks," *Dawn*, 21 May 2013, URL: http://www.dawn.com/news/1012539/nawaz-sharif-calls-for-taliban-talks (accessed on 26 July 2014).

"No Validation of Military takeover, says Chief Justice," *Dawn*, 24 December 2011, URL: https://www.dawn.com/news/682874/no-validation-of-military-takeover-says-chief -justice (accessed on 11 July 2012).

"Opposition seeks debate in Senate on media reports," *Dawn*, 29 July 2006, URL: http://www.dawn.com/news/203609/opposition-seeks-debate-in-senate-on-media-reports (accessed on 2 May 2015).

"Pak military expresses serious concern over political crisis," *The Indian Express*, 1 September 2014, URL: http://indianexpress.com/article/world/neighbours/pak-military-expresses-serious-concern-over-political-crisis/ (accessed on 15 May 2016).

"Pakistan frees Sharif to exile in Saudi Arabia," *The Guardian*, 11 December 2000, URL: http://www.theguardian.com/world/2000/dec/11/pakistan.saudiarabia (accessed on 12 April 2016).

"Pakistan Lifts Office ban on Nawaz Sharif," *The Telegraph*, 26 May 2009, URL: http://www.telegraph.co.uk/news/worldnews/asia/pakistan/5388737/Pakistan-lifts-office-ban-on-Nawaz-Sharif.html(accessed on 7 August 2015).

"Pakistanis condemn Rushdie honour," *Al Jazeera*, 27 June 2007, URL: http://www.aljazeera.com/news/asia/2007/06/2008525131447351 97.html (accessed on 17 April 2015).

"Pakistan's Khan calls for civil disobedience," *Al Jazeera*, 17 August 2014, URL: http://www.aljazeera.com/news/europe/2014/08/pakistan-protests-continue-second-day-2014817142532776182.html (accessed on 8 May 2016).

"Panama Papers: The Power Players," *ICIJ*, URL: https://panamapapers.icij.org/ the_power_players/ (accessed on 12 September 2016).

"PCO and its victim judges," *Dawn*, 7 January 2008, URL: http://www.dawn.com/news/841674/pco-and-its-victim-judges (accessed on 20 June 2014).

"PML-Q's demands fulfilled; Elahi made Deputy PM, 15 ministries granted," *Dawn*, 25 June 2012, URL: http://www.dawn.com/news/729424/demands-fulfilled-15-ministries-granted-to-pml-q (accessed on 7 May 2015).

"Poll: Who Was Asia's Person of the Year in 2012?" *Asia Society*, 20 December 2012, URL: http://asiasociety.org/blog/asia/poll-who-was-asias-person-year-2012 (accessed on 5 May 2015).

"PPP Government's Achievements," *Pakistan Peoples Party*, URL: https://www.ppp.org.pk/achievements/ (accessed on 31 January 2016).

"President Leghari's Order of November 5, 1996," *pakstani.org*, URL: http://www.pakistani.org/pakistan/leghari.order.html (accessed on 3 September 2015).

"Prime Minister of Pakistan: Mian Muhammad Nawaz Sharif," *Prime Minister's Office*, URL: http://www.pmo.gov.pk/pm_profile.php(accessed on 5 October 2015).

"Profile of Chief Justice and Judges," *Supreme Court of Pakistan*, Annual Report, April 2010-December 2011, URL: http://www.supremecourt.gov.pk/Annual_Rpt/ Profile% 20 of%20the%20Chief%20Justice.pdf (accessed on 13 January 2016).

"Provincial Apex committees formed to implement NAP," *Geo News*, 3 January 2015, URL: https://www.geo.tv/latest/46-provincial-apex-committees-formed-to-implementnap (accessed on 17 August 2016).

"PTI, allies launch Ehtesab march today," *The News*, 3 September 2016, URL: https://www.thenews.com.pk/print/147324-PTI-allies-launch-Ehtesab-march-today (accessed on 17 September 2016).

"Rangers take MQM leaders into custody, seal party headquarters Nine Zero," *Dawn*, 23 August 2016, URL: http://www.dawn.com/news/1279250/rangers-take-mqm-leaders-into-custody-seal-party-headquarters-nine-zero (accessed on 23 August 2016).

"Red Zone's security handed over to Pakistan Army: Nisar," *Dawn*, 19 August 2014, URL: http://www.dawn.com/news/1126356 (accessed on 12 April 2016).

"Religious activists out against Qadri's hanging," *Pakistan Today*, 1 March 2016, URL: http://www.pakistantoday.com.pk/2016/03/01/city/karachi/religious-activists-out-against-qadris-hanging/ (accessed on 2 August 2016).

"Retired army officers absolve MQM of Jinnahpur plot: Altaf calls for truth and reconciliation commission," *Dawn*, 25 August 2009, URL: http://www.dawn.com/news/ 849392/retired-army-officers-absolve-mqm-of-jinnahpur-plot-altaf-calls-for-truth-and-reconciliation-commission(accessed on 27 April 2015).

"SC makes public office out of bounds for Sharif brothers," *Dawn*, 26 February 2009, URL: http://www.dawn.com/news/849139/sc-makes-public-office-out-of-bounds-for-sha rif-brothers (accessed on 8 January 2014).

"Sharifs disqualified, Punjab under governor rule," *Dawn*, 26 February 2009, URL: http://www.dawn.com/news/955822/sharifs-disqualified-punjab-under-governor-rule

(accessed on 8 January 2014).

"Sirajul Haq Replaces Munawar Hassan as Chief of Jamaat-e-Islami," *The Express Tribune*, 30 March 2014, URL: http://tribune.com.pk/story/689135/sirajul-haq-replaces-munawar-hassan-as-chief-of-jamaat-e-islami/ (accessed on 7 October 2015).

"Text of Chief Justice's affidavit filed in Supreme Court,"*Daily Times*, 30 May 2007, URL: http://www.dailytimes.com.pk/default.asp?page=2007%5C05%5C30%5Cstory_30-5-2007pg7_55(accessed on 7 July 2011).

"Text of the Charter of Democracy," *Dawn*, 16 May 2006, URL: http://www.dawn.com/news/192460/text-of-the-charter-of-democracy(accessed on 17 November 2013).

"Text of the Kerry Lugar Bill," *Dawn*, 14 October 2009, URL: http://www.dawn.com/news/913717/text-of-the-kerry-lugar-bill(accessed on 4 May 2015).

"The Leninist Concept of the Revolutionary Vanguard Party," *Marxist.Org*, URL: https://www.marxists.org/history/etol/newspape/socialistvoice/partyPR46.html(accessed on 19 September 2015).

"What Altaf Said...," *Dawn*, 23 August 2016, URL: http://www.dawn.com/news/1279393 (accessed on 23 August 2016).

"Winds of change: MQM warms up to ruling PML-N," *The Express Tribune*, 26 November 2014, URL: http://tribune.com.pk/story/797358/winds-of-change-mqm-warms-up-to-ruling-pml-n/(accessed on 12 June 2015).

"Women Protection Act against Pakistani Constitution, Sharia: Siraj-ul-Haq," *The Nation*, 15 March 2016, URL: http://nation.com.pk/national/15-Mar-2016/women-protection-bill-against-pakistani-constitution-sharia-siraj-ul-haq (accessed on 12 August 2016).

Adams, Tim, "The Path of Khan," *The Guardian*, 2 July 2006, URL: http://www.theguardian.com/sport/2006/jul/02/cricket.features3 (accessed on 30 April 2015).

Akbar, Hasan, "The Rise of the King's Party," *Newsline*, 13 October 2002, URL: http://www.newslinemagazine.com/2002/10/the-rise-of-the-kings-party/ (accessed on 28 June 2011).

Ali, Muhammad Mutahir, "The History of Pakistani Street-Politics," *Pakistan Today*, 12 July 2014, URL: http://www.pakistantoday.com.pk/2014/07/12/featured/the-history-of-pakistani-street-politics/ (accessed on 12 April 2015).

Ali, Tariq, "My Heart Bleeds for Pakistan. It Deserves Better than this Grotesque Feudal Charade," *The Independent*, 31 December 2007, URL: http://www.independent.co.uk/news/world/asia/my-heart-bleeds-for-pakistan-it-deserves-better-than-this-grotesque-feudal-charade-767423.html (accessed on 15 May 2015).

Ansari, Massoud, "How the Referendum was Won," *Newsline*, 15 May 2003, URL: http://www.newslinemagazine.com/2002/05/how-the-referendum-was-won/ (accessed on 4 July 2011).

Asghar, Raja, "Sharia for Malakand as Zardari signs law," *Dawn*, 14 April 2009, URL: http://www.dawn.com/news/457187/sharia-for-malakand-as-zardari-signs-law-2 (accessed on 17 August 2016).

Azfar-ul-Ashfaque, "Spotlight on MQM 'Muscle body'" *Dawn*, 6 September 2014, URL: http://www.dawn.com/news/1130232 (accessed on 28 April 2015).

Boone, Jon and Ewen MacAskill, "More than 100 children killed in Taliban attack on

Pakistan school," *The Guardian*, 16 December 2014, URL: https://www.theguardian.com/world/2014/dec/16/taliban-attack-army-public-school-pakistan-peshawar (accessed on 12 November 2015).

____________, "Nawaz Sharif in the driving seat in battle to be Pakistan's PM," *The Guardian*, 19 March 2013, URL: http://www.theguardian.com/world/2013/mar/19/nawaz -sharif-pakistan-elections-prime-minister (accessed on 25 September 2015).

____________, "Pakistani Taliban TTP warns Imran Khan ahead of drones march," *The Guardian*, 5 October 2012, URL: https://www.theguardian.com/world/2012/oct/05/pakistan-taliban-ttp-imran-khan (accessed on 28 April 2016).

____________, "Pervez Musharraf charged with Benazir Bhutto murder," *The Guardian*, 20 August 2013, URL: https://www.theguardian.com/world/2013/aug/20/pervez-musharraf-benazir-bhutto-pakistan(accessed on 18 December 2015).

____________, "Pervez Musharraf leaves Pakistan after three-year travel ban lifted," *The Guardian*, 18 March 2016, URL: https://www.theguardian.com/world/2016/mar/18/pervez-musharraf-leaves-pakistan-for-treatment-after-travel-ban-lifted (accessed on 8 August 2016).

Bruner, Tasgola Karla, "Sharif may face Death Penalty for Hijacking," *The Independent*, 20 January 2000, URL: https://archive.is/pNT8W#selection-875.0-985.24 (accessed on 7 May 2015).

Butt, Qaiser, "Govt complicit in drone attacks: Imran Khan," *The Express Tribune*, 23 April 2011, http://tribune.com.pk/story/154987/govt-complicit-in-drone-attacks-imran-khan/ (accessed on 28 April 2016).

Cowely, Jason, "12 Great thinkers of our time," *New Statesman*, 14 July 2003, URL: http://mideastweb.org/Middle-East-Encyclopedia/abul-ala-maududi.htm (accessed on 14 August 2015).

Crossette, Barbara, "Coup in Pakistan – Man in the News: A Soldier's Soldier, Not a Political General Pervez Musharraf," *New York Times*, 13 October 1999, URL: https://www.nytimes.com/1999/10/13/world/coup-pakistan-man-soldier-s-soldier-not-political-general-pervez-musharraf.html (accessed on 4 May 2013).

Dalrymple, William, "Pakistan's flawed and feudal princess," *The Guardian*, 30 December 2007, URL: http://www.theguardian.com/commentisfree/2007/dec /30/pakis tan.world (accessed on 1 May 2015).

Dugger, Celia W., "Pakistan Sentences Bhutto to 5 Years for Corruption," *New York Times*, 16 April 1999, URL: http://www.nytimes.com/1999/04/16/world/pakistan-sentences-bhutto-to-5-years-for-corruption.html(accessed on 3 May 2015).

Ghuman, Khawar, "Imran calls for PM's resignation," *Dawn*, 11 April 2016, URL: http://www.dawn.com/news/1251383 (accessed on 14 September 2016).

Ghuman, Zulfiqar, "Article 6 can't just apply to one man: Gilani," *Daily Times*, 17 September 2009, URL: https://web.archive.org/web/20120113101523/http://www.dailyt imes.com.pk/default.asp?page=2009%5C09%5C17%5Cstory_17-9-2009_pg1_1(accessed on 18 December 2015).

Ghumman, Faisal Ali, "2,520 PTI, PAT activists in 27 Punjab jails," *Dawn*, 17 August 2014, URL: http://www.dawn.com/news/1125893/2520-pti-pat-activists-in-27-punjab-jails(accessed on 2 May 2015).

Graham, Stephen, "Court Restores Pakistan Chief Justice," *Washington Post*, 20 July 2007, URL: http://www.washingtonpost.com/wpdyn/content/article/2007/ 07/20/AR2 0070 72000562.html (accessed on 12 July 2011).

Guevara, Marina Walker, "ICIJ releases database revealing thousands of secret offshore companies," *ICIJ*, May 9, 2016, URL: https://panamapapers.icij.org/blog/20160509-offshoredatabaserelease.html?utm_content=buffercee67&utm_medium=social&utm_source=twitter.com&utm_campaign=buffer (accessed on 12 September 2016).

Haider, Mateen, "Gen Raheel dismisses 6 army officers from service over 'corruption,'" *Dawn*, 22 April 2016, URL: http://www.dawn.com/news/1253497 (accessed on 17 September 2016).

Haque, Jahanzaib, Faraz Khan and Ahmad Jung, "Navy says PNS Base under Control after Attack," *The Express Tribune*, 21 May 2011, URL: http://tribune.com.pk/story/173888/blast-on-dalmia-road/ (accessed on 7 July 2011).

Hertzberg, Hendrik, "Big News Week," *The New Yorker*, 30 May 2005, URL: http://www.newyorker.com/magazine/2005/05/30/big-news-week (accessed on 12 April 2015).

Hussain, Altaf, "India and the World: A Blueprint for Partnership and Growth," *Hindustan Times Leadership Initiative*, New Delhi, 5-6 November 2004, URL: http://www.mqm.org/English-News/Nov-2004/ah-speech-india-061104.htm (accessed on 17 April 2015).

_____________, "The Slogan of Two-Nation Theory was raised to deceive the one hundred million Muslims of the Subcontinent," 21 June 2000, London, *mqm.org*, URL: http://www.mqm.org/English-News/Jun-2000/twonation-210600.htm (accessed on 8 October 2015).

Hussain, Sajjad, "3 dead in protests, Pakistan army meets, says won't back off 'playing its part," *The Indian Express*, 1 September 2014, URL: http://indianexpress.com/ article/world/neighbours/pakistan-showdown-2-dead-over-450-injured-as-police-clash-with-protesters-roads-leading-to-nawaz-sharifs-house-shut/(accessed on 16 March 2016).

Hussain, Zahid, "How to Steal an Election," *Newsline*, 13 September 2002, URL: http://www.newslinemagazine.com/2002/09/how-to-steal-an-election/(accessed on 26 June 2011).

Iqbal, Nasir, "1,027 civilian posts occupied by servicemen," *Dawn*, 3 October 2003, URL: http://www.dawn.com/news/118233/1027-civilian-posts-occupied-by-servicemen (accessed on 29 June 2013).

Iqbal, Nasir, "CJ Suspended, Escorted Home," *Dawn*, 10 March 2007, URL: http://www.dawn.com/news/236769/cj-suspended-escorted-home-justice-iftikhar-summoned-by-sjc-on-13th-for-reference-hearing-ex-judges-call-it-a-blow-to-judiciary-s-independence-minister-defends-decision-whither-judicial-activism (accessed on 15 January 2016).

Ismail, Ali, "Pakistan: Military sponsored-PML (Q) joins PPP-led coalition government," *World Socialist Web Site*, 20 May 2011, URL: https://www.wsws.org/en/articles/2011/05/paki-m20.html(accessed on 13 March 2015).

Khan, Azam, "Demands spelled out: 48-hour deadline," *The Express Tribune*, 17 August

2014, URL: http://tribune.com.pk/story/749809/demands-spelled-out-48-hour-deadline/ (accessed on 28 September 2016).

Khan, Azam, "Parliament reposes faith in Nawaz Sharif as Imran, Qadri up the ante," *The Express Tribune*, 20 August 2014, URL: http://tribune.com.pk/story/751325/parliament-reposes-faith-in-nawaz-sharif-as-imran-qardi-up-the-ante/ (accessed on 12 April 2016).

Khan, Iftikhar A., "ECP rejects references against Imran," *Dawn*, 6 September 2007 URL:http://www.dawn.com/news/264817/ecp-rejects-references-against-imran(accessed on 1 May 2015).

Khan, Raza, "Opposition demands 'forensic audit firm' probe Panama Papers revelations," *Dawn*, 8 April 2016, URL: http://www.dawn.com/news/1250754 (accessed on 14 September 2016).

Khan, Sher, "The coining of the 'Naya Pakistan' slogan," *The Express Tribune*, 15 May 2013, URL: http://tribune.com.pk/story/549650/the-coining-of-the-naya-pakistan-slogan/ (accessed on 28 April 2016).

Khan, Zaigham, "Who will celebrate martial law?" *The News*, 15 July 2016, URL: https://www.thenews.com.pk/print/137412-Who-will-celebrate-martial-law (accessed on 17 September 2016).

Mahmood, Amjad, "Assembly backs South Punjab, Bahawalpur provinces," *Dawn*, 10 May 2012, URL: http://www.dawn.com/news/717071/assembly-backs-south-punjab-bahawalpur-provinces(accessed on 2 September 2015).

________________, "National Security Council to be dissolved: Gilani," *Dawn*, 29 November 2008, URL: http://www.dawn.com/news/431010/national-security-council-to-be-dissolved-gilani(accessed on 12 November 2015).

Mahmood, Asif, "MQM pledges 'unconditional support' for PML-N presidential nominee," *Dawn*, 27 July 2013, URL: http://www.dawn.com/news/1032084/mqm-pledges-unconditional-support-for-pml-n-presidential-nominee (accessed on 12 May 2015).

Malik, Asad and Owais Jafri, "Memogate: Nawaz threatens to move SC if govt falls short," *The Express Tribune*, 20 November 2011, URL: http://tribune.com.pk/story/294687/memogate-nawaz-threatens-to-move-sc-if-govt-falls-short/ (accessed on 17 October 2016).

Manan, Abdul and Shamsul Islam, "Faisalabad political rally: Nawaz demands urgent 'memogate' inquiry," *The Express Tribune*, 20 November 2011, URL: http://tribune.com.pk/story/294767/pml-n-all-set-for-faisalabad-rally-today/ (accessed on 17 October 2016).

Manan, Abdul, "Demand for South Punjab," *The Express Tribune*, 5 May 2012, URL: http://tribune.com.pk/story/374354/demand-for-south-punjab/ (accessed on 22 August 2015).

Manan, Abdul, "Fight Against Terrorism: Defining Moment," *The Express Tribune*, 25 December 2014, URL: http://tribune.com.pk/story/811947/fight-against-terrorism-defining-moment/ (accessed on 12 May 2015).

Manzoor, Usman, "The 22-year history of MQM about-turns," *The News International*, 29 June 2011, URL: http://www.thenews.com.pk/Todays-News-2-54968-The-22-year-history-of-MQM-about-turns(accessed on 11 April 2015).

Masood, Salman, "Pakistan Moves Toward Altering Rape Law," *New York Times*, 16 November 2006, URL: http://www.nytimes.com/2006/11/16/world/asia/16pakistan.html?_r=0 (accessed on 12 July 2015).

Mendes, Fr. Bonnie, "Political Order Apartheid in Pakistan in the Name of Religion," *Pakistan Christian Voice*, Internet Magazine, October and November 2000, URL: http://www.suffrage-universel.be/res/pkmi03.htm (accessed on 1 July 2011).

Mumtaz, Ashraf, "Graduation: Record Number of Politicians Out," *Dawn*, 19 July 2002 URL: http://archives.dawn.com/ 2002 /07/19/ top5.htm (accessed on 13 July 2011).

Nelson, Dean and Javed Siddiq, "Imran Khan 'plotted with army to oust Nawaz Sharif', colleague claims," *The Telegraph*, 1 September 2014, URL: http://www.telegraph.co.uk/ news/worldnews/asia/pakistan/11068811/Imran-Khan-plotted-with-army-to-oust-Nawaz-Sharif-colleague-claims.html (accessed on 18 May 2016).

Otten, Christina, "The Mumbai massacres and Pakistan's new nightmares," *The Hindu*, 15 December 2008, URL: http://www.thehindu.com/todays-paper/tp-opinion/the-mumba i-massacres-and-pakistans-new-nightmares/article1395432.ece(accessed on 9 April 2014).

Paracha, Nadeem F., "Abul Ala Maududi: An existentialist history," *Dawn*, 1 January 2015, URL: http://www.dawn.com/news/1154419 (accessed on 12 July 2015).

____________, "Islamic Socialism: A history from left to right," *Dawn*, 21 February 2013, URL: http://www.dawn.com/news/787645/islamic-socialism-a-history-from-left-to-right (accessed on 19 December 2014).

Paracha, Nadeem F., "Maududi's Children," *Dawn*, 11 June 2009, URL: http://www.dawn.com/news/812924/maududi%E2%80%99s-children (accessed on 3 October 2015).

Pennington, Mathew, "Lawyers Relaunch Anti-Musharraf Campaign," *The Washington Post*, 6 September 2007, URL: http://www.washingtonpost.com/wp-dyn/content/article/2 007/09/06/AR2007090600601_pf.html (accessed on 18 August 215).

Perlez, Jane, "Pakistan Court Bars President's Rival from Office," *New York Times*, 25 February 2009, URL: http://www.nytimes.com/2009/02/26/world/asia/26pstan.html (accessed on 28 August 2015).

Pitafi, Farrukh Khan, "Reminiscing 1977," *The Express Tribune*, 25 March 2016, URL: http://tribune.com.pk/story/1072846/reminiscing-1977/(accessed on 12 August 2016).

Rahman, Tariq, "The Real Ideology of the Pakistani Male," *tariqrahman.net*, n.d., URL: http://www.tariqrahman.net/newspaper/The%20Surreal%20Face%20of%20Pakistan.htm (accessed on 26 August 2011).

Rajnath, Arun, "Altaf Hussain Seeks Easier Political Asylum For His Supporters: India Rejects," *South Asia Tribune*, 8 November 2004, URL: http://antisystemic.org/satribune/ www.satribune.com/archives/nov04/P1_arun4.htm(accessed on 14 May 2015).

Ralph, Talia, "The top 9 World leaders of 2012," *Global Post*, 20 December 2012,URL: http://www.globalpost.com/dispatch/news/politics/world-leaders/121213/top-9-world-leaders-2012(accessed on 12 May 2015).

Raza, Syed Irfan, "Govt forced to withdraw ISI decision," *Dawn*, 28 July 2008, URL: http://www.dawn.com/news/313820/govt-forced-to-withdraw-isi-decision (accessed on 12 November 2015).

_____________, "ISI, IB put under interior division's control," *Dawn*, 27 July 2008, URL: http://www.dawn.com/news/313676/isi-ib-put-under-interior-division-s-control(accessed on 12 November 2015).

Rehman, Habib Ur, "Imran Khan Announce to End Islamabad Sit-in over Peshawar Attack," *The Pak Media*,17 December 2014, URL: http://www.thepakmedia.com/imran-khan-announce-ends-islamabad-sit-peshawar-attack/2014/12/17(accessed on 2 May 2015).

Riedel, Bruce, "Clueless or Complicit?" *India Today*, 12 July 2013, URL: http://indiatoday.intoday.in/story/osama-bin-laden-pakistan-abbottabad-commission-report-united-states/1/291011.html (accessed on 15 March 2016).

Rizvi, Hasan Askari, "The Civil-Military Hybrid," *The Express Tribune*, 23 February 2015, URL: http://tribune.com.pk/story/842505/the-civil-military-hybrid/ (accessed on 4 April 2016).

_____________, "The politics of top political offices," *The Express Tribune*, 11 August 2013, URL: http://tribune.com.pk/story/588790/the-politics-of-top-political-offices/ (accessed on 29 September 2015).

Rogin, Josh, "Exclusive: Secret Pakistani-U.S. memo offering overthrow of military leadership revealed," *Foreign Policy*, 17 November 2011, URL: http://foreignpolicy.com/ 2011/11/17/exclusive-secret-pakistani-u-s-memo-offering-overthrow-of-military-leadersh ip-revealed/ (accessed on 4 January 2014).

Saiyid, Aamna, "The population of Karachi has doubled in 15 years," *The Express Tribune*, 13 January 2014, URL: http://tribune.com.pk/story/658394/the-population-of-karachi-has-doubled-in-15-years/ (accessed on 2 October 2015).

Shah, Benazir, "The Right Man," *Newsweek*, 9 July 2014, URL: http://newsweekpakistan.com/the-right-man/ (accessed on 11 September 2015).

Shah, Sabir, "Altaf Hussain arrested for fourth time," *The News*, 4 June 2014, URL: http://www.thenews.com.pk/Todays-News-2-254042-Altaf-Hussain-arrested-for-fourth-time (accessed on 13 September 2015).

Shahzad, Mohammad, "The Impact of Blasphemy Law," *Dawn*, 18 July 2002, URL: http://www.thepersecution.org/ news/dawn020718.html (accessed on 5 July 2011).

Stephens, Bret, "The Most Difficult Job in the World: Pakistan's president on terrorism, India and his late wife," *Wall Street Journal*, 4 October 2008, URL: http://www.wsj.com/articles/SB122307507392703831(accessed on 10 December 2015).

Sumra, Anwer, "Destination Islamabad: Azadi march takes off," *The Express Tribune*, 15 August 2015, URL: http://tribune.com.pk/story/748978/destination-islamabad-azadi-march-takes-off/ (accessed on 28 September 2016).

Taseer, Shehrbano, "The Rebirth of Maryam Nawaz Sharif," *Newsweek*, 23 March 2012, URL: http://newsweekpakistan.com/the-rebirth-of-maryam-nawaz-sharif/ (accessed on 19 January 2014).

Tharoor, Shashi, "Bhutto's death has averted a mullah-military Pakistan," *The Guardian*, 4 January 2008, URL: http://www.theguardian.com/commentisfree/2008/jan/04/

pakistan .world (accessed on17 May 2015).
Walsh, Declan, “Imran Khan laps up acclaim in Pakistan,” *The Guardian*, 31 October 2011, URL: http://www.theguardian.com/world/2011/oct/31/imran-khan-acclaim-pakist an ?newsfeed=true (Accessed on 17 April 2015).
Waseem, Mohammad, “The Electronic Media Explosion,” *Dawn*, 6 November 2006, URL: http://archives.dawn.com/2006/11/06/ed.htm (accessed on 11 July 2011).
____________, “Joint OR Separate Electorate,” *Pakistan Christian Voice*, Internet Magazine, October and November 2000, URL: http://www.suffrage-universel.be/res/pk mi03.htm (accessed on 1 July 2011).
Wilder, Andrew, “The Politics of Civil Service Reform in Pakistan,” *Journal of International Affairs*,Vol. 63, No. 1, Fall/Winter 2009, pp. 19-37, URL: https://jia.sipa.columbia.edu/politics-civil-service-reform-pakistan/ (accessed on 23 March 2015).
Yousaf, Kamran, “On army chief’s advice, govt to pursue talks with PTI, PAT again,” *The Express Tribune*, 28 August 2014, URL: http://tribune.com.pk/story/754978/coas-asked-to-help-resolve-political-impasse/ (accessed on 30 May 2016).
Zafar, Kashif, “Countdown begins: Imran to lead ‘tsunami march’ on August 14,” *The Express Tribune*, 28 June 2014, URL: http://tribune.com.pk/story/728176/countdown-begins-imran-to-lead-tsunami-march-on-august-14/(accessed on 30 April 2015).
Zaidi, Abbas, “Whose Pakistan People’s Party?” *Gowanus*, n.d., URL: http://www.gowanusbooks.com/party.htm (accessed on 15 January 2016).
Zaman, Qamar, “Fakhruddin Congratulates Pakistan,” *The Express Tribune*, 12 May 2013, URL: http://tribune.com.pk/story/548091/fakhruddin-congratulates-pakistan/ (accessed on 20 October 2013).

Newspapers

“Hundreds held in Pakistan to foil protests against Bush visit,” *The Hindu*, 5 March 2006.
“No control over Army, ISI, Pak Defence min tells SC,” *The Indian Express*, 22 December 2011.
“Pak army officers recalled from civilian postings,” *Times of India*, 12 February 2008.
Ahmad, Khaled, “Is the PPP Dying?” *The Indian Express*, 9 October 2015.
Jaffrelot, Christophe, “The Façade of Democracy,” *The Indian Express*, 1 April 2016.
Joshua, Anita, “Military has its way; Haqqani quits over memo,” *The Hindu*, 22 November 2011
____________, “Post-Abottabad: A Failure to see the Faultline,” *The Hindu*, 17 May 2011.
Subramanian, Nirupama, “40 killed in Islamabad blast,” *The Hindu*, 21 September, 2008.
____________, “Hue and cry in Pakistan over Kerry-Lugar conditions,” *The Hindu*, 8 October 2009.
____________, “Rawalpindi Attack a Bid to Shatter Army’s Confidence,” *The Hindu*, 11 October 2009.
____________, “U.S. pushed for Pasha’s India visit,” *The Hindu*, 19 May 2011.

Appendix A

Registered Parties with the Election Commission using "Muslim League" as a Nomenclature[i]

All Pakistan Muslim League Muhammad

Awami Muslim League Pakistan

Muttahida Muslim League

Pakistan Fatima Jinnah Muslim League

Pakistan Muslim League

Pakistan Muslim League (J)

Pakistan Muslim League (Muttahida)

Pakistan Muslim League (N)

Pakistan Muslim League (Nazaryati)

Pakistan Muslim League (Qasim)

Pakistan Muslim League (Qayyum Group)

Pakistan Muslim League (Safdar)

Pakistan Muslim League (Sher-e-Bangal)

Pakistan Muslim League (Z)

Pakistan Muslim League (Zehri Group)

Pakistan Muslim League Council

Pakistan Muslim League Democratic

Pakistan Muslim League Humkhiyal (Like Minded)

Pakistan National Muslim League

Peoples Muslim League Pakistan

i. "list of political parties enlisted with ecp," URL: http://ecp.gov.pk/Misc/ListPolParties withaddresses.pdf

Appendix B

Brief Points in the Charter of Resolutions[ii]

The Sindh domicile should be given solely to those people who have lived in Sindh for at least 20 years along with their families and this domicile should be made mandatory requirement for obtaining an identity card in Sindh.

Only the local Sindhis should be recruited in the police department an all other non-Sindhi police should be transferred to their provinces

Muhajirs and Sindhis should be allowed to keep weapons with valid license.

Afghan refugees should be confined to camps near the Afghan border and not to be allowed to buy property and do business.

In order to curb the unnatural growth of population in Sindh other provinces should provide employment to their own people.

To stop the illegal settlement and land-grabbing the land allotment should be regularised and allotted to Sindhis only.

Transport system should be modernized and electric train system should be developed in Karachi and Hyderabad; student should get discounted fare and driving license should be given to literate person only.

Local Sindhis should be given priority in jobs in the province.

Non-Sindhis should not be allowed to vote in the province.

Voting age should be reduced from 21 to 18 for all types of elections.

The Muhajirs and Sindhis should be given reservation in job and educational institution according to their proportional numbers in the census.

In all of Sindh's government and private industrial organisations preferences should be given to the local labourers.

The Muhjairs who were forcefully weeded out of various government jobs by using 'special laws' should be compensated and such practice should be stopped immediately.

The Muhajirs who are stranded in Bangladesh should be recognised as citizens of Pakistan and arrangements should be made to bring them in Pakistan.

---

ii. For the details of points see Altaf Hussain, *My Life's Journey: The Early Years 1966-1988* (*Safar-i-Zindagi*) translated by Khalid Athar (Karachi: Oxford University Press, 2011), pp. 169-187.

The Khokhrapar route should be open and the federal government should have postal rates equal to the neighbouring countries.

Local students should be given preference in admission in provincial institutions and one must open one more university and medical college in the province.

There should be increased health budget in Sindh and Jinnah Hospital should be under Sindh government.

Citizens without home should be allotted plots at low prices and given loan to construct houses.

KESC should be separated from WAPDA and restored to its earlier position.

The Sindh government should be given the right to collect sales tax.

Shah Latif's death anniversary and Liaquat Ali Khan's martyrdom day should be declared public holidays throughout the country.

Appendix C

Benazir Bhutto's Handwritten Will[iii]

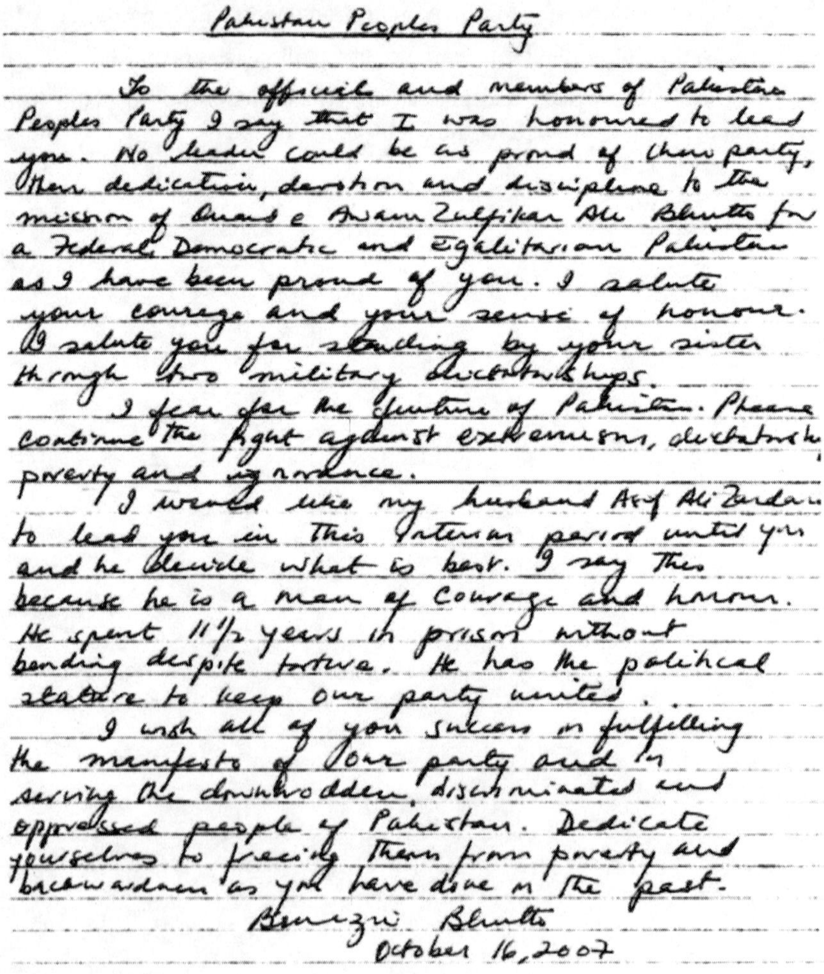

Pakistan Peoples Party

To the officials and members of Pakistan Peoples Party I say that I was honoured to lead you. No leader could be as proud of their party, their dedication, devotion and discipline to the mission of Quaid e Awam Zulfikar Ali Bhutto for a Federal, Democratic and Egalitarian Pakistan as I have been proud of you. I salute your courage and your sense of honour. I salute you for standing by your sister through two military dictatorships.

I fear for the future of Pakistan. Please continue the fight against extremism, dictatorship, poverty and ignorance.

I would like my husband Asif Ali Zardari to lead you in this interim period until you and he decide what is best. I say this because he is a man of courage and honour. He spent 11½ years in prison without bending despite torture. He has the political stature to keep our party united.

I wish all of you success in fulfilling the manifesto of our party and in serving the downtrodden, discriminated and oppressed people of Pakistan. Dedicate yourselves to freeing them from poverty and backwardness as you have done in the past.

Benazir Bhutto
October 16, 2007

iii. "Her Will," *benazirbhutto.org*, http://www.benazirbhutto.com/her-will.html (accessed on 20 December 2016).

Appendix D

Blasphemy Law

Pakistan Penal Code (Act XLV of 1860): XV of Offences Relating to Religion.

295 – Injuring or defiling place of worship, with Intent to insult the religion of any class: Whoever destroys, damages or defiles any place of worship, or any object held sacred by any class of persons with the intention of thereby insulting the religion of any class of persons or with the knowledge that any class of persons is likely to consider such destruction damage or defilement as an insult to their religion shall be punished with imprisonment of either description for a term which may extend to two years, or with fine, or with both.

295A–Deliberate and malicious acts intended to outrage religious feelings of any class by insulting Its religion or religious beliefs: Whoever, with deliberate and malicious intention of outraging the 'religious feelings of any class of the citizens of Pakistan, by words, either spoken or written, or by visible representations insults the religion or the religious beliefs of that class, shall be punished with imprisonment of either description for a term which may extend to ten years, or with fine, or with both.

295B – Defiling, etc., of Holy Qur'an: Whoever wilfully defiles, damages or desecrates a copy of the Holy Qur'an or of an extract therefrom or uses it in any derogatory manner or for any unlawful purpose shall be punishable with imprisonment for life.

295C – Use of derogatory remarks, etc., in respect of the Holy Prophet: Whoever by words, either spoken or written, or by visible representation or by any imputation, innuendo, or insinuation, directly or indirectly, defiles the sacred name of the Holy Prophet Muhammad (peace be upon him) shall be punished with death, or imprisonment for life, and shall also be liable to fine.

296 – Disturbing religious assembly: Whoever voluntarily causes disturbance to any assembly lawfully engaged in the performance of religious worship, or religious ceremonies, shall be punished with imprisonment of either description for a term which may extend to one year, or with fine, or with both.

297 – Trespassing on burial places, etc.: Whoever, with the intention of wounding the feelings of any person, or of insulting the religion of any person, or with the knowledge that the feelings of any person are likely to be wounded, or that the religion of any person is likely to be insulted thereby, commits any trespass in any place of worship or on any place of sculpture, or any place set apart for the performance of funeral rites or as a, depository for the remains of the dead, or offers any indignity to any human corpse or causes disturbance to any persons assembled for the performance of funeral ceremonies, shall be punished with imprisonment of either description for a term which may extend to one year, or with fine, or with both.

298 – Uttering words, etc., with deliberate intent to wound religious feelings: Whoever, with the deliberate intention of wounding the religious feelings of any person, utters any word or makes any sound in the hearing of that person or makes any gesture in the sight of that person or places any object in the sight of that person, shall be punished with imprisonment of either description for a term which may extend to one year or with fine, or with both.

298A – Use of derogatory remarks, etc., in respect of holy personages: Whoever by words, either spoken or written, or by visible representation, or by any imputation, innuendo or insinuation, directly or indirectly, defiles the sacred name of any wife (Ummul Mumineen), or members of the family (Ahle-bait), of the Holy Prophet (peace be upon him), or any of the righteous Caliphs (Khulafa-e-Rashideen) or companions (Sahaaba) of the Holy Prophet (peace be upon him) shall be punished with imprisonment of either description for a term which may extend to three years, or with fine, or with both.

298B – Misuse of epithets, descriptions and titles, etc., reserved for certain holy personages or places:

1. Any person of the Quadiani group or the Lahori group (who call themselves 'Ahmadis' or by any other name who by words, either spoken or written, or by visible representation- (a) refers to or addresses, any person, other than a Caliph or companion of the Holy Prophet Muhammad (peace be upon him), as "Ameer-ul-Mumineen", "Khalifatul- Mumineen", Khalifa-tul-Muslimeen", "Sahaabi" or "Razi Allah Anho"; (b) refers to, or addresses, any person, other than a wife of the Holy Prophet Muhammad (peace be upon him), as "Ummul-Mumineen"; (c) refers to, or addresses, any person, other than a member of the family "Ahle-bait" of the Holy Prophet Muhammad (peace be upon him), as "Ahle-bait"; or (d) refers to, or names, or calls, his place of worship a "Masjid"; shall be punished with imprisonment of either description for a term which may extend to three years, and shall also be liable to fine.
2. Any person of the Qaudiani group or Lahori group (who call themselves "Ahmadis" or by any other name) who by words, either spoken or written, or by visible representation refers to the mode or form of call to prayers

followed by his faith as "Azan", or recites Azan as used by the Muslims, shall be punished with imprisonment of either description for a term which may extend to three years, and shall also be liable to fine.

Appendix E

List of Elected and Appointed Prime Ministers of Pakistan

Liaquat Ali Khan	15 August 1947 – 16 October 1951
Khawaja Nazimuddin	19 October 1951 – 17 April 1953
Mohammad Ali (Bogra)	17 April 1953 – 11 August 1955
Chaudhri Mohammad Ali	11 August 1955 – 12 September 1956
H. S. Suharwardy	12 September 1956 – 11 October 1957
I. I. Chundrigar	18 October 1957 – 11 December 1957
Malik Firoz Khan Noon	16 December 1957 – 7 October 1958
General Mohammad Ayub Khan	27 October 1958 (less than a full day)
Zulfikar Ali Bhutto	14 August 1973 – 5 July 1977
Mohammad Khan Junejo	23 March 1985 – 29 May 1988
Benazir Bhutto	2 December 1988 – 6 August 1990
Ghulam Mustafa Jatoi (Caretaker)	6 August 1990 – 6 November 1990
Mian Mohammad Nawaz Sharif	6 November 1990 – 18 April 1993
Balkh Sher Mazari (Caretaker)	18 April 1993 – 26 May 1993
Mian Mohammad Nawaz Sharif	26 May 1993 – 18 July 1993
Moinuddin Qureshi (Caretaker)	18 July 1993 – 19 October 1993
Benazir Bhutto	19 October 1993 – 5 November 1996
Malik Meraj Khalid (Caretaker)	5 November 1996 – 17 February 1997
Mian Mohammad Nawaz Sharif	17 February 1997 – 12 October 1999
Mir Zafarullah Khan Jamali	21 November 2002 – 26 July 2004
Chaudhry Shujaat Hussain	30 July 2004 – 27 August 2004
Shaukat Aziz	27 August 2004 – 16 November 2007
Muhammad Mian Soomro	16 November 2007 – 25 March 2008

(Caretaker)	
Yousaf Raza Gillani	25 March 2008 – 19 June 20012
Raja Pervaiz Ashraf	22 June 2012 – 25 March 2013
Mir Hazar Khan Khoso	25 March 2013 – 5 June 2013
(Caretaker)	
Mian Mohammad Nawaz Sharif	5 June 2013 – 28 July 2017
Shahid Khaqan Abbasi	1 August 2017– May 2018
(Caretaker)	
Nasir ul Mulk	1 June 2018 – 18 August 2018
(Caretaker)	
Imran Khan	18 August 2018 – In Office

Index